RELIGIOUS DISARMAMENT

RELIGIOUS DISARMAMENT
Rethinking Coversion in India

Rudolf C. Heredia

GYAN

ISBN : 978-81-2121-252-6
Price : ₹ 990
Republished 2014
(First Published as "Changing Gods", 2007, Penguin)

Published by

Gyan Publishing House
23, Main Ansari Road, Darya Ganj
New Delhi-110002
Phones : 23282060, 23261060
Fax : 011-23285914
E-mail: books@gyanbooks.com
Website: www.gyanbooks.com

Laser Typesetting: Rudra Computer Graphics, Delhi
Printed at: G. Print Process, Delhi

Cataloging in Publication Data—DK

Courtesy: D.K. Agencies (P) Ltd. <docinfo@dkagencies.com>

Heredia, Rudolf C.

Religious disarmament : rethinking conversion in India / Rudolf C. Heredia.

p. cm.
Reprint.
Includes bibliographical references (p.) and index.
ISBN 9788121212526

1. Conversion. 2. Christianity and other religions—Hinduism. 3. Hinduism—Relations—Christianity. 4. India—Religion. I. Title. II. Title: Changing gods.

DDC 248.24 23

Contents

Preface: Positioning Oneself 9
New Preface: Repositioning Oneself 13
Acknowledgements 17

1. **Many Voices** **13**
A Complex Terrain- Atmaparivartan and *dharmantar* - Proselytising and non-proselytising religions - Indigenous and non-indigenous traditions - *Finding Common ground* – demographic distractions.

2. **The Past from Our Present** **28**
Conversion by Absorption - Evolution of Hindu traditions - Counter-point of heterodox traditions – Opposing perspectives- *Islam: Not by the Sword Alone*- Demonising the Other - Encounter with the West - Indigenisation in South Asia - Crossroads and Cutting Edges - *Christianity: From Proselytisation to Dialogue*- Historical Origins - Orthodoxy in the South - Colonial Beginnings - New Initiatives - Protestant Ventures - Beyond the Elites - Colonial Connections - Inter-religious Witness - *Whose Freedom of Religion?* - The Constitutional Debate - The Freedom of Religion Bills- *The Future of Our Past.*

3. **A Postponed Tryst** **83**
Conversion as subversion- The clash of Nationalisms- Two Perspectives - Hindu Cultural Nationalism -

Conversion as Atrocity - Lost Selves, Lost World - *A Second Axial Age* - Recovery and Reaction - Back to the Future - *Identity and Dignity* - The 'Self' and the 'Other' - Individual and Collective Rights - Inclusive and Exclusive Identities - *Diversity and Difference* - Plurality and Pluralism - Diversity in Unity - Identity and Integration – *Conversion as Freedom* - Indian Secularism - Majorities and Minorities - A Project in Progress.

4. **A Holistic Approach** 112
Personal Quest - Collective Dignity - Political and Economic Interests - Religious Worldviews - Conversion as Multi-faceted.

5. **Personal Journeys** 135
Ambedkar: Conversion as Liberation - The Inescapable Question - Contextualising a Movement - Confronting Gandhi- In Pursuit of Dignity- The Quest for Identity - Beginning Anew - Ambedkar's Relevance - A Multidimensional Analysis - A Defensive Opposition - A Holistic Response - *Gandhi: Conversion as Adharma* - *Dharmantar* and *Atmaparivartan* - Gandhi's Hinduism - Equality and Caste - Synthesis and Transformation - Positioning Gandhi - Identity and Alienation - Ascription and Choice - Reform and Liberation- Dharma and *Varna* - Disarming Opponents- *Adharma* and *Avarna* - *Ramabai: Conversion as Interrogation* -Pivotal Prototype - The Peripatetic Life The Turning Point - An On-going Journey - Challenging Patriarchy - Interrogating Constraints - Critical Integrity - Proponents and Opponents - Religious Revolutionary *Nivedita: Conversion as Dedication* - The Disciple - The Nationalist - Aggressive Hinduism - Revolutionary Nationalism - Personal to Impersonal - Revival or Reform - Ambiguities and Contradictions-A Complex Paradox - A New Seed - *Commonalities and Differences*.

6. **Connecting Contested Issues** **194**

Dalit Frustration - No Entry, No Exit - The Resilience of Caste - Meenakshipuram - Longing for Self-respect- The Wider Significance - Conversion as Protest and Quest - *Tribal Aspiration* - The Staines Murders - The Politics of Hate – the Larger Context - The Devi Cult - Conflict in the Dangs – A Complex Heritage - Assimilation - Resistance - Response - Identity Construction - Significance of Religion – Conversion as Future Aspiration - *Christian Ambiguity* - The Bishops' Dilemma - Openness of Truth - The Imperative of Equality - The Relativity of Culture - The Protestant Spectrum - The Catholic Transition - Creative Fidelity- *Hindu Tolerance*- The Irrepressible Question - The Hindu Paradox - Recovering Tolerance- Gandhian Relevance - Nehruvian Rationalism - Neutrality or Respect - Conversion to Tolerance - *Muslim Diversity* – Homogeneity and Demonisation - Unity not Uniformity - Indian Islam - Multiple Diversities - Modern Challenges– Subaltern Responses- *Comparisons and Contrasts* - Dalits and Tribals - Christians, Hindus, Muslims.

7. **Rethinking Conversion** **251**

Conversion as Process, not Event- Many Pilgrimages - Conversion to Each Other - *Conversion as Change and Affirmation* - Religious Identities - Social Space - Civil Society- Faith and Ideology- Affirming Dignity - *Conversion as Tolerance* - Mixed Motivations - Religious Options - Legal Repression - Limits and Levels – Dimensions of Understanding - Levels of understanding-*Conversion as Dialogue* - Dialectics to Dialogue - Culture of Dialogue - Inter-religious Dialogue - Domains in Dialogue - Intra-Religious Dialogue - An Equal Dialogue – Inside/Outside - Pluralism and Relativism - *Conversion as Multiple Belongings* - Singular and Multiple Identities - Beyond Dialogue - *The Journey Ahead.*

8. Religious Disarmament **284**

Models *of* and Models *for* - *Faith and Reason* - New Sutras for Old Dichotomies - Right Belief, Right Practice - *Towards a Global/Universal Ethic* - the Paradox - The Ethical Imperative - A Global Ethic - A Compelling Search - Mapping a New Landscape - *Freeing the Imagination* - Mismatches and Misunderstandings - Human Rights and Religious Liberty - Person and Community - *Many Dharmas* – Introspection and Interrogation - Beyond Introspection.

Bibliography 305

Index 325

Preface: Positioning Oneself

During the Cold War, the protagonists achieved a balance of terror with their nuclear policy of *mutually assured destruction*, with the appropriate acronym MAD. The saner option of a *mutually agreed disarmament* was considered unviable within the realpolitik of that time. Some mishap or miscalculated brinksmanship could have precipitated a 'nuclear winter', and in retrospect we now know how close we came to this. Today religious extremism and fundamentalism is whipping up another wave of terror that seems unbalanced and uncontrollable. A parallel to the MAD approach is grossly inadequate. Rather, we need to step back from the brink with a determined religious disarmament, not to dismiss or negate religion but to disarm and discard the aggression and violence of those that who indulge in, and those who seek to contain this religiously inspired madness.

In many places, religious indifference loosely unites a large part of the population; in many others, religious differences sharply divide people. Jonathan Swift once perceptively remarked: "We have just enough religion to make us hate, but not enough to make us love one another." Nowhere is this truer than in India today, and no issue illustrates this better than that of conversion.

Religion has moved to centrestage in the identity politics raging through this land, in the attempt to create convenient 'vote banks' to be manipulated for political gain. This is dangerously divisive, and the endpoint is all too often some kind of ethnic cleansing or worse, even genocide. The frequency of such instances is horrifying. Some minimal comprehension of the issues involved is necessary for any kind of harmony in our society, not just between religious traditions, but also within them.

Religious conversion is an unavoidable stumbling block for any aspiration for religious harmony, for any real hope of true religious understanding, both of which are so essential to contain a potentially divisive diversity. Such is the context and the concern this book attempts to address. I invite the readers to join this quest and carry it forward in their own varying situations.

Writing a book on religious conversion is a daunting task. For either we preach to the converted, or we inevitably run foul of the unconvertible. Extremism on either side leaves little room for a middle ground of sanity and common sense, and always less space for an awareness of the inevitable pre-judgements we bring to bear on this problem. However, it is in this middle ground and sensitised space that any possibility for a useful exchange must be located. Here I position myself, and further attempt to enlarge this common ground and open a space to engage in a plurality of conversations with those willing. Obviously, an assumption of good faith and goodwill must be the starting point for this. It is only with such an understanding that we will find or even create this common ground.

There are exclusive positions that negate such a possibility. Those clinging to them already place themselves beyond the scope of this discussion. Inclusive positions too can have their problems when they absorb other differences, leaving little room for distinctiveness. We need a starting position, and we cannot avoid beginning from where we are, within our own perspectives and commitments. Honesty demands acknowledge these at the outset. But we also need flexibility and openness to place ourselves outside these when required to seek the commonalities we all share. We must engage at this level if we are to repair the damage of the past, to heal old wounds and make anew our future. As we claim our common humanity, we open ourselves to discovering together a richness and depth that we could never have alone.

This common ground is defined not just by overlapping areas or mutually acceptable, non-contradictory positions. It must be extended to include other areas of human values and concerns that may well be outside these religious traditions and can still serve to question and critique them in turn. Nor does it exclude the secular or the non-religious insofar as this helps to further a multi-faceted dialogue.

Myself purpose then cannot be to settle all the issues that can be raised. For many of these involve some dilemmas that we can only live with, not resolve. We must find ways of living together or, as the awful events of our recent past testify, destroy each other.

Here my intention to unravel the various strands that are woven into this web and to examine the varying stands we take on these contentins matters. This can easily unsettle the status quo, threaten settled certainties, disturb old equilibriums.

An interrogation does not begin with a complete blank. There is always some knowledge that gives rise to the question raised. Some background against which the responses are received. These constitute the necessary and inevitable pre-judgements that we all begin with, but must be amenable to revision and change. We must indeed begin this dialogue with openness and trust but we will not proceed very far without perseverance and good faith. The alternative is the violence of 'might is right' which settles very little and destroys so much.

Violating a person has deeply destructive consequences for a society struggling to establish a genuinely human social order. If freedom defines the moral dimension of humans, then freedom of conscience must lie at its core. For the human is defined not so much by self-consciousness as by personal conscience. Moreover, the person is violated when human identity is denigrated or personal dignity denied. This can happen when religious conversion is promoted or opposed, or when the would-be-converts' real freedom of choice is subverted.

Yet authenticity will require that we bracket, not betray, our deep-seated beliefs and commitments, for the time being, and come back more sensitised to critique and refine them after the exchange. As this process is reiterated, openness is increased, the encounter enriched, awareness enhanced. This has been called the 'hermeneutical circle'.

However, this demands an honest and open positioning of oneself even before one embarks on such a venture. To begin then with am I as a Catholic priest and I must be sensitive to the exclusiveness of some specifics of Christian beliefs. Aware that these could come in the way and so must be bracketed before entering this common ground for a mutual encounter. I hope to then come back to my own faith to reinterpret it in new and more critical ways and perhaps even make an unanticipated breakthrough, a real conversion to a broader inclusiveness, which may well be an even deeper and more comprehensive faith. At the same time, I would like to carry forward the positive universalism I have internalised with my faith and which

I experience as so much a part of orthodox Christianity. The measure in which, I succeed in this will be the measure of the authenticity of this book. The extent, to which I fail, will be the extent to which the value of this venture is compromised.

Moreover, as a Jesuit priest, I make no claim to be a theologian, or to have any specialised competence in that academic discipline. My perspective is rather from the social sciences and my approach is that of a sociologist with faith commitments and social concerns to be honoured. I want to understand in order to be understood, to interpret creatively in order to change constructively, to bring reflection and action closer in a praxis, an action-reflection-action process, that can be shared with likeminded people of goodwill, and carried forward together.

Conversion is a complex and emotionally charged issue. Fundamentalists of all hues exploit it, liberals confuse it, many do not really comprehend what all the fuss is about, and many more just do not want to get involved. However, especially in a multi-cultural, pluri-religious society like ours, it is a problem that cannot be wished away. For like it or not, we are all in some way involved. In today's surcharged context of minority-bashing and anti-conversion laws, of majoritarian politics and minority vote-banks, the issues implied get more explosive everyday. Sooner rather than later we must grasp the nettle.

But if discretion is the better part of valour, then besides courage we will need discernment to disentangle the complications and sort out the confusion, to wrest the discussion from all those who use religion for chauvinistic or egotistic, extremist or obscurantist purposes. There are many who seek to define this terrain to their own advantage, but there are many more, I believe, who do want to facilitate a genuine exchange on a difficult and delicate problem. For me this venture has been a personally enlightening quest, an on-going conversion still in progress, and I am willing to dare sharing it with anyone who cares enough to risk the same.

I have attempted to present the argument here less as a linear one-dimensional development than a circular reiteration. Points first made are elaborated later to bring a deeper and more comprehensive understanding to the subject, and hopefully some incisive insight and decisive determination to the reader.

Rudolf C. Heredia, Delhi, 2006

New Preface : Repositioning Oneself

Religious Disarmament, the title of this new edition, is intended to suggest a stepping away from an entrenched defensive stance in encounters with other religious traditions so that even if there is a clash of horizons, there is an invitation to a fusion of horizons. Such a possibility enriches both religious traditions in their specificity, while pointing beyond to a convergence over the horizons of either tradition in their contemporary articulation. This is the fundamental basis for an open and equal dialogue, at the many levels of life, action, expression and experience between the self and the other in any human engagement of persons or groups, communities or societies. Today more than ever, this is what *Rethinking Conversion in India* must mean if our polarised religious divides are to thaw.

The earlier title, *Changing Gods,* was to make the book more accessible to a general readership. It pointed to the problematique of religious conversion, especially in a multicultural, plur[i]-religious society like India. The present title registers an attempt to refocus the discussion and impact the discourse on the issue from an alternative perspective. It is meant to appeal to more academically inclined readers. Published by Penguin, India, in 2007, the earlier version of the text was reprinted once. It is now being republished by Gyan Books with the present title. The text itself has not been altered: not much has happened to warrant this, except perhaps that the Kandamal communal pogroms only reaffirmed what the book was trying to anticipate and defuse.

The 2007 edition of the text concluded with the statement of the interreligious conference at Lariano, Italy, in 2006, on religious conversion. The Hindutva ideologue Sudheendra Kulkarni was a participant there, invited by Archbishop Felix Machado, then at the Congregation for Interreligious Dialogue at the Vatican, later bishop of Nashik, and now of the Vasai diocese, both in Maharashtra. Kulkarni wrote about this in his column in the *Indian Express* (12 October 2008), endorsing the recommendations of the Lariano Conference but calling for "a sustained and sincere all-religion debate in India on an anti-conversion law in the spirit of the above recommendations"!

Some years later, on 12 June 2009, there was another meeting in Mumbai at Archbishop's House, with Cardinal Jean-Louis Tauran, the Prefect of the Congregation for Interreligous Dialogue to which Kulkarni had been invited, following which, in his column (*Indian Express*, 14 June 2009), Kulkarni nostalgically recalled the Lariano meeting while discussing the Mumbai one. Among those present at this Hindu-Christian dialogue, he mentions the following on the first day:

> "Swami Jayendra Saraswati, the Shankaracharya of Kanchi Mutt, led the Hindu delegation, which included Sri Sri Ravi Shankar, founder of the Art of Living movement; Swami Chidananda Saraswati of Parmarth Niketan, Rishikesh; Rajayogini Dadi Janki of Brahmakumaris; Swami Nikhileshwaranandaji and Swami Vigishanandji, two senior monks from Ramakrishna Mission; Sri Venkatachariar Chaturvedi Swami of Sri Ramanuja Mission Trust and Mahamandaleshwar Swami Vishveshwaranand Giri Maharaj of Sanyas Ashram, Hardwar. Catholic participants included Pedro Lopez Quintana, the Vatican's ambassador in India; Archbishop Felix Machado of Nashik; Bishop Thomas Dabre of Pune and Bishop Raphy Manjaly of Varanasi."

On the second day this was

> "followed by an enlightening colloquium, in which eminent Muslim, Jewish, Zoroastrian, Sikh, Jain and Buddhist personalities also participated. It was organised by Shantilal Somaiya, a renowned octogenarian educationist, who has been striving for better inter-religious understanding for many decades."

These conversations were being held in the wake of the Kandamahal communal violence that rumbled through the 1990s, fuelled by the politics of hate and an ideology of religious violence deliberately manipulated to keep the communal tensions constantly on the boil. Violence erupted with disruption of the Christmas celebrations in December 2007 and began to escalate until the murder of Swami Lakshmanananda, on 23 August 2008,which was then cunningly used to ignited a conflagration. The whole sequence was so obviously modelled on Godra in Gujarat: an inadequately investigated incident, a death yatra though the country side to instigate mob violence, a sustained pogrom against a vulnerable religious minority. Tragically for the targeted minorities, this kind of religious politics can be repeated as long as it yields electoral dividends.

Kulkarni ruefully concludes that

> "The road of reconciliation and durable harmony and peace is a hard one. Several important questions need greater debate leading to convergent positions. In the months ahead, both Hindu and Christian leaders also have a duty to crystallise mutual trust and understanding into a practical and collaborative agenda of action at all levels, including the grassroots level, to remove the sources of prejudices, tension and conflict. How to move ahead?"

This must be the agenda to be followed through by all religious leaders. It demands nothing less than an interrogation of the terms of the discourse and must lead to the disarming of all the mechanisms and rationalisations that are used in the defence of our rigidly entrenched religious traditions, especially those that lean towards, and at times embrace, fundamentalism and extremism, even justifying violence in the name of their religion and their God. Whether it be the Nellie massacre of minorities in Nellie, Assam, 1983, or the ethnic cleansing of pundits in Kashmir, 1989-90, or the pogrom against the Sikhs in Delhi, 1984, or the genocide of Muslims in Gujarat, 2002, there is a hardening of the divides, an entrenchment on all sides along religious fault lines in India, that still yields electoral returns in our 'religionised' politics.

A commitment to dialogue across such positions will necessarily demand a 'religious disarmament'. An open and equal dialogue cannot be premised on a strategy of mutually assured defence (MAD, in analogy to the 'mutually assured destruction' of nuclear armament; and also plain MAD). The imperative now is rather for a mutually assured dialogue (another kind of MAD-ness it might seem) as the only sane response to our present impasse before it cascades into confusion worse confounded.

My hope is that the republication of this book, under a new title, will precipitate this much needed dialogue, not just among those concerned with the issue of conversion, either as promoters, opponents or as converts or would-be converts, and among those who look for inter-religious peace and harmony and not merely as a passive mutual tolerance—but more specifically among those who can intervene and interrogate the terms of the present discourse on the subject as an actively engaged reaching out across borders.

In conclusion, my thanks are due to Mr Amit Garg of Gyan Books for undertaking this republication, in hardcover, and many others who supported and encouraged this venture.

Rudolf C. Heredia, Mumbai, 2013

Acknowledgements

No human endeavour is ever an isolated undertaking. Among the numerous people I need to gratefully acknowledge, some must be mentioned very especially. To them I dedicate this book. Most of all to my 'panch', the five friends and companions who read and reread the manuscript refining and tightening the text: Arundhathi Subramaniam, George Gispert-Sauch, Jerry Pinto, Paul de Gueriviere, Ranjit Hoskote. Numerous others supported and sustained me on this venture in various ways, intellectually and otherwise: Ananda Amritmahal, Ananya Vajpeyi, ,Asghar Ali Engineer, Ashraf Patel, Christian Cipriani, Christopher Heredia, Dhirubhai Seth, Eddie Rodrigues, Imtiaz Ahmad, Irene Heredia, Kiran Doshi, Joseph Dias, Joseph Feliu, Larry Malarkar, Lucinda Peach, M.S.S. Pandian, Meenu Venkatswaran, Munawar Baig, Patricia Wittberg, Shiv Viswanathan, Paul Brass, Peter Ronald de Souza, Rahul Srivastava, Shiv Viswanathan, Valerian Rodrigues, Vasudha Ambiye, Vivek Pinto ... and friends and colleagues at the Centre for the Study of Developing Societies, the Indian Social Institute, Vidyajoti, ... not to mention others without whose help this book would perhaps have been completed earlier! This has been a journey with all these and many others.

1

Many Voices

Complex terrain – Atmaparivartan and Dharmantar – Proselytising traditions – Indigenous Religions – Finding common ground– demographic distractions

Soon after the Bandung Conference in 1955, Andre Malraux recalls asking Nehru: 'What is your greatest difficulty since Independence?' Nehru's spontaneous reply was: 'Creating a just State by just means, I think ...' After a pause, he added: 'Perhaps too, creating a secular State in a religious country.' (Malraux 1970) Since then, both difficulties have grown exponentially in tandem, undermining the legitimacy of both the state and religion in this society.

The religious life of a people is inevitably enmeshed in the complex interrelationships of all other aspects of personal and group living and religious conversion can never be completely isolated from any of these. Depending on where one positions oneself, negative or positive aspects are stressed. There are many voices that must be recognised to piece together a more comprehensive and nuanced understanding of this complex problem. Though burdened with possibilities for contentious misunderstanding, religious conversion can open to a deeper and enlightening reciprocal understanding, for, in the process of change, conversions critique the status quo, question traditional ways of living, challenge dated structures.

Thus, conversions can destabilise the life of a people, unsettle painfully balanced boundaries, scramble carefully constructed identities. If the affected people have imagined an exclusive nationhood for themselves, then nationalists will readily see conversions as subversive. The Reformation in medieval Europe witnessed Protestants and Catholics identifying their religion with the state to the point of violently eliminating any conscientious dissenters. Today the proclamation of an official state religion has too often led to the bloody persecution of minorities and ethnic cleansing.

Religious conversion never happens in abstraction, it is always mediated: by other persons, social institutions, group and community interactions... Thus every religious tradition has a community of believers that live in greater or lesser solidarity among themselves, and any entry or exit affects the communities concerned in multiple ways, precipitating changes on both sides. The multiple dimensions of conversion need to be sorted out, even though they are not separate and in fact overlap. For, while religious commitment is essentially a matter of personal conscience and choice, it inevitably impacts other areas and levels of individual and social life. Hence, conversion is invariably associated with resistance and rebellion, dissent and protest. It includes a spectrum of possibilities both in analysis and interpretation as well as in response and action. It can precipitate religious antagonisms that militate against community cohesion and political consensus or it can facilitate a cultural pluralism that makes for social diversity and inter-religious tolerance.

The Clash of Civilisations by Samuel Huntington (1996) popularised a contemporary reading of history that played to old prejudices and nurtured fears of the Muslim world. The Islamic world too cannot forget the barbarians at the gates in the time of the Crusades and so are understandably apprehensive that the 'war on terror', first called a 'crusade', harks back to the medieval conflicts in the Middle East. The 'war' has most recently mutated into a 'global struggle against violent extremism'. Closer home, the endeavour to erase a millennium of Muslim presence in India appeals to the same distorted logic of incompatible and hostile worldviews. The violence initiated by colonial powers, whether in the Middle East or South Asia or anywhere else, suggests a clash of barbarisms rather than anything even remotely civilised. The events of 1857 on this subcontinent, the great revolt and its suppression, were witness to this.

Such barbaric violence is fuelled by wounded memories and unresolved grievances from a long gone past, colonial and pre-colonial. All too often, these are deliberately kept alive by vengeful zealots to nurse injured collective egos. However, when it comes to religious violence, there are no precision-guided hate bombs. Rather with such 'chosen traumas' there is a sense of self-righteousness and self-justification that legitimises unlimited horrors in the name of 'the cause'. Yet to think in terms of 'teaching them a lesson' when the initial assumption is precisely that 'such people never learn', exposes the inconsistencies in this madness without method.

In situations of sharp and hostile religious boundaries between communities, conversion represents the ultimate betrayal. Yet even when inter-group or community relationships are not in conflict, conversion movements have the potential to challenge accepted wisdom and renegotiate the status quo. No wonder, in times of rapid social change, religious conversion is likely to find aggressive promoters and equally fierce resisters, even as the voices of the converts themselves are silenced. No wonder, proselytising is illegal in some countries such as Israel, Nepal, and most Muslim countries. Similarly, our own anti-conversion laws, euphemistically entitled 'Freedom of Religion Acts', border on an administrative ban on conversions. The Reformation compromise at Westphalia in 1648 of '*cuius regio, eius religio*' (the ruler imposes his religion) is being revived by an articulation of 'majoritarian' rule for the majority religion.

Religious conversion is not merely a threat to the unity of a people. There is both continuity and discontinuity implied in any process of conversion. In a plural society it can challenge the more particular and exclusive community identities, to come together as multi-layered identities under a more universal and inclusive one, as in a common citizenship in civil society or an overarching culture or civilisation. In fact, some states have successfully done this by secularising social institutions and relativising religious ones. Where secularism itself is contested, this becomes problematic and contentious. What would be the alternative in a mutli-cultural and pluri-religious society like ours? To homogenise it by converting people to a single religious or cultural tradition is to negate the rich diversity of our heritage; to freeze it in the prevailing status quo is to deny the dynamic pluralism of our tradition. This makes religious conversion the touchstone of a religiously pluralist and culturally tolerant society today.

A society as diverse as ours in its multi-cultural and pluri-religious richness, not to mention its linguistic heritage and economic divides, seems to be precariously poised in an unstable equilibrium of inconvenience. When freedom of conscience is denied in one area, such as religion, it always affects freedom of choice in others areas: from the more public freedom to choose one's politics and occupation, to the more private ones of lifestyle and personal relationships. Moral policing inevitably tends to overreach its initial brief. The fundamental right to freedom is an integral social good for a person, though always limited by the same rights of others and the necessities of public order.

There can be huge risks involved in disturbing the status quo, but freezing it has its own costs. Democratising caste hierarchy may provoke an upper caste backlash, but preserving caste domination can precipitate a dalit revolt. Conversion then is a paradoxical, confused and complex terrain. Fundamentalisms of all kinds, whether religious or otherwise, distort the issues involved and make any resolutions of the differences implied a matter of enforcement, not agreement, resulting only in violence not in harmony. We must then begin with a pragmatic openness, but pragmatism alone is never adequate to such a problem.

In 1981, the conversion of dalits to Islam in Meenakshipuram district in Tamil Nadu precipitated a hostile campaign by the Vishwa Hindu Parishad (VHP, Universal Hindu Association) against conversions. In 1992, the demolition of the Babri Masjid escalated into communal riots against Muslims across the country, with immense loss of life and property. Atrocities against Christians followed, beginning in 1998 with the Dangs of Gujarat and followed by the murder of Graham Staines and his two young sons at Manoharpur in Orissa. As recently as 2003, Udit Raj, a dalit leader, began mobilising mass conversions to Buddhism.

In such a surcharged climate, religious identities are powerful mobilisers in the game of electoral politics, even though appeals to religion and caste are forbidden by law. Today, implicitly if not explicitly, pragmatically if not programmatically, the politics of identity based on religion and caste has displaced the politics of interests premised on class and party. The resulting politics of passion is rapidly becoming a politics of hate, nurtured on a sense of self-righteous grievance and irrational insecurity. The pogrom against Muslims in Gujarat in 2002 was a murderous demonstration of this. Ashok Singal, president of the VHP, claimed in *The Hindu* newspaper (23 January, Chennai), that 'the recent communal violence in Gujarat symbolised the first positive response of Hindus to Muslim fundamentalism in 1,000 years'. The Muslim reaction has been to retreat further into a defensive religious fundamentalism. Indeed, there is little to choose between fanatics of any colour, saffron or green, red or white.

Religious nationalism and caste factionalism too often masquerade as communitarian loyalty. They have come to dominate our politics, while real economic needs, basic civic rights, genuine political participation and other legitimate demands of our people are sidetracked or hijacked. It was once thought that caste factionalism would undermine the democratic foundations of our country but now it is religious antagonisms that are the greater danger. The parliamentary election in May 2004 may presage a return to reason but it is still a very precariously balanced multi-party coalition of varying and warring interests.

There are of course many encouraging and positive aspects of our situation that we can build on. The most elementary resource we have is the basic goodwill and good sense of most of our people when they are not manipulated and panicked into unreasonable and antagonistic positions. There is still the traditional ideal of tolerance and harmony to which we aspire. The legacy of Mahatma Gandhi (1869 – 1948), his *ahimsa* (non-violence) and *satyagraha* (truth-force) has not been entirely abandoned, even though we have failed him so grossly. The social democratic traditions and the secular rational institutions that Jawaharlal Nehru (1889-1964) nurtured have not been completely lost. Procedural democracy has been stabilised over the years even though we have a long way to go with regard to a more substantive one; the economy is picking up, even though poverty and inequality are still endemic in our society; and civil society is becoming more demanding with regard to rights of citizen and duties of the state.

In this labyrinth we must find common ground spacious enough to allow for multiple players with many voices that must be heard. For these encounters are not just across religious traditions but within each one, and even with those without any allegiance to one as well. Obviously, the free and open space within a religious tradition or a secular ideology will be carried over to the common ground we are trying to construct. An inflexible and intolerant tradition or ideology will restrict the rich possibilities of an open encounter across differences and even disagreements. In other words, besides the exchange between believers from different traditions, the interaction between believers within a single tradition, as also an encounter with non-believers from secular ideologies, can sharpen and focus the discussion.

But any fruitful encounter must be within a mutually accepted framework, in which we can begin to understand and accept that we are different. This right to be different must be conceded at the start even when we may not understand or approve the difference itself. Only then can the process of exchange be sustained by consent and consensus and not be manipulated by pretence and deception.

We will endeavour to move the discussion away not just from fundamentalists and extremists, but from religious elites and erudite specialists as well, to try more to engage people of good faith and goodwill, whether religious or secular. Certainly, we must wrest the discussion from those who would exploit it for political or other narcissistic purposes, whether individual or collective. Unfortunately, conventional commonsense on this contentious issue has too often justified presumptions and prejudices that must be questioned, and not taken for granted as part of our 'unconscious ideology'. Hence, we must first clarify our starting point with some descriptive definitions and distinctions.

A Complex Terrain

A startling anomaly on the issue of conversion is that Mahatma Gandhi and the Rashtriya Swayamsevak Sangh (RSS, National Volunteer Society) apparently seem to be on the same side. But it cannot be because they have similar understandings, as they come from opposite poles. Both may perceive this as a 'colonisation of conscience' but their understandings of 'colonisation' and 'conscience' are quite directly opposed.

Atmaparivartan and *Dharmantar*

Etymologically, 'conversion' comes from the Latin '*convertere*', meaning 'to turn around' or 'turn completely'. In a religious context it is a turning away from evil and a turning towards the good, repentance for sin and a rebirth to new life. Different religious traditions might interpret this differently: for Christians this corresponds to a change of heart, a 'metanoia', 'repent and believe'; for Muslims submission to Allah, God, and acceptance of his Prophet; for Buddhists it is 'going for refuge', being enlightened; for Hindus self-purification and self-realisation.

But these understandings are mostly about conversion within one's own religious tradition. This is generally not really controversial or contested, except when there are fundamentalist divisions and extremist sects seeking to homogenise a tradition with 'orthodoxies' from within. Rather, it is conversions across religious traditions that cause the real difficulties. The first involves an *atmaparivartan*, a metanoia, or a change of heart, within the same religious tradition; the second a *dharmantar*, a change of one's religious allegiance across such traditions.

However, religious conversion either as *atmaparivartan* or as *dharmantar* implies a change in both one's religious commitment and social position. The more radical the conversion, the more drastic the change will be. Within the same tradition, this may well be a matter of degree and/or of kind. Religious revivalists often see themselves in this light, i.e., reviving, renewing the tradition from within. Conversion across traditions will inevitably implicate relations between the traditions concerned. Promoters and opponents of conversion clash on this terrain, which we seek to clear for a fruitful encounter. However, the equivalence of '*dharma*' and religion is very problematic though this is now common usage. Here we would rather speak of a religious tradition, and this is better rendered by '*parampara*', '*sampradaya*', '*panth*', '*qaum*', *mazhab*' ...

A Hindu becoming a better Hindu is likely to be positively valued, especially where there is a consensus on what this 'better' implies. But a Hindu converting to Islam or Christianity involves a change of *sampradaya* and so is likely to be disturbing, especially where such a change of religious tradition is not positively valued or hostilely rejected. Yet those opposed to conversion across such religious traditions seem willing to apply their logic of exclusion to others while they exempt themselves from its rigours. Thus, giving up one's own religion for another is viewed as 'apostasy'. Supposedly, such a turning away cannot come from goodwill or good faith and so must be the result of external force or fraud, or internal delusion or perversity. Conversion is rejected, but reconversion is accepted as a 'homecoming', *gharvapasi*.

Again, proselytising others is claimed as a right, but 'sheep stealing' by others is resented. Such people perceive 'conversions' as inherently violating persons, but only when their group is targeted, not when they are the promoters themselves. Without judging motives, we cannot help but notice how in traditionally Catholic countries of Latin America, Protestant Evangelicals have been notoriously opposed as 'wolves in sheep's clothing' by Catholics and even by the Vatican.

Indeed, there are those for whom conversion is univocally categorised as 'violence', the imposition of a conquering, dominant people on a subservient, subaltern one, or as manipulated by unfair and foul means. This is too simplistic a reading to do justice to the realities on the ground that we are attempting to explore. Much depends on how far a religious tradition is implicated or complicit with the powers that be. We must take cognisance of the historical context and be sensitive to unequal social relationships. To presume that marginalised persons and groups in a society are unable to make such religious choices for themselves, or to resist and subvert such 'impositions' on them smacks of paternalism. This is hardly congruent with serious democratic aspirations or liberal pretensions. After all, if universal suffrage presumes that people can make valid political choices, surely, religious choices, including conversion, should be equally valid for them. Imposing on would-be converts a protection they do not seek (as is now often proposed and frequently done), shows as little confidence in such people as isolating new converts in 'mission compounds' (as was once widely practised).

As with any change, religious conversion implies both continuity and discontinuity, rejection and acceptance. Even when the change is disruptive there is always a necessary negotiation between the old and the new; neither can the old be totally rejected and left behind in one big leap nor can the new be accepted and personalised in a single initiation. For even if the converts are plucked right out of the original situation and transplanted into a set of totally new circumstances, previously interiorised attitudes and orientations of individuals and groups are inevitably carried over. Such change continues even over generations and eventually results in something new and distinctive. For conversion is unpredictably creative and full of surprises for the converter and the converted, and at times even for those initially opposed to it.

Thus at the individual level, even after a conversion as dramatic as that of Saul of Tarsus to Paul the Apostle, he still remains a Hebrew, loyal to his people, a rabbi who speaks from within their traditions, only now he has another message. At the group level, the negotiations are even more complex and subtle. Thus, Indian Christians have retained their distinctiveness and differences not just from the Western missionaries who converted them but also from other Christian communities across the subcontinent as well. Muslims on the subcontinent too are not a homogenous community. They are as diverse and divided as most other people in the region.

Proselytising Traditions

To begin on the neutral ground of etymology, the verb 'convert' is used in both the active and passive voice. Much of the controversy centres on the active pursuance of converts. This is better referred to as proselytisation from the Greek 'proselytes' meaning 'new comer', rather than conversion. It is often used in a derogatory sense, going back to the condemnation of Jesus in the New Testament: 'Woe to you scribes and Pharisees, hypocrites! For you traverse the sea and land to make a single proselyte, and when he becomes a proselyte, you make him twice as much a child of hell as yourselves.' (Matthew 23:15 Revised Standard Version)

Often proselytisation has amounted to organised aggression on vulnerable peoples for not very noble motives. As such, it is deservedly condemned. But surely all religious propagation is not of this nature and there must be some legitimate space to reach out to others outside the fold. Calling to repentance, preaching enlightenment, witnessing to one's convictions, fostering religious and spiritual values, need not necessarily amount to proselytising. We have numerous examples of this in our history, of Buddhist monks, Hindu sadhus, Muslim Sufis, Christian mendicants, as also living ones today. Moreover, if religious conversion is to be restricted to within the fold only, how and where and by whom will these boundaries be drawn? Freedom of conscience will demand that these be kept porous, as indeed most borders will be in a globalising world. All attempts at promoting one's religious beliefs or spreading a religious movement must not be tarred with the same brush.

Thus Christianity, which began with a strong missionary mandate that still converts and proselytises, has been conditioned by historical circumstances that have shaped this mission in many different and diverse ways. The persecutions suffered by the early Christians resulted in a very different sense of mission than when Christianity was made the official religion of the Roman Empire. The Crusades and the colonial expansion continued this complicity of church and state, which in some countries still prevails, even in secularised societies as in the United Kingdom, and secular countries as in the United States. However, in the Eastern Orthodox Churches there has not been the same aggressive pursuit of proselytisation, especially when Islam advanced into once historically Christian regions. Now in the post-colonial period the churches are reassessing their missionary mandate, and many fundamentalist extremes are as far from the mainstream churches in this matter as are some secularised liberal ones.

Islam began with a rapid expansion out of the Arabian desert but the image of conquering hordes imposing a militant religion on subdued peoples is simplistic and superficial, to say the least. In actuality, victorious Muslims were more tolerant of other faiths, especially the peoples of the book, than the marauding Christian Crusaders were at the time. In a great many regions, including this sub-continent, Sufis and traders were more responsible for the spread and stabilisation of Muslim communities than soldiers and sultans. But this is hardly the common perception today and it needs must be challenged. The cultural achievements of Islam, which has produced more than one great civilisation, stand in direct contradiction to prevailing prejudice.

Hinduism has come to perceive itself as a non-proselytising, non-dogmatic faith. But if multifarious *panths* and *sampradayas*, sects and cults have spread across the sub-continent and beyond under an overarching Brahmanism, it surely implies an expansion that has absorbed and integrated other local religious and cultural traditions. N.K. Bose termed this 'the Hindu mode of absorption' (Bose 1994: 177) which is as gradual and untidy as the economy's 'Hindu rate of growth'. Here too there have been immense variations in the pace and manner, the content and consequences of this absorption, from implicit resistance to explicit violence, from segmented communities to hierarchical castes. The number and scope of the consequent little traditions established by charismatic *sant-kavis* (saint-poets) and their following of *bhaktas* (devotees) constitute a bewildering diversity. The legends and sagas of local or *desi* folk traditions and oral history can be mined to yield living testimony of this. Further, even the multiple great traditions of the *sanatani* (eternal) mainstream Hinduism admit many different paths or *margs* within an overall orthodoxy. The final composite of all this is more a 'parliament of religions', as Vivekananda (1863-1902) termed it, than a single homogenous religion that came to be called 'Hinduism' in the British Census in the 19th century.

The Buddhist tradition presents an interesting picture of missionary propagation without real violence or much political induction. It was spread by *bhikkus*, wandering monks, in the true *shramana* tradition they shared with Jainism and its *munis*. At times, these were politically sponsored: Emporer Ashoka sent Buddhist *bhikkus* overseas. But they were not accompanied by conquering armies. Though historically grounded in the experience of the Buddha, Buddhism was not a dogmatic religion and showed an enlightened capacity to adjust its beliefs and teachings to local cultures and traditions, to adapt its directions and orientations into new syncretic forms and innovative native expressions. Hence, among the great religious traditions of the world, Buddhism is more easily inculturated and vernacularised.

In clarifying the distinction between proselytising and non-proselytising religious traditions, we can stretch them along a continuum from aggressive and organised proselytisation to conversion by gradual absorption and integration. Effective internalisation of any religious conversion is only accomplished over a greater or lesser period, in individuals over a lifetime or with communities over generations, depending on the scope and depth of the changes involved and the corresponding extent and scale of their impact. However, when a religious tradition becomes identified with a particular group, its more universal appeal to those outside the fold is often compromised. Moreover, the group itself may find that the compulsion to 'mission' and to recruit neophytes invites a further disruption of the status quo, with perhaps unpredictable and inconvenient consequences beyond their control.

Conversion on any considerable scale into a community requires an assimilation of the converts into the new community. This demands changes in both communities, which in turn can have positive and/or negative consequences in varying degrees and ways. Yet, whether it is possible to maintain inviolable boundaries between such communities in our globalising world is a moot point.

Hence, encapsulating a community within a religious tradition and identifying the two has often enough isolated both from further religious change. The result is an 'ethnic religion', where religion and ethnic community are identified. Most often non-converting traditions belong to this category, as the Zoroastrians in India. But there are other instances too as when a religious tradition gets identified within a caste or sect, a subcultural group or some peculiar orthodoxy. There are numerous little traditions in our land and elsewhere that begin with the appeal of a founding *Sufi* or *sant* within a larger tradition and then evolve into a new religious one, which is later identified with a particular sub-caste or jati, a regional community, like the Lingayats of Karnataka, or a dispersed following, like the

Varkaris of Maharashtra. Some of these religious movements become more exclusive, others remain more open. Jainism today would be a fair example of the first, Sikhism a good model for the second.

Moreover, encapsulation is one way of compartmentalising social relationships to contain intra- and inter-group competition and conflict. Each community and individual has its own niche, its own role and function in the larger social scenario. This is what caste hierarchy is all about, and it works as long as the system imposes a legitimacy and is internalised at various levels by the different constituents. As with any change that crosses traditionally ascribed boundaries, conversion tends to disturb the status quo and precipitate unpredictable and uncontrollable consequences. Hence, the legal banning of religions conversion is proposed in the name of religious harmony between communities, but in actuality is a protection of the religious status quo.

Non-proselytising religions have often felt the need for protection vis-à-vis proselytising ones. But a strict dichotomy between these does not reflect the evolving historical reality. These religious traditions too have reached beyond their original fold to absorb and encapsulate others. Today some of these religious groups have developed a sense of mission inspired by the very proselytisers they once opposed but now imitate. The market for religious conversions is now open in many more directions than before. However, the reality of group tensions precipitated by religious conversions must be faced and defused, or better, resolved and harmonised.

Indigenous Religions

Another binary opposition being mooted in the context of religious conversion is one between indigenous and non-indigenous religions. Conversion across indigenous religious traditions is considered legitimate, but not from indigenous to non-indigenous ones. However, the category of indigenous religions is even more problematic than the concept of indigenousness itself.

The question of indigenous people and their religious traditions implies a privileged relationship to the land as its first inhabitants or rather the holy land of its especial devotees. But how far back must this go? Going back to human origins in accepted anthropology today, homo sapiens originated in Africa and migrated from there over the rest of the globe. In most habitable places, migrating peoples have followed each other, displacing, integrating and evolving into new peoples and cultures, with their own languages and religions. Seeking to freeze this process at a fixed point in time is much like the railway compartment syndrome of closing the door on others once one is safely in!

For religious traditions do in fact travel beyond their original ethnic communities and regional territories. If, as some claim, only the religious traditions that have originated in the sub-continent are to be considered as indigenous, then what happens when these emigrate beyond and more importantly when other traditions immigrate here? Is Buddhism in south-east Asia an indigenous religion after centuries of assimilation and integration there, or still a foreign one? Is Hinduism in Bali an alien religion? Will Hindus in South Africa or the West Indies, in Fiji or elsewhere in the West, always be foreigners because of their religion? Will Islam after a millennium in the sub-continent always be another 'nation'? In the postcolonial age, is Christianity forever to be conflated with imperialism in the former colonies? Or even more outrageously, is Christianity to be considered a foreign religion in Europe because it was born in West Asia, where its holy land is?

At what point in time does a people's claim to belong to the land become viable? How many generations must be born and nurtured in the place before it becomes their homeland? How long must they wait to qualify as indigenous, or must migrants always be aliens? How long before the traditions they bring, whether religious or cultural, are naturalised, accepted as part of the social inheritance of the land they now inhabit? Our tribals are perhaps the only people who can lay any valid claims to being the earliest inhabitants, the adivasis, of this land. They have been progressively displaced further and deeper into less inhabited and less habitable regions. Over time, though, they too have been Hinduised or Sanskritised, Islamicised or Christianised at different periods and in diverse places. Historically, many groups have been absorbed into the mainstream social hierarchy as sub-castes or jatis, as sub-cultures or ethnic communities, with identities very different from their original tribal ones.

The history of a continuous migration to this sub-continent cannot be gainsaid. For the less ancient ones there are intelligible and authentic records; for the more primitive ones there is decisive archaeological and linguistic evidence. They have come in wave after wave, as nomads and settlers, as craftsmen and traders, as soldiers and sailors ... They have mixed and merged, re-emerged and settled into a profuse diversity, an enriching distinctiveness. To base any claim to indigenousness on the exclusiveness of race or religion, of language or culture is no longer viable now. With the immense movement of populations within national borders, any nativist appeal to 'sons of the soil' becomes politically explosive and demographically untenable. Exclusivist appeals to a holy land for insiders that negates the claims of the 'unholy' outsiders are even more socially divisive and dangerous.

Finding Common Ground

Given the billion plus population of South Asia, the demographic impact of religious conversions cannot but be marginal. Moreover, differential fertility rates among various religious communities have little to do with religion and much more to do with economic, social and cultural factors. Amartya Sen points to the Kerala model that achieved demographic balance in a state that has a high proportion of religious minorities, without any of the draconian measures used in modern China.

Current demographic data points to one emphatic conclusion: the most pertinent variables associated most positively and robustly with declining population growth rates concern the status of women. The logic is simple: in a society, especially a patriarchal one, women carry the burden of bearing and rearing children, whereas men make the decision to have them or not. This disjunction in gender roles cannot but result in population growth rates immune to factors that do not impact such patriarchy. However, the religious demagogues who press the panic button to play on people's fears, are not the ones urging autonomy and equality for women.

Perhaps the most tragic and traumatic conflict consequent on tying religion to the land is in the Middle East where, in the words of Palestinian novelist Mahmoud Darwish, what may have begun in our present times as 'a conflict of two rights', is now careering into an unending war of a clash between 'two wrongs'. Surely, it is not impossible for such destruction and ruin to be replayed elsewhere. In this sub-continent after two bloody Partitions, in 1947 and in 1971, can we really risk anymore? In addition, is the answer to this deep-seated divisiveness an endless series of further divisions? How far is religion really the cause or merely the symptom of this disease?

There is a rich heterogeneity in the confused complexity of the religious traditions of this land. In actuality, each constitutes a family of fluid traditions and evolving institutions, of thought and experience, of practices and beliefs. They are labelled as a matter of convenience, for the sake of shorthand reference, but this is at the risk of misunderstandings and misrepresentations. For as Marxist ideologue Antonio Gramsci in his *Prison Notebooks* has reminded us: 'Every religion ... is in reality a multiplicity of distinct and contradictory religions.' (Gramsci 1996: 420) If there is no peace between these traditions, there can be no peace within them and vice versa. For what is projected to, the outside world eventually turns onto itself. Likewise, conflict within will be projected outside the fold.

Today in South Asia, conversion, both in the active and passive sense, is still more associated with Christianity and less so with Islam, though certainly not only with these two. There have been numerous and immense variations in all traditions with regard to time and place. Missionary urgency has waxed and waned, depending on historical circumstances and social scenarios. The 'non-proselytising religions' too have spread in less obvious and perhaps more gradual ways. But over a period of time these too have precipitated religious changes in peoples and places that are not different from a 'turning around', a 'conversion', even though this may not be as sharply marked by rites of passage as in other explicitly converting ones. Thus, every religious tradition must be subject to a rigorous critique that reads it against their historical background. All religious change, as in fact any social change, must be first historically contextualised and then assimilated into the present context, or it is left open to misinterpretation and misuse by fundamentalists or extremists, by rationalists or ideologues.

These in turn have fuelled communal feelings and violence. Born-again Christian evangelisers provocatively and insensitively promote conversions as their fundamental God-given right. Religious nationalists, like the *Hindutvawadis* (followers of Hindutva or Hinduness), aggressively attempt to homogenise Hinduism with communal violence and intimidation of non-Hindus. Suicidal Islamists unleash a reign of terror in the name of Allah and submission to Him. There is little effective communication across the estrangement that isolates such people and grows by the day, threatening to engulf even sane and reasonable persons on both sides in a clash of barbarisms that gets less and less civilised, a war of terror that gets more and more terrifying.

This book is an attempt to clear some of the common ground still available and reach out to the moderate middle across these divides. It is an effort to begin a dialogue to bridge the chasm before more hapless victims fall into its horrifying depths.

2

The Past from Our Present

Conversion by Absorption - *Evolution of Hindu traditions* - Counter-point of heterodox traditions – Opposing perspectives - *Islam: Not by the Sword Alone* - Demonising the Other - Encounter with the West - Indigenisation in South Asia - Crossroads and Cutting Edges - *Christianity: From Proselytisation to Dialogue* - Historical Origins - Orthodoxy in the South - Colonial Beginnings - New Initiatives - Protestant Ventures - Beyond the Elites - Colonial Connections - Inter-religious Witness - *Whose Freedom of Religion?* - The Constitutional Debate - The Freedom of Religion Bills – *The Future of Our Past*

History has been described as the passionate concern with the present. It is about discovering where we came from, so as to realise who we are and how we got here. We mine the archives of the past, not just to get at the 'facts of history', but also to find our origins in them, discover our roots there, and to reach out and grasp our future.

Certainly, we do not create the past nor can we recreate it. Yet the past is never quite dead, it lives in the present and has implications for the future. This is precisely the explosive potential of history. Not to learn from our history, is to be condemned to repeat its mistakes, to re-enact its tragedies. Those who with Henry Ford dismiss history as "bunk", open themselves in turn to be debunked by its avenging march.

We approach the past from our standpoint in the present with questions seeking answers and uncertainties begging reassurance. In this sense, all history is contemporary, that is, interpreted from the present. An exaggerated scepticism could easily fall into a paralysing cynicism or into a tired relativism. Moreover, though we are inevitably conditioned by our circumstances, we are not completely determined by them. Some measure of freedom and objectivity is still possible. However, the selection we make of the facts and the meaning we give to them will demand an honest and sensitive transparency that preconceived prejudice does not permit.

A positivist approach to history presumes to base itself on a 'hard core of facts' following the popular wisdom of 'facts speak for themselves'. But historical facts, such as they are, come to us refracted through the observer, the recorder, the transmitter ... and there may be more than one of each. 'Facts' can hardly remain 'pure' on a journey of so many possible distortions, like a game of 'Chinese whispers' down the ages, across the globe.

In trying to answer the question *What is History?*, E. H. Carr insists that "the facts speak only when the historian calls on them: it is he who decides to which facts to give the floor, and in what order or context." (Carr 1996: 11) Without a judicious selection, it is possible to drown in an ocean of detail. Our survival response to 'information overload', finally settles us into a comfort zone of oversimplified stereotypes, loud sound-bytes and colourful media images.

However, the sensitive historian must find and select facts, interpret and draw out their meaning and relevance. Of course, one's own subjectivity impinges on this and so an objectivity check against other selections and interpretations must also be put in place. Thus for Carr history is "a continuous process of interaction between the historian and his facts, an unending dialogue between the present and the past." (Carr 1996: 30) We propose such an open-ended encounter with our past for an understanding and tolerance that will endure into our future.

Colonial historians constructed a history that was more a projection of their European imagination than a faithful reflection of the sub-continental reality. They overly depended on Brahmanic textual sources and neglected subalterns ones, oral traditions and archaeological findings. This history from above supported the idea of a homogenous community of peoples that were identified as 'Hindus' in the colonial census. It greatly simplified administration and the dispensation of personal law, but hardly reflected the reality on the ground. Moreover, rather than allowing these multiple traditions to evolve on their own from within, they were frozen into a status quo from without, as Amrita Shodhan's study of *Religious Groups and Colonial Law* demonstrated. (Shodhan 2001)

The idea of a homogenous Hindu community did facilitate a cultural revival but it also encouraged the competition for political power and economic resources. This was eagerly seized on by neo-Hindu revivalists and religious nationalists in their quest for cultural and political hegemony. New understandings were projected into interpretations of the past. Later, with electoral democracy in the offing, majoritarian politics inevitable precipitated a minority one and the two cascaded into the two-nation theory that finally partitioned the sub-continent. However, culpability for this tragedy is most often reversed, depending on how one positions oneself. Little wonder then, that the Pakistani version of this history is hardly recognisable in India and vice versa.

Indian Christian communities with their affinity with the colonial West, and other minorities with their own peculiarities, had other kinds of exigencies to face. These carried their own distortions and reinterpretations. But how far any of the new or old approaches to the past are able to cope with the fluidity and prodigality of religious traditions and diverse social movements across the sub-continent over the centuries is still a moot point.

There has indeed been critical and credible history written on South Asia by a wide spectrum of authors. Much of it has come from the liberals and the Left. This too has been challenged today. We have postmodern scholars who discredit any grand narratives in favour of 'fragments' of history. But then even a fragment, in order to be such, presupposes some kind of a whole. There are also increasingly vociferous religious fundamentalists with their simplified beliefs, as also politically powerful cultural nationalist with their ideologies. In particular, Marxist scholarship is attacked by Hindu extremists, each with their political manoeuvring when in power, which later gets reversed and 'detoxified' when they fall from it. However, a comprehensive alternative to the earlier post-colonial approaches is yet to emerge as a credible, and not merely ideological or political, challenge.

A persevering Indophile and Indological scholar of great repute, A. L. Basham, has concluded: "Whatever we write about India, past, present and future, will be open to correction in the coming years, and we can only draw up an interim balance sheet." (Basham 1975: 487) He is severely critical of projecting the present into the past "to fit traditional Indian conceptions into the framework of twentieth century democracy." (Basham 1975: 490) The uncritical glorifying of the past is but an escape from the challenges of present realities. Such romanticising has been more an elitist, nationalist interpretation, a history 'from above'. However, subaltern approaches to a history 'from below' have been better at critiquing such elitist nationalism, than at constructing alternative interpretations in viable and adequate measure.

The underlying historicity of truth and the need to deal with this critically and meaningfully, must not exclude a similar approach to the obverse of this, the historicity of error. Navigating between the two is a delicate yet necessary task for any historical contextualisation. For any discussion of religious conversion to be meaningful and relevant, setting it in such a context is imperative. In attempting to sketch this in broad outline, what we leave out may be as important as what we include, for silence can scream louder than words. However, a fulsome wealth of inconsequent detail can obfuscate the bigger picture just as too superficial an exposé leaves the door open to other charges. The full picture cannot be completed in just a single venture. It must be an on-going endeavour on which we set out now with small steps but great expectations.

'Indigenous' religious traditions refer to those that have originated in the sub-continent. However, we are not positing an either-or binary opposition to non-indigenous ones. As indicated in the clarifications made in the introductory chapter, such a dichotomy would be problematic, and as we shall discuss later, it has ideological implications that have been exploited politically, particularly with regard to the question of religious conversions.

Evolution of Hindu traditions

The term 'Hindu' was originally a geographic category used in the 7th century by the Arabs for the region of the Indus valley and beyond. It has now become a construction for a multiplicity of diverse religious beliefs, and cultural practices. Only when these are deconstructed and critiqued can we realise how divergent subaltern versions and understandings are from dominant ones, and how different is their response from mainstream ones. (Omvedt 1995) In his *Myth and Reality: Studies in the Formation of Indian Culture*, (Kosambi 1962) D. D. Kosambi points to the dominance of Brahmanism as the original legitimating ideology. But this has always been contested by a rich tradition of unorthodox non-Brahmanic alternatives.

The present archaeological evidence indicates that among the earliest surviving records of human habitation in the sub-continent are those of the Harappan peoples, discovered as late as the 1920s, when Mohen-jo-daro, the Mound of the Dead, was excavated in Sindh. Much in the archaeological data is still to be decoded but there is enough evidence to conclude that their civilisation was quite distinct in culture and language from the Aryans who succeeded them. The notion of an 'Aryan' race is now discredited; rather it signifies a language category. (Thapar 2004: 351) These new people had a closer linguistic and cultural affinity to the nomadic tribes of Central Asia. It is now accepted that they came not in a concerted invasion as was thought in the 19th century, but in waves of migrations through the mountains in the north-west in the early half of the second millennium BC.

By then Harappa was already on the decline due to causes as yet unclear. Was it the deterioration of trade with the Middle East, or an ecological crisis? We may never know. With the coming of the new immigrants, its people were displaced and pushed further south, as some proponents of Dravidian culture have argued. Little, if any, real continuity between the Harappan peoples and the living cultures of today has been established even in north India, though some have suggested this. If anything, the indications are distinctly otherwise. Romila Thapar's study on "Imagined Religious Communities? Ancient History and the Modern Search for a Hindu Indentity" concluded that what we know of Harappan culture does not match with Vedic texts. For example, (Basham 1989) the Indus people knew the tiger but not the horse or the lion, whereas the Vedic hymns do not mention the tiger, but they do refer to the lion and the horse, which was introduced into the sub-continent by the Aryans.

The oldest of the four Vedas, the *Rigveda*, older than the *Iliad*, makes little mention of Indus cities. These were not popular religious texts of urban dwellers, rather they reflected a still nomadic people, at least at the time of the earlier hymns, which Basham has characterised as

> "composed by and for the religious aristocracy of an intrusive race who had entered India some time earlier and were

expanding at the expense of the indigenous inhabitants, of whom some were pushed eastward and southward by the invaders and others were incorporated as second-class citizens in the tribal society." (Basham 1989: 10)

The fourth and last Veda, the *Atharva-Veda*, already reflects a very different cultural world.

The Upanishads, interpreted by some to mean 'sitting near', were composed around 700 to 600, or even 200 BC. Philosophical reflections or doctrinal formulations begin to be articulated in this period, to which the belief in transmigration can be traced. This is first mentioned in the *Brhadraranyaka* Upanishad, the oldest and longest. Upanishadic speculation revolved on the individual *atman* as the subject of *karma* and rebirth. Here we already have intimations of the later *Advaita* Vedanta or non-dualism. But its non-dualism was opposed by the *Sankhya* system of the sage Kapil. The Lokayatas, also called Carvakas after their teacher Carvak, also espoused materialism and vigorous atheism. There is, then, very early testimony to the diversity of philosophic traditions, which were not considered completely separate from the religious ones.

But Vedic religion also evolved into the *Pauranic* traditions and its exuberant expressions of popular religiosity, as was represented in epic poems such as the *Mahabharata* and the *Ramayana*, which were eventually converted into religious texts by a Brahmin priesthood. Most famously with the interpolation of the *Bhagvadgita* in the *Mahabharata*, we have the acknowledgement of the impersonal, *nirguna* Brahman fused with the devotion to the personal, *saguna avatar* of Vishnu in Krishna, as the high point of *bhakti*, premised on *varnashrama dharma* of society. *Gitabhashyas* were common even from the time of Adi Sankara. Lokmanya Tilak (1856-1920 popularised them for political reasons, while Gandhi used them for spiritual ones. Thus, the *Bhagvadgita* has now come to be the most influential religious text among Hindus. *Bhakti* or devotional cults are more persistent and pervasive among religious Hindus today than ascetic practice or mystical spiritualism. Indeed, the myth-making capacity among devotees is still very much alive as is evidenced in the spontaneous devotional cult of Santoshi Mata. (Dwyer 2006: 46, 61)

There is a rich variety of local compositions and even oppositional narrations of conventional texts in folk and tribal religious traditions. It makes for an enormous complexity that resists any homogenising. However, this is subsumed under an overarching umbrella of a pan-Indian Brahmanism, that Sanskritises these traditions, though this was less successful with the heterodox ones, like Jainism and Buddhism. Yet, even under this umbrella, the doctrinal diversity and institutional autonomy of these sects and cults were largely maintained so that there has never been a monolithic Hinduism. Indeed, Hinduism itself is a complex construct and not an organic unity, as is sometimes projected today. Such constructs amount to impoverishment rather than enrichment for any tradition, though it may well empower the leaders even if it does not enable the devotees.

Centripetal Sanskritising forces in the Hindu traditions have never quite overcome and subdued the centrifugal de-Sanskritising ones. There have always been vigorous heterodox religious traditions within the larger Hindu fold, like the de-Sanskritising 13th century Tamil Veda, *Acharyahridayam* by Akakiya Manavala Perumal Nayanar, or the Mahanubhav Panth in Maharashtra. (Hardy 1995: 40) In fact, the major post-Vedic religious traditions, including Vaishnavism and Shaivism, which are today regarded as sects of Hinduism, were traditions as distinct in their own individuality as the heterodox Jainism and Buddhism that rejected the Vedas.

The notion of an integrated common Hindu religion originated with the European Orientalists who, as we know, had their own agenda. The idea was made to stick by the colonial administration with its codification of customary law and the official demographic census. Romila Thapar traces 'Hindu' as a self-descriptive term to the 15th century, and 'Hinduism' itself was first used in English around 1830. (Madan 1997: 177) This was taken further in colonial debates and controversies that sharpened religious self-definition and hardened religious identities. Ancient India was now imagined as the 'golden age of Hindu India'. However, even the Gupta period was hardly the classical golden age of India, but a later retrojection interpretation? As D. D. Kosambi perceptively observes: "Far from the Guptas reviving nationalism, it was nationalism that revived the Guptas" in the 19th century. (Kosambi 1975: 313)

The origins of contemporary Hinduism are still traced to the Vedic period. However, if the Vedas represent the construction of a single community then it is a literary-religious one, not a historical-political one. For these were nomadic communities in transition to settled agriculture, hardly one people premised on any religious orthodoxy, though they did have a common, syncretic cultural world. It already presages the multiple imagined communities based on varying identities and traditions. This has been the direction of their evolution, to ever-greater diversity and heterogeneity. The sense of the 'Aryans' as a single people is more a construct of 19th century Orientalism. It was at this time too that Hindus felt the need for constructing a 'Hindu community' as a requirement for political mobilisation.

Moreover, these religious traditions did interact as they spread and merged. R.C. Dutta eulogises the Aryanisation of North India, claiming that "the circle of civilisation spread wider and the zone of unreclaimed barbarism receded farther and farther ... It is a story of the spread of Hindu civilisation among hitherto unknown countries and aboriginal nations." (Dutta 1906: 198-200) Sarvepalli Radhakrishnan's *The Hindu View of Life*, based on his Upton lectures delivered at Oxford in 1926, establishes how the missionary impulse very early led to the absorption of whole tribes:

> "In this sense Hinduism may be regarded as the first example in the world of a missionary religion. Only its missionary spirit is different from that associated with the proselytising creeds. It did not regard it as its mission to convert humanity to any one opinion. For what counts is conduct not belief." (Radhakrishnan 1927: 37-38)

N. K. Bose called this the "Hindu method of absorption", (Bose 1994: 177) not by rejecting earlier beliefs or demanding doctrinal assent, but by integration in the caste hierarchy and conformity to the Brahmanical way of life.

R. C. Majumdar tells the story of *Hindu Colonies in the Far East* as far as Cambodia and through the Malayan archipelago to Bali and Borneo. (Majumdar 1963) E. R. Tambikuttu's *History of the Tamils from Prehistoric Times to AD 1800*, (Tambikuttu, n.d.: 8) speaks of "Brahmin missionaries" settling in *Dravida*, south India, to become "pioneer missionaries" there, like the sage Agastya in the *Ramayana*. The *bhakti* cults too spread with their *sant-kavis* (saint-poets) and *bhaktas*: at times evolving into distinct even unorthodox religious sects, like the Lingayats of Karnataka; at times converting other Hindus and even Muslims to form more conventional ones, as Chaitanya did; at times establishing a new and syncretic religious tradition, such as Kabir (1398– 1448) and Guru Nanak (1469–1539) did. Moreover, there are *tantric* practices at the edge of conventional ritual and practice, and even beyond that more mainstream Hindus would earnestly disclaim and perhaps disdain.

However, the present legal situation is even more open-ended. The Indian Constitution in Article 25 (2) explains the term 'Hindu' as including Jain, Buddhist and Sikh religions and this is repeated in all the relevant subsequent legislation. The Hindu Code Bill of 1955–56 brought together previous personal law in a single Act and the three religions mentioned, included under the term 'Hindu" in Section 2 (1) any other person who was not a Muslim, Christian, Parsi or Jew. The term then is defined negatively. Any Indian by birth, who is not of another religion and does not explicitly reject Hinduism, is a Hindu in law, and comes under Hindu personal law.

D. D. Kosambi in *An Introduction to the Study of Indian History* claims that Brahmins pioneered the transformation of a forest-based, hunter-gatherer people into caste-based peasant agriculture. Those still outside the caste system, such as tribals and adivasis, were regarded as "backward Hindus" by the doyen of Indian sociology, G. S. Ghurye, in one of the earliest post-Independence studies of *The Scheduled Tribes* (Ghurye 1963: 20). Other anthropologists regarded them as animists echoing the early colonial censuses from 1871. With the 1911 Census, the term was discontinued. The Census Commissioner, E. A. Gait, in a circular proposed to exclude, from the category "Hindu", lower castes and others not served by Brahmin priests and not allowed temple entry. Conservatives initially welcomed this but later it was opposed and aborted (Sarkar 2002: 84).

Faced with the syncretism of multiple beliefs and practices and even self-definitions, Gait in 1911 ordered the census enumerator to assign "the persons concerned to one religion or other as best he could." (*Census 1911, Volume I, i (India Report), p.18*) (ibid. 225) Sudipto Kaviraj explains how the 'fuzzy boundaries' between communities began to be replaced by more rigidly defined ones as the Census began to construct them as 'enumerated communities'. Including the Scheduled Castes and Tribes within the Hindu fold was not just a practical or a speculative question; it was an urgent political one with the anticipation of electoral representation.

Yet these peoples have preserved their religious traditions and identity, and many among them today are no longer content to be labelled as 'backward' or as 'Hindus'. Neo-Buddhist converts are a telling indictment of this and their numbers are increasing. Adivasis are now claiming their own distinct religious identity outside the Hindu fold, though in the Census their *Sarna* religion, an animist faith, is not officially acknowledged, while the tribes in the northeast are choosing to see their identity at the margins of the Hindu fold or even outside it, if they convert to another religion.

In modern times, we have explicit missionary movements within the accepted Hindu tradition that convert, or re-convert as the case may be, in a deliberate and organised manner. The Ramakrishna Mission, the Arya Samaj, the Chinmayananda mission, the Krishna Consciousness movement, and others are modern-day missionary enterprises recruiting new members to their cause, at times apologetic and defensive, at others assertive and aggressive, but certainly committed and engaged. Interestingly, the Ramakrishna Mission in West Bengal even filed a petition in the High Court in 1981 claiming minority status as a religion distinct from Hinduism, which the court upheld in 1985, but which was finally rejected by the Supreme Court in 1996.

Radhakrishnan's *Hindu Way of Life* as a spiritual quest, not a doctrinal creed, provides the crucial insight into the underlying unity that grounds the diversity of the Hindu religious traditions. Indeed, it is difficult to reject or exclude someone who claims to be a Hindu. Already in 1910, the *Daily Hitavadi* in Bengal on 5 November concluded a discussion on this topic thus: "whoever calls himself a Hindu is a Hindu"! (Sarkar 2002: 84) Belief was not relevant, though social customs were to be respected. It is a religion of orthodox practices, not of orthodox Doctrine.

This has been the great strength of Hindu religious tradition down the ages, and its great weakness too. However, the perception as to which is greater varies with where one positions oneself in the heterogeneity versus homogeneity debate. Any attempt to homogenise such a rich and multi-faceted tradition under a hegemonic hierarchy will impoverish it religiously and devastate it culturally, even if it yields short-term political gains.

How distant this is from V. D. Savarkar's 1923 definition in *Hindutva: Who is a Hindu?* in terms of 'pitru bhumi' and 'punya bhumi', fatherland and holyland! A seriously committed Hindu academic, Arvind Sharma, opines that "the great challenge Hinduism faces in our times is to ensure for all Hindus an equal opportunity in determining what Hinduism should be for our times." (Sharma A. 1996: 22) But first Hindus will have to challenge the legitimacy of self-appointed arbiters of their faith. Jyotirmaya Sharma's response to Hindutva could well be their shibboleth: "Every Hindu decides what is Hinduism. That space ought to remain inviolable. It is a space worth living for and dying for." (Sharma J. 2003: 13)

What we have then is a core of Brahmanic beliefs and practices expressing a minimal orthodoxy in terms of a personal/impersonal understanding of the cosmos, the practice of *varnashrama dharma* and the acceptance of caste hierarchy. But around this core there is a vast expanse of heterodox sects and cults that distance themselves either by default or with deliberation, to the point of being more in opposition than in continuity with this minimal orthodoxy. These are today claiming an identity of their own. There is no linear progression in this evolution, no recognised founder, no organised church, but rather a mosaic of cults and deities, of rituals and myths, which form a rich and distinctive pattern. They intersect and interact, and draw on a common Indic civilisation for their symbols and beliefs, which run the whole gamut from atheism to animism, from *bhakti* to *tantra*, from *jnana* to karma. A "Parliament of Religions" as Swami Vivekananda characterised Hinduism.

Eventually, *Vedapramanya*, the acceptance of the Vedas as revealed texts, is the only recognised criteria of orthodoxy for the *sanatan dharma*, (eternal religion) of mainstream Hinduism. This puts a question mark on the numerous religious traditions, now assumed Hindu, that are not founded on this *Vedapramanyam*. It becomes particularly pertinent for those communities that have not been completely Sanskritised, or rather Brahmanised, such as our tribals and dalits. and now have begun to contest their cooption into Hinduism with a new awareness of their own identity.

Much earlier, Jainism and Buddhism were regarded as heterodox traditions, not because they were considered to be *nastik*, or atheist, but because their explicit rejection of the Vedas placed them outside Hindu orthodoxy.

The *shramana* traditions of Jainism and Buddhism were spread all through the land by wandering ascetics, surely the earliest evidence of missionary monks in our land. But legally all such persons are Hindus today, even those belonging to these heterodox traditions that in their founding origins unambiguously rejected the Vedas as inspired scriptures, pointedly discounted Brahmanism and did not accept caste hierarchy or *varnashram dharma*.

Jain sects spread during the 7th century BCE but it was Mahavir who gave shape to them in the 6th century BCE. (Thapar 1966: 64) The rigorous ascetism of Jainism and its teaching of *ahimsa* (non-violence) and *anekantavad* (many-sidedness of truth) was counter-poised to the Brahmanism of the time. But it was not able to support the warrior ethic of a conquering class on its way to dominance or the exigencies of peasant culture for long. In South India, Jainism was the dominant mass-based religion. Indira Viswanath Peterson gives a convincing description of this for the Tamil region.

Here Digambar Jainism was widely prevalent even in the remote countryside from the first to the 6th century CE, as reflected in Tamil literature of that period. Peterson draws on Tamil sources to reconstruct how Jainism began to be perceived as "Sramanas Against the Tamil Way of Life: Jains as Others in Tamil Saiva Literature". (Peterson 1998: 163-185) By the 6th or 7th century, with the rise of Shaiva temple religion in the Kaveri delta, a coincidence of interests emerges between the settled agriculturalists and the Brahmin priests. Moreover, the Jain ethic with its privileging of *ahimsa* and asceticism, was in dissonance with the growing warrior ethos. To consolidate their hegemony, the Chola kings decisively linked the royal cult with Tamil Shaivism, which became identified with Tamil culture almost until the 19th century. The story of the impalement of 8,000 Jain monks at Madurai is indicative of the hostility and violence associated with the disappearance of Jainism is the South.

David Ludden's *Peasant History of South India* (Ludden 1989: 204) is relentless in his harsh judgement: "Tamil literature makes it painfully clear that the foundations of the medieval synthesis were soaked in blood from the battles that established the temple-centred devotional Brahmanic ceremonial practice at the centre of the agrarian order." Tamil Jains held their own until the 12th century. Today Jainism survives in small communities in the north and especially in the west. They have retained their ancient religious heterodox tradition and their distinct identity to become a closely-knit and prosperous people.

Buddhism converted masses of people across the sub-continent to its egalitarian and liberating message with its critical and rational discourse. In the 3rd century BC, it received imperial sponsorship in the Mauryan Empire with the conversion of Emperor Ashoka (265–232 BC), who issued the first recorded edict for tolerance, the famous 12th major rock edict:

> "On each occasion one should honour another man's sect, for by doing so one increases the influence of one's own sect and benefits that of the other man ... Again, whosoever honours his own sect or disparages that of another man, wholly out of devotion to his own, with a view to showing it in favourable

light harms his own sect even more seriously. Therefore concord is to be commended, so that men may hear one another's principles and obey them." (Thapar 1961: 255)

However, with the eclipse of the Mauryas, Buddhism practically disappeared from our land. This saga of the spread and disappearance of Buddhism, and its resurgence again in our time is yet to be fully told. To an enormous extent, after the first millennium BCE, which was its formative period, Indic civilisation was dominated by Buddhism, to the point that some scholars would insist that ancient India was Buddhist India. (Ovedt 2003: 118)

Indeed, Buddha's message was essentially universalist and inclusive, non-dogmatic and rational. No wonder it was so readily adopted by other cultures and adapted to other lands. Its rejection of caste hierarchy and critique of Brahmin ritual, especially animal sacrifice as practised at the time, converted masses of people to its egalitarian and liberating gospel, and it spread from Afghanistan in the north to Sri Lanka in the south, all through south-east Asia and into China, reaching Japan.

It was in the more egalitarian villages of south Asia that Buddhism spread and established itself. In the more stratified societies of China and Japan, it remained a minority religion. However, in India itself, at the material level, Buddhism could not displace the economic foundation of caste in an inegalitarian society; hierarchical Brahmanism suited this better. At the ideological level, *advaita* philosophy subsumed Buddhist ideas into an internal critique, thus countering its external challenge and alternative vision of society, and finally eclipsing it.

The impressive Buddhists monuments so widespread throughout the sub-continent are a testimony to the pervasive influence and popular support it had for nearly 1,500 years. However, neither of the heterodox religious traditions could destroy the caste system. For, even though their teachings were in emphatic opposition to caste, and their religious organisation embodied egalitarian and communitarian features from an earlier tribal period, they did not undermine the political economy, which reproduced and sustained the system. During the turmoil and disruptions of the Gupta period (BC 300-700), the quest for royal legitimacy, through Brahmin-controlled genealogies ensured that "the status of the Brahmin was firmly established." (Thapar 1966: 166)

The decline of Buddhism in India is testimony to the absorptive capacity of Brahmanic Hinduism, which eventually converted and integrated Buddhism. By the 9th century BC, Buddha becomes the ninth *avatar* of Vishnu and the inherent contradictions between the two religious traditions are resolved by one driving out the other. Brahmanism was not tolerant of Buddhist heterodoxy. The basic tolerance of the Upanishadic and the early Buddhist period turns to paranoia and insecurity with the *Puranas* of the Gupta period. Buddhism was seen as a threat to Brahmin religious hegemony and a competitor for popular support and royal patronage.

In spite of its humanising and liberating potential, Buddhism had its institutional centre of gravity in the monasteries, not in the life of the people. The Tibetan Buddhist chronicler, Taranath, writing in the late 16th and early 17th century, mentions three hostile rulers who opposed Buddhism: Pushyamitra Shunga at the end of the Mauryan period, Mihirakula, who raided north India in the 6th century, and finally the Turks in the 12th century. The final blow was struck, according to Babasaheb Ambedkar and others, by the "sword of Islam", which destroyed the great Buddhist centres of north India like Nalanda. Gail Omvedt insightfully points out that Brahmanism adapted to the new rulers. It did not offer the same kind of challenge to Islam as Buddhism did, not militarily but more profoundly, since both were competitors as universal and egalitarian, missionary and communitarian religions, whose peoples were engaged in international commerce and trade. (Omvedt 2003: 175) Thus while there was no single decisive battle, this was a millennium-long war.

V. D. Savarkar echoes the dark sentiments of the anti-Buddhist *Puranas* even as he claims to humbly admire the Buddha. He regards him as one, who came before his time, too soon to be of help to India or of use to humankind in general. He bemoans how Hinduism was emaciated by Buddhist pacifism. For Savarkar "Buddhism had its centre of gravity nowhere." (Savarkar 1964: 18)

The absorption of Buddhism into Hindu religious traditions was not without its tensions. Vivekananda made a gallant attempt to overcome this by positing a reciprocity between the two:

> "Hinduism cannot live without Buddhism and Buddhism not without Hinduism ... The Buddhists cannot stay without the brain and philosophy of the Brahmins, nor the Brahmin without the heart of the Buddhist ...Let us joins the wonderful intellect of the Brahmin with the heart, the noble soul, the

wonderful humanising power of the Great Master." (Vivekananda 1962: 366)

Gandhi saw the Buddha as a 'Reformer of Hinduism", not as the founder of a new religion. He wrote in *Young India*, (24-11-1927) that in his opinion: "the essential part of the teachings of the Buddha now form an integrated part of Hinduism ... for Gautama was himself a Hindu of Hindus. ... The Buddha never rejected Hinduism, but he broadened its base. He gave it a new life and a new interpretation." Sarvepalli Radhakrishnan too considered Buddhism and Jainism to be "protestant movements" in *The Hindu View of Life*.

In India, we take pride in 'Bhagwan Buddha' as a son of India – actually his birthplace, Kapilavastu, is in modern-day Nepal, once the only officially designated 'Hindu' state. Hindus now seem to accept the Buddha, though once they rejected the Buddhists. However, Ambedkar and the neo-Buddhists, whose conversion was precisely a rejection of Hinduism, emphatically reject the Hindu claim to Buddhism as part of Hinduism, and certainly Buddhists in other countries too would affirm this as earnestly.

Nehru and Ambedkar make distinctly different conclusions on the Buddhist and Hindu periods of our history. Nehru's 'unity in diversity' is a nationalist reading of our history by an upper caste-class leader. Ambedkar's awareness of division and hierarchy comes from his conscientisation at the bottom of these social strata.

In Nehru's *Discovery of India*, there is both "continuous growth and often conflict", (Nehru 1947: 89) a continuing dialectic of synthesis and unity in "a vivid and growing national life". Eventually, he sees not a decline of Buddhism in India so much as its absorption into "a Brahmanism or (to use a later word) Hinduism, which became a symbol for nationalism." (Nehru 1947: 105)

Ambedkar regards the Buddha as a revolutionary who challenged the Vedic-Brahmin tradition. (Gore 1993: 292) His incomplete manuscript on *Revolution and Counter-Revolution in Ancient India* (Moon ed. 1987a, Vol. 3) demystifies this early Aryan history as "the worst kind of debauchery: social, religious and spiritual" (ibid. 151-52) and claims Buddha as "the first Social Reformer and the greatest of them all" (ibid: 164). In recognising the rights of shudras and women, it released an enormous vitality, suppressed till then, and engendered a vigorous religious and artistic revival. But eventually, "The Triumph of Brahmanism" (ibid: 229-30) heralds "the Birth of Counter-Revolution." (ibid. 266-332)

The religious traditions we have here called 'indigenous' have their own distinctiveness, and identity, but they do share a certain commonality in their world-view, and especially in its philosophical underpinnings. Thus they understand the concept of dharma as 'righteousness', though the content and expression of this righteousness may widely vary. They accept the concept of karma as a universal law even as some treat it with less rigidity than others do. They all seek moksha, nirvana, as liberation from the cycle of re-birth, the ultimate human quest for the ultimate Reality, and yet there is much variation in their religious ethic, from otherworldly to this worldly.

The two religious traditions we will now turn to, began with decidedly different world-views from the ones we have just considered. Their distinctiveness from indigenous traditions is more in evidence than their commonality with them. However, over the centuries these too have inevitably evolved and found their place in the larger entity of a sub-continental culture that we can validly call Indic civilisation.

Islam: Not by the Sword Alone

The demonisation of the 'other' is often the result of a perceived threat, real or imagined. The rapid expansion of Muslim rule westward soon after its founding by Muhammad made Christian Europe feel encircled. They launched the Crusades to recover the Holy Land but more so to break the Muslim dominance of the trade routes to Asia. This failed, but eventually, Europe's mercantile nations opened the sea route to the East, putting the Muslims on the defensive and affecting their trade disastrously. Jerusalem was eventually retaken in 1917 and General Allenby made his historical remark that the Crusades were now finally completed! In 1920, Damascus was taken and the French commander went up to the tomb of Salaudin in the Great Mosque and cried: *Nous ravenous, Salaudin*! (We are back, Salaudin!).

With substantial immigration into Western Europe in the second half of the last century, Muslims are now a significant and vocal minority there, but their integration into European civil society is still problematic. The animosity between the two protagonists has not been resolved and the 'War on Terror' is perceived by extremists on both sides as the latest Crusade. In such circumstances, religious conversion from either side only heightens hostility and perpetuates prejudice.

For the preservation of culture and religion is a sensitive issue in a pluralist and secular modern world. The desire of Muslims to retain their distinctive identity and traditions is surely a legitimate one in any truly democratic and liberal society. Too much attention focuses on Islamic fundamentalists and extremists, rather than on the genuine struggle waged within this community by moderates and modernisers to adapt without necessarily compromising the essentials of Islam. Muslim communities the world over are now on the defensive from without and within. However, this has not always been their story and we need to set the present in the context of the past.

The prevailing perception of Muslim 'jihadis' as religiously inspired, has generated a wave of xenophobia against Muslims in the West. "All Muslims are not terrorists. But why are so many terrorists Muslims", expresses a common prejudice, as though there was some kind of monopoly involved. Yet the Irish Republican Army (IRA) was not accused of 'Christian terrorism' in the West, nor is the United Liberation Front of Assam (ULFA) named 'Hindu terrorists' in India! Moreover, what is too readily dismissed is the role of the West in the present revival of jihad, which means 'struggle' rather than 'holy war'.

For instance, the CIA (American Central Intelligence Agency) with its sponsorship of the mujahidin fostered the concept of 'jihad' to fight the Soviets in Afghanistan, which was then condemned as a terrorist state. Osama bin Laden was trained by the Americans and he went on to found Al Qaeda that is now the main target of the American war on terror. Today Islamophobia in the West, especially after the terrorist attack on the United States on 11 September 2001, is reinforcing the historical misrepresentation of Islam, which goes back many centuries to the Crusades and before.

In 632, the newly converted Arab *Ummah*, the community of believers, under a united command, burst out of the desert and filled the vacuum left by the Byzantine and Persian empires, which had fought themselves to exhaustion. They beat the Byzantines at Yarmouk in 634 and the Persians at Qadisiya in 637. The Moors swept through North Africa and occupied Spain. They crossed the Pyrenees in 718 and Abd al-Rahman overran Burgundy as far as the cities of Lyons and Besancon. However, they were finally turned back at Poitiers in 732 by Charles Martel and expelled from France in 759. Only in 1492 after the fall of Granada were the Moors expelled from Spain by Ferdinand and Isabel of Castile.

In the 11th and 12th centuries, the Crusades did recover the Holy Land for a while, but their short-term success left long-term antagonisms, even after their final defeat at Acre in Syria in 1291. These antagonisms were further exacerbated when the Ottoman Turks conquered Asia Minor, advanced into the Balkans and took Constantinople in 1453. Suleiman the Magnificent laid siege to Vienna but failed to take the city in 1529. The defeat of the Turkish fleet at the battle of Lepanto in 1571 marked a turn in the tide, though the Saracens were once again at the gates of Vienna as late as 1683, where they were finally turned back.

In such circumstances, the Christian polemic directed against Islam and its Prophet was a defensive reaction of a people who felt threatened by the Muslim other. The Enlightenment brought a more even-handed though a rather paternalist perception of Islam. The colonial expansion into the Middle East, with Napoleon and after, did little to assuage mutual suspicions. Now the Arab Muslim world was at the receiving end.

Given the once dramatic expansion of Muslim conquests and now the alienation of the Muslim world, it is hardly surprising that defensive and threatened antagonists would perceive each other in negative terms. The conventional wisdom in the West, carried over into their colonies, is that the 'sword of Islam' was the main instrument for its spread. This remains the popular prejudice even after Muslim empires have collapsed and Muslims nations, subjugated by the West, are intimidated by its modernity.

Muhammad himself did not expect Jews and Christians in Muslim territories to convert, unless it was out of conviction. What is perceived as Muslim intolerance came much later, and it was inspired more by prevailing political realities, than Quranic religious injunction. Such confusion between religion and politics is not peculiar to the Muslim world. Religious traditionalists of all persuasions have not always respected the separation of religion from politics. Even mature democracies in the West often honour this more in the breach than in practice, as appeals to the 'moral majority' makes evident even in a post-Christian West.

The early Caliphs, the supreme civic and religious heads among Muslims, especially Umar-ibn-Khattab, who launched the *Ummah*, the Muslim community, outside the Arabian Peninsular to set up an empire, showed little interest in conversions. The expansion of Muslim conquests did spread the Islamic faith, but it was only after the boundaries of the early Muslim Empire were stabilised with the

Umayyad (671-750) that a process of consolidation and conversion began.

Sufism, which came to express the mystical contemplative aspect of Islam in numerous sects and fraternities, began as a protest movement against the wealth and power of this period as it was a departure from the simplicity of the early Muslim community and its inspiration towards justice and equality. The Sufis took their name from the course woollen ('suf') garments they wore after the habit of Christian ascetics. They were also influenced by Neoplatonism and the agnosticism of the time. This was the formative period of Islam, when the main divide between the Sunnis and Shias was formed.

The classical period under the Abbasids of Baghdad (750-1258) followed, during which the study of theology and philosophy was established and various schools of jurisprudence and law flourished. Indeed, it was the Arab encounter with Greek philosophy that preserved it through the Dark Ages in Europe, to be recovered only in the medieval period via Spain. Prominent among these Islamic philosophers was the Aristotelian Abu Ali ibn Sina (980 – 1037), and Abu al-Wahid Ahmad ibn Rushd (1126-1198), known as Avicenna and Averroes in the West respectively. Unfortunately, they were less popular in the East. Eventually in the Muslim world, it was the anti-philosophical theologians who prevailed over Greek philosophy.

The classical period ends with the sack of Baghdad by the non-Muslim Mongols in 1258, a trauma from which the Arab Muslim world never quite recovered. Their centres of learning were destroyed, and even after the conversion of the Turkish tribes to Islam, Timor-I-Lang sacked the city again in 1401.

However, Islam expanded beyond its political boundaries mainly into Central Asia, where a number of Turkish tribes accepted the faith, though many pre-Islamic practices continued. This was mainly the work of wandering Sufis. In sub-Saharan Africa, Islam travelled mainly along the trade routes, from Timbuktu to Sudan, and as far as Uganda. (Goddard 1995: 128) The Turks in turn furthered the expansion of Muslim rule under the Great Seljuks (1038-1194) and the Rum Seljuks (1077-1307), while Ottomans Turks completed the eclipse of the Byzantium with the fall of Constantinople in 1453.

Turkish dynasties were also established on the Indian sub-continent with the rise of the Ghaznavids in the 10th century, and Muslim rule reach its zenith with the Mughalss (1526-1858) ruling most of the sub-continent except the far South. In Southeast Asia,

Muslim traders settled and established their rule through indigenous local leaders. (Robinson 1999: 38)

In these later phases of the expansion of Muslim rule, once again conversion followed conquest. There are great advantages for a subject people in adopting the religion of their conquerors and vice versa, for the rulers to have subjects of the same religious persuasion. However, the survival of significant minorities of Jews and Christians under centuries of Muslim rule is testimony to its tolerance towards people of the book. If they were not treated as complete equals, for example in regard to the *jizya*, the poll tax on non-Muslims, they were assured security of life and property and allowed to practise their faith, which is more than we can say about how 'infidels' were treated in some parts in medieval Europe. While it is true that Latin Christians did not survive in North Africa, after the Reconquest of Spain Muslims were given the choice of conversion or expulsion. In the East, Oriental Christianity survived even though it did not thrive, and the Jews did not experience the anti-Semitism and periodic pogroms that ravaged them in Europe.

In the later conquests, the process of Islamisation was incomplete as in the Sultanates in Indonesia, where pre-Islamic culture and beliefs are still vibrant today. (Geertz 1973) In the Indian sub-continent too, centuries of Muslim rule have not resulted in an overall majority of Muslims. This again is evidence of the gradual growth of the Islamic faith, not just by the soldiers, but also by itinerant Sufis and traders who settled among the indigenous population.

In sum, Islam as a universal faith spread not by the conquering sword so much as in the wake of Muslim rule that created a favourable environment for the conversion of subject peoples. Many did convert to take advantage of the benefits of the official state religion. Those, who chose not for forfeited these, but were allowed to practise their faith. Obviously, there was an inducement to convert and when the alternatives to refusal were extremely stark, it could easily amount to compulsion. Moreover, political resistance was often met with religious reprisals but Muslims rebels were not exempt from such political vengeance. Shia-Sunni relations illustrate this.

In practice, the difficulty with relations between the ruler and the ruled, when they are of different faiths, is to separate the religious from the political, and Muslims rulers were not exceptional with this conflation. Religious differences with other religious traditions or within the Islamic fold were generally tolerated when they posed no political threat. Much of this changed as the decline of Muslim rule put it on the defensive in the colonial world and more so in the post-colonial one.

The 17th century witnessed the decline of the three Muslims empires: the Ottomans, the Safavids and the Mughals, but it also overlapped with a period of reform led by men like Muhammad Baqir Majlisi (1628-1700) in Persia, Shah Wali Allah of Delhi (1703-1762) and Muhammad bin Abd al-Wahhab among the Arabs (1703-1792).

Colonial dominance was as varied in its impact as the diverse colonising powers. The scholars responded to this Western challenge by calling for a revival of Islam. Muhammad Abdu (1848-1905), the grand Mufti of Egypt, argued that Islam had not failed the Muslims. The Muslims had betrayed Islam. He called for a return to the sources. In India, the Deoband School was founded in 1887 and still thrives today. However, with decolonisation came the birth of political Islam. The Wahabis, named after the radical reformer Abd al-Wahhab, gained control of Saudi Arabia and its immense oil wealth, the Muslim Brotherhood was established in Egypt in 1928 by Hassan al-Banna (1906-1949), and the Jamaat-i-Ismaili (the Muslim Party) was found in 1941 in India by Abu 'l-Ala Mawdudi (1903-1979). Islam became the rallying cry but it was generally subservient to the emerging new nationalism. (Robinson 1999: 51)

These new states were a colonial legacy in which the politicisation of religion was hardly exceptional. However, their failure to meet the rising expectations of their people left them disillusioned with the promise of progress and alienated in the modern world. Their seething discontent set off a resurgent Islamism that had pan-Islamic pretensions, with an ingrained animosity to the West. Such movements are more correctly read in the language of social protest against injustice or as defensive reactions to adverse change, than as merely religiously inspired reform or revival. Ayatollah Khomeini in Iran with his Hizb-Allah (Party of God) and the Taliban in Afghanistan are obvious examples of this.

However, these were by no means the only responses or even the most dominant ones at the beginning of this decolonisation of the Muslim world. Mustafa Kemal Pasha (1881-1938) also known as Ataturk (Father of the Turks), founder of the secular Westernised state of Turkey, was the exact opposite of this Islamism. In India, the Sunni Tablighi Jammat, founded by Muhammad Ilyas (1885-1944), is an apolitical quietist revival movement that has now branches in ninety countries.

Today, Christian and Muslim religious leaders are moving towards a more conciliatory inter-religious dialogue, but political tensions have further escalated, with the Muslims nations feeling increasingly marginalised and disillusioned by the modern world, dominated as it is by the West. Francis Fukuyama was positive about the eventual victory of democracy and modernity in the Islamic world in *The End of History*. (Fukuyama 1992: 46) However, more prevalent today is the theory popularised by Samuel Huntington of the inevitable *Clash of Civilisations* (Huntington 1996) between Christianity and Islam. This has become a self-fulfilling prophecy, expediently reinforcing old stereotypes and prejudices. Conveniently forgotten are the vicious clash of ideologies and interests mainly within Western civilisation itself in the last century, with two world wars and the threat of a third. Even today, Western interests are aggressively pursued by neo-conservatives with their new and self-serving doctrine of preventative intervention and the pre-emptive strike, as has happened in Iraq.

The West once perceived the Moors and Saracens as a threat. Today the Muslim world is seen to be a problem. Muslim rulers, once amazed at the uncivilised Crusaders from Europe, now in the post-colonial age are struggling to catch up with modern civilisation. There are more complexities here than can be addressed in this review. However, the encounter of the Muslim and Western worlds will demand much soul-searching on both sides for any real understanding or meaningful rapprochement, and this must include both Islam and Christianity as religious faiths. A beginning has been made, but there is still a long way to go.

The challenge confronting the Muslim world today cuts deeper than even the crisis precipitated by the sack of Baghdad by pagan Mongols in 1258. For eventually, the Mongols were converted and Islamic civilisation regenerated in other empires of even greater power and prestige. Some radical extremists may still dream of a similar resolution to the present crisis when the self-sufficiency of Islam is being put to question as never before in the modern world.

In the sub-continent, British colonial rule replaced Muslim dominance. This was further consolidated and brought directly under the crown after the brutal suppression of the Great Revolt or Uprising of 1857. Thereafter to stymie any such 'mutiny' in the future, British divide-and-rule policy set Hindus and Muslims against each other. At the time of Indian independence in 1947, this culminated in the Partition of British India, which precipitated more problems than it resolved for both new nations. There was tragedy and trauma for the religious minorities, who were left, isolated, and for the emigrants, who had to leave everything behind with no place to go. The horrendous violence and bitterness of that experience still fuels mutual antagonisms. A second division between West and East Pakistan in 1971 has left three nations in the sub-continent. This has certainly questioned the religious basis of the first Partition but it has not helped to defuse inter-religious communal tensions.

Past memories still surface and are reinforced by communal riots of increasing intensity and frequency. These brutal ethnic cleansings intensify religious and ethnic divisions. Not surprisingly, religious conversions are likely to have an explosive fallout. Simplistic stereotyping will not help us to address such complex and emotionally charged situations. A careful historical critique will be just the first step to unravelling the complexities and coping with the continuing tragedy.

The West's encounter with Muslims in the Middle East has inevitably carried over to the perception of Islam elsewhere in their colonies. Yet the largest number of Muslims is found east of Karachi. According to the 2011 Census of the two countries India with a Muslim minority (177.2 million) is still the third largest Muslim nation after Indonesia (205.8 million) and Pakistan (178.0 million). The prevailing perception of Islam and Muslims in India, especially since the colonial period, and now in the post-colonial one has been much influenced by the West's, and then read into the events of the past. The resulting entanglements are difficult to sort out and disengage, even as they must not be ignored. However, neither must the distinctiveness of Indian Islam be dismissed.

For it is precisely in the enduring encounter between living religious traditions that India so uniquely affords, that we can all learn, not just to cope, but to mature into a society striving towards being a modern, secular democracy. The risk of failure is great and it would be disastrous, but even a modest measure of success would be a challenging example to the world

There are two opposite readings of the encounter of Muslims and Hindus in the sub-continent. The first concludes to insurmountable antagonisms and unbridgeable chasms between them; the second, in contradiction, sees centuries of coexistence that have brought about a composite sub-continental culture. We reconstruct historical events depending on how we position ourselves about this divide, but if we are to constructively engage each other across our divisions, we must learn from the mistakes stressed in the first reading, and also be open to the possibilities uncovered by the second. This will set the stage for better mutual understanding and a more meaningful exchange.

The Arab Muslims first came to India as traders who settled along the west coast. In 629 AD, in Kodungallur, Kerala, they built the first mosque in India, and the second in the world where Juma prayers were recited. It was based on Hindu architecture and resembled temple. Conquerors followed later. Muhammad bin Qasim, a young Arab general, occupied Sindh in 711 when the local ruler failed to protect Arab dhows from local pirates. Muslim invaders from the North came later but eventually these marauding hordes, first Afghans and later Turks, settled to found the Delhi Sultanate, which held power from the 12th to the 16th century. Babur (1483-1530) defeated Ibrahim Lodi at Panipat in 1526 and Muslim rule reached its zenith with the Mughals, cutting off further invasions from the North. The extent of their suzerainty was exceeded only by the British, who finally deposed the last Mughal figurehead in 1858 after ruthlessly suppressing the Great Uprising of 1857.

Earlier invaders, from Alexander's Greeks to the Asiatic Huns and after, had settled and been assimilated into the all-absorbing cultures of the sub-continent. However, Islam with its characteristic traditions and distinctive doctrine was not so easily assimilated. The early Muslims invasions saw a spate of temple destruction and looting. A careful analysis of these events over centuries of Muslim rule indicates two motivations for temple desecration: to show dominance in newly conquered territories, when temple patrons were disloyal to the ruling power. (Smith 2003: 49) However, this does not amount to a theology of iconoclasm. Certainly, the political ideology involved is not to be justified today, but it was not peculiar to Muslims at the time. Religious wars in Europe and elsewhere resulted in much the same thing.

Under the enlightened Mughals, a workable synthesis was envisaged. Akbar the Great (1556-1605), Babur's grandson, ruled from the Hindu Kush to the Bay of Bengal and from the Himalayas to the Arabian Sea. Humayun Kabir (1906-1969), politician-philosopher, argues convincingly that Akbar's was "the first conscious attempt to formulate the conception of a secular state" (Kabir 1955: 21) in the country. However, this was not followed through by his great-grandson Aurangzeb (1658-1707). His policy of Islamisation finally led to the disintegration of the empire after his death, the Marathas gaining control of the south and the Sikhs coming to prominence in the north. Finally, the British united the whole sub-continent under their imperial rule.

A significant though too little noticed anomaly about conversion in pre-colonial India is this: whereas the longest period of Muslim rule was at the centre of its dominance in the north around Delhi, it was not here but in the peripheral areas of east Bengal and in the north-west that Islam became a majority religion. Surely if conversions were mainly by force, then the majority of them should have been in and around the centre of Muslim power, where force could more easily induce the local population.

Richard Eaton examines three possible explanations for this "inverse relationship between the degree of Muslim political penetration and the degree of conversion to Islam." (Eaton 2004; 106) The sword of Islam as the principle instrument of conversion, a theory dating back to the Crusades, does not stand up to these geographical facts. Political patronage too is an inadequate explanation because it would obviously decrease, not increase from centre to periphery. A more attractive and recent theory is that of social liberation, but this projects our present values and concerns onto a people's past perceptions and preoccupations. A careful reading of Persian sources suggests that in the presentation of Islam, monotheism against polytheism, not the ideal of social equality against caste hierarchy, was emphasised. (Eaton 2004: 109)

Eaton's own theory is more nuanced and close to Robin Horton's studies in Africa (Horton, 1975). Here the constructive role of social change is stressed in the larger context of the socio-cultural and ideological changes taking place. Thus, preliterate peoples at the margins of an expanding agricultural society are acculturated and absorbed into the religious ideology of that society. (Eaton 2004: 110) The process is gradual and facilitated by various agents of the new order; in coastal areas they were merchants and traders, more in the interior were village Qajis, or judges. However, it was the Sufis, who received the most attention and exercised the most influenced more so, when their tombs became centres of pilgrimage and blessings, *Baraka*. All this adds up to a gradual assimilation of Islamic religious belief and cultural practice.

In Bengal, Muslim rule arrived in the 13th century, when Mohammad Bakhtiyar led his Turkish cavalry down the Genetic plain in 1243-1244. He overran the Buddhist monasteries in north Bihar and took the royal city of Nadiya in the north-west of the delta. However, Muslim society emerged only two centuries later. Eaton's careful study of *The Rise of Islam and the Bengal Frontier, 1204-1760*, (Eaton 1994) traces the expansion of Islam into the Ganges delta to illustrate this. In the west delta, Muslim rulers co-opted local leaders of already arable lands. In the east delta, agriculture was expanded through the semi-Hinduised tribes. This resulted in a process of Sanskritisation in the West and of Islamisation in the East.

Thus in east Bengal Islam is not considered a foreign religion by the peasant masses. It was not identified with the urban *ashraf*, the noblemen who came from outside, but rather as a 'religion of the plough', which the *ashraf* disdained. This distinction between the 'high' religious culture of the elites and the 'low' religious traditions of the rustic masses, a distinction neither peculiar to Bengal nor to Islam, illustrates how new religious traditions introduced into a society often get acculturated and indigenised among the lower strata and gradually become acceptable in society at large. Many would argue that this was rather similar to what happened with Christianity in the Greco-Roman world and after.

In the provinces on the north-west periphery, the prominence of Islam was mainly due to immigration by Muslim tribes from the north, Afghans and Turks, who settled and intermarried. However, west Punjab was Islamised by a process of acculturation and assimilation similar to that in east Bengal. Here a nominal commitment to Islam was not an unusual consequence of a political and economic integration into a regional Indo-Muslim state. A second order of integration then followed with Sufis and other agents of Islamisation.

The southern periphery in the Tamil region was not islamised as was east Bengal and west Punjab. Susan Bayley's survey of *Saints, Goddesses and Kings: Muslims and Christians in South Indian Society, 1700-1900,* (Bayley 1989), concludes that Islam was spread there more by merchants and teachers, *mullahs* (theologians) and *pirs* (holy men) than by soldiers and kings. For already in the 9th and 10th centuries there were maritime Muslims communities all along the Coromandel Coast with close links to the Middle East and South East Asia. These centres created a Tamil-Arabic culture to rival the Mappilas of Malabar, as the more prominent merchants came to share in the royal schemes of patronage and affiliation.

The eventual ascendancy of the British colonial power brought new challenges to both Muslims and Hindus. However, the Muslim encounter with the British in India was rather different from that of the Hindus. The colonisers brought with them the old European prejudices about Islam, whereas the Hindus tradition and culture were being discovered by them at close hand for the first time. Enthusiastic Orientalists, led by William Stanley Jones, Max Mueller and others, constructed a golden Vedic age and precipitated a Hindu renaissance in the 18th century reform movements led by a spectrum of remarkable persons, especially in the Bengal and Bombay Presidencies.

Muslims leaders, on the other hand, suffered from a sense of loss with their displacement from political dominance, which coloured their response to colonial challenges. After the merciless suppression of the Great Revolt of 1857, they withdrew from, rather than engage with, the colonial government. The struggle against colonialism did spark reformist and revival movements, like the more westernised Sayyid Ahmed Khan of Aligarh (1817-1893) and the more polemical Munshi Meheru'llah (1861-1907) of Jessore in Bengal. Political competition between Hindus and Muslim communities was encouraged by the British, determined to retain their power. They then established themselves as the mediators and guarantors of peace. Old antagonisms revived and intensified, and not even a Gandhi could contain them. The Partition of 1947 and its aftermath is something that both communities are still struggling to come to terms with, complicated further by the break-up of Pakistan and the birth of Bangladesh in 1971.

Muslims in India have always been a religious minority in spite of centuries of political rule, especially in the heartland of the North. Among Muslims themselves, the 'men of the pen' and 'men of the sword' were always an elite minority. The majority of the Muslims have always been part of, and still belong to our toiling masses as artisans and cultivators, the rural peasantry and the urban working class. In *Islam Today,* Akbar Ahmed (Ahmed 1999: 207) points to three types of Muslims in India: the critical, the defensive, and the confused. Too few Muslims are constructively critical, too many are defeatist and defensive, and most are oppressed and confused. Thus, the real issues affecting the community get lost in a passionate politics of identity from which only the political and religious elites are advantaged.

Certainly, the encounter of Muslims and Hindus has been unfortunately skewed by colonial rule, but to put all the blame on the British is escapist, to say the least. There is always violence and many atrocities that conquerors wreak on the conquered, and history is written by the victors to enhance their own glory, until others in turn replace them and then change the story.

Several scholars like Sumit Sarkar (Sarkar 2002: 222) have pointed out that Persian chronicles were used as legitimating devices and not unexpectedly boast of the defeat of infidels and the destruction of their temples. Regional language texts use ethnic rather than religious terms for the conquerors, most commonly "Teresa" or Turk. We can hardly pretend innocence to the destruction and brutality of the conquerors, whether Muslim or otherwise. Nevertheless, we also need to examine the present orgies of communal violence that have put Muslims so acutely on the defensive. To ascribe all this to religious differences between the protagonists and miss the real political exigencies involved is surely an exaggerated, one-sided perspective.

Islam in India has distinctive features of its own. The assimilation processes have affected both Hindus and Muslims to form a composite indigenous, if not a completely integrated new culture, which goes beyond mere separate coexistence. Islam has not just adapted to, but also even adopted, many of the particular characteristics of caste, notwithstanding the egalitarian ideals of Islam. *Bhakti panths* (devotional sects) have surely been inspired by the fraternal features of Islam. Sufi and *bhakti* movements have interacted and merged to open new traditions in our religious consciousness. Urdu, a new language spoken by both communities, was born in the north. There are remarkable areas of cultural integration. Indo-Saracenic architecture has given us the Taj Mahal and more, as enduring symbols of this synthesis. Indian classical music and Kathak dance are other remarkable aesthetic achievements.

However, there are cultural fault-lines that can and has been activated for political gain, more so in recent times. Religious conflict is grounded in civic strife, but once secular battle lines are sharply drawn, then theological justification is readily invoked to legitimise violence and more. However, this is not the monopoly of any single religious tradition.

Coming back then to the two readings of this history referred to earlier, we can identify Akbar and Aurangzeb as two 'ideal types' from this past who represent two real possibilities for our future: a secular and civic tolerance or a religious and political fundamentalism. Revivalists and extremists see that the Muslim community in decline and threatened by the non-Islamic world. The pan-Islamism they advocate as a response represents a shift from the low Islam of the local masses to the high Islam of the Arabised elites.

The tension between the *Ulema*, the community of Islamic scholars, and rationalist philosophers is not new to Islam even in Islamic states. It goes back to the controversies over the *Shariah* (law) and *Falsafah* (philosophy) in early Islam. The power tussle between religious and political authorities is not a modern phenomenon. These go back to the *mullahs* and the sultans. A further conflation between the religion and politics, the sacred and the secular as envisioned by fundamentalists can only revive and intensify the old tensions and struggles, as in fact is happening today.

Sufi movements with their affinity to the *bhakti* traditions in India have the potential to soften the polarities between Muslims and Hindus and among Muslims themselves in the sub-continent. Unfortunately, these are being sidelined by fundamentalist *maulvis* and *mullahs,* clerics and scholars, from within the community. They, of course, have their own stakes, but if Islam in India abandons its quest for pluralism, both within and among the numerous religious traditions and sub-cultures of the land, there is a real danger of a pan-Islamist homogeneity overtaking the community.

Islam has certainly been resilient in retaining its distinctive identity in South Asia. Being the religion of the rulers over vast areas and long periods certainly helped to resist assimilation and absorption into the indigenous religious traditions. Muslim elites especially were in a position of advantage to preserve their identity even as they acquired indigenous characteristics and nuances. The Muslims mass in spite of upper class patronage were hardly in the same situation and the local variations and influences are even more in evidence here.

This has given Muslims in South Asia a unique position in the Islamic world between Arabisation and indigenisation. Pan-Islamism today has become a politicisation of religion that demands a closed option for the first. However, there is other more authentic and viable interpretations that have favoured more open options for the second. Every religious tradition has a core that anchors its singular uniqueness. Yet, there are also specific particulars that contextualise and enrich it as well. If Islam is at the crossroads in the modern world, then Islam in India could well be at the cutting edge of a breakthrough to a creative and constructive response to the challenge.

Christianity: From Proselytisation to Dialogue

The expansion of Christianity in the West is popularly far better known than its early spread in the East, where it took root among Arabs and Persians in the domains of the Zoroastrian rulers. It reached Central Asia by land and South Asia by sea in the early centuries of the Christian era, even before it had reached many parts of Europe. It was the official religion of Armenia much before it was so in Rome (Frykenberg 2003: 33). However, much of this history was lost when first the Arabs, and later the Mongols, overran the territories of the Byzantine and Persian empires.

The historical origins of Christianity are in the Orient and the earliest doctrinal articulation was by the Eastern Fathers of the Church, its first theologians. The first seven Ecumenical Councils of the Church up into the 8th century AD were all held in the East: two in Nicea in Asia Minor, in 325 and 787; three in Constantinople in 381, 553 and 680-681; one in Ephesus in 431; one at Chalcedon near Constantinople in 451. These universal Councils of all the bishops of the Church represent the foundational definitions of Christianity in the first millennium before the Great Schism between the Orthodox and Latin Churches in 1054.

In the West, after centuries of persecution in the Roman Empire, Christianity became an officially accepted religion with Constantine the Great in 313 AD. The conversion of Europe spread over a millennium, promoted not as a centralised movement but by the varied efforts of wandering monks and missionary bishops. By the late middle Ages, numerous monasteries and much political patronage established and stabilised Christianity. By about the 14th century, Europe was called Christendom, the Kingdom of Christ. However, the Protestant Reformation in 16th century Europe divided Christendom, and to this day, numerous sects have sprouted and grown from closed conservative ones to open progressive ones, some even beyond the horizon of mainstream churches. After the Enlightenment, modern Europe has become progressively post-Christian. The rejection of any explicit mention of Christianity in the proposed Constitution of the European Union, in spite of pressure from the Vatican, is a rather unambiguous comment on how far Europe has come from its mediaeval identification with Christianity. This is a distant cry from Hillarie Belloc who famously opined, "the Church is Europe and Europe is the Church."

All this flies in the face of the misconception that "Christianity is essentially European and European religion has traditionally been

Christian." (Frykenberg 2003: 5) Yet in India, the identification of Christianity with the West, and particularly with Europe, lingers as a post-colonial hangover enormously difficult to shake off.

In our own time, based on sober demography projections, Walbert Buhlmann sees *The Coming of the Third Church* (Buhlmann 1977) already on the horizon. This will certainly not be a European or a North American Church. Such a trajectory of change is not surprising, when we consider that Christianity has never had a single sacred language, nor was it practically or doctrinally tied to a specific location. In its history, geographically and linguistically, culturally and theologically, there has been proliferation of centres and pluralism at the peripheries. It is in this mosaic of the universal church that Indian Christianity has its distinct and special place.

Christianity came to India much as Islam did, first with traders from the Middle East and much later with colonial conquerors from the West. The Acts of St. Thomas, though an apocryphal gospel attributed to one of the original twelve Apostles, may be a romantic tale, but rests on sound historical probability. The Syrian Christians in South India trace their origins to St. Thomas. This is substantiated by the flourishing exchange between the Middle East and the West Coast of India at that time. Thus, when the Portuguese came seeking 'Christians and spices' on their arrival in Travancore, Vasco da Gama was surprised to be greeted on the streets of Cochin in Spanish by a Jew expelled from Toledo!

The tradition of St Thomas's sojourn in the South goes back to his landing in Kodungallur near Kochi in 52 AD and his death in Mylapore in Chennai in 72 AD. (Fernando and Girpert-Sauch 2004: 59) The copper plates found in Malankara in Kerala date to the 345 AD, claim Christians to be Nambudhiri Brahmin converts, equal in status with the Nayars, a Kshatriya caste. (Frykenberg 2003: 131)

These Christian communities were well established and integrated into local society even as they kept their own identity and some minimal contact with the Chaldean patriarchate in Mesopotamia. They had their niche in the local caste ecology, and were granted ritual status equivalent to the Nayars. This ethnic Christianity made no organised effort at proselytising. They lived in harmony with local communities, but did not spread beyond.

The coming of the Portuguese disrupted this harmony. For the Portuguese these Indians were 'imperfect' Christians. They attempted to latinise them, subjecting them to a colonial episcopacy through the decrees of various ecclesiastical councils, as at the Synod of Damper in 1599. This was vigorously resisted by the Syrian Christians, for it would have compromised their status in the caste hierarchy, reducing it in the eyes of the Hindus to that of the recent low caste converts in the Latin rite church. Eventually this resulted in a schism from the Roman Church in 1665. The bitter memories of that period have since sustained the separation between the Syrian Orthodox churches of Kerala and the Roman Catholic one. Some of these churches did later come to accept communion with Rome, while retaining their Orthodox status. Others have remained outside this allegiance, within the Orthodox tradition but separated from Rome.

The Portuguese changed the balance of power between the local Christians and their rulers in areas where they held sway. Though their dominance at sea did not survive the Dutch onslaught and they were replaced on the east coast by the French, they did leave their mark in their colonies of Goa, Daman and Diu on the west coast. Landing in Calicut in 1498, Vasco da Gama (1460-1524) sought to control the sea trade in the Indian Ocean. In 1510, Portuguese commander Afonso de Albuquerque (1453-1515) at the request of the local Hindus in Goa to free them of Muslim rule from Bijapur, took Goa after defeating Adil Shah and went on to consolidate Portuguese possessions in the Estado da India (the state of India).

Albuquerque began with a pragmatic policy of non-interference in religious affairs. This was contested once the Franciscans arrived in 1517. The Charter of 1526 accepted local customary laws of inheritance and included the maintenance of temples. However, legislation that is more coercive was to come in 1540, somewhat ridiculously called the 'Rigour of Mercy'. A policy of 'convert or leave' was put in place following the logic of church-state unity, which did not allow for 'strange gods' before them. Their images were to be broken and destroyed. However, in the lucrative port city of Diu, in Gujarat, they were more pragmatic, sparing the temples there lest the flight of the Hindu bania (merchant) community brought commerce to a halt. (Robinson 1998: 65)

Portuguese oppression did meet with some violent resistance as the massacre of some Jesuits missionaries and their collaborators at Cuncolim in 1583 testifies. However, many Hindus did migrate across the borders and settle outside of Portuguese territories, most chose to stay and accept the new religion. However, their gradual Christianisation after conversion was a syncretic process over generations in which local custom persisted with Christian practice, as Rowena Robinson painstakingly shows in her study of *Lived Christianity in Southern Goa* (Robinson 1998).

To force the pace of religious assimilation, the infamous Inquisition was instituted in 1560, abolished for a while in 1774, and reinstated in a new form a few years later, to be finally suppressed in 1812. However, contrary to popular credence, its records confirm that it was directed against the defective faith of Christians rather than the beliefs of non-Christians. These drastic measures of ritualised terror were only likely to produce horror and internal resistance. They were not geared to a stable internalisation of the faith.

Anthony D'Costa describes the slow and painstaking process undertaken by the Jesuits, who had arrived in Goa in 1542, and local clergy and catechists, for *The Christianisation of the Goa Islands*, over which the Portuguese held sway at the time (D'Costa 1965). In many places, whole villages converted to maintain village unity, which was necessarily implicated because of the lands it held in common. This, according to the legend recorded by Henry Heras, happened in Divar, while in other villages; leaders persuaded their people to convert, as in Chorao (Heras 1933: 39-44). By the end of 17th century, Christians were in a majority in the old conquests of the Goa islands.

New territories were added in the second half of the 18th century. By then, inspired by the European Enlightenment, a measure of religious equality and tolerance was introduced by the prime minister of King Jose I the Marquez de Pombo, with the 'Law of Equality' in 1761 and his 'Instructions' in 1774. These guaranteed local uses and customs and mitigated discrimination against non-Christians.

The Enlightenment also inspired political aspirations in Goa, which registered one of the earliest anti-colonial revolts in the sub-continent, the Conspiracy of 1787, sometimes called the Uprising of the Pintos, after the main protagonists. Three priests and some army officers met in Candolim to plan a revolt with the Bardez and Salcette regiments of mostly Goan soldiers. They were betrayed and brutal reprisals followed public executions, exile, and imprisonment.

The Christianising influence of the Portuguese was not confined to Goa and its possessions to the north especially around Bassein, now Vasai, near Mumbai. It stretched all along the Malabar and Coromandel coasts in South India, where conversions were mainly among the fisher folk and the lower castes. The missions were subject to the jurisdiction of the Archbishop of Goa, who in 1886 was given the title of Patriarch of the East Indies. The Portuguese government sustained these missions under the *Padroado Real*, the royal right of the patronage that allowed the Portuguese government to name bishops to the seas in their territory in return for their material support of those churches. For such communities as the Mukkuvars and Paravas at the bottom of the caste hierarchy, there were obvious advantages in aligning with the Portuguese. These were not just economic and political, for religious conversion further affirmed a new cultural identity even if this was still a socially contested one.

However, as Portuguese power waned so did their support to the missions. In response, the Congregation for the Propagation of the Faith was founded in 1622 under the direct jurisdiction of the Papacy in Rome, thus beginning a new era in Church history. Conversion to Christianity in Goa was dependent on ecclesiastical and political power. Without colonial patronage, this could not be replicated in territories outside colonial dominance. Moreover, too close a reliance on colonial governments presented its own serious limitations in terms of political interference and compulsions of expediency, but more so in terms of the theological and cultural premises on which this missionary enterprise was founded.

In overcoming such limitations, the Jesuits successfully initiated a bold and far-sighted venture in religious adaptation and cultural dialogue. They sought to disengage Christianity from its western cultural moorings and present it, not as the local religion of Europe, which was so much a part of the earlier missionary endeavour, but as a universal religion with a message for all humankind. They avidly studied the alien cultures they encountered in an effort to understand in order to be understood.

In China, Matteo Ricci (1552–1610) entered as a Buddhist bonze in 1583, but eventually adopted the dress and style of a Chinese mandarin in Beijing. The Chinese rites he initiated attempted to acculturate an indigenous Chinese church, and for a while, it flourished under the patronage of the Emperor himself. In Goa, Thomas Stevens (1549–1619) attempted to make the New Testament story more accessible to the indigenous population with his *Krista Purana* in the local language. This is now an acknowledged classic, an epic poem in the traditional *pauranic* genre. Rudolf Acquaviva and his companions were in Agra at Emperor Akbar's invitation, engaging others scholar in religious debates for which his court was well known for some time.

Further south, Robert de Nobili (1577-1656) came to the Madurai mission in 1606 and soon distanced himself from low caste 'Parangis' and colonial missionaries to set up his ashram and adopted the lifestyle of a *sanyasi*, an acetic. He mastered Tamil and Sanskrit and discovered the Vedas. He was given the title of *Tattava Podhakar*, Teacher of Reality, by which he is still known today, though he is buried in an unmarked grave. Max Mueller regarded him as the first European Sanskrit scholar.

De Nobile's vision was of a completely indigenised church, situated within Indian cultural traditions, served by a Christian *sanyasi* priesthood, using Sanskrit as its ritual language. However, he had to compromise on caste, eschewing contact with lower polluting castes to make himself acceptable to the higher castes. This is not something we would condone today. Even then, he had to justify his methods at the Synod in Goa in 1619, presided over by the archbishop. For a while, his arguments prevailed. However, he too had to adjust by introducing a band of '*Pandarasamis*' in 1640, missionary priests to administer to the low castes.

Like the Chinese rites, the Malabar rites were an expression of an indigenous church that flourished in numbers, with scholars such Constance Busch (1680-1746), who wrote the first Tamil grammar, and martyrs like John de Britton (1647-1693). These were bold and innovative ventures far ahead of, and out of tune with the colonial church. After a long and bitter struggle, the Malabar rites were suppressed by Rome in 1704 and the Chinese ones in 1707. Eventually, the Society of Jesus too was suppressed in 1773. An epic era in the history of the missions ended. The church in Asia had failed to break its colonial moorings to western culture. Only when colonialism was breathing its last did the Roman church withdraw the oaths required of missionaries against the Chinese rites in 1939 and the Malabar rites in 1940.

The Protestant Reformation in Europe in the 16th century did not inspire a missionary undertaking until almost a century later. The Lutheran missionaries arrived in India some 200 years after the Portuguese captured Goa. Two German Lutherans, Bartholomew Ziegenbalg, who was twenty-four years old at the time and Henry Plütschau, who was twenty-nine, landed at the Danish port of Tranquebar near Madras in 1706. By 1707, nine Tamils were converted, the Bible translated into Tamil in 1714 and the first Tamil pastor ordained in 1734. The Protestants followed the earlier trail of the Catholics as they covered Thanjavur, Mayavaram, Cuddalore and Ramanathpuram.

In 1799, at Serampore near Calcutta, William Carey with two young colleagues, Joshua Marshman and William Word, began the specialised study of Indian languages. The Bible was translated into a dozen Indian languages and Carey himself became a professor of Bengali and Sanskrit at Fort William College in Calcutta (now Kolkata). Protestants acknowledge Carey as the father of the modern missionary movement and Serampore College continues his work even today.

In its early period, the British East India Company did not welcome Christian missionaries since it felt their proselytising would antagonise the local population and compromise their commercial interests. It took a struggle to get the 'Pious Clause' proposed by Charles Grant, allowing missionaries into the territories controlled by the Company, accepted into the Company Charter in 1813. Grant argued that "Christianity of the English sort might keep Indians passive, just as it had induced contentment in the English lower working order" (Cited Horne 1967: 13). Later the Christianising role of the missionaries in the colonies was perceived as complementary to the civilising mission of the British. As sharing a 'white man's burden' an effective force for the civilising responsibilities of the colonial administration. However, officially the Government adopted a neutral stance visa-vis religion. Not all missionaries, as we shall see, were collaborators, but largely people found it difficult to distinguish the 'white man who ruled' from the 'white man who preached'.

After the Great Revolt of 1857, the reforming zeal of the Government seems to have waned. The missionaries too, somewhat disheartened by their lack of success with the people at large turned, to more indirect methods, like education and charitable 'works of mercy'. Alexander Duff had predicted that education would be the time bomb ticking at the roots of Hinduism and would blow it to bits. However, this turned out to be more a damp squib. For once again local religious traditions proved quite resilient even as western education was accepted. Caste was a major obstacle to religious conversion. People's social relationships were inexorably tied into the hierarchical system that ruled their lives.

However, the threat of Christianity and the challenge of Western colonialists were far more radical than that presented earlier by Islam and Muslims invaders. For not only was the colonial power politically and militarily dominant across the region, it was perceived as a more progressive culture and a more effective scientific civilisation. Religious revivalists and social reformists did respond to this with varying measures of success. Some even speak of a Hindu 'Renaissance', with Ram Mohan Roy and others who challenged local traditions while criticising colonial practice. Eventually, though Christian converts remained a small minority in the sub-continent, there were some remarkable regional successes.

In 1704, the Malabar rites initiated at the beginning of the 17th century by the Jesuits in the Madurai mission were suppressed. This was a devastating setback for the Catholic Church in south India. The Protestants were even more uncompromising on caste and local religious practice than the Catholics were. Upper castes, especially Brahmins, were less opposed to converting, when they were allowed to keep their ritual caste purity on which their social status depended. Their conversion in any significant numbers became a distant dream and the 'downward percolation theory' of Alexander Duff was discredited and discarded. Attention now shifted to the lower castes and marginalised peoples from the folk and little traditions. These had already begun to approach the missionaries in different places seeking their help for various reasons, and were favourably received.

The tribal church in Chotanagpur, covering the present state of Jharkhand, Chhattisgarh and parts of Madhya Pradesh, West Bengal and Orissa, represents a well established indigenous Christianity. Its story goes back to 1845, when the first Lutheran missionaries arrived from Calcutta and took up residence on the outskirts of Ranchi, a district town, now the state capital of Jharkhand. For five years, no one approached them until one day four tribals of the Kabir Panth came seeking to know about Jesus, whom they had read about in a Hindi pamphlet featuring extracts from the New Testament. On 9 June 1850, the first adult baptism took place.

Outsiders had come into the tribal hinterland as moneylenders and stayed on as property owners under the Mughals, and a process of acculturation had begun. The Kabir Panth promoted a third way between Mulims and Hindus and attracted some tribals. In 1765, the defeated Mughal Emperor conceded the *divanis* of Bengal, Bihar and Orissa to the British. However, more interested in revenue than reform, the East India Company implemented an administrative system very much in contradistinction to traditional tribal law. The subsequent land alienation and massive immiseration resulted in numerous revolts by the tribals here and elsewhere. All of these were ruthlessly repressed by the colonial administration. However, once the tribals perceived the missionaries to be on their side, they began to join the churches enthusiastically.

The Catholics were late arrivals on the scene, mostly Belgian and German missionaries, and not so completely identified with the British. The Jesuit Constance Livens (1856-1893) and his companions began in 1885 with elementary education and health services, but soon Livens realised the tribal's were unable to defend themselves in the colonial legal system and so were losing their lands and becoming bonded labourers. After preparing himself with a study of the history of land possession in the area, he had great success in defending these simple people in the courts. He was relentlessly opposed by moneylenders and government officials, and even denounced in Calcutta, then the colonial capital. Eventually, he was sent home to Belgium to recover his health, where he died a year later at the early age of thirty-seven.

The German Jesuit, John Baptist Hoffmann (1857-1928), built on and carried forward Livens's work. In 1909, he started a Catholic Cooperative Society and a grain bank a few years later to provide the tribal's with a safety net against the loan sharks, who exploited them with exorbitant interest rates. Today, the Catholic Church in Chotanagpur is more than a million strong, and has several tribal bishops and even its own cardinal.

From Serampore in Bengal, the Protestants launched their mission in the northeast in the 1820s and 1830s. The New Testament was translated into Assamese and Khasi. In 1836, the American Baptists established a mission in Manipur though they were more successful with the Nagas in 1872, when E. W. Clark (1830-1911) arrived in their hill country. However today there was no coordination with various missionaries and the organisation, which has left a legacy of rivalry among them that, lasts until today.

Education and medical work were seen as a positive contribution by the local people and welcomed by the government, which was extremely stretched and precariously placed in these far-flung parts. Though the British had annexed Assam in 1842, they established an office in Kohima only in 1878 and brought the country of the Ao Nagas under their administration later in 1889.

However, the modernising tribal elites stood by the missionaries, and so did the government as long as they were no threat to the colonial administration. When missionary activity threatened political stability, the colonial government unhesitatingly curbed it. In turn, when the government interfered with their work, the missions would delink themselves from it. We have here an ambiguous relationship between local churches and government that was quite typical of other places in the country.

Such tensions have carried over into the present situation in the northeast. For these tribal peoples the concept of nation, of control by a distant national government, was alien. Even the colonial government was not much of a presence here. The Japanese invasion in World War II opened for them a window on the world. At the battle of Kohima in 1944, the Nagas fought with the British. However, to think they were battling for the colonial government is a misconception. They were just defending themselves from the brutalities of the Japanese army. Nor did the tribal's take much part in India's freedom struggle. In fact, in 1929, the Nagas had expressed their desire to the Simon Commission not to be under Indian control. (Marak 2000: 190)

In 2001, Nagaland was a state of 1.74 million people, of which almost 90 per cent are Christian, predominantly Baptist. However, the decadal census shows that most of the increase came between 1941 and 1951, from 17.9 per cent to 45.7 per cent, an increase of 27.8 per cent. Over the next two decades, it increased by 23.3 per cent to 66.7 (Sarkar 2002: 232). The colonial government surely cannot have facilitated this. More likely, the trauma of the war precipitated it. With immigration and demographic changes today, tensions between locals and outsiders, between tribes and government have accentuated.

Richard Eaton in his study of "Conversion to Christianity among the Nagas: 1876-1871" (Eaton 1984) argues that the peculiarities of the Naga cosmology, its evil spirits and high god, their social relations that privileged village unity, facilitated their conversion. Once the Christian God was perceived as more powerful than their high god was, conversions followed. Initially, village leaders would oppose them as breaking the unity of the village. However, when the movement reached a critical mass they would join or even lead the conversions. This is not an uncommon pattern in cultures with a strong communitarian life, which absorbs the individual. However, this can work both ways as it does with caste-based society.

Like tribal peoples, the backward castes too were oppressed and exploited in various degrees and in multiple ways. The worst were the 'Depressed Classes' or the 'Untouchables' at the very bottom of the caste hierarchy, the outcastes who today are called 'dalits', the oppressed. Tribal conversions were mainly in areas of tribal concentration, Chhotanagpur in central India and in the North East. The dalit communities are more widely distributed through the land, and their conversion pattern reflects this.

The early missionaries, like the early Orientalists, focused on the high castes, to which they had access through sacred texts and learned pundits. Theirs was a top-down model of social control and changed derived from their own feudal past. Not surprisingly, they made similar assumptions about caste society. Winning over the high castes, especially the Brahmins, they believed, would win over the others. However, the *savarna*, the twice born high castes, were far more resistant to missionary persuasions, and the strategy failed. Attention then shifted to the *avarna*, the lower castes, and an interest in their folk religion and popular culture.

De Nobili had already seen the need for this when he instituted the *pandarasamis* to minister to the Paraya castes in Madurai. Caste was seen as a socio-cultural structure, comparable to the medieval estates or the classes in Europe. However, this was a compromise with the egalitarian teachings of Christianity, though at the time it was thought to be a transitional one. In hindsight, the transition did not happen and there is no support for such a position in the Catholic Church today.

The Protestants, however, were much less willing to compromise with the caste system, even as a temporary transition to a more authentic Christianity. In 1853, George Uglow Pope and his High Church missionaries of the Society for the Propagation of the Gospel in Foreign Parts called upon government officials in Thanjavur to publicly flog 'Hindu Christians' for refusing to give up caste rules (Frykenberg 2003: 15). In the second half of the 19th century, hundreds of 'shudra' Christians were forced to leave the Anglican Church in this district over the caste issue, even though these dissidents continued to report themselves as Christians in the Census (Oddie 1977a: 5). Some Protestant churches were at times willing to expel groups that refused to accept other lower castes into their church.

The first dalit conversion movement in the United Provinces began in 1859 with the Mazhabi Sikhs, regarded as lower castes even though Sikh tenets reject caste. By the 1880s and 1890s, the movement spread to the Lal Begs and the Chamars, both outcaste groups. In the Punjab, the United Presbyterian Mission made a breakthrough in the 1870s with the Chuhras, a caste that traded in hides. The movement gained momentum in the 1880s and carried over into the 1920s. By 1931, there were 4, 00,000 dalit Christians among this group.

In the south, the Parayas and other 'Depressed Classes' were converted by various churches like the Church of Scotland, the Methodists, the Reformed Church, the Anglicans, the Salvation Army. In Andhra, the Baptist Church had begun work with the Madigas near Ongole in 1866, while the Anglicans and Methodists worked with the Malas in that state. In western India, there were lesser movements: in Gujarat among the Dheds, and in Maharashtra around Jalna, Ahmednagar and Kolhapur, mostly among the Mahars and Mangs.

The colonial presence had precipitated changes in the late 19th century and these castes were seeking new identities to shake off their oppression and take advantage of the opportunities opening up before them. Conversions proceeded despite the resistance of caste, but caste survived in spite of conversion to Christianity. For caste was too strong a factor in Indian society, too firmly embedded in its socio-cultural and eco-political structures, to be overcome by either the egalitarian ideology of Christianity or of Islam.

In a caste society, conversion meant an immediate excommunication and inevitable alienation from their caste community. This was the only community the individual had, thus making individual survival apart from the group unviable. It was especially so with vulnerable outcaste groups, more dependent on higher castes for their livelihood and wellbeing. Hence, conversion was feasible for groups, rather than individuals. This of course only renders such collective conversions even more problematic.

Given the dominance of caste in traditional communities, collective movements across caste boundaries were a rational way of self-protection against caste structure. Isolated individual ventures could hardly survive such social compulsions, but groups did have a chance and were even able to preserve some of their cherished customs and old traditions in their new situation.

The complexity of conversion among the lower castes is best illustrated in Andhra Pradesh, where many of the churches were involved. The movement began with the conversion of Venkayya, a robber chief, in 1849. (Hodge 1946: 27) Over the next eighty years, groups of 50-200 converted, (Graham 1946: 55) from about 75,000 in 1851 to 300,000 in 1891. (Sarkar 2002: 232) In 1901, there were 29,186 Christians in the Krishna district, in 1928 there were 1, 22,500, (Hodge 1946: 28) and still growing in numbers.

The story of Vedanayagam Samuel Azariah (1874-1945) is necessarily entwined in the complications and ambiguities that are inevitable in a mass conversion movement like this. He was the first Indian to be ordained to the Anglican episcopate in 1912 as Bishop of Dornakal. A Nadar, a Tamil caste once considered backward, he laboured tirelessly for the dalits in Andhra Pradesh. He worked at the grassroots with the poor and the outcastes, the ordinarily discounted people, who are more spoken of, than spoken for, and who remain voiceless while others ventriloquise on their behalf.

Azariah argued in favour of, and supported these conversion movements because he knew that, once expelled from their caste community, converts could only survive in groups. Moreover, he felt he could not refuse entry to those knocking at the door, for here the case was more of being sought after than of seeking out. He would have readily understood Ambedkar's mass conversion movement to Buddhism. With Gandhiji, he opposed reserved constituencies for the Depressed Classes. He felt this would eventually lead to their further isolation. Azariah admired Gandhiji for bringing back India to her religious ideals and the two had worked in tandem on the question of reserved seats for the Depressed Classes, but they fell out on the issue of religious conversion, and a meeting in 1937 in Nagpur failed to bring about reconciliation.

In 1936 Ambedkar, well aware of all that the church had done for the outcastes of Hindu society, met him and asked, if in becoming Christians the 'Harijans' ('Children of God', the name Gandhi gave to the outcastes) would be united as one people in one church, free from prejudice. Azariah later admitted that he had never felt so ashamed in his life because he could not answer 'yes', but could only come away in disgrace! This epitomises the contradictions of mass conversions in caste society.

Azariah was a complex person, deeply religious and dedicated, but caught in the complicated situation between his commitment to his church and the political exigencies of his time, as many of his Christians contemporaries were then. C.F. Andrews is perhaps one of the best known among these. Coming from a Tamil convert family, Azariah became a missionary in Andhra to the Telugu people; belonging to the Nadar caste, he devoted his life to the dalits, being a colonial Indian he became an Anglican bishop. However, for all this, he was rooted among his people. His commitment was to an indigenous form of Indian Christianity rather than to a Christianised version of nationalism, which he knew all too well had precipitated horrific wars even among 'Christian nations', two world wars in his own lifetime. He supported India's freedom struggle but was apprehensive of a nationalist chauvinism, as Gandhi and Tagore also were. However, today in our world of secularism and nationalism, Azariah has fallen off our radar screen.

Colonialism was founded on an ideology of superiority, both racial and religious. Its legitimacy was premised on its supposedly civilising mission, of which Christianising was but a part. However, the colonial involvement in the missionary enterprise is too easily and uncritically taken for granted. While it cannot be dismissed, it needs to be fine-tuned and contextualised. The compulsions of the colonial government were not always compatible with the goals of the missionaries. There was the inevitable conflict of interests between religious conversions by the missionaries and the political order and economic profits of the colonial state. The most obvious example was evangelising China, which missionaries promoted, and the Opium Wars, which colonialists waged. Even when the colonial governments were sympathetic to the missions, their priorities were not easily compromised, and often opposed by the missionaries.

Hence, the simplistic conflation of colonialism with Christianity leads to the crude assumption of an alien religion forced on hapless natives against their will. This is still used as a rhetorical device even against Islam. Once again, it is the voice of the dominant classes and castes, who speak for the subaltern ones, supposedly misled by force, fraud and inducement. Giving no real and effective agency to the oppressed as actors in their own history and the changes that affect them reflects an elitist mindset, one not too different from the colonial ideology itself.

Though most Christian converts in the 19th century in India were dalits and tribals, it is difficult to hear them speak directly in the records of their own religious conversion and in the controversies that followed. They were too unlettered and considered too unimportant to have their say then. Today, they are more vocal and speak for themselves, but the dominant voices on this, as on other such matters, is still not theirs.

The religious conversion of subalterns involved a self-assertion that underscored a positive change in self-esteem. Moreover, it opened up prospects of better healthcare and education that could not have been unattractive to people long deprived of minimum human needs and basic human rights.

Colonialism facilitated some changes and stymied others, and so the relationship between the colonial officials and the missionaries was quite ambivalent. Most missionaries were rooted in Western society and often had strong nationalist sentiments, as became apparent when their colonial countries went to war against each other, or when, with their governments, they opposed the freedom struggles in the colonies. No doubt, there were notable exceptions. However, in this regard, much missionary practice was not in keeping with its preaching. It stood exposed when challenged by their converts, who associated what they had learned from their mentors with progress and modernity.

Yet in spite of — or maybe because of — this interaction with colonial rule, which at times their churches supported and at others opposed, Indian Christians developed their own distinctive identity with its own peculiar characteristics. Some carried over from its indigenous past, some derived from the colonial masters, both with variations across geographic regions and religious denominations. There are many Christianities in India and many different mission theologies. However, the abusive arrogance of some of the early proselytisers cannot be justified. It belongs to the religious imperialism of a colonial past.

The rich encounter between Christianity and the religious traditions of India is best illustrated by the men who truly represented this dialogue. De Nobili had once envisioned a Sanskritised version of an Indian church. Brahmabandhab Upadhyay, who started out as a nationalist terrorist, eventually converted and saw himself as a modern Hindu-Christian, while reverend Narayan Vaman Tilak was a Marathi convert, a Christian *sant-kavi*. Bede Griffiths, an English monk and Swami Abhishekananda, a French one, have both been emphatic about their debt to Hinduism and have blazed new trails at the cutting edges of this encounter.

With the Second Vatican Council (1962-65), for the first time, other religions are described positively and appreciatively in an official document of an Ecumenical Council. In 1997, the World Council of Churches (WCC), in its statement from the Hindu-Christian Consultation held in Varanasi, has condemned aggressive proselytising in the pursuit of numbers that takes advantage of vulnerable people. I hope that now; such misled missionaries will be outdated, at least for the mainstream churches.

This transition from proselytisation to dialogue is aptly summed up by Raimon Panikkar as he describes the historical evolution of

Christianity through five sequential self-understandings. (Panikkar 1987) These are not discrete periods in time, but perspectives that follow on each other, even as they overlap with, and persist in, each other.

For the primitive church, to be a Christian was to be a witness, a martyr, joyfully testifying to, and faithfully interpreting the founding events and experiences of their faith. Christians were a small and ruthlessly persecuted minority, but their faith was irrepressible and contagious. With the change in imperial policy of Constantine in the 4th century, Christians came into their own. They gradually became the dominant majority, and there was little room for martyrdom. The emphasis shifted to conversion, a *metanoia*, a radical change of heart and turning to God, saying 'no' to the world and worldliness as best exemplified by the desert hermits in Egypt.

From the 8th century until the Renaissance, the very real danger of being overwhelmed by Islam led to an aggressively militant Christianity that gave rise to the Crusades to retake the Holy Land. But with the advance of colonialism the balance of power changed and the crusading spirit was channelised into a *mission*, to colonise and rule, to civilise and exploit, to Christianise and convert as new worlds began to open up to the colonial powers. The experience of this period is still alive in the historical consciousness of the colonised and continues to influence their perceptions.

In the post-colonial period, there is now a greater mutual respect and the approach to other religious traditions in and through *dialogue*, not as a strategy for the older 'mission', or a substitute for the earlier 'crusade'. Rather it must be as an authentic return to 'witnessing' to one's faith and a genuine 'conversion' of heart, learning from and enriching each other in an inter-religious encounter. There are still crusading evangelical sects focused on proselytising, for whom there is no salvation outside their 'church'. These are still living with a colonial mission, albeit a religious one. There are more extreme fundamentalists, who seem to crave the 'palm of martyrdom' like the early Christians, but end up caught in their own fanaticism. There are contemplative Christians who seek their own 'conversion' and withdraw from a this-worldly engagement to otherworldly spirituality. However, across the broad spectrum of the mainstream churches, the movement has been from proselytising to dialogue with varying degrees of commitment and multiple levels of engagement.

Who is Freedom of Religion?

When Atal Bihari Vajpayee, then Prime Minister, visited the Dangs in Gujarat after they had been rocked by violence against tribal Christians, he neither condemned the atrocities against Christians, nor did he console affected tribals there. Instead, on 10 January 1999 he called for a 'national debate on conversions'. Was he using a diversionary tactic to obfuscate the real import of what had happened? Was he trying to get at the root cause of the 'disturbances'? Was he trying to revive an issue already settled but not to the liking of those of his own persuasion? In reality, he was glossing over the fact that there had already been an extensive debate on this issue in the Constituent Assembly some fifty years earlier, which finally resulted in the Right to Religious Freedom in Article 25. Then his Bharatiya Janta Party (BJP) was unhappy with the Constitution itself and had set up a Constitution Review Commission even when many agreed with then President K. R. Narayanan, who said that it is not a Constitution that had failed us but vice versa.

Many of the issues that appear new to us today, were anticipated, discussed and decided on then. We need a dialogue to contextualise the religious freedom that we then gave ourselves, not a debate to whip up the kind of religious extremism that is now threatening to take it away. Such extremism divided the country once. Pursuing religious dominance will only deepen religious divisions again. Today, we need inter-religious harmony to keep the country united.

In 1947, the Constituent Assembly met under extremely difficult and critical conditions. To their credit, the founding members produced a remarkable document. What were the issues, and who were the protagonists? Where were the sticking points on this right to religious freedom at the time? The members were concerned particularly with the issue of conversion, though the word does not feature in the final text. The discussion was mostly between Christian and Hindu members and it focused mainly on 'the right to freely profess, practice and propagate religion'. Muslims seem not to have been very involved in this discussion, particularly with regard to the freedom to propagate religion. K. M. Munshi and B. R. Ambedkar were prominent members of sub-committee drafting 'Fundamental Rights'.

A series of anti-conversion laws had been passed by various princely states particularly in adivasi areas: the Raigarh State Conversion Act, 1936, the Patna State Freedom of Religion Act, 1942, the Surguja State Apostasy Act, 1945, the Udaipur State Anti-conversion Act, 1946. All of these restricted the freedom of the converter and the would-be convert. Christian members were apprehensive and wanted protection against such laws, which they felt compromised their freedom of religion. Although it was not in the first version, they wanted the word 'propagate' to be added to the text. Hindu members felt that non-proselytising religions needed protection against any abuse of this freedom, particularly for the weaker sections. They were not happy with the freedom to 'propagate religion'. After some discussion, the word was included in Clause 13 of the final draft.

A further clause specified that conversions 'brought about by coercion or undue influence shall not be recognized by law and the exercise of such coercion or influence shall be an offence.' (Rao 1967 Vol. II: 174) Legal recognition had consequences because of Indian personal law. K. M. Munshi proposed that 'fraud' be added to 'coercion and undue influence'. At the time Jerome D'Souza a Catholic member, pointed out that the phrase 'undue influence' was vague and open to distortion, and categorically affirmed that Christians did not intend to use conversion for political purposes.

Munshi also raised the issue of the conversion of minors, since this would bring in many complications with regard to its implications in Indian civil law. However, Ambedkar opposed this because of the many difficulties involved in its implementation. If minor children were not allowed to convert with their parents, he explained, this "would lead to many disruptions, to so many evil consequences." (CAD 1948 III: 502)

Hence, the whole clause was sent back to the drafting committee and finally dropped at the suggestion of Vallabhbhai Patel who wrote to the President of the Assembly, Rajendra Prasad: 'this clause enunciates a rather obvious doctrine which it is unnecessary to include in the Constitution and we recommend that it be dropped altogether.' (Cited Kim 2003: 49) The Assembly met on 30 August 1947, at the height of the communal violence consequent on Partition, and voted to delete this clause altogether.

After the publication of the Draft Constitution, the Assembly meet on 3rd December. There was still much opposition to the word 'propagate'. T. T. Krishnamachari argued convincingly that the right to propagate is meant for all religions, subject to public order, as indeed all freedoms in a civilised society must be. Finally, Munshi, earlier the main protagonist, carried the day, when he endorsed

Krishnamachari's arguments. Insisting that in independent India religious conversion posed no political threat; he conceded, "so long as religion is religion, conversion by the free exercise of the conscience has to be recognised." (CAD 1948 VII: 838)

The willingness of Christians to give up reserved seats in the legislature, which had been included in the Draft Constitution of October 1947, was a positive affirmation that Christians were not pursuing political privileges consequent to their religious affiliation. And so on 26th November 1949, the Right to Freedom of Religion, as we have it today, was adopted by the Assembly. Article 23 (1) now reads: 'Subject to public order, morality and health and to the other provisions of this Part, all persons are equally entitled to freedom of conscience and the right to profess, practice and propagate religion.' The unanimous conclusion is remarkable in that there were just seven Christians in the Assembly of 296 members. No wonder Jerome D'Souza remarked that it 'is so reassuring and so encouraging to the minorities that we have no reason at all to quarrel or to ask for stronger assurances. That attitude must provoke, on the part of minorities, an equally trustful attitude which I hope will inspire future relations and future discussions.' (CAD 1948 III: 4970)

It would seem that the Constitutional debate was more a dialogue and the conclusions mutually agreed on were not a compromise lacking conviction, though some have insinuated as much; they were much more a compact based on mutual trust. However, there were underlying differences in approach and perspective, which needed to be sorted out with sensitivity and understanding. If the Christians had made their point and got it accepted, they had to win the trust and goodwill of the others. If the Hindus accepted the assurances given by the Christians and showed tolerance, this had to be verified on the ground. There was room for misunderstanding and political pressures, and expediency could play these up.

Hindus understood religion in terms of dharma and freedom here meant freely to fulfil one's ascribed dharma. 'Freedom of religion' is then understood as freedom for dharma, to do one's duty in terms of dharma. Christians understand freedom as a matter of a person's choice not being determined from the outside. Freedom of religion here would mean freedom from influences that restrict that choice in matters religious. A tension here demands a sensitive resolution. A dharma, ascribed by birth, that allows no choice, whether this concerns religion or caste or other social affiliations, cannot be compatible with fundamental or human rights. However, a personal choice that negates one's duties, or does not show tolerance to others, cannot be justified by such rights.

The compact underlying the Constituent Assembly's consensus implied a certain restraint and transparency on the part of Christians as well as an openness and tolerance on the part of Hindus. Such a compact is not justiciable, not liable to legal redress. It must be supported and sustained by civil society as a vital part of its social capital of trust, or it will collapse. The distrust in some sections of our society seems to have reached this point. However, this did not happen in one big leap, but rather in smaller incremental steps.

The expectation was that in the post-colonial period, the climate would not be favourable for conversions and the status quo would obtain. However, when tribals and dalits continued to convert, the first cracks in the compact began to appear. The Indian Converts (Regulation and Registration) Bill, 1954 was proposed by Jethalal Joshi to 'regulate and provide for registration and licensing of a person aiding any person to become a convert'. This was strongly opposed by Muslim member Pocker Sahib, and when Nehru spoke against it, arguing that the real approach would be tolerance and respect for the others' religion, the bill was rejected on 2 December 1955.

However, in Madhya Pradesh, there were complaints about foreign missionaries proselytising in Surguja and Raigarh district, where earlier princely states had anti-conversions laws now invalidated by the Constitution. The Christian Missionary Enquiry Committee was set up on 16 April 1954, chaired by Bhawani Shankar Niyogi, a retired Chief Justice. It had only one Christian member who was persona non grata with Christians because he was known to be against conversion. The committee failed to win the confidence and cooperation of the churches. When the report came out in 1956 it expressed the darkest fears of Hindu Nationalism against conversion, which was perceived as a direct challenge to its own Hindutva ideology, that identified Indian with Hindu, an ethnic nationalism in direct conflict with the territorial nationalism of the Nehruvian consensus.

In the report, proselytisation was seen as a threat to 'national unity', undermining 'the principle of peaceful coexistence' and intending 'to create a Christian party in the Indian democracy along the lines of the Muslim League ultimately to make out the claim for a separate State, or at least to create a "militant minority"', (Niyogi Report 1956 Pt. II. Ch. III, no. 27 p. 59-60). The demand for Jharkhand was taken as evidence of separatism, and even an 'agitation for

Adivasisthan ... with a view to forming a sort of corridor joining East Bengal with Hyderabad, which could be used for a pincer movement against India in the event of a war between India and Pakistan.' (Niyogi Report Ch. 1. p. 9) Ironically, in November 1999, both Jharkhand (on the 15th) and Chhattisgarh (on the 1st) were established as states of the Union by the BJP-led Central Government. The Christian political party has not yet materialised, and East Bengal ceased to a part of Pakistan in 1971.

The report was rejected by Christians and failed to win support among moderate Hindus. However, the report did bring to public notice the well-organised and funded effort at evangelisation and conversion in the tribal heartland of central India. Such endeavours certainly did not go down well even with the moderate majority. It is here that, from Rammohan Roy to Gandhi, Christian missionaries have been so incisively challenged. However, though the recommendations of the Niyogi Report were not implemented immediately, they did resurface in the Freedom of Religion Act of Orissa and Madhya Pradesh.

More recently, there have some efforts to draw attention to the Niyogi Report to stir up anti-missionary feeling among Hindus, but no mention is ever made in this context of Niyogi's own conversion to Buddhism, as reported in the *Enquiry*, 21 October 1956, in the wake of the neo-Buddhist conversion movement led by Ambedkar.

In 1958, the State Assembly rejected the Madhya Pradesh Prevention of Religious Conversion Act. Again, in 1963, a private member introduced a Madhya Pradesh Conversion Bill based on the recommendations of the Niyogi Report. It was thrown out because the matter belonged to the Central, not the state government. However, the Orissa Freedom of Religion Act was passed in 1967. In its statement of objectives and reasons, it affirms: "Conversion in its very process involves an act of undermining another faith," and that the Act was intended "to provide for the prohibition of conversion from one religion to another by the use of force or inducement or by fraudulent means". The Madhya Pradesh Dharma Swatantrya Adhiniyam 1968 (Freedom of Religion Act) was almost identical but it substituted 'allurement' for 'inducement', and further required the reporting of a conversion to the district magistrate.

The Orissa Act was challenged in the High Court by the Catholic Union of India and on 24 October 1972 found to be ultra vires of the Constitution. The Court argued that Article 25 (1) extended to the right to propagate religion and "conversion into one's own religion must be included in the right so far as Christian were concerned." (AIR, Orissa, 1973:120) However, the Madhya Pradesh chief justice in a verdict on 23 April 1974 upheld the validity of the Act there, as actually 'establishing the equality of religious freedom for all citizens by prohibiting conversion by objectionable activities such as conversion by force, fraud and by allurement' (AIR, Madhya Pradesh, 1975:163).

Inevitably this difference between two High Courts came up before the Supreme Court on 17th January 1977 and it sided with the Madhya Pradesh High Court affirming that what the Article grants 'is not the right to convert another person to one's own religion, but to transmit, or spread one's religion by an exposition of its tenets ... There is no fundamental right to convert another person to one's religion. Because if a person purposely undertakes the conversion of another person to his religion... it would be impinge on the "freedom of conscience" guaranteed to all the citizens of the country alike' (AIR, Supreme Court, 1977, 908-12).

With the legal hurdle out of the way, more such acts were legislated in other states. The Arunachal Pradesh Freedom of Indigenous Religions Act 1978 included certain forms of Buddhism, Vaishnavism and nature worship as indigenous. Lok Sabha member O.P. Tyagi sought to extend the Orissa Act to the whole country in a private member's Bill, presented to Parliament on 22 December 1978. However, the government fell in February 1979, and the Bill was never discussed. More recently, the All India Dravida Anna Munnetra Kazhagam (AIADMK) Government passed The Tamil Nadu Prohibition of Forcible Conversion of Religion Ordinance, 2002 on 5 October, followed by the BJP government in Gujarat with The Gujarat Freedom of Religion Act, 2003, on 9 April, with even more stringent measures, requiring prior permission from the district magistrate. However, after AIADMK's debacle in the Lok Sabha elections of May 2004, the ordinance, which became an Act after the governor's approval, was hastily withdrawn, though the Acts in other state are still in force.

The crux of the matter is the negation of the fundamental right to convert as included in the one to propagate religion, and affirmation of the equality of all religions and freedom of conscience as guaranteed by the Constitution. What the Supreme Court judgement affirms is the Constitutional right to propagate one's religion but negates any fundamental right to convert another. Further, it affirms the Constitutional guarantee to follow one's conscience, and consequently the freedom to be converted. Clearly, the Court was trying to maintain a delicate balance, but this has not found agreement all around.

A Christian lawyer, E.D. Devasason, opined that the Constitutional guarantee of equality of religions 'only means that the state cannot discriminate one religion from another and the state is bound to treat all religions alike. It does not impose an obligation that the citizens should treat all religions alike.' (Devadason 1977: 437) Indeed, it would be inevitable that for a believer, one's own religion would be treated more equally than others would. Eminent Hindu lawyer Ram Jethmalani speaking in Bombay on 18 March 1979 on the Orissa Act was emphatic: 'as a student of law, without committing contempt of court, I am free to say that the Supreme Court is wrong. I have no doubt that someday the Supreme Court, more properly informed about the legal provisions, will reverse that decision.' (Cited Mathew 2002: 36)

Certainly, conversion is a matter of more than just legislation. Political scientist Bhanu Pratap Mehta finds the 'anti-conversion legislation is illegitimately paternalistic. It sets up the state as an agency that is in the business of saving our souls by putting it in judgment of our motives when we "choose" our religion' (Mehta 2003: 56). For if, the motivation is political or economic, accordingly to these laws the choice would be illegal. 'But then', Mehta rightly insists, 'that is exactly why conversion needs to be protected. If indeed, conversions are political, should not a democracy protect them as legitimate expressions?' (ibid.) However, once the courts have constructed 'religion as a site of passion and unreason', (ibid. 54) their paternalism steps in to protect people from themselves or from others, since they seen as are incapable of doing either. Mehta concludes: 'The court seems to assume throughout that people are not capable of managing religious ideas they receive, particularly if they are from the lower castes' (Mehta ibid. 55).

Ultimately, it would seem that the question is whether the freedom to convert as a fundamental right guaranteed by our Constitution must be constrained by the freedom from conversion as a necessary protection provided by the state. Certainly, force, fraud and other unfair and unethical means are taboo, but is there no legal space for ethical persuasion in matters religious? Alternatively, is this to be confined only to matters within, never across religious traditions? What happens when there is a plurality within a tradition, especially in a country like India, where all our religious traditions are complex and multiple? Will the status quo be frozen with anathemas and excommunications, fatwas and edicts...? Surely, there are complicated and confusing issues involved that cannot be addressed with any kind of rigid extremism or atavistic fundamentalism. Here we arefacing the profound dilemmas of rights and duties, of freedom and responsibility, of liberty and tolerance. We will certainly need all the sensitivity and openness, all the compassion and trust we are capable of to begin to live with these ambiguities constructively, even creatively.

The Future of Our Past

If there is one thing obvious in these brief historical sketches, it is the inevitable and necessary entanglement of religious traditions in other institutional systems of society, not the least of which are political ones. Once religion becomes a marker of political identity in an age of nationalism, this becomes an explosive mix. The long and brutal religious war after the Protestant reformation in Europe and the Armageddon of the nations in the 20th century has left an aftermath, which has discredited religion in a secularised post-Christian era in the west. Islam too has its history of violence as religion and politics are entangled, and this has left both a reaction of religious fundamentalism as well as disillusionment in its wake. Hinduism may be a latecomer to these aberrations, but it has surely arrived there today.

In the Indian sub-continent, the national freedom struggle could not bypass the religious question. The first to propound the two-nation theory was V.D. Savarkar in his presidential address to the Hindu Mahasabha in Ahmedabad in 1937, when he said: "There are two antagonistic nations living side by side in India." (Savarkar 1971: 24) However, it found no real echo among Hindus then, for they were mostly with the Indian National Congress. Gandhiji never countenanced such a theory. He appealed to Indian nationalism, and even here, he was apprehensive of possible chauvinism. He never appealed to religious or Hindu nationalism, though he publicly professed to be both a devoutly religious and committed Hindu.

However, his attempts in the 1920s with the Ali brothers to mobilise the Muslims on the Khilafat issue was dangerously close to spilling over in a religious nationalism with its battle cry of 'Islam in danger'. In 1940, Mohammed Ali Jinnah espoused the two-nation theory and blatantly used it to appeal to Muslim nationalism. This became the more successful obverse version of Savarkar's religious/cultural nationalism. Separate electorates for religious minorities were part of the British divide-and-rule policy, taking advantage of old prejudices and new ambitions, in the vain expectation of perpetuating their own dominance. It only succeeded in fanning religious antagonisms into one of the bloodiest communal clashes in our history.

The sub-continent has still not come to terms with the tragedy of the Partition in 1947. Hindu nationalists dream of reversing history, of turning the clock back to an undivided India, with some convenient ethnic cleansing, no doubt. Others, more moderate and sensible, prefer to move beyond the status quo in which we are mired now, to a more viable South Asian Association for Regional Cooperation (SAARC), which was founded in 1985 but has still to really take off. However, wounded memories are all too easily manipulated by religious fundamentalists and political chauvinists to precipitate violent expressions of their brooding, unsatisfied rage and dangerously unreasoned fears.

Meeting in the long dark shadow of the barbaric violence that followed in the wake of the Partition, the Constituent Assembly of India affirmed the secular understanding of the state in spite of some inevitable compromises as the debate on religious conversions shows. The Preamble of the Constitution on 26 November 1949

Solemnly resolved to constitute India into a sovereign democratic republic and to secure to all its citizens:

Justice, social, economic and political;

Liberty of thought, expression, belief, faith and worship;

Equality of status and of opportunity;

And to promote among them all,

Fraternity is individual assuring of the dignity.

Later in 1976, the Constitution was amended to add 'socialist' and 'secular' to the definition of the republic and to assure the 'unity of the nation' with the dignity of the individual. This is a part of the fundamental structure of the Constitution now. It cannot be abrogated, even by Parliament. It was meant to stymie the Hindu Right that had begun to mobilise ominously by then. When it did come to power in the late 1990s, it even called for a review of the Constitution.

Elsewhere in the sub-continent, religious nationalism has been disastrous, if not worse. In Pakistan, the tolerance and magnanimity of an Akbar is no longer evident. Bangladesh was born as a secular republic, amidst fratricidal violence from their co-religionists in the west, but it did not survive as such. In Sri Lanka the Sinhala, who are Buddhist, and the Tamils, who are Hindu, are locked in a civil war that neither can win nor afford to lose. Nepal, until May 2006 the only officially Hindu state, is under serious threat. Myanmar, for all its heritage of Buddhist compassion, is ruled by a repressive military dictatorship.

Indian secularism has its own contestations and controversies, through which it has evolved its own distinctive understanding of what is means to be 'secular' in a religious society. It is not the western separation of church and state, or the privatisation of religion and its exclusion from the public life. It is not so much the Nehruvian dharma nirapekshata, equal distance from all religions, but the Gandhian sarvadharma samabhava, equal respect for all religions. The Constitutional debate on religious conversion and freedom of conscience must be placed in this context. Unfortunately, we seem to be careering down a road where Nehru's secular neutrality is becoming equal disrespect for religions and Gandhi's religious egalitarianism is becoming unequal distancing from them.

3

A Postponed Tryst

Conversion as subversion – The clash of Nationalisms – Two Perspectives – Hindu Cultural Nationalism – *Conversion as Atrocity* – Lost Selves, Lost World – *A Second Axial Age* – Recovery and Reaction – Back to the Future – *Identity and Dignity* – The 'Self' and the 'Other' – Individual and Collective Rights – Inclusive and Exclusive Identities – *Diversity and Difference* – Plurality and Pluralism – Diversity in Unity – Identity and Integration – *Conversion as freedom* – Indian Secularism – Majorities and Minorities – A Project in Progress

The debate in the Constituent Assembly on religious conversion illustrates the difficulties in legislating in the sensitive area of freedom of conscience and religious liberty. The Constitution adopted a sound basic secular perspective, though in a statutory document not all nuances could be spelt out, nor all consequences adequately anticipated. Secularism is still an evolving concept and a much contested subject. Many consider it the single most crucial issue in our identity politics today. Liberals and rationalists promote secularism militantly, while religious nationalists and fundamentalists challenge it aggressively.

The Partition of 1947 precipitated a genocidal ethnic cleansing unprecedented in the sub-continent. We have not yet come to terms with the human cost of this tragedy, wounded memories have not healed, and outraged honour still seeks revenge. If we refuse to learn from our history, we condemn ourselves to repeat it. After the first Partition, the sub-continental Islamic state broke into two, and neither seems able to come to terms with its religious minorities, or even with dissenters from the same religious tradition. Indian secularism too is under threat from the aggressive quest for a Hindu rashtra (state). Religious and ethnic violence has now become dangerously endemic in South Asia, where deadly communal riots have become premeditated means for political ends. (Brass 2003)

There is a tectonic fault-line between the two perspectives of a liberal secular nationalism and a fundamentalist religious one. When activated, this has disastrous consequences. How will this collision between two mutually exclusive templates affect the fundamental dignity and cultural identity of persons and communities? Will the rich religious pluralism and endless cultural diversity of South Asian society survive these self-created seismic tremors? Alternatively, will we all be washed away in the tsunami that follows in its wake?

The compact made in the Constituent Assembly represented a precarious consensus, a notional assent to utopian ideals. We still have a long way to go to institutionalise this effectively in civil society. The fate of the Hindu Code Bill, intended to codify and reform Hindu personal law, exemplifies the conservative reaction to reform. In spite of Nehru's backing, a Parliament dominated by his party rejected the Bill in 1954, and Ambedkar resigned as law minister in protest. Later, the Bill was modified and passed in 1955. This was an early indication of the serious resistance to legislative reform by elected representatives of dominant classes and castes.

The Constitutional goal of a common civil code is still a distant dream. Changes in Muslim personal law are resolutely resisted, even when these favour greater gender justice. More and worse has followed in the religious nationalism that have emerged on the sub-continent to challenge the Constitutional compact. The struggle for purna swaraj (complete self-rule/freedom) is still distressingly incomplete. Gunnar Myrdal in his classic *Asian Drama: an Inquiry into the Poverty of Nations* (Myrdal 1968) speaks of India's postponed revolution that betrayed the high hopes and bright expectations of that magical moment when our nation was born. As Jawaharlal, Nehru reminded us then, 'Long years ago we made a tryst with destiny.' Now we seem to be caught in a time warp and unable to redeem our pledge.

Conversion as Subversion

As an ideology, nationalism originated in the west with the nation-state. It has been a powerful mobiliser for state making as well as for state-breaking. A people often use religion to identify themselves as distinct from others, but when such a religious community seeks political expression in a nation-state of its own, religion functions as a political ideology rather than a spiritual faith. When these two compelling motivators coalesce in a religious nationalism, it has a doubly compounded potential, for better or for worse.

The 20th century has been witness to the murderous clashes of nationalisms in Europe that engulfed the world in two horrendous Armageddons. Yet the new nations in the postcolonial age have striven to mobilise their masses with a nationalist ideology. As the political projection of a peoples' right to self-rule, nationalism has become the legitimising creed of the modern state's claims to authority.

Modernity necessarily involves rapid and radical changes in traditional societies. These precipitate a volatile discontent that is easily manipulated and politicised. A failed modernity, or even a tardy or untidy one, brings new injustices and inequalities, unfamiliar dominations and exploitations, whose severity can eclipse the memories of earlier atrocities. A successful modernity inevitably brings insecurities and uncertainties, alienation and anomie, with which traditional society is unprepared to cope. It is not surprising that a modernising state becomes the target of this discontent. In the quest to redress and escape from present miseries; the past is revived and reconstructed into a 'golden age'.

Religious revivalism quite naturally follows, since religion is so much an intrinsic part of these traditions, overlapping with and reinforcing other divisions, whether ethnic, racial, linguistic or tribal. Once these are politicised, disaffected people readily attempt to subvert and seize state power in pursuit of their own interests. All too often, such ethno-nationalism brings with it the horrors of ethnic cleansing. Religion is the most common and most effective of the many identity markers that characterise such movements, providing an explosive mix of religion and politics in religious nationalism.

The compulsion to create a national identity has been murderously homogenising. Religion can become a part of this compulsion, as in the forced conversion of Jews and Muslims to Christianity in 15th century Spain, or the elimination of Jainism by Tamil Shaivism in South India by the 12th century, or the ethnic cleansing, communal riots and pogroms in our own times. Such religious nationalism is generally authoritarian and chauvinist. It produces and reproduces the enemy because it survives best on politicising differences, not in reconciling them. It flourishes on heightening hurtful and hurt feelings, not in calming passions and healing memories.

Religious nationalism politicises religion but it seldom democratises it, except to establish an authoritarian 'tyranny of the majority'. It puts a premium on religious homogeneity in its quest for a national identity. Dominant groups exploit this to establish their hegemony over others in the name of national unity. Tolerance is perceived as weakness, if not a betrayal of national interests and religious concerns.

However, modernity thrives best in an atmosphere of diversity and openness. Religious tolerance is best supported by a social pluralism and secularism, which opens spaces for diverse religious traditions in society. Eventually, religious nationalism may use modern means and technologies rather effectively, as Ayatollah Khomeini did with audio tapes to communicate with the Iranian masses from Paris, or as Osama bin Laden does with his messages on video tapes to be televised to the world. However, religious nationalism remains intrinsically discordant with modern values and institutions. This is really the core of the contradiction between religious nationalism and secular modernity.

However, the search for alternatives, fuelled by the disaffected, does vary. It may begin as a moderate conservative populism, in which people seek protection and refuge from internal anxieties and external domination, at times isolating themselves from public confrontation and strife; but it can later explode into a trenchant and radical engagement such as a liberation struggle against alien ideologies and foreign powers.

These are not unchanging choices. The 'Moral Majority' in the United States began with the popular conservatism of the Bible belt in the south against unChristian values and secular liberalism in a largely permissive society. It is now vigorously supporting the war on terror, in which it perceives threatened Christians pitted against aggressive Muslims. On the other hand, in Iran, Khomeini's overly radical Shiite revolution against the modernity of the Shah's 'white revolution' is now moderating itself with a more pragmatic Islam. (Armstrong 2000: 244)

The roots of the reactionary resistance to western colonialism in India go back to the 19th century 'renaissance' that began in Bengal and spread to the Presidencies of Bombay and Madras. At one level, this had an 'Orientalist' agenda popularised by Max Muller (1823–1900) and others. In reaction to the colonising west, it projected an idealised India, unsurpassed in its timeless genius and originality. Thus Swami Vivekananda preached a *'sanatan dharma'* (eternal religion), whose universal spirituality surpassed all other religions. In 1903, Bal Gangadar Tilak (1856-1920), describing the *Arctic Home in the Vedas*, promoted a Vedic civilisation as the most ancient and advanced, a resource to regenerate a decaying West.

However, besides this revivalist strands, there was another level, critical rather than reactionary that also originated with this 'renaissance'. This was oriented to change rather than restoration, beginning with the reformists Ram Mohan Roy (1772-1833) in Calcutta and Justice Mahadev Govind Ranade (1842-1901) in Mumbai and becoming more radical with Mahatma Jotirao Phule (1827-1890) in Pune.

The first perspective projected a nationalism that was more Hindu than Indian, with a definite inclination to religious revivalism. Though somewhat subdued in the freedom struggle, it found an echo in the Hindu Right as it gained ground in the post-Nehruvian period. Today this finds effective political expression in the Bharatiya Janta Party (BJP), not to mention the Sangh Parivar, the extended family of numerous front organisations promoted by the Rashtriya Swayamsevak Sangh (RSS, National Volunteer Association). Their ideology of Hindutva (Hinduness) claims to be a 'cultural nationalism' and seeks to establish a 'Hindu rashtra'.

The second perspective found expression in the freedom struggle, dominated by the Indian National Congress and its leaders, especially Gandhi and Nehru, whose liberal secularism and democratic socialism is enshrined in the Constitution after the Partition of India in 1947, a monumental concession to the Muslim nationalism of Mohammed Ali Jinnah. Now Hindu nationalists attack Gandhi and Nehru as pseudo-secularists and demand concessions to the Hindu majority, thus making other minorities extremely insecure. Their coming to power at the Centre and in some states has intensified rather than moderated the majority-minority divide, precipitating violent communal conflicts.

There was an inherent ideological tension in the freedom struggle: between a vision of an idealised ancient past prioritising religious and cultural revivalism, and a dream of an enabling new future centred on social transformation and concern for Gandhi's last and least Indian. The dominant Nehruvian consensus of the early independence era was premised on the second, but it never could quite contain or defuse the lure of the first.

In the sub-continent, Muslim religious nationalism has painted itself into a corner. Having got its demand for Pakistan, Mohamed Ali Jinnah, the Qaid-e-Azam (The Great Leader) and founding father, was more pragmatically concerned with the secular interests of Muslims than theologically involved with the religious practices of Islam. Addressing the Pakistan Constituent Assembly meeting for the first time on August 11th 1947, Jinnah dreamed of the time, when 'Hindus would cease to be Hindus and Muslims would cease to be Muslims, not in the religious sense, because a matter of the personal faith of each individual but in the political senses as 'citizens of the State' (Jinnah 1948: 10).

Now the dream lies shattered in the religious terrorism that is holding Pakistan to ransom, while military dictatorships legitimise themselves as the only effective force restraining the terrorists (as President Musharaf claims now), or encouraging them (as President Zia-ul-Haq did earlier). Bangladesh, having debunked the two-nation theory for a three-nation one, is still struggling to establish credible secular credentials. There are many distinctly different Muslim communities in the sub-continent and religion is not always the most unifying factor among them. Indeed, pan-Islamism rather than Muslim nationalism is now the more pressing threat in South Asia. However, today the most ominous challenge to our Constitutional compact on religion is from Hindu nationalism within the Indian Union.

Hindu nationalism is not particularly religious. In its present avatar, it claims to be 'cultural nationalism'. Its founding father V.D. Savarkar was himself a rationalist atheist, who wanted his body cremated after his death without any religious ceremonies. Yet he was fanatical about Hindutva or Hinduness, which he first formulated in 1923, and deliberately set in opposition to other religious traditions not originating in India, such as Islam and Christianity. Sarvarkar's early projection of Hindu-Muslim unity with his *War of Independence of 1857*, published in 1909, was completely reversed during his transportation to the Andamans from 1911-1921. His *Hindutva* was articulated as a political ideology of ethno-religious nationalism to include culture and race (Savarkar 1989). It was designed to unify and mobilise the inegalitarian classes and hierarchical castes among

Hindus under a communal banner. In 1941, his birthday wish was expressed in the slogan: 'Hinduise all politics and militarise all Hindudom' (cited McKean 1996: 71).

Hinduism refers to a religious faith tradition that is far easier to describe than define. With Sarvarkar, there is an emphatic distinction between Hinduism as a religious system and Hindutva as a political ideology. 'What is Hinduism?' and 'Who is a Hindu?' are questions better answered in inclusive rather than exclusive terms as we have earlier discussed, in regard to both culture and religion. Savarkar politicises these questions, answering them in terms of a nativist, sacred geography.

Thus for him 'Hinduism must necessarily mean the religion and the religions that are peculiar and native to this land and people.' (Savarkar 1989: 104) He defined Hindu in terms of 'the three essentials of nation (Rashtra), race (Jati) and civilization (Sanskriti)' (Savarkar 1989: 101). The first important qualification of a Hindu is that 'the whole continental country from the Sindhu to Sindhu, from the Indus to the Seas', (Savarkar 1989: 82) 'is not only a Pitribhu but a Punyabhu, not only a fatherland but a holyland' as well (Savarkar 1989: 111). In his speech to the Hindu Mahasabha at Nagpur in 1938, he insisted that 'India must be a land reserved for the Hindus.' Others were here on sufferance as lesser citizens.

Sarvarkar is the first and principal ideologue of this extreme Hindu nationalism. Others like M.S. Golwalkar (1939), who followed with *We or Our Nationhood Defined* (1980) and later *A Bunch of Thoughts*, drew on him but repeated rather than advanced his argument. Hindutva overlapped and conflated with Hinduism in the popular projection. Justice J.S. Verma in his remarks in a Supreme Court judgement in 1995 concerning the political use of religion opined an explicit equivalence between the two: Hindutva is nothing but Hinduism. This has been much quoted by the Sangh Parivar to legitimise its intolerant and aggressive ideology. Later, however, shocked by the horror of the Gujarat pogrom in February-March 2001, Justice Verma claimed he had been misunderstood on this account.

Hindutva is now projected as Bharatiyata, Indianness, equivalence that Savarkar himself had rejected: 'the term Hindu cannot be synonymous with Bharatiya or Hindi and mean Indian only.' (Savarkar 1989: 84) The change in name proposed is merely to make it more acceptable to the unsuspecting. Ultimately, as an ideology of religious nationalism, the basic content, the first premises and final a conclusions of Hindutva remain the same.

From its very origins, the project of Hindu nationalism has been to mobilise Hindus into a politicised ethnic group and to construct this into a dominant majority. Non-Hindus would become subordinate minorities and/or sub-nationalisms, provided they present no threat to the Hindu majority. However, the way it exclusively equates 'Hindu' and 'India' is far from being the most significant interpretation, or the most dominant expression of Hindu culture and religious traditions.

Religious nationalisms thrive on religious homogeneity: one creed, one code, one cult. They then attempt to translate this into a political hegemony: one ideology, one party, one nation. However, the inherent diversity among Hindus, of caste and tribe, of language and region, of gods and sages, has proven extremely resilient to any externally imposed uniformity. Nevertheless, the endemic hierarchies of caste and insoluble inequalities of class need serious commitment to affirmative action for the last and the least.

Obviously, conversion across religious traditions will be anathema to any project for religious nationalism. It represents a subversive threat. As a change in religious allegiance, it undermines the very foundations on which such nationalism is premised, for porous boundaries are subversive of exclusive loyalties. Inter-religious marriages, especially of women in a patriarchal society, where the family system is patrilineal and patrilocal, are opposed for similar reasons. Conversion across religious communities epitomises this, especially when it is in groups or large numbers. Not surprisingly religious communities resist such conversions to other religious traditions, even though they favour conversions to their own. Religious nationalisms politicise and sharpen the resentment, making it more strident and even violent.

The Hindu opposition to proselytising in colonial times has carried over in the anti-conversion laws. Hindu nationalism has made an issue of conversions to Islam and Christianity and supported re-conversion movements to redress this. More recently, the dalit conversions to Islam in Meenakshipuram in Tamil Nadu in 1981 provoked strident hostility and violent retaliation. The Christian tribals in the Dangs in Gujarat where subjected to brutal atrocities and savage intimidating in 1998 and 1999. Christians too have been angered at conversions from their own flock to other religious denominations. However, they are not as sensitive when proselytising others for their own church. In the northeast of India, this had led to much inter-sect violence. In many Muslims communities, conversion to another faith results in excommunication and ostracism but conversions in the opposite direction are welcomed.

When the majority religion is politically dominant, conversion to another religious tradition is seen as positively anti-national, as happened when Anglicans in England converted to Roman Catholicism, or Catholics in France to the Protestant Huguenots. In India, conversion to non-Hindu religious traditions still invites the anti-national suspicion from those Hindus, who project themselves as a national political majority and not just a religious one. 'After all,' Gauri Viswanathan emphasises, 'nationalism's recourse to concepts of ethnicity, race, religion and language is precisely what conversion contests' (Viswanathan 2001: xv) by making group boundaries fuzzy and porous. Clearly, perceptions of subversion are selective and there is room here for much soul-searching all round.

Conversion as Atrocity

Fundamentalism in its etymological sense means going back to the fundamentals. There are many such fundamentalisms, each with its own distinctiveness. For instance, economic fundamentalism may be premised on an inalienable commitment to the market, political fundamentalism can be a dogmatic faith in a rigid ideology. Religious fundamentalism exhibits some common characteristics with these, as also across various religious traditions, even though there is an enormous range of differences in degree and kind. Even within a specific religious tradition, fundamentalism is never a unified whole. Shia and Sunni fundamentalists are often at each other's throats. The Protestant Mennonite Amish in the Midwest have little in common with the Southern Baptists. The Hare Krishna sect would not see eye to eye with some Arya Samajis.

Religious nationalism is a response to the discontents of modernity, and as the term itself suggests, it has two dimensions. Nationalism is surely one of the most powerful ideas to have moulded our modern world. Religion now adds another more compelling dimension. However, in the wake of modernising nationalisms, secularism was expected to displace religion to the private domain. The Enlightenment in Europe, in which modernity is grounded, was to liberate people from oppressive dependencies. The shibboleth, 'Man come of age', epitomised its spirit. Reason was to be the true source of legitimacy; traditions were to be put to the test of rationality.

However, modernity betrayed its liberating promise, wherever it was experienced as an aggressive invasion destroying the old familiar world and replacing it with an unfamiliar fluid one. This leaves people insecure and fearful, unable to cope with the new and so longing for the old. In their anxiety and disorientation, their 'old time religion' seemed a more reliable assurance than the promise of this 'brave new world'. As people began to mine their lost world for answers in their struggle to find their lost selves, the religious backlash against this disenchanting secular modernity could no longer be ignored.

Modernising societies subject their people to a growing socio-cultural homogenisation; this devalues and threatens their traditional identities. Moreover, such societies subjugate the masses to the expanding eco-political hegemony of the upwardly mobile elites. This subordinates and excludes the older, more static ones. Eroded identities and displaced elites are a volatile, explosive mix. Moreover, the feeling of being marginalised and alienated undermines people's self-respect and violates their sense of dignity, leaving them with feelings of inferiority that give further credibility to their perceived grievances. The middle class too is disoriented by rapid modernisation in spite of being relatively advantaged. It has lent strong support to revivalist and fundamentalist developments.

In this uncertain and unforgiving world, religion becomes a place of refuge and solace, a haven in a heartless world. However, the remedies sought and promoted vary across a wide spectrum of responses, from passive withdrawal to aggressive assertion. For the loss of a sense of identity is readily translated into the pursuit of otherworldly promises, seeking religious remedies for secular problems. When this is compounded by resentment against one's violated dignity, it can further be transmuted into this-worldly anger and rage that does not stop at violent responses to their perceived predicament. This is how religious fundamentalisms are born, whether in the form of an apolitical withdrawal or a politicised engagement.

Historically, when left to themselves, apolitical religious fundamentalisms tend to withdraw into their own isolated world and be marginalised. Today, isolation is no longer a viable option as the modernising state reaches into the lives of its citizens with a comprehensive regime of civil rights it endows, and civic duties it imposes, the impact it has and the control it exercises. Interaction with the surrounding situation becomes inevitable. This will affect even the most withdrawn religious fundamentalisms. When, these interactions are perceived to be at odds with the beliefs and practices of a religious tradition. Then resistance, or even escape, will not be possible without a political engagement with the state.

This encounter can be dangerously subversive for a modern secular, liberal democratic state. The coalescence of a strident religious fundamentalism and a committed religious nationalism is a serious concern today, and not just on this sub-continent. For every major religion has its share of fundamentalists, though there are obvious differences of intensity and intent. Already too many floundering nation-states have been overtaken and put to risk by this backlash of politics and religion, further compounded in our imploding global world.

A Second Axial Age

Karen Armstrong in *The Battle for God* describes religious fundamentalism as a 'militant piety' (Armstrong 2000: ix) that transforms anxiety and fear into anger and rage. It is a defensive reaction, and unless we can understand where it is rooted, we will not be able to contain its aggressive militancy. On the contrary, repression only confirms the worst suspicions on both sides and provokes a bitter and excessive response, kicking off an escalating spiral of violence. This is a classic case of a self-fulfilling prophecy. In the final analysis, aggressive religious fundamentalism and assertive secular modernity are locked into a relationship, which neither can negate nor escape; each represents its own rejected, yet still threatening other. This is a scene set for confrontation.

The roots of such religious fundamentalism run deeper than the politics of religious nationalism. For with modernity, we are going through a transformation similar in scale and scope to the Axial Age of the 8th to 2nd century BC, when different and distant peoples across the globe experienced the inadequacy of their localised religion and its particular cults. (Armstrong 1994: 27) As their agricultural economies stabilised and trade expanded, they underwent radical changes in their civilisation. The old sustaining religion, with its myths and rituals, was no longer relevant to the new, universal worldview opening before them. Their intuitive understanding of their world poetically and metaphorically expressed, their 'myths', had changed and it needed a rational articulation in terms of a more viable philosophy and/or theology, a 'logos'. The dissonance between the two keeps mounting until the tension is no longer sustainable or stable.

Eventually, prophets and charismatic individuals, persons of religious genius, blaze a new trail, make disciples and gather followers, and found a new tradition in which such tensions are creatively resolved and carried forward. All the major religions of the world derive from this period or trace their origins to it: Buddhism, Taoism, and Confucianism, the Upanishadic, Zoroastrian, and Abrahamic religions.

Modernity has precipitated a similar 'culture-quake'. The mythic imaginative grasp of one's world (the old 'myths'), is undermined by a science that explains how it works and a technology that demonstrates how it can be manipulated (the new 'logos') (Bultmann 1961: 5). Traditional religion becomes less persuasive and new theologies vie with each other to fill this credibility gap. The displacement of popular religion leaves behind 'a God-shaped hole', in the evocative words of the existentialist Jean-Paul Sartre. The fear of social annihilation in this black hole can be terrifying.

Today, masses of people are moving out of their earlier isolation into a world they cannot quite comprehend. Those who can cope with such disorientation and are committed to the changes, often because they benefit from them, will develop new pertinent 'myths' and relevant theologies and/or ideologies. What the great confessional faiths once did must be done again in this second Axial Age. 'Myths' is what makes our world meaningful; 'logos' explains the meaning and its implications for our lives. We need both to cope with our everyday life. Having lost our old religious myths and abandoned our traditional religious beliefs, we are still in quest of a new 'myths' and a corresponding 'logos' is consonance with our age.

Religious fundamentalism is a quest for certainty and security in an unpredictable and changing world. It is a defensive reaction to fears and grievances that may well be legitimately founded, but when politically compounded can turn dangerously violent. This is not really a reactionary regression into the past, but a proactive project for the future. It is an attempt to recover the 'fundamentals' of a religious tradition, believed to be in danger of being lost. It is a determination to re-sacralise the world and rebuild the lost utopia. Religious fundamentalists make a selective, or more correctly a protective, retrieval of belief and practice from a sacred past, an endeavour that is both derivative and innovative. We cannot pour new wine into old wineskins without risking both.

Fundamentalists are not averse to the pragmatic use of modern rationality for their religious purposes. They create their own religious theology and political ideology; they promote charismatic leaders and evolve action-plans. However, whether their earlier intuitive grasp of their old world now passing away will be adequate to, and in consonance with the new one coming to birth in their midst is extremely problematic. For the real world does indeed change, as well as and the human understanding of these changing realities. As our worldview undergoes paradigm shifts and radical changes, religious understandings can remain unaffected. If theologies articulate these understandings, these too cannot escape the need for rethinking and new articulations. Indeed, at any given time in any complex situation, there are multiple religious understandings and many theologies, prevailing and expressing different perspectives even within one faith, and change will demand reform and renewal.

However, the fundamentals of the tradition are recovered, once they are abstracted from their context they tend to become non-negotiable and dogmatic. This negates the metaphoric nature of religious language. All language is symbolic, religious language even more so. We cannot ever express religious mysteries in conceptual formulae, no matter how verbally elegant. Without a contextual interpretation, the literalism espoused by fundamentalists inevitably leads to an unacceptably static understanding of tradition. 'There is no text without context' is a basic principle of interpretation that the literalism of the fundamentalist negates. A living tradition must be constantly reinterpreted in radically changed contexts, or it will become irrelevant and die. Religious fundamentalism negates this inevitable pluralism within, and across religious traditions. It sees all differing views as betraying its one truth and will not come to terms with the plurality of our world today.

However, the very multiplicity of traditions will give rise to many different fundamentalisms. Fundamentalisms based on 'right belief' develop in religious traditions that stress orthodoxy or doctrinal fidelity. They dismiss their differing coreligionists as heretics or apostates. Fundamentalisms based on 'right practice' develop in traditions that stress orthodox behaviour or the observance of law and ritual. Their non-conforming co-religionists are considered impious or polluted.

With a rich plural religious tradition, the recovery claimed by the fundamentalists cannot but be selective, even though they may claim a 'narrative fidelity' to their authentic religious heritage. For to be effectively mobilised it must be cohesive, and for this uniformity greatly helps. Then it loses a broad based appeal. Moreover, once the internal diversity of a culture is compromised, it becomes easy prey to fundamentalism. Thus non-dogmatic inclusivity traditions have been less hospitable to fundamentalism than dogmatic exclusivist has ones, just as monoculture peoples are more prone to ethnocentricity than multicultural ones.

Unitary dogmatic religious traditions are more prone to fundamentalism than plural non-dogmatic ones. The inherent plurality of Hindu religious traditions would explain why the revivalists become enclosed in sects like the Arya Samaj, and why Hindu fundamentalism is more recent than most others, and its appeal is more political than religious. As a crude endeavour to homogenise Hindu traditions, Hindutva must be seen in this context, as also the pan-Islamism, which threatens to reduce the multiplicity of religious traditions of Muslim communities to a unidimensional Arabised one. Christian fundamentalism too easily becomes a project of western religious imperialism. This was more obviously so in the colonial period but it continues more subtly in the neo-colonial phase. Hindu fundamentalists seek a return of Ram Rajya, the mythic utopia of Valmiki's epic. However, in pursuing this today they have projected a Ram Raudra, the angry avenger that is in obvious contradiction to the original Ram Saumya, Ram the gentle. Gandhi's Ram Rajya was surely more faithful to the *maryada purusa*, the complete man, but then Gandhi was a reformist, not a fundamentalist. Not without reason, Ashis Nandy calls Hindu fundamentalists 'misbegotten children of the Raj who have managed to escape the orphanage of history,' (Nandy 1993: 6) seeking now to replace colonial racial dominance with a hierarchical religious one. However, their construction of a single Hindu community has not transcended the internal divisions of caste, nor come to terms with the rich diversity of sects.

Muslim fundamentalists dream of an Islamic state which will end the secularist separation of religion and politics, and where the Shariat will hold sway. The inspiration goes back to the early days of the Prophet in Medina, when he combined in his person both religious and secular power in a way that no one else could since. Early Shiism tacitly condoned the secularisation of politics (Armstrong 2000: 51) with another-worldly emphasis that was apolitical, and many of its numerous sects still keep up this tradition. From its earliest origins the Shariat has developed a sophisticated body of jurisprudence of contextual rather than literal interpretation, with four Sunni schools of law: the Hanafi, Maliki, Shafii and Hanabilah.

Today, the ideally fundamental religious state seems much beyond the horizons of the pluralism a modern society needs and demands. In this regard, fundamentalist Islam seems to be on a violent collision course with modernity. The present story of radically Islamic states is evidence enough of this.

Christian fundamentalists exclude all others in their comprehension of the 'kingdom of God', and pursue a numbers game that is more political than religious, more commercial than ethical, as they proselytise the unfortunate mortals outside their fold, who are considered 'damned' if they do not convert. Sikh fundamentalists too have demanded the unity of the sacred and the secular, *piri-miri*. This too has proved to be more violent than viable.

Fundamentalism, then, is a negative reaction to rapid change that attempts to freeze traditions and beliefs in a literalism wherever these are undermined and/or challenged. In struggling with the negative consequences of modernity, the resounding cry is not that our religion has failed us, but that we have lost our identity and dignity because we have been unfaithful to our religion. Hence, 'return to fidelity', 'back to the future', becomes the prelude to a counter-offensive by a religion of rage deeply rooted in fear.

Once again we see the relationship between modernity's discontents and fundamentalism, especially in the developing world. In Asia and Africa, Nandy finds that 'fundamentalists are the illegitimate children of modernity, claiming to be the legitimate children of tradition' (Nandy 1993: 6). Religious fundamentalism today is evidence enough that modernity in its misguided rush to displace rather than transform pre-modern identities and traditions has run into a roadblock. The abstract individualism institutionalised in its culture has not proved adequate to contain the disorientation of change, or the eclipse of a concrete sense of community belonging that traditional societies once provided. Individuals need this to connect with each other and cope in an alienating and unequal world. Religious fundamentalism becomes a language of protest and opposition and offers a tempting alternative with no dearth of organic intellectuals or displaced elites to articulate and lead it. How viable will this be in addressing the real issues of alienation and anomie seems dangerously precarious.

'Religion in danger!' is the rallying cry of such groups. In such a 'politics of passion', religious nationalists use riots and pogroms as ritual performances to construct and sustain such divisive and hostile borders, of which they become boundary-keepers. Conversion across such divides inevitably renders them porous and diffused, and not surprisingly is perceived as more than just a subversive betrayal. It amounts to a threat of annihilation, an atrocity against the group, which must now counter this with atrocities of its own in order to survive by reinforcing group boundaries.

For similar reasons, inter-caste marriages are seen as a threat to the particular caste community and its traditions, and meets with the same violent opposition when communal boundaries are ascribed and inviolable. The fundamental freedom of individual choice is sacrificed to community solidarity, and collective norms are imposed that restrict individual rights.

Closed communities under threat react defensively to reinforce group boundaries, and individual transgressors pay a heavy price in violence, ostracism, and even death. Whether against their own (as in the burning of heretics at the stake, or honour killings), or against the other (as with the execution of 'infidels', or the murderous enforcement of caste taboos), perpetrating atrocity becomes an instrument of boundary-maintenance between religious groups.

Identity and Dignity

Religious nationalism and fundamentalism have a remarkable affinity. They feed on each other, politicising and radicalising one another. Both respond to the modernising secularists but address different aspects: the religious nationalists challenge the eco-political hegemony that discounts human dignity and impoverishes people. The religious fundamentalists contest the religio-cultural dominance that disregards traditional religious identities and undermines self-respect.

Identity and dignity are intimately connected. Identity answers to 'Who am I?' dignity to 'What respect am I do?' The affirmation or the negation of one carries over to the other. The right to identity must include the right to dignity. One's identity is never developed in isolation but in interaction with significant others. However, this is never an entirely passive process. I discover myself, my horizon of meaning and value, with and through others. 'Who I am' is always reflected off, and refracted through others. 'What I am due' is always in a social context mediated by them. The denial of recognition and affirmation amounts to a negation of my human identity.

Indeed, the other is more-integral to oneself than one might want to admit. The other helps to make sense of experiences, but also interrogates my world. For the other always puts a question to one's self, and when the other is different the question can be threatening. One can ignore the question only for a while, one may even be tempted to destroy the questioner, but the questioning cannot be so easily silenced. History bears witness to how dominant persons and groups have sought 'final solutions' to eliminate or subordinate others in genocide and ethnocide, in cultural assimilation and religious conversion. Most of these attempts have failed.

As with individuals so with groups. The individual is affirmed, or negated in the group, as the group is in society. At the individual level, this mediation is essentially through interpersonal interaction; at the social level it is also through myth and symbol, values and norms, collective memories and popular history. (Kakar 1993: 50)

Modern development brings rapid and radical change. The strain and stress can precipitate a disorientation in personal identity. In such situations, a crumbling self can lean on group support, as a dilapidated building is trussed up by scaffolding. In a world increasingly characterised by anxiety, uncertainty and disorder, there is an urgent need for the reassurance of security, trust and a sense of solidarity in a collective identity. Such identities become 'vehicles for redressing narcissistic injuries, for righting of what are perceived as contemporary or historical wrongs' (Kakar 1993: 52). Collective action is resorted to in order to redress individual insecurities. The group solidarity then becomes a substitute for lost attachments, a support to heal old injuries and right historical wrongs. Such collective remedies to individual trauma easily become totalising and aggressive. Confirmed in their self-righteousness, leaders manipulate and mobilise groups, disregarding the dignity of other groups as well as the dignity of their members. Thus in any social breakdown, it is easy to see why extremist responses come into prominence.

This construction of the sense of self in the context of a hostile other is necessarily a function of the needs of the insecure individual and the group. What is unconsciously disowned and rejected in ourselves is projected on and demonised in the other. What is desirable in the other is denied and attributed to oneself. We are non-violent, tolerant, chosen and pure; the other is violent, intolerant, polluted, damned. They may seem strong, compassionate, devout, but they are aggressive, devious and fanatical.

To contain and defuse such collective passions, we must recognise and guarantee both equal dignity and unique identity for every individual person and each human community. The first is founded on human rights and is committed to enforcing equitable rights for all individuals, e.g., the right to life and liberty of conscience. The second is premised on collective rights and is responsible for ensuring the cultural identity of each group, e.g., the right to language and religion.

The dilemma between individual and community becomes evident when individual and collective rights are not in consonance. Treating all equally could lead to some becoming more equal than others in violation of the rights of more vulnerable individuals. This happens in modernising societies when the relationships between individuals are unequal, as in caste communities, where lower caste individuals are more deprived. Conceding some kind of cultural rights to groups can be oppressive for individuals in them, as in patriarchal communities, where empowering men further disadvantages the women. However, we can and must find ways in which human rights are sensitive to the cultural specifics of a community, which in turn do not violate fundamental rights of individuals.

In other words, a homogenizing universalism cannot be so absolute as to negate cultural and religious diversities. It must respect and even celebrate these differences within the limits set by collective rights. However, whether religious, or cultural, these rights cannot be unconditional or in violation of more fundamental human rights and freedoms The 'non-recognition', or worse the 'misrecognition' of either, becomes oppressive and distorting, projecting a negated, wounded identity. This is precisely what prejudice is all about.

Identities that are defined negatively against others in terms of 'what one is *not*' will tend to be exclusive and dismissive of others. This creates in-groups and out-groups, stereotypes and scapegoats. Those affirmed positively, prescinding from others in defining 'who one *is*', will tend to be inclusive and not disregarding of others. This allows for openness and receptivity. 'We *are not* like that' is less open to a broader inclusion in a larger common ground than 'this is how we *are*'. Exclusive identities emphasise differences and set up oppositions and polarities with the other.

Sudhir Kakar, the psychoanalyst, explains how they help increase the sense of narcissistic wellbeing and attribute to the other the disavowed aspects of one's own self (Kakar 1992: 137). Inclusive identities are inclined to affirm similarities and complementarities with the other. These make for tolerance and flexibility. For example, identifying with one's language or religion need not mean hostility to other languages and religions. Yet when used thus, language and religion have been among the most effective markers to divide a society into 'them' and 'us'.

Secular nationalisms have used a national language to promote a linguistic uniformity in their societies, just as religious nationalisms seek to revive and impose their religious tradition. Without a vigorous multi-lingualism and a vibrant religious pluralism, the cultural and religious diversity of a society will not survive. Linguistic nationalism was among the earliest threats to our unity-in-diversity in India, when Hindi was sought to be imposed as the national language. Allowing space for regional languages has defused this threat. Religious nationalism and fundamentalism are now a greater threat to our religious diversity and political unity.

In South Asia, the most prevalent exclusive and antagonistic collective identities are caste and/or religion based. All claims to individual and collective rights are demands by the claimants to have their identity recognized and their dignity affirmed. The denial of one or the other, as often happens to religious groups in secularised societies, is perceived as a threat of annihilation, whether intended or not, and inevitably this generates dangerous political passions. Religious nationalism and fundamentalism thrive on such negative politics.

Diversity and Difference

Modern societies are inevitably plural because of their complexity and scale. However, plurality has characterised other societies, including traditional ones, especially where these have been in contact with different peoples and diverse cultures, as in ancient empires, where one dominant group ruled over numerous dispersed subordinate ones. Plurality implies diverse social groups coming together in some kind of more inclusive social order. As a positive response to such complexity and diversity, pluralism attempts to integrate rather than negate this plurality. Today no single worldview can conveniently contain the diversity and differentiation of our complex world. In a free and open society such as we aspire to be, imposing a dominant perspective or worldview is no longer possible. Homogenising plurality by suppression or force can only make for an unstable and potentially violent situation. An open democratic society must be premised on consensus, not coercion.

The necessity of pluralism today is not to be perceived as an unnecessary evil to be repressed before it engulfs us further; or tolerated as a necessary one to be constrained, since it cannot be dismissed. Rather it is an inescapable challenge that will not go away. It must be constructively met or it will disable, if not destroy us. We can no longer settle conflicting differences between groups and peoples by enforcing uniformity. This only escalates the spiral of violence. Too much blood and tears have been shed for this already.

In any society, structure and culture are necessary dimensions. Structural plurality implies a set of distinguishable and diverse interrelated social institutions incorporated into an integrated social system. Cultural plurality refers to distinct cultures or subcultures with distinctive individual and collective identities within an overarching civilisational unity. Structurally, the market and the state, the economic and the political system integrate diverse groups in a common social order. Culturally, a common religion, language or historical tradition becomes the basis for a more inclusive civilisation unity.

In so-called 'mature western democracies', plurality is more structural, whereas in post-colonial societies, especially in South Asia, plurality is decidedly more cultural. More often than not, the cultural dimension is more resilient in its segmentation of a plural society. Caste or race, religion or language groups have more stable and less porous boundaries than class or interest groups, political parties and ideological movements. There is an obvious interaction between the two dimensions. Indic civilisation has served as a common meeting ground for diverse historical or religious traditions, different regional, caste and language groups of the sub-continent. It is the basis for the Union of Indian, the state, which now provides a common economic and political order for the country. So too is European culture the basis for the European Union today.

Some such common basis is necessary for socio-cultural integration, involving some minimal orientation towards cooperation rather than conflict, lest the common meeting ground becomes the occasion for misunderstanding and hostility. Europe was such a battleground in the last century. South Asia is a good example of such an implosion in our globalising world today.

We are coming to value diversity as something potentially enriching and even uniting at a higher level of unity. This is certainly true of the rich religious traditions of this land, when they are not manipulated for narrow political gain or subversive communal interests. Such an enriching unity must inspire us to reach out to each other in a common concern and in a shared faith, bringing us together with our differences into a unity in diversity, one that does not negate our peculiarities, but rather accepts and respects, even celebrates them.

In India, unity in diversity is official policy. Yet today, such multiculturalism is under a menacing threat from rationalist secularism and religious fundamentalism. Democratic pluralism is no quick fix solution to the rising expectations of our people, but it seems to be the only feasible alternative if this reality of diversity and difference is to be accepted and not suppressed.

Ultimately, our response to pluralism must begin with rejecting inequalities and accepting differences, affirming equal dignity for all and respecting the unique identity of each, reaching out to live and celebrate similarities and differences as parts of a larger organic social and cultural whole. Our pluralism is not so much to promote our unity over and above the reality of our diversity, but rather to protect our diversity in our quest for unity. Not unity-in-diversity so much as diversity-in-unity.

Structural plurality becomes the basis for a 'politics of interests', mobilising groups around 'what they want'. If this is not integrated into a system that protects fundamental rights and promotes equitable distribution, it engenders class conflict. Cultural plurality is fertile ground for the 'politics of identity', mobilising groups are based on who they are. If this is not incorporated into a pluralism that recognises cultural differences and affirms collective rights, it breeds collective passions. Exclusive identities, whether based on religion, caste, race, or any other common ethnic trait, once imposed, easily become an effective basis for group mobilisation and ethno-politics. The identity politics precipitated by religion has been among the most violent and destructive.

Unique identities pertain to the cultural domain. When these are aggregated from the individual to the group, they can become more intractable and uncompromising than ever. This is precisely what happens with exclusive and total identities. They subsume all other individual identities into the group one, and oppose this to the identities of other groups. This is the death knell of any kind of cultural pluralism in society. Religious nationalisms and fundamentalisms are prone to this.

Rather, we need inclusive multiple identities both for individuals and groups, identities that are layered and prioritised according to the context around a core identity that gives stability and continuity to the person and the group. This will demand flexible identities and overlapping porous group boundaries. Gandhi, as we shall see, is a remarkable example of such a rooted yet open person (*Young India*, June 1921: 170).

Identity politics is an effective motivator for individuals and a powerful mobiliser for groups. However, in recognising 'who we are' we have to discover 'what we want'. If the politics of identity is not rationalised by the politics of interests, it can oppress others and suppress its own. For both individuals and groups, we need an integrated and holistic approach that will recognise the universal demand of equal dignity for all, and comprehend the particular exigencies of the unique identity of each.

Democratic pluralism cannot exclude identity politics, though its relationship with the politics of interest is certainly a problematic one. Collective identities mobilise group interests. These interests in turn consolidate corresponding identities. A constructive integration will demand that a larger concern and a deeper unity direct and subsume both. Caste communalism and religious fundamentalism have severely undermined such a politics of integration. These have deliberately exploited communal riots and civil disturbances to polarise our society for electoral gains. This further multiplies the divides and deepens the fissures in society.

The politics of integration must be a quest for an egalitarian, just and free society. In our quest for economic equality, creating class-consciousness is never merely to invert class divisions and perpetuate them. It is to mobilise a class struggle for a classless society, where social inequalities are abolished. In our quest for social justice, mere positional change in the caste hierarchy without an attempt to eliminate it will only perpetuate casteism. Rather, caste mobilisation must be for a casteless society, where caste hierarchy has been demolished. So too if religious identities are activated in our quest for religious liberation — it must not be for dominance or isolation, but to create a free and inter-religious pluralism, where religious differences are complementary, not antagonistic.

Conversion as Freedom

The secular ideal was an integral part of the freedom struggle in this country. The separation of politics from religion was considered essential to the process of building a modern nation. There were dissenting voices of Muslim separatists and Hindu nationalists, but with the trauma of the Partition and the assassination of the Father of the Nation, secularism was written into our Constitution and later defined as part of its basic structure that cannot be changed.

Today, this secularism is mired in controversy. The state and civil society have become increasingly and violently communal. Rather than abandoning our Constitutional secularism, we need to critically contextualise and reaffirm the old broad-based consensus. For secularism is not just the sine qua non for tolerance in a multi-cultural society, it is also a project for liberation in a religiously oppressive one. Although secularism as an ideology may be foreign in its origins, it is not alien to the aspirations it inspires among our people. Here we can already anticipate where support and opposition to it might come from.

In the Christian west, secularism has meant the separation of church and state, especially where the state was unable to impose a single official faith on the multiplicity of its warring churches. The Enlightenment began a radical rationalist critique of religion with the undisguised goal of displacing all religion from public life and all faith from private life as well, replacing both with a new secular consensus as the basis of the national community. For science and technology brought a new autonomy to 'Man come of age', who no longer needed the tutelage of institutional religion.

Yet even in advanced modern societies, the widespread religious revivalism today demonstrates that the 'decline' or the 'demise' of institutional religion is far more complex and contested than was once thought. A simplistic identification of secularism with rationalism and progress, and religion as obscurantist and reactionary is not tenable any more.

The role of religion is problematic in any complex society, though the concrete context may indeed make for more specific and significant differences. Cultural and religious traditions cannot but reflect the ambivalence and contradictions of their own society. The understanding of secularism in a pluri-religious, multi-cultural society like India, will certainly be different from that in the west, a difference not just in degree but also in kind. Historically, the Indian situation is far more complex. Yet in the pluri-religious consciousness of our inclusive traditions, we can find some basis for a relevant concept of secularism for our present situation.

One can argue that the Upanishads were a philosophic secularisation of Vedic religion. That Jainism and Buddhism were Kshatriya attempts, which for a time offered an egalitarian alternative to Brahmanic hierarchy. The *bhakti* movement beginning in the Tamil south and, spreading north, expressed not just explicit longing for salvation in the next world, but also implicit protest against religious oppression in this one. The *Sufi* tradition is also close to such expressions and aspirations, and Sufi-*bhakti* poetry remains a treasure trove of these traditions. Kabir, Guru Nanak, Tukaram, Mirabai and many others are testimony to this. More recently, diverse liberation theologies have begun to articulate the liberative, this-worldly dimensions of our religious traditions. Among the earliest to anticipate this trend in a modern, secular context was Babasaheb Ambedkar's interpretation of Buddhism, his Navayana (new vehicle). Asghar Ali Engineer for Islam, Swami Agnivesh for Hinduism and George Soares-Prabhu for Christianity, among others, deserve special mention.

However, a reactivation of our lost national consensus cannot be separated from the social processes in which it must be grounded. Imposing it from above as part of a dominant hegemony, as the liberal middle-class and modern rationalists are wont to urge, will not be truly liberating for our religiously oppressed masses. It might easily be counter-productive. A dichotomy between the 'secular-minded elite and religiously-oriented masses' would be alien and oppressive, and only precipitate a further regression, as some anti-secularists have argued.

In fact, Indian secularism has leaned too heavily on a Nehru's rationalism, and remained an imposition from the outside even though it could claim Constitutional legitimacy. Nehruvian secularism was understood as dharma *nirapekshata*, or indifference/neutrality towards religion. This was hardly ever likely to have much sustained mass support. Gandhian secularism of *sarvadharma samabhav*, equal respect to all religions, is much closer to the reality of the ingrained multi-faceted religiosity of our people. It implies an essential tolerance and the openness that is more in tune with our Constitutional protection to the rights of religious minorities.

Nehruvian dharma *nirapekshata* and Gandhian *sarvadharma samabhava* represent the two most significant models of secular ideology that were subsumed into the national consensus. There were others too, like Tagore with his deep humanism, Ambedkar with his commitment to rationalism that mostly supported and nuanced this consensus. For secularism in our Constitution, though not adequately defined, has meant at least minimally, a guarantee of equitable treatment to all religious communities by the state. However, our secular state is also committed to the reform of religious communities in view of establishing the fundamental rights of its members.

Indian secularism, then, is not centred on the separation of religion and the state, as in the west. It is peculiarly Indian, both pluralist and reformist, not a completed project yet but a struggle for religious tolerance and freedom of conscience. Religious nationalists who want to homogenise our society with a cultural nationalism will inevitably be at odds with such a pluralist secularism. Religious fundamentalists who see their religious traditions endangered by reformist interventions of the state will surely oppose it. However, those who value equal respect and space for conscience and choice for all, will be its mainstay.

Hindu nationalists now dismiss both the Nehruvian and Gandhian versions of secularism and champion instead its very antithesis, namely, the 'positive secularism' of 'justice for all, appeasement of none', a slogan that hides far more that it reveals. They argue that since Hindus are the majority community, Hinduism must mean nationalism, and vice versa. To them, true nationalists can only be Hindus, culturally if not religiously as well. This would sacralise the state into a theocracy, where the survival of religious and other minorities would depend on the goodwill of the religious/ cultural majority. However, the Hinduism of our people is a multiplicity of religious traditions held together in broad civilisation worldview, whereas Hindutva of the fundamentalists is a narrow communal ideology of Hindu religious nationalists.

Minority and majority communities are not a matter of demographic numbers. Like all groups, their identities are constructed by self-definition and by the perception of others. It is in the interaction between the two, whether opposed or compatible, that a group finally identifies and positions itself in society. In this sense, both can be called 'imagined communities', following Benedict Anderson, (Anderson 1983) be they national, sub-national or even smaller 'ethni-clones'.

In fact, class and subculture internally differentiate all majorities, which have more different than similar, more divergent than convergent political concerns and economic interests. This is especially so with assumed religious majorities. For in spite of commonalities, as T.N.

Madan correctly insists, no religious community is undifferentiated, the Hindus least of all (Madan 1997: 251). Nevertheless, the danger of religious 'majoritarinism' must not blind us to the provocation of vesting minorities with veto powers. For Constitutional protections are meant for the vulnerable, not as privileges over others.

Because the majority-minority syndrome is constructed both from without and from within these groups, the minority definition can at times be imposed on a group by outsiders. Dipankar Gupta has characterised this as 'minoritisation', a process by which new minorities are created, and from which no community is completely safe (Gupta 1999: 76-77). An alarming illustration of this is the minoritisation of the Sikhs that climaxed in the horrendous pogrom of 1984 in Delhi. Would anyone have anticipated such an atrocity on the Sikhs, once considered 'the sword arm of Hinduism', the militant defenders of the Hindus at the time of the Partition riots, less than four decades earlier? Once we begin to exploit identity politics, there is no limit to cultural differences that can be constructed and the cultural divides that may begin to surface. South Asia already provides more than ample proof of this. Everyone here belongs to some differentiated minority, depending on how the social cake is cut, and we cannot quite anticipate where the knife will fall next.

Similarly, 'majoritisation' too can be precipitated by the aggressive self-assertion of a minority group, whether defensive or dominant, straining the tolerance of the larger community into hostile reaction. Muslim communities and dalits have often been thus accused, but in majority-minority conflicts, it is obvious who are the more vulnerable and disadvantaged, and on whose side the numbers add up. The official death toll in communal riots is convincing evidence of this, whether it will be Delhi in 1984, or Mumbai in 1992-93, or Gujarat in 2002. In all these instances, the argument of self-defence is an unconvincing post factum rationalisation.

In situations of hostile and competitive inter-community relations, extremism on both sides feeds on each other, just as trade union rivalry escalates industrial conflict. Majority and minority groups become locked into a process of violent confrontation that spirals out of control, though it is mostly the leaders and elites on both sides who benefit from the polarisation. Most ethnic and religious conflicts in South Asia, as elsewhere, are rather an obvious illustration of this process, often deliberately manipulated and pursued. In Sri Lanka, this has led to a continuing and irresolvable civil war. The lesson for the rest of us is too obvious to ignore.

In colonial times, the system of separate electorates was more than a divide-and-rule disaster; it was an invitation to competing identities that militate against an overarching pan-Indian one. In the competition for the new opportunities and resources opening up in the colonial period and after, group identities were mobilised and consolidated. This has reached critical proportions in the postcolonial period, especially in the context of our skewed development and misdirected modernity.

Some view our present predicament of endemic communal conflict as due to the pragmatic or tactical communalism of pseudo-secularists, who have used the communal card to appease minority communities. Others explain it as the well-planned programmatic or strategic communalism of extremists, who manipulate religious sentiment to their own advantage. Modernists see this revival as a failure of rationality and a regress into tradition, while postmodernists blame the homogenising nationalist state for precipitating a communal reaction.

The ambiguities of our Constitutional secularism have become a multifaceted instrument. This has been put to a variety of contrary purposes. Religious minorities have sought protection under its umbrella of neutrality, used it to preserve their collective rights, but resisted when it has been cited in favour of reformative changes they resent. Hindu nationalists have denigrated it for privileging religious minorities and discounting the Hindu majority. Rationalists have promoted it as a means of aggressive reform from above. Conservative traditionalists have blamed it for the marginalisation of religion and the consequent moral vacuum.

No society can function without some consensus on the underpinning worldview that must sustain it. In a religious society, a rationalist modernity would not be popularly acceptable to the mass of our people, nor would a traditionally religious one be adequate to the changes to they are subjected. Post-modern anti-secularists have diagnosed the aggressive homogenisation by the modern state as the cause of the severe backlash precipitated in traditional religious societies. However, they have not convincingly demonstrated how adequate the tolerant pluralism that they hope to find in the older religious traditions will be to the strains and stresses of modernity and its multiple impacts, or how able to resist the hegemonic nationalist state. On the contrary, religious nationalists and fundamentalists have been quick to politicise these traditions in the opposite direction of exclusion and violence.

The founding vision of our state is now under serious threat. How we understand and institutionalise our Constitutional guarantees will dictate how we define our future. Our development and modernisation processes have accentuated discontent and differences, that religious nationalists and fundamentalists have seized on, and so compounded our problems further. However, benign neglect is no longer viable in a globalising world when others are ready to rush in where we have failed to act. We need a pluralism that will celebrate and reconcile our differences, affirm and subsume our identities in a larger organic whole. The historic strength of Indic civilisation has been its capacity to tolerate difference and allow such diversity. Indic traditions have demonstrated a resilient identity in spite of the drastic changes they have faced. This continuity in change has given an overaching civilisation unity to our cultural diversity.

Constitutional secularism was intended to underwrite an inclusive pluralism with the fundamental right to 'profess, practice, and propagate' one's religion. Locating religious conversions within this context of a tolerant pluralism is problematic and contentious. For religious nationalists, conversion is subversive and must be suppressed; for religious fundamentalists, it is an atrocity that provokes their retaliation. However, religious conversion essentially concerns the freedom of conscience of individuals and groups. We have clearly a constitutionally guaranteed right to such a freedom of religion, but we must also find in ourselves the equally fundamental duty of religious tolerance.

However, religious nationalism and fundamentalism in India with their politicisation recently have become more strident and aggressive. The compulsions of political compromise, when in positions of responsible political power, were expected to moderate their extremism, but the adjustments have been more tactical than strategic, tentative not lasting. For as long as extremism yields electoral results, it will be used at the hustings. Diminishing returns do serve as a reality check, as happened with the general election in May 2004. We owe this reversal more to the good sense of our common people rather than the religious sensitivity or social conscience of their leaders.

The response of religious nationalism and fundamentalism to our present predicament is more a misreading of our history than a legitimate interpretation. The attempt to rewrite our history to legitimise such extremism is a grotesque distortion that has little academic credibility. If we compare the history textbooks of India and Pakistan, we are left wondering if both are talking of the same sub-continent. We need a certain distancing from, and an honest analysis of, destructive historical events and compromised social structures, not self-righteous defensiveness. Today, this has an increasing urgency, situated as we are in an 'India shining' for the few, while the majority are excluded from this charmed circle of light.

As with any change, conversion unsettles group boundaries and threatens the status quo. The state may be tempted to respond by freezing the inter-group boundaries or imposing a 'national' homogeneity. Neither is workable in a society as complex and heterogeneous as ours. A constructive approach would be to create an encompassing unity, larger than the community, which will contain and restrain, both sectarianism and fanaticism within a just, democratic, secular state. This is our challenge as a new and diverse nation with an old and rich heritage.

There are many players in this performance and multiple dimensions to the play. Sorting these out is a delicate but necessary task for any in-depth understanding and honest critique of religious conversion.

4

A Holistic Approach

Personal Quest - Collective dignity - Political and economic interests - Religious Worldviews - Conversion as Multi-faceted

There are several approaches to understanding religious conversion and various ways of responding to it. Perceiving conversion as subversion, as atrocity, or as freedom comes from inherently different perspectives. Each has evoked very different responses. When protagonists are not asking the same questions, how can they ever comprehend, let alone agree on the answers? Those promoting and those opposing religious conversions are two entrenched opponents, who have monopolised the debate for too long. We need to consider a third player, the converts themselves, who have been silenced far too often.

Given the emotional charge it usually carries, the discussion on religious conversion is frequently fragmented and unfocused. In attempting a holistic approach, we will distinguish four levels of understanding: the psychosocial, the socio-cultural, the eco-political, and the socio-religious. These levels are distinct but not separate. They overlap and interrogate each other. Moreover, a comprehensive discussion must imply an interdisciplinary approach. Though in any particular instance one or the other level may be privileged, no level can be given an exclusive priority in an inclusive framework of understanding.

At each level, the presentation here will proceed in the following steps. First, we will explain what conversion involves, elaborate its implications, and discuss the issues that arise. Next, we will examine the role of the three players we have identified and the interaction between them. Finally, we will draw out the consequences of the discussion for our common citizenship and our civic rights.

A holistic approach to a complex issue cannot but be multidimensional. In teasing out the levels of understanding and identifying the actors involved at each, we can bring a sharper focus to our analysis. In drawing together the manifold but related aspects of the question, we hope to bring a broader comprehension to the discussion. Our overarching concern will be for social identity and human dignity, for personal freedom and individual respect, as affirmed by our common citizenship. Here we position ourselves in this discussion.

Personal Quest

At this psychosocial level, conversion is a question of personal choice. It involves a rejection, a change or an adaptation of one's identity. An internal reconstruction or an external imposition can precipitate this. A complex set of motivations is involved. Individuals looking for personal space often opt for a changed religious identity that allows for such space, whether psychological or social, intellectual or emotional.

The change is the result of a personal quest, which may be more than a religious or spiritual one. Positively, this is experienced as liberation; negatively, it could be an escape. Breaking away from one's community or even family, when these are experienced as too constraining, can mean a change of religion. This is especially so when a religious tradition is perceived as affirming individual equality and dignity against an imposed hierarchy, whether of caste or class, race or ethnicity. Thus, escape from one's tradition to a more affirming one takes on religious overtones, though there are non-religious motivations operative as well, like self-improvement and upward mobility.

The rejection of the old identity and the adaptation to the new implies a critique or an interrogation of both. This can be a painful process for the convert, particularly where one's personal identity is enmeshed in a network of dependencies and responsibilities. It can also be threatening to, and resented by the group the convert leaves behind. They may feel rejected by the change, especially when critical numbers or significant individuals convert. When identities are inflexible and group boundaries impervious, conversion becomes an emotional issue and can even precipitate violence. Obviously then, open and inclusive identities and groups are better able to cope with such change than closed and exclusive ones.

The danger is to have a single, consolidated identity, inflexible and rigid. It leads to all kinds of personal crises, with inevitable changes that affect one's life. This is what 'life's passages', the necessary discontinuities in one's life, are all about. No life can be evenly continuous, especially in times of rapid social change. Old and stable identities are eroded, creating new insecurities and anxieties that become aggressive and even violent. Religious conversion as personal change cannot but imply a new rearrangement of such evolving identities. The different protagonists have different takes on such identity change. This involves more than just the religious or the spiritual.

At this personal level, religious conversion is not merely a renunciation, even though confessional narratives by converts often emphasise this. It is also a transition from the old to the new. This necessarily involves a negotiation of both the consonance and conflict between two identities, two traditions that may at times be more, at others less contrary to each other. The negotiation is generally fluid and flexible. It can sometimes be very subtle and unconscious, at others almost a struggle for survival. It can be a defensive self-justification or an aggressive protest, a spiritual liberation or a leap of faith.

Beginning with the converts, their old identity is not erased; rather, the new one is overwritten on it. They often undergo much role strain and stress in their new situation, which may show up in unanticipated and critical ways. Conversion may even involve a reorganisation of personality that could be quite radical. Less acknowledged is that at times such a change also involves a critique of the very tradition the convert chooses to join. New entrants are often marginal persons who represent alternative perspectives on, and a critique of the old traditions they have left, as well as the new ones to which they commit themselves. This is precisely the complex transition they must negotiate, whether conversion happens in an assimilative or an oppositional context.

Converts may also experience an inner psychological urge that drives them to religious change. Sometimes these are interpreted as a spiritual and religious quest and it may indeed be so, but it will be truly so in the measure in which it is internally free from psychological and other compulsions.

We will take up some controversial conversions in the next chapter, but we mention a few examples here by way of immediate illustration. Thus, John Henry Newman (1801-1890), whose conversion from Anglicanism to Roman Catholicism in 1845 not only confounded his old Anglican Church and the Oxford movement he had espoused, but ironically left him under suspicion in the Roman Church. The autobiographical account of his conversion *Apologia Pro Vita Sua* (A Defence of My Life) published in 1864 was better received by most Anglicans than by many Catholics. Narayan Vaman Tilak (1961-1890) was at odds with his American Baptist Mission in his search for an indigenous Christianity after he converted in 1895. Brahmabandhab Upadhyay (1861-1907), who converted in 1891 and died in a Kolkata hospital, charged with sedition by the colonial government, was a man far ahead of his time with his ideal of a Hindu Christianity that neither community was ready for at the time.

Coming now to those promoting conversions, in one scenario at this psycho-social level, these converters could be projecting, extending and imposing their own religious identity on the converted. If this is by force or fraud or unfair inducement, then it is a violation of the person, an illegitimate dominance over another. This can happen with all kinds of identities, political or ideological, cultural or ethnic, linguistic or numerous others. For religious identities are never in isolation but embedded in the social context of a person's life-situation.

At times, converters could be motivated by their own uncertainties and doubts, and persuading others becomes one way of keeping faith themselves. Newman's *Essay in Aid of a Grammar of Ascent* (Newman 1979) elaborates how this 'intellectual anxiety' works itself out, in the need to disseminate and even impose one's own convictions on others, who may stand as a question mark against them. It may at times be done unconsciously, but when it becomes a self-centred imposition on the other, then it clearly amounts to an unacceptable violation. Newman himself did not engage in proselytising the Anglicans from whom he converted to Catholicism. His life and work was witness enough to his openness to the pursuit of truth, and it still inspires us today.

On the other hand, a converter may also be reaching out to others with an enabling religious alternative that helps them cope with their own situation, bringing them to experience a greater freedom.

Propagating alternatives is not exclusive to religion, it happens in many other areas of life. Thus commercial advertising can be a less offensive, even a helpful example, while political propaganda a more offensive, even an abusive one. With religion, this has often involved the arrogance of converters, who denigrate another tradition to propagate their own, but it need not be so, for respect for another's religions does not exclude responsible freedom to propagate one's own. Ashokan Buddhists monks were certainly more respectful of the people they preached to than colonial's missionaries.

Those who oppose religious conversion perceive it as an unfair imposition that violates a person's identity and dignity. The greater the violation involved, the greater the need to oppose it. Historically, this has certainly happened, and subjugated or colonised peoples still have bitter memories of this. Such 'a colonisation of consciousness', which is not confined to the religious sphere and was endemic to colonialism, is still a part of a neo-colonialism in our post-colonial world, where economic dominance still commands affiliation, religious or otherwise. Ashis Nandy explores the psychological dimensions of *The Intimate Enemy* we have internalised (Nandy 1983). Marxian 'false consciousness' explores the socio-political dimensions of the phenomenon and Antonio Gramsci explains how it works towards the hegemony of the dominant classes (Gramsci 1996).

But then again opposition to personal conversions also comes from communities and groups that are defensive about converts leaving them. They perceive it as a rejection and negation of something they value, as undermining their dominance or compromising their interests. Their defensiveness can become aggressive, precipitating violence against the converters and the converted. This escalates the spiral of violence rather than putting a stop to the conversions, because the root causes of the conversions are not addressed.

The need to oppose unjust violence cannot be contested. Nevertheless, when persons feel violated in the community or tradition they find themselves in, forcing them to belong or denying them an alternative outside the fold is as much a violation of their freedom as converting them by force, fraud or inducement. Proponents and opponents of conversions are often locked in a battle where the real casualty is the freedom of the would-be convert caught in between. Unfortunately, religious violence is not the only violence converts are subject to, and yet for the other two protagonists, religion becomes the overriding preoccupation. This too must be questioned, as we will in a later chapter.

In terms of citizenship, the real issues involved concern the individual's fundamental human rights and civil liberties. A liberal secular democracy must negate the presumption of ascribed status. Persons are not born to be locked into a given identity and role. Human dignity demands the right to express one's individuality and freedom. This 'freedom of conscience' must embrace both the right to change for the converted, as also the right to propagate for the converter, always respecting the need for reasonable restrictions that all civil liberties and democratic rights must be minimally subject to.

This is well articulated in the Marxian expression: 'The freedom of each must be the condition of the freedom of all.' Otherwise, there is great danger of the so-called imperative for 'law and order' being used repressively, rather than to support and protect a liberal regime of human rights. Unfortunately, at times, some opponents of conversion deliberately create, or threaten to precipitate, a law and order situation, and then call for restrictive measures, not against themselves but against those who have supposedly provoked their violence with 'proselytising'. Atrocities against vulnerable religious minorities or caste groups are examples of this kind of vicious manoeuvring.

However, there is also the question of collective rights, a community's right to unique identity as sanctioned by our Constitution, so long as this does not violate the fundamental rights of individuals. For individual freedom is in tension with, but not necessarily in contradiction to, community solidarity. Religious freedom is one of the most sensitive areas of this tension. Hence, the protection of identity and dignity, whether of the individual or the community, will need more than a regime of political rights. There is also the need for civic space in which both can flourish and the individual-community tension meaningfully resolved. This is an issue of tolerance that cannot be legislated and so all the more concerns our civil sense.

Collective Dignity

At the socio-cultural level, the question is of social advantage or disadvantage, of affirmation or discrimination, of a sense of privilege or deprivation that a group — or the community — experiences with regard to its cultural identity and its collective dignity. This is a different level of articulation, not just of numerical aggregates but social groups of interacting. Collective rights reside in the group, not the individual. These cultural or community rights are consequent on cultural or community identities. However, while they are distinct, they are never separate from — much less in opposition to — individual rights and identities. They must be complementary, never contradictory to them. Thus, protecting a community's identity and safeguarding its dignity is a legitimate exercise of these rights. The freedom of choice for individuals or of groups to reject, accept or change their own allegiance, and consequently their identity, cannot be rightfully denied. Group belonging must be voluntary and never indelibly ascribed by the collective.

Religion in a society is always culturally expressed. Hence, conversion across religious traditions implies a change in one's cultural identity. This often involves a distancing from, or even a rejection of, allegiance to the old socio-cultural tradition and consequently to the group or community identified with it, or a transfer of this allegiance to a new socio-cultural tradition, or even the creation of a new one.

Anxiety over such a change of allegiance is hardly surprising, particularly when there is a close identification between community and religious tradition as happens with ethnic religions, as we have seen earlier. It implies a threat to the tradition and the collective identity of both communities affected by the change: the one left behind, where feelings of anxiety and rejection may be greater than for the one that the converts join, where the neophytes may not always be welcome. Thus, the conversion of dalits is resisted by dominant castes as a rejection of hierarchy, even while dalit converts have often been resented by upper caste Christians as undermining their community status in the larger society. History records many instances of this.

In some circumstances, the anxiety and resentment even yields to a narcissistic rage, especially with religious extremists, whether fundamentalists or nationalists. Religious wars and religious terrorism are ghastly demonstrations of such rage, and it is always the weakest and most vulnerable who suffer its harshest consequences. In this country, dalits and tribals have been mute victims of this wrath, at times, less valued by some religious leaders than other holy cows.

However, not all conversions necessarily imply drastic socio-cultural change. Often, there is cultural continuity after the conversion, though more often than not there is a certain rupture. The transition from the Sikh to the Hindu tradition via the Guru Nanak Panth, and vice versa, has for long been unproblematic; so too has the passage between many liberal Protestant denominations. However, what colonised and conquered peoples underwent in their conversion to the religious tradition of their masters was often a violent cultural alienation — and worse. Converts were left doubly alienated: from the old tradition, which they had not fully left behind, and in the new one, in which they did not completely belong. Colonial Christianity has left an estranged heritage and its memories still haunt us even today, particularly in Asia.

Such violence is not inherent to the process of conversion as seen in religious traditions that have spread without conquering or subduing a people. Violence is not integral to any of the major religious traditions; if anything, it is an aberration and an abuse of power. Yet historically, violence has unfortunately often compromised these traditions. We still have a long way to go in exorcising this demon from our religious world, where extremists legitimate this. We are at the crossroads between religious antagonism, religious tolerance and the future of our children hangs in this balance.

If the prevailing social divisions and cultural fault-lines are not bridged, they tend to intensify with competitive identity politics and electoral compulsions, especially in times of rapid change and continuing crisis. This can reach the point of no return, precipitating irreversible divides, and ultimately a vivisection of a people, as we know from our bitter experience of the Partition in 1947.

Religious conversions can further exacerbate the cultural tension in such a situation, but they can also be the focus of interrogation between the opposing traditions. If they are not hijacked for partisan purposes, they can provide a point of integration in a larger overarching unity. For religious conversions challenge our understanding of - and commitment to - a pluralist society, and point to the need - and perhaps the necessity too - for a secular state. Here interrogating the gender divide and caste patriarchy in terms of a larger human unity across sexual and other divides are parallel and pertinent examples.

As with persons, so with groups: the converts may well be seeking a new social identity as an escape or liberation from a self-understanding no longer adequate or acceptable. Conversion becomes a passage to a new social identity that empowers and frees the group. The converts do not attempt to reform the old. They have lost hope in this regard. Their choice is a social protest directed, not to reform the old, but to reject it, inspired by hope for a better future elsewhere.

It may also happen that converts are moved more by 'pull' rather than 'push' factors. There is the attraction of a new future promised and the example of those already there. The pull of upward social mobility too is apparent, as when converts choose the religious tradition of a dominant group or ruling class. Such a quest for self-improvement and upward mobility can happen within the same religious tradition, as with the Sanskritisation of Hindu lower castes and tribals, or it can reach beyond the fold. However, the transition may have begun, negotiations that are more complex follow, and many hopes may remain unfulfilled or even betrayed. For the motivations involved in such conversions are quite complicated, and need to be carefully and respectfully disentangled.

Religious conversion implies social change. Those at the very bottom of the social hierarchy may want a change for the better but are too vulnerable to take such a risk. Rather it is those a little higher up, yet closer to the bottom than to the middle, who are the most likely to convert. These have more room to manoeuvre and hence an openness to change. Thus, the 19th century in south India saw the backward castes' movement to Christianity. These were less backward than the Scheduled Castes. In the 20th century, the mass conversion to Buddhism in Maharashtra was of the Mahars, who were the better off among the dalits.

The converter in this context may be imposing a new dominance, or protecting, or even extending the dominance of the old community and its tradition by assimilating new and marginal groups, thus domesticating the alien. However, in the process, internal contradictions come to the fore. New converts may incisively interrogate a religious tradition attracting converts because of its egalitarian promise, if they do not experience this equality. The prevalence of caste among Christians and Muslims in India exemplifies this anomaly.

Sometime there is an internal attempt to adapt and even reform the tradition to better cope with the neophytes' expectations. However, this too has often been opposed by the old orthodoxy's refusal to distinguish essentials from non-essentials, real content from incidental context. The resistance to indigenise or inculturate a religious tradition illustrates this. As we have seen, the Malabar rites were at the time opposed by the Roman Church. Islamisation has too often meant Arabisation and Hinduisation is made equivalent to Sanskritisation.

On the other hand, the converter could be genuinely sharing or offering a new socio-cultural liberation. This can sometimes happen even within the tradition, as with liberation theology in Latin America, which really represents a renewed tradition transforming popular religiosity in that continent. In Asia, such a liberation theology is beginning to make inroads as we have seen in the last chapter. Not surprisingly, empowering the poor is as threatening to the dominant establishment here, as it was in Latin America, even though there such change represents a *metanoia*, rather than a *dharmantar*, i.e., a change within — not across — traditions. However, when the liberating power of a religious tradition finds expression in conversion across traditions, a *dharmantar,* it is doubly provocative to the status quo.

Considered at this cultural level, those opposing conversion have a fear of cultural, even demographic extinction. However, this fear of ethnocide is better addressed by reforms in the community that improve the lot of the oppressed there, than by resistance to their opting out of the fold and others welcoming them in theirs. At times, the opposition may have little to do with cultural or even religious concerns and more with economic interests and political dominance. The apprehension in the west towards conversions to eastern religions, especially to Islam, needs some introspection in this light, as do conversions to western religious traditions in the east.

In the context of citizenship, the issue is one of collective and cultural rights, in terms of both protective and affirmative action, for non-dominant minorities and disadvantaged groups. The religious traditions of many of our tribals, as also of some religious sects and subcastes, are tied into their own distinctive culture and language, or at least a sub-culture and dialect. Our Constitution guarantees their protection, and our governments are supposed to be committed to promote their collective rights.

Conversion by force, fraud or undue inducement is a violation of these rights. However, leaving people trapped within an oppressive and imposed fate is no less perverse. Surely, human solidarity would require that we facilitate a process whereby those in need are enabled to draw on their cultural and religious resources to change their fate. Romanticising their culture and traditions and sealing them off against change only keeps them as exotic exhibits in a museum, or a zoo, something we would hardly want for our own community and culture. Change for the better is a fundamental human aspiration in our world. People themselves must be the subject of their history and choose their future as best they can. Religious change, whether offered as a choice, or chosen as an alternative, cannot be excised from that future.

This is the minimum respect they can legitimately demand. Those who promote and those who oppose conversions cannot in good conscience deny this respect.

However, in today's discourse of 'cultural nationalism', with the battle cry of 'justice for all, appeasement of none', these collective rights are being contested in the arena of religion, but it certainly will not stop there. For such contestations, once politicised, do not readily set themselves any limits, religious, cultural or ethical. Our experience with what has come to be derogatorily called 'moral police' originates in such a censoring mentality.

What can such a 'national culture' mean to dalits who witness their families being lynched? Or, tribals who have their habitat destroyed? Alternatively, the poor, who are condemned to a sub-human subsistence? As Antonio Gramsci has shown, 'nationalism' as an ideology is essentially a hegemonic imposition by the dominant classes on the subordinate ones. In India, 'cultural nationalism' is basically for an upper caste-class instrument for dominance. More liberal democratic groups, especially subaltern ones, including all Scheduled Castes and Tribes contest this, when they are not co-opted by an identity politics against their own best interests. When such nationalism is religious and fundamentalist, conversion will be among the most sensitive arenas of the conflict.

However, cultures and identities are not static, singular life forms, which are easily destroyed when changed. They are constructed in a context and can be deconstructed and reconstructed in others. Some may be more organically integrated than some others may. They do evolve, very gradually at times, but they also mutate rapidly and unpredictably at others. No single cultural tradition can fully express the rich human potential of a people — and by extension, no religious tradition can fully satisfy all human spiritual aspirations. For precisely as a human social tradition, it is subject to inevitable human limitations. Even when a religious tradition claims divine inspiration, it cannot escape communication in a culture and language, and institutionalisation in a society. This necessarily brings its own human limitations.

Given the burden of our history, we need to privilege social diversity over uniformity, cultural heterogeneity over homogeneity, civic tolerance over political dominance. Culture is indeed a primary good but not an ultimate one. It must not compromise human dignity but enhance it. We must emphasise both the right to one's culture and the freedom from being imprisoned in it. We have a duty to respect other cultures and other religious traditions, as also the need to be inter-cultural and inter-religious as well. The issue here is not just one of rights and duties, but one of tolerance and dialogue, a theme to which we will return in a later chapter.

Political and Economic Interests

Separately or together, politics and economics cannot satisfactorily explain religious behaviour, though they do help enlighten the context in which it must be interpreted. To reduce religious conversion to a matter of political concerns or economic interests is a dangerous oversimplification of complex phenomena, which a multi-dimensional approach must shun.

The question here is one of justice or fairness, spelt out in terms of economic opportunity and equality, of political participation and control. This raises the issue of relative deprivation and just reward, of fair play and a level playing field, and how far religious communities are, and ought to be, implicated in all this.

Conversion at this level will involve the realigning of stakes and centres of power. For in changing one's religious allegiance, one changes many other circumstances as well, because human interactions are interdependent. However, not all these changes may be positive for the parties involved.

Conversion could mean a passage from subaltern to dominant eco-political groups, as when gypsies converted to Christianity in Europe, or Christians to Islam in Muslim-dominated West Asia; or vice versa, as when the first proud Romans were initiated into primitive Christianity, or Anglicans into Catholicism in England. The second is surely more likely to be religiously motivated than the first.

Conversion could involve the cooption of a subjugated people, domesticating the alien, as happened with colonialism. Alternatively, it could be to empower a coalition of otherwise disparate individuals and groups that come together under the umbrella of a larger religious brotherhood to strengthen their allegiance, for what could well be non-religious purposes. This could be local leaders converting to the religion of their conquerors and then joining the ruling elite, or conquerors adopting the religion of the vanquished leaders and consolidating a joint elite.

Thus, joining a 'church' or an organised religion or a religiously dominant group may facilitate promotion in the establishment, just as converting to a non-dominant religious community may be a renunciation of social status. The first is more likely to become a social movement than the second. However, the church that marries the state in one generation may well be widowed in the next.

The real issue here is how conversion will affect other levels of social interaction. Will the status quo prevail, or will there be increased dominance and oppression, and for whom? Will conversion create an openness to positional and structural change for group and community mobility in occupation and status, or will it rather cause an alienation and even regress? Though conversion may essentially be a religious change, it has inevitable consequences for the political economy of a society, when this involves a change across religious traditions.

Human motives are notoriously mixed. Converts may be economically or politically motivated, even when they project other motivations. Historically, a colonised or subjugated people have found it convenient to adopt the religion of their masters, even when not under compulsion to do so. The larger percentage of converts in such territories would testify to this. Sometimes their leaders have led them into the new fold, as when a tribal chief or the village elders convert. However, to assume that all groups convert for such material reasons denigrates people who often pay a heavier price than the material benefits they may gain.

Conversely, converts are often protesting political and economic repression and seeking to escape it. Conversion from the lower castes and tribes is ample testimony of this. However, this too has met with resistance, even in our post-colonial world. Here again, reforming the repressive status quo rather than resisting the converts' efforts to escape, would be a more credible and human response, addressing upstream causes rather than downstream effects.

Opposition to conversion is often carried over to a prejudice against the converts. Only a deep cynicism would believe that material advantage is the sole, or even the most dominant motivation of these human beings. Homo Sapiens does not live by bread alone!

The exploitation of subject peoples has all too often been legitimised by the religion of the subjugators. When religious converters followed in the wake of political power, there were enormous ambiguities not easily explained in religious terms. In this sub-continent, Muslim raiders invaded to destroy idolatry, but then retreated home laden with rich booty, leaving more than just broken idols behind. The Portuguese came seeking 'Christians and spices', and certainly sought economic profit from the spice trade, and to consolidate their rule by finding and making Christians among the people they colonised. The English came to trade but then stayed to rule, and legitimised this as a mission to civilise, which for many meant to Christianise their colonial subjects. Even peaceful monks and Sufis, missionaries and social reformers, often inadvertently, have become an extension of political or at least cultural influence where they were welcomed. The critical question is whether this left people better or worse off.

At times, converters seek to defuse social contradictions and tensions in society by converting disaffected groups to another-worldly ethic. Often such missions are sponsored by the establishment with precisely this intention. Religion then becomes the 'opium of the people' that allows the free market to function or an authoritarian regime to have its way. When worldly 'bread and circuses' fail then it will be another-worldly 'pie in the sky' that is promised. The quest for individual salvation in the next world becomes instrumental in dissipating tensions in this one; this-worldly liberation is displaced by other worldly salvation; oppression suffered now is accepted as *punya* for moksha, merit gained now for liberation promised later. Much of the revolutionary potential of the devotional bhakti traditions in this land have been co-opted in this manner, as Jayant Lele (Lele 1995) and others have shown.

The converter can also be motivated by a sense of economic justice and political liberation for the oppressed. Where the real issues are indeed economic and political, we must face them with a secular agenda, interpreting our religious traditions creatively to draw inspiration from them. Making such interventions conditional on conversion is to compromise them, as Gandhi rightly insisted. Indeed, ethical prophets, especially in the Old Testament, as in other varied religious traditions, particularly the Quran, have thundered against injustice inflicted on the poor. Such injustice was an evil to be suppressed, not a condition to be taken advantage of, for religious or other purposes. Such prophetic justice is meant for life in this world even as it reaches out to life in the next.

As we have already seen, this is precisely what liberation theologies today try to do for oppressed peoples in various contexts. In Latin America, it transformed popular religiosity within the Christian tradition in that continent with its 'preferential option for the poor'. In Asia, it has reached beyond the Christian to other religious traditions as well. Indeed, this inspiration was central to the Islamic concern for equality and justice, and the Gandhian *antyodaya*, uplifting the last and least.

In most religious traditions, preachers have addressed issues of injustice and won people over. Their beliefs were convincing because their actions authenticated them. Missionaries too have done this, sometimes even against the colonial government, rushing in where the government feared to tread. As we have seen, peasant and tribal movements were supported by missionaries in Jharkhand. C.F. Andrews (1871-1940), Samuel Evans Stokes (1882-1946), Verrier Elwin (1902-1964) and others supported the freedom struggle and the weakest among our people, though perhaps these were more the exception than the rule. All were in turn deeply marked by the India they so loved. Andrews remained an Anglican, though not quite in favour, Stokes eventually joined the Arya Samaj, and Elwin gave up organised religion. However, their commitment to their people never faltered.

Opposition to religious conversions at this level is articulated in terms of protecting the would-be converts from violence to their conscience, culture, and religious allegiance. Violence of any kind, whether by force, fraud or inducement, must be opposed. Converters, as we know, have not always been innocent of this, particularly when religion and politics mixed.

However, to assume that religious conversion is inherently violent is not just to deny to converters the freedom to propagate their faith fairly and respectfully. It negates the freedom of converts under the guise of protecting them. It is blind to the violence the weak and vulnerable already suffer from dominant groups, supposedly protecting them from force, fraud and inducement.

In fact, oftener than not, those opposing the conversion of these groups are motivated less by the concern for the converts than by the threat they perceive to themselves. Such prejudice and discrimination can be played out subtly and unconsciously, even with secular-minded liberal persons. With religious nationalists and fundamentalists, it reaches paranoid proportions. 'Nation at risk', 'Religion in danger' becomes their battle cry, resulting in brutal atrocities. Few religious traditions can claim innocence in this matter, once they are politicised.

Once again, the civic issue is one of freedom of conscience: should a change of religious allegiance affect the civil liberties and economic rights of citizens? Alternatively, if I find turning the issue around that changing my religion promotes my economic opportunities and democratic rights, or my upward social mobility in some way, should I be prevented by the state or other citizens? Is not this choice within civil liberties that must be protected? This may not be a truly religious motivation, or a very noble one, but can a democratic, secular government or its constituents forbid their citizens to sell their religious heritage for a mess of pottage, if that is the value, they place on it?

Nevertheless, if the converts' freedom is really the issue, they must be protected against those who convert, as also against those who prevent their converting, when either of these use force or fraud or undue inducement. Both being led beyond the fold, or being made to stay within it, are violations, when such means are used. Genuine concern for freedom of conscience will demand a level playing field here.

To pretend that some citizens are incapable of such freedom and need state protection against being misled is dangerous paternalism in a secular democracy that has seen fit to privilege its citizens with universal franchise. Certainly, voters mobilised by muscle and money power in our elections are not any the freer from such force and fraud, not to mention very dubious inducements. However, this cannot be reason enough for abandoning or banning competitive electoral politics. Rather the challenge is to prevent aberrations and make the process more transparent and responsive to voters. This is being urged by our Supreme Court but is resisted by the very politicians who claim to speak for the voters. Is there not a similar stake when it comes to the politics and economics of conversion?

Further, the right to improve one's material condition cannot be limited or constrained within hereditary occupations as ascribed by the caste hierarchy or a religious tradition. In a just and democratic society, this must be left to free choice and fair competition, and in a secular and liberal one such choices cannot be restricted even when this involves a change of religious allegiance.

Our Constitution sanctions reserved electoral constituencies and quotas as instruments of affirmative action to level the playing field for backward classes at the expense of the forward ones. This is part of the collective rights of the weaker sections of our society. The rights of minorities must also be seen in this light as protection for vulnerable communities, religious and linguistic. However, just as affirmative action is not intended to violate the fundamental rights of other individuals, so too minority rights must not be used against the majority.

Religion cannot be banished to the private sphere. It is never just an individual or family affair, but has necessary community and social dimensions. When it steps into the public domain and demands its political rights as guaranteed by our secular, democratic Constitution, religion must also constrain itself with the consequent political and civic duties, not just by respecting the rights of others, but also being sensitive to their sensibilities, including religious ones. This is especially so when it comes to preaching and propagating religion, for insensitivity here degrades both one's own and the other's religious tradition as Ashoka's rock edict, quoted earlier, emphasised centuries ago (Thapar 1961: 255).

Religious Worldviews

Considered at this level of understanding, religious conversion across traditions implies a change in a religious worldview and its root paradigm. In terms of our earlier discussion of 'mythos' and 'logos', this is a change in the intuitive grasp of one's world and the rational articulation of it. Often this can be a wrenching experience, and even famous converts have been known to long resist the plunge. For it involves reconstructing one's life and context in new and unfamiliar ways.

It took the horrific carnage of the battlefield for Emperor Ashoka to convert to Buddhism, and a long drawn out struggle and a mother's prayerful pursuit for Augustine of Hippo to convert from his dissolute pagan life to Christianity. However, as Bernard Lonergan has pointed out, at times 'conversion is not so much the denial and destruction of value systems and root paradigms as their restatement and transvaluation.' (Lonergan 1978: 13) Thus John Henry Newman considered his conversion to Catholicism an affirmation of his earlier Anglico-Catholicism, a coming home not a going away; or with Brahmabandhab Upadhyay and Pandita Ramabai, for whom conversion to Christianity did not negate being Hindu. This is the issue of multiple belongings, to which we will return to in a later chapter.

Religious pluralism can only be premised on a viable socio-cultural one. Essentially, it must be grounded in individual and collective freedom of choice. Today, such pluralism is the only viable alternative to both the relativism that undermines religious commitment with permissiveness, as well as the absolutism that subverts it into extremism. For pluralism allows for fidelity to one's own tradition, while requiring respect for that of others. It privileges diversity over uniformity, favours liberalism over dogmatism.

At the level of the religious community, a change of worldview and of the root paradigm will undermine the foundational myth of a people's religious tradition. The change and corresponding challenge is likely to be much greater for a dogmatic tradition than for a non-dogmatic one, and its impact rather different in a theistic tradition than in a non-theistic one, in a historical religion than in a non-historic one. Further, the impact of such change is the greater when a society identifies with, or privileges the religion and culture of one community over others, as happens with some ethnic religions. When a dominant or hegemonic social group identifies with a religious tradition, then the status quo is the more affected by such religious change. The greater the change, the greater the threat, the greater is the corresponding resistance.

The real issue here is the one of religious pluralism, and the tolerance and dialogue this must entail. Should boundaries between religious communities be porous or sealed? Should we have an open, inclusive understanding of religion or a closed exclusive one? Flexible, non-antagonistic expressions of our religiosity, or rigid, hostile ones? Should we be tolerant of religious differences and dialogue across them towards understanding and harmony, or seek to impose homogeneity and uniformity on others and ourselves? Where does organised group or mass conversion stand in this regard? These are essentially religious issues, but politically explosive ones, the more so today in our contentious social context.

At this level of understanding, the religious motivation of the convert is the focus of concern, though once again the motivation can be more or less mixed. The decision to convert may come after a long quest, as with Gautama, who spent many years in his quest before he became the Buddha, or as a sudden experience, as with Saul of Tarsus, who on the road to Damascus is struck down and becomes Paul, the Apostle. The primacy of the spiritual and religious quest is hardly in doubt with such persons, or with other more ordinary mortals who have journeyed along this path in openness and honesty, to find beyond the fold what they had sought within it.

This kind of religious conversion is an intensely personal matter of conscience. It is difficult to see how group or mass conversion can fall in the same category. This is not to deny any spiritual motivation in these other conversions. Yet certainly, within such an aggregate, there cannot but be varying levels of motivation and other levels of understanding that come into play. Such conversions may not be truly 'religious', but then, even in religious matters, religion is not always the primary motivation. How far they are authentically religious will depend on the extent to which they are truly free and spiritually motivated.

At times, persons may feel so constrained by their own tradition that they may long for an escape into something more fulfilling for their spiritual and religious desires. At times, it is these very desires, nurtured in one tradition, which may seek their fulfilment in another. Here again conversions of significant persons from the dominant group, even for primarily religious reasons, may then be seen as undermining the group and its dominance, and similarly conversions into the group as extending, and sharing in its influence.

In the case of the converters too, the primacy of a religious motivation may not always obtain. Certainly some converters are but proselytisers, who function like travelling salesmen selling religious wares; but there are others, like wandering minstrels, who sing the divine praises for all to hear; and still others like the garden rose, who's enchanting fragrance suffuses all around. There are the martyrs, who witness with their lives to the truth, in which they believe, and the fanatics, who impose their truth on others' lives. There are organised efforts at converting others and an informal absorption of others into a community.

In this country, among the Sufi-bhakti traditions we have the best examples of a witness to a faith that invites others without propagandising them, that gently touches hearts and 'converts' them, without hard sell 'proselytising'. We have also known here and elsewhere, missionaries of various persuasions, who have felt justified in bullying people into their religious 'heaven' without any real concern for the 'hell' they were creating for them in the bargain. Such violence must be condemned.

Those opposing such conversions are certainly justified in doing so, though they do no good to their cause when they use violence of their own to resist that of the others. If this is truly a religious outrage, then it is difficult to legitimise the use of irreligious means to address religious ends. It only escalates the violence and confirms the desecration on both sides. Caught in between are the hapless converts and would-be ones, who become so much cannon fodder in this religious war.

However, some are opposed to any religious conversions even when conversion is a free and spiritually motivated decision. Religious functionaries and elites, who have the most to lose with the exodus of their flock, often resist their leaving. But then neither can we expect shepherds to encourage their sheep to leave? Yet, the freedom of the flock in such religious matters should be of paramount importance. Shepherds competing over the sheep too often forget this.

In addition, others oppose religious conversions in principle. There is a real concern that religious conversions may eventually destroy a community's unique cultural identity and undermine a society's multicultural diversity. Such opposition would logically mean compelling people to find their religious and spiritual fulfilment in their own tradition, and negating the possibility of their finding this elsewhere. These opponents seem to discount what conversion may mean to the converts in terms of their own personal understanding and quest.

Affirming social identity and diversity should not stand in contradiction to personal freedom and dignity. For neither identity nor diversity need be frozen and static, they must be allowed to evolve and change into new identities and new diversities. Communities and peoples themselves must be enabled to freely steer their own future course. Imposing a uniformity, or freezing a status quo would precisely be a violation of their freedom and dignity, whether by opponents or proponents of conversion.

Here again the issue of citizenship concerns religious liberty and freedom of conscience within the charter of human rights and freedoms. Too often, religious freedom is included so generally that it gets observed more in the breach than in fact. Given the preoccupation with anti-conversion laws, euphemistically labelled 'Freedom of Religion Acts, the time has come for such an explication of what is implicit in our Constitution.

For if there is a 'Freedom of Religion Act', its logic should work both ways: preventing the use of force, fraud and unfair inducement in converting people, and equally, preventing such use from hindering people who want to convert. Both these constitute a violation of the freedom of choice, especially in the case of vulnerable peoples, whether it is a matter of conversion, no conversion or even reconversion. In such a sensitive matter, the onus of proof must be equitably distributed without a prejudiced assumption in favour of one side or the other.

Religious nationalism and fundamentalism are caught in this escalating spiral of violence involving both the proponents and opponents of conversion. Only a secular, democratic state can provide a supportive context, in which such issues can be addressed within a regime of pertinent civil rights. However, dealing with religious prejudices is more than a matter of protecting and promoting civil liberties by law. Coping with divergent religious understandings, and more especially misunderstandings, is a matter beyond such civil rights and civic duties. It is much more an issue of religious tolerance and dialogue, where people can connect with each other precisely by drawing on and reaching out from within their religious traditions, to a point of convergence beyond each, yet where all meet.

The mystics in every major tradition have long ago grasped the ultimate convergence of the human quest for transcendence, by whatever name it is called. We have still much to learn from these mystics, as they struggle to communicate what they have encountered. For by its very definition and nature, the divine transcends all human expression and comprehension. The mystical experience grasps something of this surplus of meaning. As Karen Armstrong's *History of God* so convincingly demonstrates in describing 'The God of the Mystics', (Armstrong 1994: 170-208) we find an amazing cross-cultural and trans-religious harmony and consonance among these mystics, Sufis and saints, across and beyond all their different religious traditions, 'deep calling to deep'!

Religious nationalists or fundamentalists are closed to such transcendence. Whatever may be their pretensions, in fact they negate this mystical potential in every religious tradition that opens to it. In the end, their extremism is self-destructive. Muslim terrorists destroy authentic Islam, Christian fundamentalists distort true Christianity, Hindu extremists degrade genuine Hinduism…

Conversion as Multi-faceted

The various players in this conversion drama have their own ambiguities and anomalies, as also their genuine interests and concerns. However, in an area as sensitive as religious conversion, when there is little understanding and much antipathy between the protagonists, one stance is readily pilloried as manipulation or pathology by another hostile one.

Converters may assume their own altruism as much as they doubt that of others, with little awareness of the own self-centred preoccupations. So too, those opposing conversion may be pretending to protect the would-be converts, while failing to see they are actually projecting their own interests and fears. In all this, the converts become the sheep caught and torn between the wolves. Opposing the violence of the converters is certainly justified, but to consider all religious conversion as violence betrays one-sided prejudice. Worse, opposing it with violence of one's own is an unjustifiable negation of religious freedom and tolerance. Yet there are ways of preaching with respect and of propagating one's religious persuasion without propagandising others into it, as Sufis, bhaktas and many missionary monks have long done. This is truly how genuine religious conversions ought to be.

However, the converts may have their own mixed motivations and often use conversion as an instrument of protest and escape from this-worldly circumstances as much as a quest for other-worldly liberation and fulfilment.

Group and mass conversions complicate the issue of religious motivation even further. Though non-religious motives may be justified on non-religious grounds, it is for the converters to question their own religious motivations when they propagate such conversions. Opposing such conversion on religious grounds may well be justified, but when the non-religious issues are left untouched, then the motivations of these opponents must also be questioned. Large-scale conversions are mostly associated with the perception of large-scale injustice and oppression. Attributing them to force, fraud or inducement, too conveniently misreads the situation from the top, while not duly acknowledging the reality at the bottom. Addressing the upstream causes with appropriate reforms is a more viable and authentic response than trying to contain the downstream effects with vehement opposition.

When conversions are organised and backed by political and economic power, they can hardly be truly religious. The arena then changes to the political, and here the state must contain the players within politically permissible and constitutionally sanctioned limits. This is critical for any secular, democratic state. Yet, there is a crucial role for civil society to go beyond regulations and laws and create a common ground, with tolerance and compassion for dialogue and understanding.

Otherwise, there is great danger of continued religious strife. When this is violent and vindictive, people get disillusioned with religion itself, and eventually with their leaders, religious or otherwise. Certainly, the religious wars of medieval Europe did not make people more religious; rather the 'Age of Faith' gave way to the 'Age of Reason' and eventually brought about a post-Christian Europe today. Will there be a similar trajectory towards a post-religious South Asia?

Here we must further distinguish between the elites and the masses. The elites have a great stake with regard to change in society, older elites in retaining the status quo, the newer ones in restructuring it. Conquering, colonising elites once had such a stake in religious change, in spite of their pretensions otherwise. Local religious elites resisted and contested this as far as they could. In the post-colonial age, they still have their own vested interest in religion, a reversal on some counts to the pre-colonial past. In this context, it is the *savarna* higher castes, rather than the *avarna* outcastes, who have been the most opposed to conversions, from their own communities or that of others.

When oppressed people find their voice and hope for change, religious betterment can be a part of this aspiration. If this is not made possible in their own religious tradition by effective reform, to prevent them from seeking it elsewhere is to betray and leave them trapped. Certainly, this is not the only oppression they suffer. If religious conversion does not address their other oppressions, then this too betrays their hopes.

If people are the real concern and not just religious institutions and traditions, if the approach is to be holistic and authentic and not partisan and truncated, then both proponents and opponents of conversion must confront this issue of oppressed peoples. The converts and would-be ones already do, for they cannot escape its clutches. They must now be allowed to speak for themselves. We need to listen to them rather than speak in their name. This is what the case studies in the next chapter will try to do.

5

Personal Journeys

Ambedkar: Conversion as Liberation – The Inescapable Question – Contextualising a Movement – Confronting Gandhi – In Pursuit of Dignity – The Quest for Identity – Beginning Anew – Ambedkar's Relevance – A Multidimensional Analysis – A Defensive Opposition – A Holistic Response – **Gandhi: Conversion as *Adharma*** – *Dharmantar* and *Atmaparivartan* – Gandhi's Hinduism – Equality and Caste – Synthesis and Transformation – Positioning Gandhi – Identity and Alienation – Ascription and Choice – Reform and Liberation – Dharma and *Varna* – Disarming Opponents – *Adharma* and *Avarna* – **Ramabai: Conversion as Interrogation** – Pivotal Prototype – The Peripatetic Life – The Turning Point – An On-going Journey – Challenging Patriarchy – Interrogating Constraints – Critical Integrity – Proponents and Opponents – Religious Revolutionary **Nivedita: Conversion as Dedication** – The Disciple – The Nationalist – Aggressive Hinduism – Revolutionary Nationalism – Personal to Impersonal – Revival or Reform – Ambiguities and Contradictions – A Complex Paradox – A New Seed – **Commonalities and differences**

The case studies here focus on exploring religious conversion in diverse contexts. The persons chosen are well-known historical figures, with their own understanding of religious conversion. The stance taken by such significant public persons does have wider implications for the rest of us. They challenge us to question ourselves, and explore other understandings of religious conversion.

Micro-narratives are contextualised in the macro-narrative, and critically question the 'validity' of our macro-level perceptions, where our unconscious biases are often located. Each helps us to examine the other for a better understanding of both. However, we must listen closely and empathetically, and only then respond critically and creatively.

To the extent that the case studies here are grounded in such listening they will be able to speak to the issues, and help to discern the real human concerns involved from the entangled vested interests projected, so often by so many. We cannot pre-empt the right of others to speak for themselves, or presume to speak in their stead but we hope that through these case studies we can begin to listen and speak to each other with more understanding and empathy.

Ambedkar: Conversion as Liberation

Any discussion today on religious conversion has to come to terms with the conversion of Babasaheb Ambedkar (1891-1956) from Hinduism to Buddhism, which cuts to the heart of the controversy in this country. His ruthless interrogation of caste Hinduism is still incisive today. The only way Brahmanic Hinduism and many middle class *savarna sanatanis*, mainstream upper caste Hindus, cope with such a conversion is denial: Buddhism is still Hinduism so Ambedkar did not really convert, his conversion is an *atmaparivartan* not a *dharmantar*!

However, Ambedkar was decidedly unambiguous about his quest for an alternative when he announced at Yeola on 13 October 1935, 'It was not my fault that I was born an untouchable. But I have determined that I will not die a Hindu.' (Gore 1993: 126) This cri de Coeur situates his conversion and implicates us all in an introspection of our own. When he was asked on the eve of his conversion exactly twenty-one years later, why he was converting, he shot back: 'Why do you not ask this question yourself to your forefathers as to why I am getting out of the Hindu fold and embracing Buddhism?' (Cited Pal 1990: 61)

Bhimrao was born in Mhow in Central India, the fourteenth child of Ramji and Bhimabai Ambedkar, on 14 April 1891. His family hailed from Ambavade, of Ratnagiri dirstrict in the Konkan plain in Maharashtra. His father was the headmaster of the military school and both his grandfathers had been employees in the colonial military, which at the time had mandated schooling for their children. This early start set Bhimrao on an extraordinary trajectory. The degrading experience of growing up as an 'untouchable' stamped him with a life-long determination to fight the evils of caste. In spite of the seemingly insuperable obstacles that no untouchable before had overcome, he managed to get himself educated to the highest level, a degree in economics from Columbia University, New York, and a doctorate in law from London. This already is a testament to his resolution and strength of character. He finally returned to India at 32 and devoted himself to the cause of his people until his death on 6 December 1956, in Delhi, exhausted and broken in health, almost a pauper but richer than ever in the love and respect of his people.

In Maharashtra, Mahatma Jyotirao Phule (1827-1890) had first mobilised the non-Brahmans against the caste oppression of traditional Hinduism. In other parts of the country, early dalit radicals took up the protest: the *Ad-Dharm qaum* of Mangoo Ram in Punjab in the 1920s, the *Adi-Hindu* identity of Acchutananda in Uttar Pradesh., and the *Adi-Dravida*, *Adi-Andhra*, *Adi-Karnataka* movements in the south. In Maharashtra, Kisan Faguji Bansode (1870-1946) was a pre-Ambedkarite dalit leader who sounded the revolt against the higher castes in 1909.

However, the anti-caste movement began to fragment and lose its edge, as it was increasingly subsumed and absorbed into the nationalist movement, which was itself emerging under a dominant middle-class, upper-caste national elite. The Left's preoccupation with 'class struggle' failed to incorporate and respond to the problem of caste conflict with an adequate understanding. Whereas by reinterpreting caste and stressing Hindu unity, Hindu nationalism succeeded in co-opting many non-Brahmin and even dalit leaders, like M.S. Rajah of Tamil Nadu and G.A. Gavai of Vidharbha to the Hindu Mahasabha, a radical Hindu organisation (Omvedt 1995: 40).

At the turn of the century, there were two diverging paths open to the dalit movement: an integration into a reformed mainstream Hinduism, through Sanskritisation and a rejection of the Brahmanic tradition with an assertion of autonomy. The two orientations were not easily reconcilable, driven as they were by opposing forces. The first, represented by Bansode and Gavai drew on the *bhakti* traditions. They petitioned religious leaders and political rulers for better treatment and equal opportunities. The second, led by Ambedkar was rooted in the *Satya Shodhak* (Truth Seekers) movement of Phule. This was a non-Brahmin movement to claim their rights as a matter of justice, not largesse. The first was the path of uplift and unity but it yielded too little, too late, and still leaves many dalits disillusioned. The second sought a more radical alternative in separation and autonomy, and is gaining ground today.

This latter alternative required dalits to organise independently and define their non-Hindu, non-Aryan option, to articulate their stance on British rule and their position in the nationalist movement, to choose the social group and political allies with whom to work for their cause. It was no mean task and Ambedkar provided the ideology and leadership for this. A mass movement is never just the creation of a single charismatic leader. The ground realities of a society have a significant, at times even a decisive role to play.

In Maharashtra, the dalits were mostly labourers rather than peasants, though they were usually the most exploited among the landless and poor. In the industrialising urban areas of the Bombay Presidency, especially in textile mills in Mumbai, migrant workers were an emerging working class, with a significant number of dalits. This provided a relatively strong base for a social movement linked to the rural hinterland. (Omvedt 1994: 142), thus, urban-industrial labour helped to radicalise its leadership, while the reformist movements in western India helped to legitimise its struggle.

Ambedkar's own history is inextricably interwoven with that of the movement, he led and is reflected in the trajectory of his life. As a young academic at Columbia University (1917), he wrote in a graduate school paper, 'I venture to say that there is no country that can rival the Indian peninsula with respect to the unity of its culture.' (Zelliot 1996: 81) It was such a long journey before he eventually comes to the opposite conclusion in an unfinished manuscript at the end of his life. 'It must be recognised that there is never a common Indian culture, that historically there have been three Indias, Brahamanic India, Buddhist India, and Hindu India, each with its own culture ... It must be recognised that the history of India before the Muslim invasions is the history of a mortal conflict between Brahmanism and Buddhism.' (Moon ed. 1987a, Vol. 3: 275) For him India was still a nation-in-the-making, and the Constitution he fathered was to be the basis for the new society being born.

On his return to India in 1920, Ambedkar began his political career in association with Shahu Maharaj, his one-time patron. His entry into politics was cautious. He began as a moderate claiming the heritage of the non-Brahman movement, but his experiences in the struggles of his people increasingly disillusioned him with caste Hinduism and progressively radicalised the movement he led, with his assertion for dalit autonomy and the claim to a separate identity for them in Indian society. He saw as the only viable path for dailts in the face of upper caste resistance to reform.

In 1924, together with a few upper caste sympathisers and some Mahar youth, he formed the *Bahiskrit Hitakari Sabha* (The Untouchable's Welfare Assembly). The motto Ambedkar gave them was 'Educate, Agitate, and Organise.' With the Mahad Conference and the subsequent *Satyagraha* against caste Hindu violence in 1927, Ambedkar emerged as the leader of a growing mass movement. However, he was not yet pursuing an agenda beyond the Hindu cultural and religious fold; his priorities were clear and uncompromising. Writing in the *Bahiskrit Bharat* at the time (Ganaveer 1981: 78-82) he insisted: 'We want equal rights in society. We will achieve them as far as possible while remaining within the Hindu fold, or if necessary, by kicking away this worthless Hindu identity.' He affirmed: 'We do not value Hinduism, we value human dignity.' (Ganaveer 1981: 240) The decisive break with mainstream Hindu society came with Ambedkar's confrontation with Gandhi and the Poona Pact.

Gandhi's fears of a divided Hinduism, with the granting of separate electorates for the untouchables, were more those of a Hindu representative than a secular national leader. Speaking to the All India Suppressed Classes Conference at Lahore in 1926, Gandhi urged them to secure their rights by 'sweet persuasion and not by Satyagraha, which becomes Duragraha when it is intended to give a rude shock to the deep-seated prejudices of the people.' (Punjab Acchut Udhar Mandal Report 1926-31, Lahore, p.18, cited by Prashad 1996: 555)

On the other hand, Ambedkar was convinced that only political clout, and not just appeals to a change of heart, would give this most vulnerable people the necessary means to protect themselves against caste oppression in a hierarchical system, which he characterised as 'an ascending scale of hatred and a descending scale of contempt.' (Moon ed. 1987a, Vol. 3: 105)

The Ramsey MacDonald Award in favour of separate electorates was made on 16 September 1932. Gandhi began his fast unto death on the 20th, forcing Ambedkar to back down. The Poona Pact was a compromise sealed on the 24th and announced on the 25th: reserved seats and a joint electorate in a two-tier system, in which untouchables chose the candidates, from among whom the general electorate would vote the Depressed Class representatives, now doubled from 71 to 148 in a total of 780. On the 26th, Gandhi broke his fast.

Ambedkar emerged as the undisputed leader of the dalits. Gandhi was praised by mainstream nationalists for maintaining the integrationist nature of Hindu society. However, he was condemned by revivalists for selling out, and blamed by the Left for distracting attention from the main anti-imperialist struggle. However, the basic tension between the two approaches remained unreconciled. Gandhi's approach to end untouchability was to reform Hindu society by persuading Hindus to give the dalits their rightful place. Despairing of such reform, Ambedkar's endeavour was to liberate dalits by establishing their rights through political power, even going beyond the Hindu fold.

For a while, the Poona Pact did goad the conscience of caste Hindus. The temple entry movement for Harijans gained some momentum. Ambedkar and Gandhi worked on the common platform of the Untouchability League, which later became the *Harijan Sevak Sangh* (Harijan Volunteer Association), but they could not work together for long. Gandhi was willing to take direct action against the British but not against caste Hinduism, while Ambedkar had different priorities for external freedom and internal equality. Even as late as 1943, he points to the contradictions in Indian nationalism and challenges Gandhi's integrationist approach.

Commenting on *Mr. Gandhi and the Emancipation of the Untouchables*, Ambedkar says 'The nation does not exist, it is to be created and I think it will be admitted that suppression of a distinct and separate community is not the method of creating a nation.' (Moon ed. 1991: Vol. 9: 412) Words that still ring so true today, when we have *Nationalism without a Nation in India*, as G. Aloysius has convincingly argued, (Aloysius 1997) or rather nationalisms of various kinds, sub-, pseudo-, cultural ... and still no real sense of a national civic community of equal citizens.

The Poona Pact marked a tragic parting of ways for Gandhi and Ambedkar, and their later attempts to work together for the common cause were not without some reservations. It was more than a misunderstanding between two great and good men; it was really a contest between two radically different and opposed perspectives. Gail Omvedt sums up the differences thus: 'The real issue was not

Gandhi's nationalism versus Ambedkar's separatism, it was rather that of Dalit autonomy within the broader national community' (Omvedt 2000: 84). Once universal suffrage was accepted, Ambedkar was no longer in favour of separate electorates. The divide between the two reflected a deep emotional chasm, which remained unbridgeable to the end. For Ambedkar, Gandhi was an outsider, an upper caste patron; for Gandhi, Ambedkar was a misled, uncompromising sectarian leader.

Their first meeting at Mani Bhavan in Mumbai on 14 August 1931 already seemed to presage this distance between the two leaders. Ambedkar had testified in favour of separate electorates before the Simon Commission in 1928. By the time of the first Round Table Conferences in 1930, Ambedkar was the most prominent dalit leader, while Gandhi claimed to speak for all Hindus. Gandhi appealed to Ambedkar 'for the sake of the country' not to press his demand, provoking this tormented *cri de Coeur* from Ambedkar as he left the meeting: 'Mahatmaji, I have no country!' (*Times of India*, 18 Aug. 1931. *Source Material* 1982 Vol. I: 52). The outcome of the meeting is summed up on the one hand, by Gandhi in his dismissal later: 'Those who speak of the political rights of untouchables do not know their India, do not know how Indian society is constructed' (Moon ed. 1982: Vol. 2: 663). Moreover, on the other, by Ambedkar's final comment on the Poona Pact: 'Mahatmas only raise dust' (Phadke 1993: 276).

Ambedkar's final disillusionment with Hinduism, even as proposed by the best and most reformed Congress leadership, ultimately brought him to a radical commitment to dalit autonomy from Hinduism itself. He was convinced that caste was an inevitable consequence of Brahmanic Hinduism, and untouchability it's most degrading expression. Its eradication demanded the abolition of caste, something he now felt was not possible even for the reformist Hinduism of Gandhi or the Congress.

Brahminism involved a complex set of cumulative oppressions, psychological and social, eco-political and religious. Louis Dumont has rightly stressed how the untouchable outcastes at the bottom of the caste hierarchy were functionally necessary to sustain the purity-pollution ideology legitimising the Brahmins at the top; the indignities at the bottom sustained the dignities on the top. Besides rural feudal structures, capitalist industrialism accentuated class as a category of exploitation. Indeed, the cumulative caste-class inequalities were fundamental to the structure of Indian society, to which colonialism added a further political dimension.

Ambedkar's attempt to address these inequalities in pursuit of dalit dignity began early in his political career with his involvement with peasants and workers. One would have expected a natural alliance of Ambedkar's movement with the Left. However, Leftists of all hues, including Congress socialists and others, gave little priority to the issue of caste and the struggle against it. Therefore, Ambedkar distanced himself from the Left trade unions as much as from the religious reformism of Gandhi. Both have failed to understand caste hierarchy adequately, just as they failed again with patriarchy. Given the relationship between the two, it is not surprising that caste insensitivity and gender blindness go together. If Ambedkar saw the Congress as a Brahman-Bania party, the Communists for him were just 'a bunch of Brahman boys'. In his final disillusionment he even dismissed Nehru as 'just another Brahman'! (Cited Omvedt 1994: 325). Unfortunately, there was no dialogue to help towards a more inclusive perspective of caste oppression and class exploitation.

It became increasingly clear that neither the Congress on the right nor the Communists on the left would support the interests of the dalits in the electoral politics being initiated at this time. Who would represent the dalits? This was the core issue in his fallout with Gandhi. For Ambedkar, it could be neither the reformist Congress, nor the revolutionary Marxists. Dalit autonomy required its own electoral response and so in 1936 Ambedkar established the ILP (Independent Labour Party, Swatantra Mazdur Paksh). It was to be an alternative political project, a party of the labouring masses, endeavouring to create peasant and worker unity by fighting caste 'to establish an identity separate from the communist led unions in the labour field and from the Indian National Congress in the political arena.' (Gore 1993: 150)

But Ambedkar could not find allies for such an alliance. The non-Brahman movements were joining the Congress all over the country. The Left too was opting to wage the battle against imperialism by working with and within the Congress. However, Ambedkar did not give the nationalists' struggle first priority, and he found himself increasing marginalised in the freedom movement. He himself was more an inspirer than an organiser. He could not forge a common front with labourers of other castes. In the 1937 elections, his party showed strength in Bombay but was weak in other provinces. Finally, when he wound up the party in 1942, he himself admitted the failure 'of its great mission of struggling for the freedom of the great non-

Brahman community.' (*Bombay Sentinel*, 14 July 1942, *Source Material*, 1982: Vol. I, 253)

In July 1942, Ambedkar constituted The Schedule Caste Federation at the All India Depressed Classes Political Conference in Nagpur. This was to be a dalit front on an all India basis, a pressure group within a democratic framework, and to act as a special interest group in a statist-capitalist economic structure. However, already this marked a gradual retreat from his earlier radicalism of the 1930s. Gail Omvedt (1994: 256) sadly concludes: 'the significant period of the 1940s and 1950s thus appears as a basic defeat of Ambedkar's major revolutionary project, that of creating a revolutionary and equalitarian mass political platform.'

Nevertheless, it was the period that prepared the way for the Republican Party of India, which was envisioned by Ambedkar as a united front of all the exploited and oppressed, and not just dalits. However, the party was only formally constituted after his death. The political and economic emancipation that Ambedkar struggled to achieve for the oppressed all through his life-still remains an unfinished revolution, a continuing pursuit for human dignity.

In his submission to the Round Table Conference in 1930, Ambedkar argued that the Depressed Classes 'must be regarded as a distinct and independent minority...We cannot be deemed part of the Hindu community,' but he moderated his stance to plead for them to be categorised as 'Protestant Hindus' or 'non-caste Hindus' (cited Zelliot 1996: 132). However, after his fateful decision at Yeola in 1935, a great deal of Ambedkar's intellectual energy and moral endeavour was focused on constructing a neo-Buddhist identity, and inventing a new social tradition for his people. Phule stayed within the Hindu fold though he rejected Brahmanism. He never converted out of Hinduism, though he was not part of its mainstream. He reinterpreted old symbols and rationalised new aetiologies. Ambedkar went beyond to reject Hinduism and demythologise the *Riddles in Hinduism* (Moon ed. 1990b, Vol. 8).

In his first published work on *The Annihilation of Caste* in 1936, he shifts from Phule's racial conquest theory of caste to a systemic consideration of cultural conflict, political manoeuvring and ideological deception. His query on *Who Were the Shudras?* in 1947, sees caste in terms of class conflict between Brahman and non-Brahmans. This discourse is elaborated further in *The Untouchables* in 1948, who are considered to be conquered tribals, the 'broken men' whose association with Buddhism brought them degradation from a victorious Brahmanism. Reflecting on *What Congress and Gandhi Have Done for the Untouchables*, in his Ranade lecture in 1945, he makes a direct attack on both, and warns the untouchables: 'Beware of Mr. Gandhi' (Ambedkar 1945 ch. 10)

His major theoretical analysis, published posthumously in 1956, traces the conflict between Buddhism and Brahmanism in terms of *Revolution and Counter-revolution* (Moon ed. 1987a: Vol. 3) Here his analysis follows the lines of Phule's search, but with greater scholarship and depth. It was meant to 'serve an ideological purpose in his fight against the Hindu caste system and strengthen the legitimacy of his resolve to convert to Buddhism.' (Gore 1993: 242) Conversion to Buddhism, into which he eventually led a large number of his followers, was seen by them unwarrantedly 'as a social rebirth, a gaining of a new identity, a way in which the Dalits were leading, not simply joining a movement for the recreation of India.' (Omvedt 1994: 248)

If Ambedkar's search for an alternative religious identity begins with his definitive rejection of Hinduism at Yeola in 1935, the final decision to convert was declared only at Colombo in May 1950, and his actual *diksha* took place on 14th October 1956 in Nagpur. His conversion to Buddhism was the conclusion of a long process, discerned carefully, thought through critically, planned diligently, and timed deliberately. He was acutely aware that however personal his religious convictions might be, his conversion could not be just a private affair. It would inevitably be a public event that affected to lakh peoples of necessarily and crucially.

Other alternatives, like Sikhism, Christianity and Islam, were also considered, and the leaders of these faiths made many overtures. However, all these three had internalised, to a greater or lesser extent, the institutionalised inequality of the caste system. Besides Christianity suffered from the colonial connection; Islam was engulfed in a surcharged communal climate; Sikhism was more inculturated in Hindu society but the depressed condition of the Mazhabi Sikhs, the low caste in the community, deterred him. None of these religions presented the chance of a new beginning for the converts, an opportunity to be part of a new religious community without the baggage of past prejudice. Buddhism had been extinct as a mass religion in the Subcontinent for centuries, so it offered him the challenge of beginning anew, still within Indic, though not Hindu culture, as he perceived Ambedkar and his neo-Buddhists were opting to re-establish themselves with an ancient religious identity and a new human dignity.

The Buddha and His Dhamma, published posthumously in 1957, reinterprets Buddhism more in terms of a political and liberation theology rather than as a religious spirituality. *The Buddha and Karl Marx*, completed in 1956, brings out the socialist content of Buddhism, which for Ambedkar was more 'in consonance with Liberty, Equality and Fraternity, in short Democracy', (Moon, ed. 1979: Vol. 1: 77) than Hinduism or Marxism. His Buddhism is rightly described as *Navayana*, a new vehicle, which offers a threefold challenge, to Brahminism, Marxism and Buddhism. (Omvedt 2003:1)

For his dalit followers this 'conversion as a gateway to self-respect' (Gore 1993: 99) was the culmination of a long and agonised struggle for identity and dignity, for liberation from caste oppression, so institutionalised in Hindu society and legitimated by religion.

Once again, we see a subaltern movement of great promise splinter and dissipate. Not all the dalits followed Ambedkar into Buddhism. At the time, this would have put them beyond the pale of protection given to the Scheduled Castes. The Neo-Buddhists, were mostly from his own Mahar caste, which dominates the Republican Party. Here again it was caste rather than class that was the basis of mass mobilisation.

However, the biggest constraint on Ambedkar's movement was the lack of a resource base with which to impose itself on 'the stronger and larger 'nationalist' political leadership' (Gore 1993: 215). Their 'post office socialism', as John Kenneth Galbraith characterised it, left the structures of economic exploitation and social discrimination intact. An electoral politics of caste-based vote banks strengthened rather diminished the influence of what G.S. Ghurye called 'caste patriotism' (Ghurye 1969: 407).

Ambedkar's relevance is not just local, for the dalits, or national, for this country; it is global as well, even though his cultural and historical context is very specific. In Ambedkar we have a liberal and rational ideology to draw on in our struggle against traditional social caste, imposed cultural homogeneity, revivalist religious fundamentalism, unequal economic classes and vested political interests. More significantly, there are resources here to complete the revolution he began in reconstructing the dalit community and reinventing new traditions for them, on their long odyssey to their 'tryst with destiny'.

Ambedkar's conversion was not a precipitate decision. In May 1929, he told his followers at Jalgaon in Maharashtra, that it was impossible for them to overcome their disabilities within the Hindu fold. However, in October of 1930 he declared that he would not abjure Hinduism, but already in February 1933, he told Gandhi he could no longer honestly call himself a Hindu. In the summer of the same year he scotched rumours that he was about to convert to Islam (Sangharakshata 1986: 59). Then on 13 October 1935 came the final fateful announcement, which rocked the Hindu establishment more than the burning of the Manusmruti had done on 26 December 1927 at Mahad.

Today, Ambedkar is crucially important, for he sets the issue of religious conversion in a multidimensional context that we must not ignore, and interrogates us in a manner we cannot escape. The depth of his questioning is matched by the scale of his followers' response. The neo-Buddhists movement is the largest mass conversion of the 20th century and no longer restricted to the Mahars of Maharashtra. It has already spread to the Jatvas of Uttar Pradesh and beyond.

Ambedkar's conversion was a rejection of Brahminism, with which he had come to identify Hinduism itself. He saw caste as intrinsic to Hinduism and concluded, 'there can be a better or a worse Hindu. But a good Hindu there cannot be.' (Moon, ed., 1979: Vol. 1: 86) His was an intense personal quest for dignity and identity in a new religious tradition but he came to the *dhamma* of the Buddha with the same critical mindset that made him reject Hinduism.

Moreover, as a leader it was a quest that could not but affect his followers: 'I advise you to sever your connection with Hinduism and to embrace any other religion. But in doing so, be careful in choosing the new faith and see that equality of treatment, status and opportunities will be guaranteed to you unreservedly' (*Times of India*, 16.10.1935).

However, the Buddhist identity he affirms is in no way separatist or secessionist. He clearly wants to be within Indic culture and the Indian nation, even though he is emphatic about rejecting the Brahmanic tradition for a common democratic citizenship, which Ambedkar defined as 'one man, one value'.

For Ambedkar, there could be no equal dignity in the economic-political sphere without a positively affirmed identity in the cultural-religious one. Hence, his conversion was not just a political protest but a cultural critique and a religious indictment as well.

Ambedkar's conversion was decidedly a religious event, a personal conviction he came to after a long and arduous search, and he urged his followers along the same path. However, neither intellectually nor emotionally did his religious quest isolate him from the other levels of discourse and intervention. He began his efforts at reform with attempts to change the religious attitudes of his own people and caste Hindus too. He realised the inadequacy of this and moved on to include economic and political strategies. In the end, he realised the limitations of these and came back to religion, no longer as a Hindu reformist but as a Buddhist convert.

However, he commented on Buddhism with equal rigour and from the same value, commitments that made him reject Hinduism. His *Navayana* Buddhism is a this-worldly ethic, which he explained in terms of 'liberty, equality and fraternity'. This becomes a critically relevant liberation theology for today. Indeed, his life's pilgrimage was for the liberation of his people, and not just for otherworldly nirvana. Convinced as he was of the emancipatory potential of religion, he is surely one of the earliest contemporary representatives of the 'engaged Buddhism' that is coming into its own today.

Ambedkar's Buddhism has the potential to be the functional equivalent in South Asia of what Robert Bellah called 'civil religion' in North America, a religion for civil society, or as some would prefer, a post-religion religion (Menon 2004: 1816).

The Hindu reaction to Ambedkar's conversion is instructive. Not expectedly, the Hindu Mahasabha and many Arya Samajis and even C. Rajagopalachari (1989-1972), the veteran Congress leader from the south, condemned him. They accused him of abandoning the reform movement within Hinduism to create his own constituency outside, much as other proselytisers were doing. Yet, these reformers had failed to quicken the pace of social reform, which still seems to be in slow motion even today. The Mahabodhi Society of Calcutta too had second thoughts but finally did welcome him. (Sangharakshata 1986: 62)

Gandhi regretted Ambedkar's announcement that he would not die as a Hindu but he empathised with his plight and still hoped he would not go through with it. Thus Gandhi:

> 'I can understand the anger of a high-souled and highly educated person like Dr Ambedkar over atrocities such as

was committed in Kavitha and other villages. However, religion is not like a house or a cloak, which can be changed at will. It is a more integral part of one's self than that of one's body. Religion is the tie that binds one to one's Creator, and whilst the body perishes as it has to, religion persists even after death.' (*Times of India*, 16.10.1935)

Gandhi's comment on Ambedkar's conversion makes it quite apparent that he was essentially opposed to a change of religion for whatever reasons, and Ambedkar's situation did not warrant an exception. Ambedkar's reply was pointed and sharp:

> We have decided one thing and that after due deliberations and with deep conviction that the Hindu religion is not good for us. Inequality is the very basis of it and its ethics such that the depressed classes can never acquire their full manhood. He agree with Gandhiji that religion is necessary, but I do not agree that man should have his ancestral religion if he finds that that religion is repugnant to his notions of the sort of religion he needs as a standard for the regulation of his own conduct and a source of inspiration for his advancement and wellbeing. (Moon, ed., 1979, Vol. 1: 90)

This in the end was the crux of the disagreement between the two: whether one's religion should be ascribed at birth, and remain unchanged as one's dharma, or be chosen freely and responsibly after due deliberation, as one's refuge (*sharanam*).

Ambedkar's own conversion was truly a holistic transformation, an *atmaparivartan* and a *dharmantar*. He wanted the same for all his neo-Buddhists. Any mass movement is in danger of losing its way once the charisma of the leader wears thin. Ambedkar was acutely aware of the possibility of recidivism into Hinduism that might overtake his followers once he was gone. Had not something similar happened to their ancient Buddhist predecessors. To make the break with Hinduism complete and irreversible, he added to the three refuges and five promises in the initiation ceremony, twenty-two vows, specifically intended to spell out the Buddhist *dhamma* in terms that stress its differences with the dharma of Brahmanic Hinduism.

Here we reproduce them all, though the last four vows sum up their basic thrust quite starkly: (Das 1963: 272-274)

(1) I will not regard Brahma, Vishnu or Mahadev as gods and I will not worship them.

(2) I will not regard Ram or Krishna as gods and I will not worship them.

(3) I will not honour Gauri, Ganpati or any god of Hinduism and I will not worship them.
(4) I do not believe that god has taken any avatar.
(5) I agree that the propaganda that the Buddha was the avatar of Vishnu is false and mischievous.
(6) I will not do the ceremony of *shraddhapaksh* (for the departed) or *pindadan* (gifts in honour of the deceased).
(7) I will do no action that is inconsistent with the Dhamma of Buddhism.
(8) I will have no rituals done by Brahmans.
(9) I regard all human beings as equal.
(10) I will strive for the establishment of equality.
(11) I will depend on the Eightfold Path declared by Buddha.
(12) I will follow the 10 vows declared by the Buddha.
(13) I will have compassion for all creatures and will care for them.
(14) I will not steal.
(15) I will not lie.
(16) I will not follow any addiction.
(17) I will not drink alcohol.
(18) I will carry on my life based on the three principles in the Buddhist Dhamma of dhyana, shila and karuna.
(19) I renounce the Hindu religion which has obstructed the evolution of my former humanity and considered humans unequal and inferior.
(20) I have understood that this is the true Dhamma.
(21) I consider that I have taken a new birth.
(22) From this time forward I vow that I will behave according to the Buddha's teachings.

Ambedkar's Buddhism was 'cleansed of the Brahmanic interpolations of the doctrine of karma and rebirth.' (Gore 1993: 259) His rationalist demythologising, lacked a reinterpretation of popular religiosity and beliefs, as Phule had attempted, and so it left the door open to new superstitious among his neo-Buddhists. Beyond Phule, what he attempted, and in some measure achieved, was 'a conscious non-Hindu identity, a collective material and radicalizing force in India,' (Omvedt 1994: 249) as the basis for dalit dignity. The 'wave of revolution', that the radical groups of Dalit Panthers wrote about and longed for, still remains beyond the horizon, waiting for a 'culture-quake' and a dalit tsunami to roll over and engulf 'Brahman Alley'.

How would the anti-conversion laws apply to Ambedkar and the followers he led into Buddhism? It would be a challenge to do a creative exercise and imagine Ambedkar facing trial under these laws. Perhaps a dalit playwright will attempt this.

For Ambedkar's conversion to the Buddhist *dhamma* challenges us to rethink the Hindu concept of dharma. He understood it in the context of caste hierarchy as binding or rather bonding one to the system and he rejects both Hindu dharma and caste.

For Gandhi, dharma transcends Hinduism and religious traditions as such. It is a spiritual universal in the wider human condition. He understands conversion in this context, as a *dharmantar* that breaks these bonds. Gandhi is a counter-point to Ambedkar in the sense that each helps to enlighten us about the other. They must be read, not just together, but against each other as well.

Gandhi: Conversion as *Adharma*

If ever there was a person most sensitive to, and appreciative of, all other religions, it was Mohandas Karamchand Gandhi (1869-1948), and yet his inclusiveness places him in opposition to conversion to a religious tradition other than one's own. Here Gandhi seems to typify the mainstream Hindu position. Yet his own understanding of Hinduism is a radical reinterpretation, though he claimed to follow the *sanatan dharma*, the 'eternal religion' of Hindus. Religious fundamentalists and nationalists have co-opted him to their own purposes on the issue of religious conversion. The very people, who uncompromisingly condemned Gandhi for making too many concessions to the Muslim minority, praise his opposition to Christian missionaries. However, their espousal of Gandhi even on the specific issue of conversions is selective and distorting. For the two have quite different preoccupations. The openness and tolerance of Gandhi is concerned with integral Hindu wholeness; the exclusiveness and aggression of Hindu fundamentalists and nationalists is interested in political dominance.

On the issue of religious conversion, neither Gandhi nor Ambedkar can be ignored. Yet, the premises they begin from are very different and the conclusions they arrive at quite the opposite. Besides being a crucial counter-point to Ambedkar, Gandhi still remains a powerful critic of Christian missionaries. He was all for an *atmaparivartan*, a change of heart, but not for a *dharmantar*, a change of religious tradition. He was a reformer not a proselytiser. Indeed, to both converters and converts he represents a most genuine challenge to deeper and more honest introspection.

At a birth centenary celebration for Tolstoy in South Africa in 1928, Gandhi affirmed: 'Three men have had a great influence on my life. Among them I give first place to the poet Raychand, the second to Tolstoy, and the third to Ruskin' (Gandhi, Collected Works, CW, Vol. 26: 261). With the perusal of the *advaita-vedanta* texts, and of the *Bhagvadgita*, Gandhi came to some basics regarding religion that marked his searching thereafter: scriptures were fabricated, miracles did not constitute proofs, spirit and matter are opposed, and liberation is the freedom of the spirit from the bondage of matter.

Gandhi's opposition to conversion must be located within the context of his understanding of Hinduism in particular, and religion in general. His interpretation, or rather reinterpretation of Hinduism has a Socratic subversiveness about it. Little wonder that traditional and extremist Hindus were hostile to the point of wanting to eliminate him. All the three attempts on Gandhi's life were made by Hindu nationalists, for whom religion was more a political ideology than a faith tradition. (Nandy 1995: 59)

Gandhi locates himself as an insider to mainstream Hinduism. The radicality of his re-interpretation goes unnoticed because of this. Gandhi does not reject, he simply affirms what he considers authentic, and allows the inauthentic to be sloughed off. His profound redefinition of Hinduism gave it a radically novel reorientation with his *sevamarg*, the path of service, adding a new dimension to three *mars* of traditional Hinduism: *jnana-*, *karma-* and *bhakti-* . This is just one of his radical reinterpretations, as Bhikhu Parekh demonstrates (Parekh 1995: 104).

Gandhi re-works the *nish-kama-karma*, detached engagement, of the *Bhagavad-Gita* (ibid. 82) to become the basis of his *ahimsa* and Satyagraha! Only ahimsa can make the quest for such truth viable. Gandhi uses this quest in his strategy of Satyagraha, or truth-force. He makes no ethical separation between means and ends, for the goal is already foreshadowed in the means used to achieve it.

The ultimate goal that unifies his entire this-worldly agenda is to seek this God and Truth wherever this led him. 'Ahimsa in my God and Truth is my God. When I look for Ahimsa, Truth says, 'Find it through me'. When he look for Truth, Ahimsa says, 'Find it through me'' (*Young India* 4-6-1925). Realising this Truth through ahimsa was his moksha.

Moreover, Gandhi did not separate religion from politics. He brought a religious ethic to politics rather than political militancy into religious communities. Savarkar's Hindutva was the antithesis of Gandhi's Hinduism. Hindutva defines India as Hindu and wants all Indians to be Hindus. Indeed, it is but a contemporary avatar of an older and more chauvinistic Brahmanism. In contrast, Gandhi's Hinduism gives space to all.

For him 'unity in diversity' was the integrating axis not just of Hindu, but of Indian culture, and of all humanity as well. Once conceded, this becomes a foundational truth, and tolerance a necessary consequence. This is not a negative tolerance of distance and coexistence, but rather one of communication and enrichment.

In cultural matters, Gandhi himself is a remarkable example of such an open yet rooted person: 'I do not want my house to be walled on all sides and my windows to be stuffed. I want the cultures of all the lands to be blown about my home as freely as possible. But I refuse to be blown off my feet by any of them' (*Young India*, June 1921: 170).

In religious matters, his *sarvadharma samabhava*, equal respect for all religions, implies not just a radical faith in the validity of all religions, but also further a fundamental faith in the adequacy of each religion for all those born into it. However, Gandhi's own understanding of religion transcends religiosity. It is essentially a spiritual quest for moksha, but one rooted in the reality of service to the last and least in this world. This was Gandhi's understanding of Indian civilisation, its culture and religion. I believe, he had grasped the fundamental strength and profound secret of its survival over millennia!

In contrast to Ambedkar's single-minded critique of caste, which focused on its exploitative and oppressive character, Gandhi tries to reform the worst of these aspects by urging the abolition of untouchability. His idealisation of the varna system, as 'the law of life', is really an attempt to steer clear of a class system, ridden with struggle and conflict, for a more co-operative and harmonious social order. Yet, the voluntary acceptance of one's dharma as the underpinning for such a society is an individualist coping mechanism, which completely avoids the structural issues of inequality and discrimination. Some have sensed a subtle and implicit hegemony here.

For Gandhi, the *varnashrama* dharma he was committed to implied status by ascription, not by choice. It was a matter of one's duty to the welfare of the community, and all callings were to be considered of equal value, whether Brahmin or 'bhangi' (scavenger): 'there is no calling too low and none too high. All are good, lawful and absolutely equal in status. The calling of a Brahmin – spiritual teacher – and a scavenger are equal, and their due performance carries equal merit before God, and at one time seems to have carried identical reward before man.' (CW 63: 153) However, good intentions apart, this inevitably ends up with some castes being more equal than others are.

Perhaps Gandhi had a shrewd sense of how far he could push his reformist ideals against orthodox Hinduism at the time before a backlash made his best efforts counter-productive (Jaffrelot 2005: 67 -). How far ahead of their people, can leaders go without undermining their own support? Ambedkar too had to face this dilemma. Certainly, by the end of his life Gandhi's ideas on the varna and dharma imposed by birth had changed, from his original defence to a redefinition and a final rejection as the basis for social organization.

In his later years, Gandhi reversed himself to urge that the 'classless society is the ideal, not merely to be at aimed at but to be worked for.' (*Harijan* Feb. 17, 1946, p. 9) He was even hoping 'there would be only one caste known by the beautiful name Bhangi, that is to say the reformer or remover of all dirt.' (*Harijan* July 7, 1946, p. 212) Thus, if Tagore would have all Indians to be Brahmans, Gandhi would want all of us to be shudras, workers, or rather bhangis, cleansing reformers.

In his last years, he was promoting inter-caste marriages: 'If I had my way I would persuade all caste Hindu girls coming under my influence to select Harijan husbands,' (*Harijan*, 7 July 1946) in order to dismantle caste hierarchy. In fact, in a symbolic statement very typical of Gandhi, M. S. Gore tells us that 'he solemnised inter-caste or inter-religious marriages in his own ashram'. (Gore 1993: 283) This certainly had a powerful potential to de-legitimise not just the *varnashrama* dharma but also undermine his own case for the ascription of dharma by birth. However, it was too little, too late to have the effect of reversing his earlier legacy on this issue. The dalits of today have neither forgotten, nor forgiven him for this.

For, though Gandhi's reformism did arouse some resistance and much guilt, which helped towards de-legitimising the grosser aspects of the caste system, it could not meet the hopes of the dalit leaders then, much less 'the revolution of rising expectations' of the avarna, the masses of outcastes today. With his critique from within the tradition, Gandhi becomes the great synthesiser of contraries, if not of contradictions, within and across traditions, even as some see him as radical and others as reactionary.

Not since the time of the Buddha, some have argued, has such a synergy between the philosophic and the popular in our traditions been experienced. Thus, Gandhi integrates the Upanishads and the Tulsi Ramayan in his religious synthesis. When it comes to bridges across traditions, Gandhi brings the Gita together with the 'Sermon on the Mount' and reads one into the other. In fact, if he has Christianised Hinduism he has certainly also presented us with Hinduised Christian spirituality.

Because Gandhi re-interprets Hinduism from within, he can do much effectively and authentically integrate into his synthesis elements from without. Though he had internal contradictions, Gandhi was neither a conservative nor a progressive. He was not compulsively driven by the need to conserve past traditions or pursue contemporary innovations. He transcends such dichotomies and he is critical of both as he strives to reconcile meaningful faith and reasonable modernity. In the best traditions of this land, he combined both faith and reason, implicating each in the other. For Gandhi, blind faith or a fundamentalist, revivalist version of religion was quite unacceptable. He would constantly analyze faith to ascertain whether it was meaningful and reasonable in terms of basic human value commitments. So too, he would demand of reason the same fidelity to these values.

However, the ascetic dimension of Gandhi's integration at times loses the aesthetic one. A criticism of Gandhi's ashrams was that they grew only vegetables, not flowers! (Parekh 1995: 209) Yet, at times celebrating beauty can provide some relief even to the overly burdened. Stressing asceticism as Gandhi had done, does not preclude celebrating beauty, as Tagore wanted. For it is only in celebrating such an authentic synthesis that we will be able to bring some wholeness to, in Iris Murdoch's unforgettable phrase, the 'broken totality' of our modern world.

The whole effort of the modern world in dealing with violence has been to control the other. Gandhi's attempt begins with controlling oneself. This is the basic meaning of swaraj, self-rule, or rather self-control. The modern world gave primacy to rights and privileged freedom; Gandhi privileged duty and gave primacy to conscience. His concern was with 'socialising the individual conscience rather than internalising the social conscience'. (Iyer 1973: 123)

One of the great contributions of Gandhi was his centring of the periphery: in politics with *antyodaya*; in religion by de-brahminising Hinduism, de-institutionalising practice and personalising belief; in education by his proposal for *nai talim* or basic education; in the economy by symbolically promoting khadi and urging trusteeship. Not all these efforts were successful or even practical, but they did make a critique and a contribution, which are still relevant today.

No one can claim that Gandhi's reformist appeal has fulfilled the 'revolution of raising expectations' of our masses. However, neither the revolutionary call of the Marxists against class exploitation. Ambedkarites against caste oppression has empowered neither the workers nor the dalits effectively enough for them to claim their place in the sun.

Gandhi is certainly a counter-cultural inspiration, very relevant to our times. However, all too often he is made into a counterfeit idol. We need an open-ended critique of Gandhi, not a close-ended 'ism', as seems to have happened with some of the official Gandhians. Ernest Renan (1823-1892) once said that when fate could not destroy a great man it sent him disciples in revenge. We may need to save Gandhi from such a fate.

There can be no doubt that Gandhi was an authentic 'organic intellectual', articulating and symbolically expressing the people's aspirations. He was no less a uniquely transformative leader, who changed persons and structures, and transformed a people and their culture, albeit for a while. Here was a *yugapurush*, a man for the ages, if ever there was one in our times.

Yet, Gandhi's views on caste and religion stand in marked contrast to those of Ambedkar. In this study, we have taken both Gandhi and Ambedkar as dialogue partners. A critical appreciation of the one must be read against a fine-tuned comparison with the other, for any fair-minded analysis that is both sensitively and subtle. We must not be careful not to co-opt Gandhi to our own stance, nor must we always agree with him. He himself never hesitated to change his mind once he was otherwise convinced. He was never an authoritarian fundamentalist or a dogmatic extremist.

As with caste, so with religion, Gandhi's position is reformist and innovative, never fundamentalist or extremist. His eventual position on inter-caste and inter-religious marriage was not fully developed against his original espousal of varna and dharma ascribed at birth. Hence, Gandhi's multidimensional positioning on these issues will require an adequately complex analysis, especially on the issue of conversion, where he is concerned mainly with Christian missionaries of various persuasions.

For Gandhi religion is a personal concern, not a matter of labelling but of belief and action. It is thus a quest for a moral and spiritual identity:

> I believe that there is no such thing as conversion from one faith to another in the accepted sense of the term. It is a highly personal matter for the individual and his God. We may not have any design upon our neighbour as to his faith, which we must honour even as you honour. For the regard all the great religions as true, at any rate for the people professing them, as mine is true for me.... In addition, seeing that it takes all resources in trying to bring our practice to the level of our faith and in preaching the same to our co-religionists, our do not dream of preaching to the followers of other faiths (*Harijan*, 28 September 1935).

Religion to him was not something you can change even after death. Such an understanding of religion has problematic implications for conversion across porous religious boundaries and allegiances involving multiple belongings, for inter- and intra-religious dialogue...These are some themes we will come back to later in this study.

He is concerned that conversion to Christianity seemed to involve an unfortunate change of identity, an Europeanisation of the converts, an awkward cultural alienation to the point of disowning their past. He noted 'As I wander about throughout the length and breadth of India I see many Christian Indians almost ashamed of their birth, certainly of their ancestral religion, and of their ancestral dress' (*Young India*, 20-8-1925). Further, this led to a certain political alienation that he decried: 'the moment a person here turns Christian, he becomes a Saheb log'. He almost changes his nationality ... and begins to fancy himself a limb of the ruling class. What the Christians are afraid of losing, therefore, is not their rights but anomalous privileges' (*Harijan*, 13-1-1940). However, as R.C. Das a prominent convert in north India (*The Guardian*, 20 September 1928, pp. 448-450) rightly claims, this estrangement was also the result of ostracism and excommunication that especially higher caste converts experienced.

However, Gandhi's concern is the proselytiser as well. In an address to foreign missionaries, Gandhi was convinced that 'every nation considers its own faith to be as good as that of any other. Certainly, the great faiths held by the people of India are as adequate for her people. India stands in no need of conversion from one faith to another' (*Young India*, 23 April 1931, p. 83).

Gandhi says little on conversion to Islam, but his comments on Ambedkar's conversion show that his opposition was more than a matter of cultural estrangement. For even as he regrets Ambedkar decision, it is rather on the grounds of exiting Hinduism, not accepting Buddhism, which could not represent a cultural alienation from Indic culture and civilisation.

Gandhi concedes that 'cases of real honest conversion are quite possible. If some people for their own inward satisfaction and growth change their religion, let them do so' (*Young India*, 19-1-1928). However, for him even oppression within one's religious tradition was not a sufficient reason for abandoning it. His response was reforming it. Yet he would not prevent anyone one from leaving even if it were for the wrong reasons. For he was firmly convinced that 'whether they - the missionaries - and we wish it, or not, what is true in the Hindu faith will abide, what is untrue will fall to pieces. Every living faith must have within itself the power of rejuvenation if it is to live' (*Harijan*, 28-9-1935).

Yet Gandhi is clearly appalled at institutionally organised efforts at conversion. In such a highly personal matter, any outside intervention is presumptuous. He would urge missionaries to live rather than preach their faith, for 'a life of service and uttermost simplicity is the best preaching. A rose does not need to preach. It simply spreads its fragrance. The fragrance is its own sermon. If it had human understanding and if it could engage a number of preachers, the preachers would not be able to sell more roses than the fragrance itself could do. The fragrance of religious and spiritual life is much finer and subtler than that of the rose.' (*Harijan* 29 Mar 1935)

He proposes the example of 'that most Christ-like of all Christians, Albert Schweitzer, who gave Christianity a unique interpretation when he himself resolved 'not to preach any more, not to lecture any more' but to bury himself in Equatorial Africa simply with the view to fulfil somewhat the debt that Europe owes to Africa' (*Harijan* 25 January 1935). For those like Miraben (Madeleine Slade,

1892 - 1982) and others who came to him for religious guidance, he would urge not a *dharmantar* out of one's own religious tradition, but an *atmaparivartan* within it. This would mean urging Hindus to become better Hindus, Muslims better Muslims, Christians better Christians ...

In so far as dharma implies duty, it is also a matter of social belonging and of moral responsibility for others and one's own varna. For Gandhi a quest for religious identity is moral and spiritual, and within the context of one's varna and dharma. Both are ascribed at birth and he cannot see people making a change of identity in either. It would be against this dharmic order. However, this is what is being contested by the convert and the converter.

Gandhi was unrelenting on untouchability. In his autobiography he wrote in 1925: 'If untouchability was a part of Hinduism it could only be a rotten part.' (CW Vol 39: 33) It had to go or Hinduism itself would rot, but he did not approve of dalits seeking to better themselves by religious conversion.

He felt that missionaries were unconscionably exploiting the vulnerability of the untouchables in converting them. However, when he goes to the extent of comparing 'Harijans' to cows his patronising gets dangerously ahead of himself: 'when I was arguing the question of the masses of Harijans with Christian friends, I said, "The majority of Harijans can no more understand the presentation of Christianity than my cows"' (*Harijan*, 13-3-1937). When asked to clarify his statement he reiterates his stance. 'I stand on unassailable ground when I assert that it is a travesty of religion to seek to uproot from the Harijans' simple minds such faith as they have in their ancestral religion and to transfer their allegiance to another, even though that other may be as good as and equal to the original in quality' (ibid.).

In fact he insists on 'equality of status, a common platform. There cannot be a common platform as between inferiors and superiors, or the enlightened and unenlightened, the regenerate and the unregenerate, the highborn and the lowborn, the caste-man and the out-caste. My comparison may be defective, may even sound offensive. My reasoning may be unsound. But my proposition stands.' (ibid.)

Gandhi's intention may well have been to protect such people, whom he saw as all too vulnerable from over-eager proselytisers. However, his paternalism towards dalits seems to deny them any agency in such matters. Today he has come to be resented more by the dalits themselves than the missionaries against whom his criticism was directed in the first place. For the dalits, Gandhi remains an outsider to caste oppression.

Nevertheless, to be fair to Gandhi and honest with ourselves, while we reject his awkward comparison of Harijans to cows, we need to look beyond this to what he was trying to get across to the missionaries, whom he was addressing. Gandhi was quite emphatic in his anguished protest against their proselytising and propaganda taking advantage of the vulnerability of such people and demanded that 'no matter what may be their policy under normal circumstances, they must withdraw from the indecent competition to convert the Harijans.' (cited Kumarappa, ed. 1941: 147)

It seems to us that Gandhi was really pleading for an equal encounter, and this is surely something too few missionaries have respected. There were of course exceptions that Gandhi was happy to acknowledge, like C. F. Andrews, whom he held up as an exemplary missionary, even though he did not always agree with him on religious conversions.

Overtly at least Gandhi is here protecting Harijans and not so much Hinduism, which he feels confident can stand on its own. His tolerance is unbounded: 'I do not expect the India of my dream to develop one religion, i.e., to be wholly Hindu, or wholly Christian, or wholly Mussalman, but I want it to be wholly tolerant, with its religions working side by side with one another.' (*Young India*, 22-12-1927)

However, quite apart from his paternalism towards 'Harijans', Gandhi's understanding of varnadharma implies a social identity that cannot be alienated. This is what Ambedkar and the avarna castes contest and this logic extends to all ascribed status and identity, including caste and religious ones.

Gandhi's critique of the missionaries must be taken seriously even today. However, his insistence on following the varna and dharma, the vocation and religious tradition one is born into, is no longer acceptable, for it militates against the freedom of choice that he himself was so sensitive to in other matters. As with all great men we do find contradictions, and this is not the only one in Gandhi.

As far as varna goes, he himself did not follow his own dharma, his *svadharma*. Ambedkar elaborating on *What Congress and Gandhi Have Done for the Untouchables* was emphatic in reminding him of this. Anyone co-opting Gandhi on conversions must take on board his stand on varna, especially his insistence on status by ascription at birth as one's own *svadharma*, one's bounded duty in life.

Yet, even when we reject his stance on varna and dharma, in refusing to come terms with Gandhi we deny ourselves a powerful resource in decolonizing our minds in numerous other areas of our lives from the '*Intimate Enemy*' within (Nandy 1983), the alien and alienating 'other', the oppressor we have so internalized that we scarcely recognise this anymore. If our own analysis is to be more incisive and our understanding more comprehensive, we need a more fine-tuned appreciation of Gandhi's views on caste and conversion, and a critical comparison of this with Ambedkar's legacy (Hardiman 2003: 136).

Gandhi's response to the political and economic motivators of conversion is to propose a comprehensive agenda for social reform that would have an impact on these and other levels. He sees as already compromised any charitable work done with such an ulterior motive: 'he holds that proselytising under the cloak of humanitarian work is, to say the least, unhealthy...Conversions have nowadays become a matter of business, like any other. I remember having read a missionary report saying how much it cost per head to convert and then presenting a budget for the next season' (*Young India*, 24.9.1931).

Gandhi is too much a liberal, even an anarchic one, to want to restrict another's freedom of choice even in the matter of religious conversion. What he did demand was purity of motivation in missionary service and informed consent from the converts. Here his opposition seems to derive from the suspicions he had on both counts. Once again, rather than a summary rejection or even a hasty cooption of Gandhi, an honest introspection is called for by all concerned, one that would allow Gandhi's stance to interrogate our own positions on conversion.

The British had espoused religious freedom, but the separate electorates based on religion introduced by the Government of India in 1909 initiated a powerful competitive politics into relationships between religious communities. For Gandhi, religious proselytisation and conversions had the potential to further heighten tensions and precipitate destabilising consequences: 'It is impossible for me to reconcile myself to the idea of conversion after the style that goes on in India and elsewhere today. It has an error, which is perhaps the greatest impediment to the world's progress towards peace. 'Warring creeds' is a blasphemous expression. In addition, it fitly describes the state of things in India, the mother – as our believe her to be – of

Religion or religions. If she is truly the mother, the motherhood is on trial (*Harijan*, 30-1-1937).

He was particularly exercised by missionary interventions: 'If I had the power and could legislate, I should stop all proselytizing. In Hindu households the advent of a missionary has meant the disruption of the family coming in the wake of change of dress, manners, language, food and drink' (*Harijan* November 5, 1935).

This was at the time of his greatest opposition to them, when, as Gauri Viswanathan points out, Gandhi still 'believed Christian conversions were the instruments of British colonialism and therefore must be resisted as vigorously as British rule' (Viswanathan 2001: xii). His judgement was very harsh: 'Christianity in India has been inextricably mixed up for the last one hundred and fifty years with British rule. It appears to us as synonymous with materialistic civilization and imperialistic exploitation by the stronger white races of the weaker races of the world. Its contribution to India has been, therefore, largely negative.' (*Young India*, March 21, 1929)

However, when explicitly asked about this later he had changed his mind, for he felt that in Independent India there was no longer any need to forbid religious conversions or have them legally banned, even though he remained opposed to them. When asked, 'Will you under Swaraj allow Christians to go on with their proselytizing activity without any hindrance?' He paused for a reply. 'No legal hindrance,' replied Gandhiji, 'can be put in the way of any Christian or of anybody preaching for the acceptance of his doctrine'' (*Harijan*, 13-1-1940).

For Gandhi is too sensitive and moral a person to deny that freedom is essential to the moral wellbeing of a person. If he wants people to stay with the religion they were born into, their ascribed dharma and varna, he wants it to be a morally free choice for conscientious reasons, not a matter of compulsion or convenience. He makes this a matter of moral duty over legal right, and for him the first was always to be privileged over the second.

Gandhi's reformist appeal did bring a slow change in the conscience of the caste Hindus. Ambedkar's revolutionary call did conscientise the dalits with desire for liberation. Nevertheless, neither has been able to overcome the prejudice and oppression of caste in India. If anything in post-Independent India, caste has been politicised and even strengthened. Gandhi saw a bleak future for Hinduism unless untouchability was eradicated. It has been constitutionally abolished, but he survives in new avatars. Ambedkar saw no possibility of dalit liberation within the Hindu fold. Much has changed and been reformed, but the dalits are still at the bottom of the caste-class hierarchy, even after their conversion to Buddhism.

Obviously, there are practical limits to Gandhi's reformist appeal to change a tradition, as well as realistic constraints on Ambedkar's revolutionary challenge to begin a new one. In either case, only a living tradition, whether religious or cultural, can reform or challenge itself from within. Fundamentalism is too often the attempt to revive the 'fundamentals' from a dead past. Yet, when pressure to change from without puts people on the defensive, it can hardly be the best way of coping with a changing future.

Gandhi reinterprets both popular and philosophical Hinduism rather radically to transcend any particular sectarian or *panthic* religious denomination. Religion for him becomes more a matter of spirituality. Perhaps that is why the socio-cultural and economic-political effects of a religious tradition are not as central to religious concerns as they are with other religious fundamentalists and religious nationalists.

Theologically, Gandhi does not privilege any one religion over another, not even his own. He is emphatic about giving them all equal respect, and opposed to the confrontational approach of Dayanand Sarasvati and others. Thus, he asks in his autobiography: 'What was the meaning of saying that the Vedas were the inspired word of God?' 'If they were also inspired, why not they have Bible and the Koran?' (CW 39: 33) He was a Universalist who cannot reconcile himself to conversion: 'For me the different religions are beautiful flowers from the same garden, or they are branches from the same majestic tree. Therefore, they are equally true, though being received and interpreted through human instruments equally imperfect. It is impossible for me to reconcile myself to the idea of conversion after the style that goes on in India and elsewhere today' (*Harijan*, 30.1.1937).

Hence, even to 'secretly pray that anyone should embrace my faith,' he finds reprehensible, and he would exclude these from membership in an inter-religious fellowship (*Young India* 19-1-1928).

Though not a converter himself Gandhi had a remarkable effect on others. He is so open and close to other religious traditions that he compels them to an internal self-critique, at least when they are receptive to the challenge he represents. Even when he opposed them, the missionaries could not but respect him. Most were deeply affected, except perhaps the more extreme and dogmatic religious fundamentalists.

Indeed, Gandhi led a more inspiring religious life than most of those preaching and promoting their own religions, whether Christian, Muslim or even Hindu, and so he had the remarkable effect of disarming his religious opponents. In his encounter with Gandhi, C. F. Andrews certainly undergoes an *atmaparivartan* though not a *dharmantar*, as did E. Stanley Jones. Verrier Elwin, following Gandhi's instruction to work with the tribals, converts out of the Christian fold eventually to a tribal religion, it would seem. Certainly Maulana Azad was inspired by Gandhi in his understanding and interpretation of Islam.

Gandhi himself always claimed he was a well-wisher and sincere friend of the missionaries. His criticism was honest and meant to be constructive. He was aware of the great good they were doing, but he refused to be blind to the hurt he felt they were causing. The missionaries were most appreciative of Gandhi's integrity even when they could not agree with him on religious conversion.

His encounter with V. S. Azariah, the first Indian bishop of an Anglican diocese, Dornakal in Andhra, illustrates the impasse. Azariah had supported Gandhi in his opposition to separate electorates for religious minorities, even though he condemned Gandhi's protest fast unto death in September 1932. He praised Gandhi for bringing India back to religious ideals in an age of materialism. However, on the issue of the conversion of lower castes to Christianity the attempt at reconciliation in February 1937 failed. The two met in the presence of four silent observers. Confidentiality was guaranteed so the conclusions were never published.

However, in claiming the 'Depressed Castes' for Hinduism, Gandhi's 'no exit' position on religious conversion had other unanticipated and unfortunate consequences, arming another set of his most extreme opponents, who co-opted him to their cause on this issue. The consequences of this are still with us today. Gauri Viswanathan insightfully observes: 'The fear of conversion produced a strange marriage between Gandhi and the Hindu nationalists, who in all other instances denounced him for making concessions to Muslims but nonetheless heralded him as the voice of reason when he opposed Christian proselytization' (Vishwanathan 2001: xii).

For Gandhi, 'conversion should mean a definite giving up of the evil of the old, adoption of all the good of the new, and a scrupulous avoidance of everything evil in the new. Conversion should therefore mean a life of greater dedication to one's own country, greater surrender to God, and greater self purification.' (*Young India*, 20 August 1925)

His understanding of varnashrama dharma does not allow for a *dharma*ntar. For him there can be no changing your dharma. This would amount to adharma. It is much like changing your mother. Your mother may be bad so, you may try to reform and improve her, but you do not, or rather cannot, ever change her for another. For even an adopted mother can never ever become the birth mother. This coloured his whole attitude to caste and conversion. He was a committed reformist, who wanted people to reform their own religion, and become examples of it rather than abandon it to join another one.

Fortunately, Gandhi himself is not consistent. He treats his own *svadharma* rather flexibly. He wants everyone to follow their varnashrama dharma but he does not follow his own *samaj* dharma, his social duty as a bania, and gets into *rajkaran*, the political arena, which is for the kshatriyas. However, he was less than forthcoming when it came to others changing their dharma, not even the scavengers whose calling was so crucial even if considered degrading. Indeed, he did not consider many capable of such an informed choice and here his paternalism, not just with regard to dalits, is quite apparent.

As a religious reformer Gandhi remains a Hindu, no matter how radical is the reform he wants to achieve. *Dharmantar* for Gandhi is adharma, seldom moral even if always legal. However, it is not by ascribed dharma alone that religious traditions are reformed. This requires a constructive critique from within and without. Precisely as a marginal person, the sensitive and conscientious convert, can effectively provide both. However, Gandhi misses this.

There was no Hindu temple in the ashrams Gandhi founded. There was a prayer hall welcoming all faiths. Here was a deeply religious person who was truly inter-religious. Yet, if we disagree with him even on many religious issues, he inspires us on others. For Gandhi's own transparency compels a critical self-introspection on all who allow themselves to be interrogated by him, his life and message. I hope we do not sidestep this.

In the final analysis, Gandhi's stance on conversion is founded not on the denial of any rights, e.g., the freedom of choice and the freedom to preach; but on his concept of duty, the obligations imposed by one's dharma. For him duty is first and must constrain rights.

Hence, the obligations of duty limit the exercise of rights. Gandhi's opponents, both the converts and the converters, position themselves based on their rights. For them rights come first and define duties. We have here the counter-positioning of rights versus duties, freedom versus tolerance. This is the discussion we must come back to and take further.

Ramabai: Conversion as Interrogation

Pandita Ramabai (1858-1922) crosses the *Lakshman rekha* of Brahmin and Anglican patriarchy and exclusiveness, and straddles religion and culture, Hindu and Christian, East and West. Disillusioned with Brahmanical Hinduism, she came into a close association with the reform movements at the time, the Brahmo Samaj in Bengal and the Prarthana Samaj in Maharashtra. However, her search compelled her beyond the limitations she found in this reformism, to her baptism in the Anglican Church, and finally outside the Anglican fold, to a more universal catholic non-sectarian Christianity.

Though she claimed to have remained culturally Hindu and religiously Christian, she was perceived as a treacherous subversive by the conservative patriarchy in both traditions. They thought her to be confusing and contradictory. Revivalists were outraged and rejected her criticism, reformists were alarmed and distanced themselves from her after her conversion, and the missionaries were embarrassed by her 'self-chosen faith'. At the time, a few more liberated and less patriarchal men rallied to her support, like Mahatma Phule (1927-1890) and Maharshi Karve (1858-1962) among the Hindu reformists, and Fr Nehemiah Goreh (1825-1885), a Chitpavan convert like herself.

In her *Centenary Souvenir*, Karve eulogised her as 'one of India's most illustrious women... very learned and highly intelligent...' (Adhav 1958: 25) Prof. A.B. Shah in his 'Introduction' to *The Letters and Correspondence of Pandita Ramabai* is more lavish and praises her as 'the greatest woman produced by modern India and one of the greatest Indians in all history.' (Shah, ed., 1977: xi) Prof. Ram Bapat establishes her 'as one of the makers of modern India. Her acceptance of the Christian creed added a unique dimension to her personality and to her endeavours. Her complex and fascinating personality and achievements have yielded a rich harvest of biographies and other accounts.' (Bapat 1995: 224)

Certainly she is a pivotal figure in the reform movement of her time and in the social history of Maharashtra. Her contribution is yet to be fully acknowledged in our still prevalent patriarchal society. However, more recently her critique of patriarchy and the oppression of women have surfaced as an inspiration for the women's movement, in its struggle for gender equality and women's rights.

Three sets of accounts provide an insight into her life and mission: the missionaries, her admirers and her opponents. However, the rich body of writing she left us is the best source on this extraordinary woman. As someone who might too easily be identified with patriarchy, in accessing this resource, I will here position myself with three women scholars. For Meera Kosambi, 'Ramabai shared the ethos and psyche of her reformist contemporaries, but transgressed the boundaries of space, culture and religion – and even of time – through her vision of a gender-egalitarian society' (Kosambi 2000: 3). For Gauri Viswanathan 'Ramabai seemed always to be outside the system of which she was ostensibly a part' (Vishwanathan 2001: 118). For Uma Chakravarti 'Ramabai crossed two *Lakshman rekhas*: first, she mounted a scathing critique of Brahmanical patriarchy at a time when even contemporary male reformers were shying away from confronting its structure; second, as a high-caste Hindu widow herself, she 'chose' to become a Christian, 'betraying' her 'religion' and thereby her 'nation' in the eyes of nineteenth century Hindu society. (Chakravarti 1998: ix)

We may disagree with her agenda for reform, but she did name the beast, social patriarchy and religious exclusiveness. Her quest was for freedom from social oppression for women and freedom of religious choice for all. On both scores, she is still relevant, for even though hers was another idiom in another context, she still interrogates us today. To many in her own generation she was an inconsistent rebel, but to later generations of women in India, she is the prototype for feminist aspirations in our country.

Ramabai's early life can only be constructed from the testimony she left many years later. When the British took Pune in 1818, Anant Shastri Dongre, a Sanskrit scholar at the court of the Peshwa, had to leave in search of new patrons. After returning to Malherambi, Mangalore, he travelled through Mysore, Benares and Nepal, and on his way back, the forty-four year old widower married nine-year-old Lakshmibai. He had failed to teach his first wife, but his new bride was an able pupil.

However, for this he was threatened with excommunication from his Brahmin sect though he managed to defend himself with his knowledge of the scriptures. He then set up his ashram in the forest of Gangamala near Mangalore, where his wife bore him six children, of whom only three survived childhood. Ramabai was the youngest. Here began the Sanskrit education of Ramabai and her siblings.

To support his family, her father had to travel through the countryside as a *pauranika*, a public narrator of the *Puranas*, supported by gifts from the people who listened to his recitals. This peripatetic life freed the family from the constraints of traditional control, giving them some independent space. Thus the 'orthodox reformer', as Ramabai calls him, continued teaching his children until he was too old. Then his wife took over. Ramabai was saved from an early marriage because her elder sister's marriage had failed when the groom refused to join the Shastri family in their travels.

Caught in the great famine of the Madras Presidency in 1876-77, Ramabai lost father, mother and sister within a few months of each other. She was just sixteen at the time, alone in the world with her brother Srinivas. They travelled together for thousands of miles on foot, *pauranikas* on a *padayatra*, a walking pilgrimage, reaching Kashmir and eventually Calcutta in 1878, which marked a turning point in her already remarkable and unusual life. It was here she was given the title of '*Pandita*', learned woman, in recognition of her Sanskrit scholarship.

In Kolkata, the remarkable and unusual pair was welcomed by Hindu reformists into their inner circle. At the suggestions of Keshab Chandra Sen (1838-1884), Ramabai began to study the Vedas, which she had not read till then. Soon she was moving beyond this charmed circle of 'high Hinduism' to question the foundations of Brahmanic traditions, particularly on gender.

When her brother died of a sudden illness, leaving her alone and homeless in the world, she married one of his friends Bipin Bihari Medhavi, a young Brahmo Samaji in a civil court in 1880 at the age of twenty-two. She had rejected a proposal of an eligible Brahmin from the Bombay Civil Service, who had come all the way to press his suit, for a more compatible marriage to a person from a lower caste, a *pratiloma* marriage, against the injunctions of the Shastras and regarded with great horror at the time. Ramabai herself says her husband was a shudra, though Padmini Sengupta claims he was a Kayastha. Two years later, in 1882, she was widowed, alone once again with her little daughter, Manorama.

However, even this did not break this spirited woman. She would not be confined in a domestic space but plunged further into public life. At the invitation of Justice M.G. Ranade (1842-1901) and R.G. Bhandarkar (1837-1925), both early leaders in the Prarthana Samaj, she returned to Maharashtra and set up the Arya Mahila Samaj, a society for women, in 1882 in Pune. Moved by the plight of a five-year-old child widow cast out by her in-laws, she began to focus her work on Hindu widows. However, she was without a social base in this traditional town and isolated by the orthodox Hindus there.

Ramabai now had to support her work by lecturing and writing. She published *Stree Dharma Niti*, a book in Marathi on morals for women. It was close to the reformist position, but mostly about women's self-cultivation than the companion-wife. Already she was moving beyond the Hindu reformists, their spirituality could not fill her void. At this time she confessed: 'I was desperately in need of some religion. The Hindu religion held out no hope for it. The Brahmo religion was not a very definite one. For it is nothing but what a man makes for himself. He chooses and gathers whatever seems good to him from all religions known to him' (Ramabai 1907: 22).

She now came to contact with some missionaries and read a Marathi translation of the Gospels. Suspected of becoming a Christian, she denied any such intention in Pandharpur in late 1882. However, disappointed with her countrymen and handicapped in her work, she decided to seek support and further training abroad. Her book paid for her passage and in early 1883, she sailed for England with her daughter and a friend, Anandibai Bhagat. Five months later, on 29 September 1883, she and her daughter were baptised. However, it was a traumatic transition.

In England they stayed with the Anglican religious community of Saint Mary the Virgin at Wantage. Ramabai was deeply touched by the work of the sisters with 'fallen women', but even then she had said that she would never become a Christian because a good Brahmin is quite as good as a good Christian (Bapat 1995: 234). She was in correspondence with Fr Goreh, whose 'humble, sweet voice' stilled her doubts and gave her strength to take the final step. For Nilakant Shastri Goreh, a Chitpavan Brahman, who himself had converted in 1848, was a scholar in both traditions. He knew the tradition and philosophy from which she was coming and could guide her to where she was going.

Yet, even though she had found an anchor in her new faith, there were still tragedies to come. Anandibai, terrified and fearful of conversion, in a fit of temporary insanity attempted to strangle Ramabai one night and then committed suicide herself (Sengupta 1970: 135). She was baptised on her deathbed, apparently to respect an earlier wish she had expressed (Kosambi 2000: 9). The trauma brought Ramabai to the brink of a nervous breakdown. She herself is largely silent about these events, and the accounts we have are from the Anglican sisters and Max Muller, with whom she went to convalesce at Oxford (Muller 1899). However, she could not begin her planned medical studies there because her hearing was severely impaired by the stress.

Ramabai's conversion brought the same critical interrogation to bear on her newfound faith as she had done with her earlier religious beliefs. Tempered and steeled by her life-experiences, she was too resilient a person to be intimidated or cowed by her new mentors.

When the sisters sought to silence her questioning, charging her with being arrogant and proud, she stood her ground. She had a mind of her own and insisted on following her own conscience, for she argued that both were God-given powers and meant to be used. She would not let anyone dictate her relationship to God or to her past. She still treasured her cultural heritage and was happy to be called a Hindu. However, she would not impose her faith even on her own daughter. She wanted young Mano to brought up among her own people and decide her own religious allegiance among the various Christian sects, which Mano eventually did, joining the Methodist Church. Having emancipated herself from one constraining patriarchal tradition, she was not about to submit to another, and so from being a prized convert for the Anglicans, she became an embarrassing dissenter.

In 1886, she left with Manorama for America, hoping to be less confined by Christian denominationalism there and find some support for her work in India. Ramabai travelled widely in the United States for two years, writing and speaking in an effort to collect money for her widows' home. Before setting sail for India in 1888, she succeeded in setting up the Ramabai Association in San Francisco.

In 1889, Sharada Sadan (Home of the Goddess of Learning) was inaugurated in Bombay, and shifted a year later to Poona, which was less expensive. A Christian woman convert having custody over young Brahmin widows was not something that went down easily with traditionalists like Tilak, who vociferously opposed her. Moreover, though Ramabai would never impose her beliefs on others, she wanted her girls to have the same freedom of choice that she had: full religious freedom regarding their ancestral religion as well as access to the scriptures of others. The real issue, as Uma Chakravarti points out, was the agency of women and the right of custody over them. This raked up a virulent controversy. Ranade and Bhandarkar resigned from the board and once again Ramabai was isolated.

The famine of 1897 precipitated further change. She went into the worst affected areas in Central India and brought back hundreds of abandoned girls to Poona. However, they could not be kept in the plague-stricken city, so she set up a relief home at Kedgaon, called Mukti Sadan, home of freedom, on a hundred acres, forty miles outside Pune. Here she experimented with new ideas in a less constricting social climate. There were 300 girls when they began, but continuing drought and poverty swelled the numbers to about 1,900 by the turn of the century.

Ramabai had now begun to turn away from the elite intelligentsia of Bombay and Poona and move further afield. Having taken on the Governor of Bombay, Lord Sandhurst, over the highhandedness of the anti-plague measures and the consequent invasion of privacy, Ramabai alienated some of her Anglican support, but she refused to be browbeaten by the colonial state. She found herself wedged between the high caste elite, suspicious of her Christianity, the missionaries wary of her Indian roots, and the government confronted by her nationalism.

In her last years at Mukti Sadan, Ramabai's faith began to turn inwards to a more Gospel-based Christianity. The *kirtans*, Marathi ballads of Narayan Vaman Tilak (1862-1919) another Brahmin who had converted in 1895, were popular at the home. She learnt Greek and Hebrew to translate the Bible into Marathi. This was printed by her girls at the press there. The British government now recognised her social contribution with the award of the Kaiser-i-Hind gold medal in 1919 (Kosambi 2000: 13).

Fittingly, Mukti Sadan was her final home. When her daughter Manorama, now a medical doctor at Miraj, died unexpectedly in 1922, it was one tragedy too many for her. She died a few months later. She had found inner peace. There were no more battles for her to fight. The epitaph chosen for Manorama could be hers too: 'Her life was sweet incense unto God.'

The status of women during the *Peshwai* rule (the Brahmin ministers who displaced Shivaji's heirs) in Poona is the backdrop against which the revolt of Ramabai must be situated. There were counter-cultural movements to the caste order much before the *Peshwas*. The *Mahanubhava Pant*, a religious sect founded by Chakradara in the 12th century, harked back to the pristine tribal life. The Pandarpur cult founded by Pundalik was crystallised by Jnanadev's (1275-1296) epic *Jnaneshwari* and developed into the *Varkari Pant* popularised by Tukaram (1608-1690). There were many women *sant-kavis*, saint-poets, too: Muktabai, (1279- ?) the sister of Jnandev, Bahinabai, (1628-1700) Janabai (1270-1350); and some low castes ones like, Namdev, the tailor (1270-1350) and an outcaste Chokamela (14th century). Such *bhakti* cults were essentially more egalitarian and non-hierarchical in their construction of a community of *bhaktas*, but they had neither the economic base nor the political strength to change the caste hierarchical order fundamentally.

Whatever the challenge the political power of Shivaji and the Marathas might have posed, the Brahmin order was restored and the caste hierarchy strengthened by the Peshwas. Pollution taboos were enforced, and the purity of high caste women jealously protected. Brahmin patriarchy and caste hierarchy demanded the control of women by men. Their sexuality was the property of their husbands and to be closely guarded. The *Yati Dharmastapana* in 1735 decreed that Brahmin girls were to be married by the age of seven to ten years, and widow remarriage was forbidden to high castes. The bereft widow represented a sacred indissoluble sacrament, a privilege not to be shared with inferior castes. What began to control female reproductivity and consolidate family property, was idealised into a high caste privilege. The Peshwas not only permitted widow remarriage in lower castes but even debarred upwardly mobile castes from enforcing celibate widowhood (Chakravarti 1998: 26).

The colonial government's personal law remained inherently patriarchal, reinforcing many retrograde practices. In their eagerness for Brahmin endorsement, the Regulation Act II of 1827 restrained the civil courts from jurisdiction in caste matters. This was to sacrifice the human rights of women to the proprietary privileges of men. Case law verdicts of the time are shocking illustrations of this. In spite of attempts at reform, the colonial government stood by the local patriarchy in denying women any free agency of their own.

The revivalists saw any attempt to change the status quo as a threat to their traditional dominance. Tilak and his newspaper, the *Maharatta*, espoused notoriously conservative traditional views. He himself refused to sign the pledge against untouchability or support the Agricultural Relief Act, 1891, to protect the *raiyati*, the peasants, from moneylenders, many of whom were Brahmins (Chakravarti 1998: 105).

The 19th century reform movement was male-dominated, and though it did try to address the issue of women's equality and gender justice, its stand on women's agency in the context of male patronage was left somewhat ambiguous. However, Mahatma Phule stands out as a radical and uncompromising reformer, and he was critical of his colleagues in the non-Brahmin movement with regard to the subordination of women.

The reformist had welcomed the abolition of sati in 1828 and the Widows Remarriage Act of 1856 as part of their progressive agenda even though it went against the orthodox ideal of the ascetic, prayerful widow. They regarded Ramabai as a new Maitreiyi, the mythical woman Sanskrit scholar of the Shastras. Her father's 'reformed orthodoxy' had sensitised her to constraints of patriarchal dominance and women's oppression, supposedly sanctioned by the Shastras. However, she used her *Pauranic* learning to defend her stand for equality against oppression and dominance. Her exposé of *The High Caste Hindu Woman* (1887) was a biting critique of the degrading conditions to which they were subjected, and a direct challenge to Brahmin orthodoxy of the time with its androcentric and misogynist bias. Understandably, this alienated the traditionalists and angered the revivalists. Outraged, they pilloried her as an inauspicious and polluting widow.

Already her acceptability was being questioned, but when Ramabai converted, the revivalists used this against her to denigrate her feminist agenda. Tilak's *Kesari* vociferously attacked her. She stood accused of betraying her cultural heritage and religious tradition, but the real issue of freedom of choice even in religious matters was lost in the suspicion and intolerance her conversion provoked. The reformist too balked, though once again Phule was unhesitating in his support and publicly defended her.

Ramabai's reports on the status of Indian women, sexually exploited as hapless widow and deserted wife, were published in the international arena. She was welcomed in the United States as a heroine. Rachel Bodley, dean of the women's Medical College in Philadelphia, introduces Pandita Ramabai's *The High-Caste Hindu Woman* thus: 'The silence of a thousand years has been broken, and the reader of this unpretending little volume catches the first utterances of the unfamiliar voice. Throbbing with woe, they are revealed in the following pages to intelligent, educated, happy American women' (cited Vishwanathan 2001: 146).

But her transparency was discredited as anti-national by Hindu nationalists particularly, who were in denial of the dehumanising exploitation of women in India. They were unwilling to have any negative impression projected abroad. Ramabai was regarded as misguided or worse, having a disguised Christian agenda.

Swami Vivekananda, who was in Chicago at the time of the World Parliament of Religions also collecting funds for his work, publicly contradicted her, claiming that widow oppression was the exception, not the rule. His 1895 lecture on the 'Ideals of Womanhood – Hindu, Mohammedan and Christian', affirmed that contrary to the Semitic races, the Aryan ideal was of women as mothers not as wives. Men and women were priests and 'co-religionists' (Chakravarti 1998: 333). He went on to outline a spirituality of the act of reproduction in which a marriage not consummated in prayer would be considered adulterous (ibid: 334). The widow's life of asceticism and poverty represented spiritual and moral values higher than of matrimony.

All this was in keeping with the Swamiji's grand agenda of projecting the superior spirituality of Hinduism. However, such an insensitive male construct of widowhood as an informal order of nuns would outrage feminists today. It certainly was not something acceptable to Ramabai even then. She had experienced another reality: 'There are thousands of priests and men, learned in the sacred lore, who are spiritual rulers and guides of our people. They neglect and oppress the widows and devour their houses...Thousands upon thousands of young widows and children are suffering untold misery and dying helpless every year throughout the land., but not a philosopher or a Mahatma has come out boldly to champion their cause ...' (Shah, ed. 1977: 308)

She pleaded that her 'learned brothers and comfortable sisters' look beyond the 'poetry' of India's 'sublime philosophies' to the 'prose' of women's lives as beggars in their dirty huts (Shah, ed. 1977: 588-9).

The agenda for women's rights was getting distorted in the nationalist project of Hindu womanhood, and in this controversy between gender and nation, Ramabai and Vivekananda were clearly on opposite sides. Ramabai's conversion, which Vivekanand strongly disapproved of, further obfuscated this controversy between cultural nationalism and gender rights. Her own critique of *The High Caste*

Hindu Woman tries to balance an incisive criticism of the Indian woman's inferior status in Hindu patriarchal society, with a nationalist defence of India vis-à-vis her western reader, as Meera Kosambi emphasises (Kosambi 2000: 28).

Ramabai took issue with the British too on their patriarchal colonial law. In response to a suit for the restitution of conjugal rites, a court order in 1887 had reversed an earlier one of 1885 and ordered Dr Rakmabai, who had filed for divorce in Bombay, to return to her husband. She had married at the age of eleven, though the marriage had never been consummated. On this issue of woman's free agency, the British supported the traditional Indians. Tilak's *Maharatta* and other conservatives urged Rakmabai to serve her husband, who was suffering from lung disease, and so attain immortality like Savatri, who married Satyavan though she knew he was dying.

However, Ramabai bitterly observed: 'A Hindu woman – unless she is a widow and destitute of friends and relatives – cannot follow even the dictates of her own conscience' (Shah, ed. 1977: 176) and she lambasted the English Government:

> 'It is not from any earthly government or law that the oppressed Hindu woman must expect justice ... It is false to expect any justice for India's daughters from the English Government, for instead of befriending her the Government has proved to be a worse tyrant to her than the native society and religion. It advocates on one hand the education and emancipation of the Hindu women, when the woman is educated and refuses to be a slave in soul and body to the man against whom her whole nature revolts, the English Government comes to break her spirit allowing its law to become an instrument for riveting her chains' (Shah ed. 1977: 178).

A pertinent observation comes from Ram Bapat, who perceives Ramabai's feminist stance as focused on the high caste woman and not inclusive enough of other women; emphasising the spiritual and religious and not the material conditions in which these are grounded (Bapat 1995: 250). Bapat further criticises Ramabai for not using the non-Brahmin folk traditions of the counter-culture in Maharashtra as resources in her challenge to caste patriarchy, but by the 19th century, as Jayant Lele points out, these had already been co-opted into the Brahaminc hierarchy (Lele 1995). Yet, her critique remains fundamental and does not disappear with her conversion. It is carried over into an equally stringent one of Christian patriarchy in the Anglican Church, and this was not the only issue on which she engaged her newfound faith.

Ramabai's anguished longing for her *Ishtadevta*, her chosen God, did not end with her baptism, rather it began anew much to the chagrin of the sisters at Wantage. She was too much of a Protestant in spirit even for the Anglican Church. This was part of the Hindu heritage she must have imbibed from her father, a discomfiture at being doctrinally constricted. His dying injunction to her was never to depart from the way of righteousness, but for her this could never be a path others dictated to her: 'When people decide anything for me without consulting with me about it, I do of course call it interfering with my liberty and am not willing to let them do it. Would you feel bound to accept every word or rule which comes from the bishop as an expression of the will of the Most High? Perhaps you would... However, we do not, and will not (Shah, ed. 1977: 59).

She was emphatic that: 'Obedience to the law and to the word of God is quite different from perfect obedience to priests only. I have just freed myself from the yoke of the Indian priestly tribe, so I am not – at present – willing to place myself under another similar yoke by accepting everything which comes from the priests as authorized command of the Most High.' (Shah, ed., 1977: 59)

She refused to have her relationship to her God ruled by others or her lifestyle controlled by the sisters. She was still fiercely loyal to the good in Hinduism and was critical of missionaries focusing only on its negative aspects. She challenged the sisters and even Fr Goreh, when they changed to Latin the Sanskrit inscription for an emblem designed for her: 'Whatever may be in other's opinion, all the good old things are very- very dear to me, and if I do not find anything in them that is contrary to our blessed Religion, I will not and must not part with them. I do not want ... from others what is not wanted, and also what is not good for my country' (Shah, ed. 1977: 28-29).

She remained a vegetarian even though this was regarded as a caste hangover and false pride. When she was refused permission to teach Marathi to the missionaries destined for India. She vigorously protested and was heard: 'I am not anxious to give lessons to young men, but I am anxious to do away with all kinds of prejudices, which deprive a woman in India of her proper place in society ... Unless I begin to have a regular and pure intercourse with men, I shall in vain hope and try to help my country-women' (Shah, ed. 1977: 59-61).

But there were still more basic issues on which Ramabai interrogates her mentors and found no satisfying answers, at critical moments in her life, even from Sr Geraldine, (1843-1918), who had spent five years in Poona and whom she affectionately called her *aji*, grandmother, or Fr Goreh, her spiritual guide. She had reservations and difficulties with the various religious controversies and denominational differences among the many Christian churches. They appeared to be similar to the sectarianism among numerous Hindu traditions. However, Ramabai ever remained a relentless seeker: 'For five years after my baptism I studied these different doctrines and made close observations during my stay in England and America. No one can have any idea of what their feelings were at finding such as Babel of religions in the Christian countries and at finding how very different the teaching of each sect was from that of the others' (Shah, ed. 1977:27).

Her complex relationship, both to her Hindu past and her Christian present, sensitised her to the conflation she observed of Anglicanism and England. How could the Kingdom of God be compared to the English nation, as Sr Geraldine had done? She had resisted at home such a fusion of religious and national identity and was certainly not going to countenance the same abroad. Her religion had no room for nationalist overtones or racist/casteist colouring.

She found an affinity to the English tradition of antinomian dissent, which at the time expressed itself in proliferation of non-Anglican denominations, such as the Unitarians and others. She was acutely aware of the fractured nature of Christianity into numerous separated churches and she was not convinced of the Anglican claim to catholicity, pointing out that while Anglicans considered other dissenting churches as heretical, they themselves were so considered by Roman Catholics from whom they had separated (Shah, ed., 1997: 170).

She had seriously difficulties with the Church's teaching on the mysteries of the Trinity and the Incarnation, and would not accept the thirty-nine articles of the Anglican Church. Rather she insisted on affirming five of her own: belief in one God, love of neighbour, belief in Jesus Christ as saviour, witnessing to this, sharing Eucharistic fellowship with Christians (Adhav 1979: 176-7). This put her, like other dissenters, beyond the Anglican fold. Sr Geraldine was wary of Ramabai's 'self-chosen religion' and felt it 'has no claim to the name of Christianity' (Shah, ed., 1977: 114). What the missionaries once thought was a prized acquisition now became a contentious example for others. However, Ramabai was convinced that her search was valid and that 'the door of the Universal Church of God is not shut against her, for the Universal, the Holy Catholic Church is not confined to the Anglican Church' (cited Adhav 1979: 15).

Though Ramabai's outspoken interrogation punctured the secure certainties of the sisters' Anglican tradition, she had no compulsion to proselytise others in order to boost her own hard-won convictions. She was grateful for the sisterly bonding she experienced in the Wantage community, but it could not contain her quest. She left for the United States where there was a greater religious pluralism and even when she returned to India she remained a searcher to the end. Indeed, Ramabai is an excellent testimony of conversion not as a straightforward event of assimilation and integration, but as a process of negotiation and critique.

Whether we agree with her conclusions or not, there is little doubt about the integrity of Ramabai's quest: her courage in the face of personal tragedy, her perseverance against bitter opposition, her openness in her quest, her transparency in her convictions. Her first encounter with Christianity was at the age of seven, when her heard the name of Jesus for the first time — and kept repeating it, as she later recalled, until her mother stopped her. When a missionary, Isaac Allen, got her interested in the Bible in Calcutta, she first felt attracted to Christianity, but her husband was severely disapproving: 'He was very angry and said he would tell Mr. Allen not to come to our house anymore. I do not know just what would have happened had he lived much longer' (Shah ed. 1977: 23).

Already we see that although Ramabai's conversion is directed by her own decisions, it could not be without its stresses and stains, considering the context and the inevitable fallout. Her *dharmantar* was the consequence of a long drawn out *atmaparivartan* that continued after she was baptised. Fr Goreh and the Wantage sisters provide her with much needed guidance and solidarity.

Yet from the Anglican point of view, her conversion was thought to be a failure. From a heroic example she became a heretical dissenter. Here more sharply than elsewhere we see the dilemma of missionaries, who want religious freedom and encourage converts to think, but then want to contain the freedom within certain bounds. However, religious conversion often releases processes that reach beyond the converter's and the convert's expectations and intentions. If directed by conscience, this will necessarily be an open-ended process.

The sense of betrayal in the Hindu community at Ramabai's conversion was to be expected and is quite understandable. The reformers wanted to change Hinduism from within, not have it changed from without. With Ramabai's conversion, they lost a very pertinent and effective promoter for their cause. The strident traditionalists and revivalists, mocking her femininity and, damning her fickleness, seem to echo a male conservative chauvinism. These wanted to revive and preserve the old status quo and their stake in it. They belittle and dismiss Ramabai, when they are not vociferously opposing her, supposedly on religious grounds.

Vivekananda was critical of her conversion and his guru Sri Ramakrishna Paramhansa (1802-1886) denounced her as egotistic and ambitious (Sengupta 1970: 163, Chakravarti 1998: 319). The Marathi journal *Indu Prakash* wrote disparagingly on October 22 1881: 'Oh Rama Bai. You are after all a woman...You have disappointed a number of friends and admirers, be assured' (Chakravarti 1998: 319). A month later on November 19 it was even more caustic: 'Pandita Ramabai was in the first instance a Hindu, then she became a Brahmo, now she has become a Christian. This shows and proves she is of unstable mind. We should not be surprised, if she becomes a Muslim soon.' (Chakravarti 1998: 319).

There are dilemmas and ambiguities here among the proponents and opponents of Ramabai's continuing conversion that cannot be ignored. Max Muller, sums these up in his inimitable way:

> 'What I feared when Ramabai became a Christian has happened: She has impaired her power of doing useful work among her countrymen. Her native friends do not quite trust her, her European friends do not always remember what they owe to her...What has become of the toleration of which the Hindus used to be so proud, which, even in the days of Upanishads, formed the glory of the true Brahmans? What has become of the freedom of thought, if freedom to choose one's own religion is to be no longer allowed in India, the home of the Vedanta philosophy? I did not persuade Ramabai to become a Christian, because she was Christian with her heart, which is far better than Christian by profession (Adhav, ed. 1979: 12).

Ramabai's life is deeply tragic yet extremely inspiring, unusually significant and prophetically subversive. She was proud of the cultural heritage of Hindu civilisation and identified with her people as a true patriot, but she rejected oppressive and patriarchal traditions. She believed in Christianity as an emancipatory and liberating faith, but her commitment to Christ would not be contained in a patriarchal and exclusivist church.

Ramabai's incisive interrogations of both Hindu and Christian traditions created dilemmas and provoked ambiguities for patriarchs of all hues. Revivalists and reformists, nationalists and colonialists have still not quite come to terms with her forceful critique. Some never forgave her for converting to Christianity, others regretted her loss to Hinduism. Neither could she be accommodated in the Anglican Church, nor did she seek to join any other denomination. The Indian nationalists found her Christianity compromising; the English colonialists found her nationalism treacherous, patriarchs found her feminism discomforting. So what did her legacy add up to amidst all these controversies?

For Bapat, Ramabai is a revolutionary, but more a religious than a social or a political one, for her revolt against oppression was spiritually inspired and religiously motivated even when it engaged in social and political issues. Yet 'Ramabai's critique of patriarchy is so fundamental – the kind of stereotypes which she wants to demolish...' that she anticipates later feminists (Bapat 1995: 251).

Maharishi Karve had been himself inspired by her to start a widow's home 1896, and his wife had been the first widow pupil of Sharda Sadan and an intimate friend of Ramabai. In the centenary celebrations for her in 1958, some thirty-four years after her death, the Maharishi, himself a centenarian at the time, has perhaps the last word:

> 'In sincerity and selfless work for the most humble, none could surpass Ramabai ... It was our own fault that this great woman, like the late Dr. Ambedkar, was lost to the Hindu religion. Pandita Ramabai Saraswati must be classed as one of the great builders of modern India. Let Indians, therefore, atone for their past mistake and support the work started by Ramabai for the down-trodden and the poor. After all, that human work is for all Indians even if Christians are carrying it on. It is work for the uplift of India and it has therefore, my heartfelt blessings' (cited Sengupta 1970: 327-8).

Pandita Ramabai's religious quest is ultimately a restless and continuing interrogation: of traditional patriarchy, which refuses to change the status quo; of institutional religion when it restrains the primacy of individual conscience; and also of feminine bonding where it submits indiscriminately to patriarchal and institutional constraints. It was hardly to be expected that her incisive critique would have brought about an overall consensus in the circumstances she confronted. However, if it is faced in the same spirit in which it was made and authenticated with her life, it certainly has a revolutionary potential for our own lives today.

Nivedita: Conversion as Dedication

Margaret Noble (1867-1912) was born on 28 October in North Ireland, the eldest daughter of Samuel Richmond and Mary Isabel. She schooled at Halifax in England, and later trained as a teacher, becoming interested in the innovative child-centred methods of Freidrich Froebel (1782-1852) and Johann Pestalozzi (1746-1827). In 1892, she started her own school, The Ruskin School, at Wimbledon. During these years, her political and moral beliefs were formed: the value of independent work, the importance of art and crafts; she wrote about working class poverty and supported women's education, as an enhancement of their role at home. In 1892, she met the Russian anarchist Prince Peter Kropotkin (1842-1921), who became a reference point in her political beliefs. In London society she was well known as an innovative pedagogue and one involved in social and charitable work.

Not expectedly, her growing social and political awareness precipitated a crisis of faith, for her Christian beliefs seemed inadequate to the new sensibilities and the quest on which she now set out. After two serious disappointments in love that only deepened her distress, she joined various discussion circles in London, like the Sesame Club, which was associated with Lady Ripon, the former vicereine of India, Thomas Huxley, Bernard Shaw and others. However, her search for a deeper fulfilment was satisfied neither by her religion nor by her social involvement.

In 1893, she met Swami Vivekananda after his success at the Parliament of Religions in Chicago. Later, at one of his discourses in London in February 1895, she was struck by what she later referred to as the 'strangeness' and 'dignity' of the philosophic and spiritual vision that he presented with such lucidity and conviction. Here was someone speaking from a deep inner experience, which she was determined to pursue for herself in India. During the Swami's second visit, he invited her to work for the education of the women of India, for he too was impressed by her. This was but the beginning of a deep and lasting bond between the guru and his disciple. On 29 July 1897 he wrote to her in a frequently quoted letter: 'Let me tell you frankly that I am now convinced that you have a great future in the work for India. What was wanted was not a man but a woman; a real lioness, to work for the Indians, women especially. India cannot yet produce great women, she must borrow them from other nations. Your education, sincerity, purity, immense love, determination and above all the Celtic blood make you just the woman wanted' (Atmaprana, ed. 1961: 117).

A month after she arrived in Calcutta in March 1898, Margaret Noble was initiated into the Ramakrishna Mission by Vivekananda, and given the name 'Nivedita', the dedicated or the consecrated one. She had used the name herself as a pen-name, but now it was meant to capture her newfound dedication to Hinduism and India that would define her spiritual quest. This was one of the most moving experiences of her life.

Vivekananda founded this Mission at Belur near Calcutta in 1897. It was committed to a 'practical Vedanta', his interpretation of Hinduism that meant nation-building through man-making through self-help. It was an ethic of this-worldly engagement, not just other-worldly spirituality. To prepare for this practical engagement, Nivedita now toured North India extensively with Vivekananda and two other women, Sara Chapman Bull and Josephine MacLeod, who became her confidante later. These were journeys of instruction, on which she imbibed the neo-Vedanta teaching of her Swami and experienced the reality of India.

During this probationary period, Vivekanada had urged Nivedita to 'Hinduise' herself. Later she recalled his injunction: '*You have to forget your own past, and to cause it to be forgotten. You have to undo even its memory*' (Nivedita 1904: 395 emphasis in text), She was to work for India as an insider, not a foreigner. Yet her latent English patriotism and 'island' mentality led her to 'the blindness of a half-view', as she termed it, and a presumed civilisational superiority. This seemed to undermine the lesson in cultural relativity that her guru tried to instil in her and once provoked a stern rebuke from him: 'Why do you insist on comparing this country with [your own], what is suitable here with what is done there? Really, patriotism like [yours] is sin' (cited Reymond, 1953: 116.).

Back in Calcutta, her education work began with the school she founded in Bosepara Lane in November 1898, where she also worked for the plague-stricken. At the end of her probationary year, she was confirmed as a Brahmacharini in February 1899. She had found the object of her inner devotion, though it still was a difficult emotional journey for her. In June 1899, she made a trip with Vivekananda to England and America to raise funds for the Mission. She described this voyage as 'the greatest occasion of my life' and made notes on the 'one continuous impression of his mind and personality' (Nivedita 1910: 230) he had given her. This she put together in 1907 in the very personal study of *The Master as I Saw Him*. Already she felt she was 'but the bridge, between him and that countless host of his own people, who would yet arise and seek to make good his dreams' (Nivedita 1910: 254).

From the beginning Margaret's involvement with Vivekananda had been intense and personal. Not long after their first meeting she had expressed her desire to unite her life to his and work for India, but the Swami had drawn a clear boundary protesting: I am a monk. (cited Boehmer 2002: 74 nt 91) Painful as this rejection must surely have been, Nivedita sublimated her feelings into a self-dedication of her love for him with her unwavering resolve: 'to make myself a servant of his love for his people' (cited Reymond 1953: 49).

In spite of the emotional distance he kept from her and the anguish it caused her, she continued to experience the 'great salt tides' of personal love for him 'rise' in her (Reymond 1953: 149). Sensing her tortured situation Vivekananda encouraged her with the paradoxical double blessing to be both mother and servant of India, leader and helper. He advised his smitten disciple to dedicate herself to Kali as he himself had done. As she recalled his earnest urging later in *The Master as I Saw Him*:

> 'The heart must become a burial ground,
> Pride, selfishness, and desire all broken into dust,
> Then and then alone will the Mother dance there!'
> (Nivedita 1910: 231)

Eventually, she confessed: 'I understood, for the first time, that the greatest teachers may destroy in us a personal relation only in order to bestow the Impersonal vision in its place' (Nivedita 1910: 139). In this self-dedication she sublimated her love for her master and achieved the emotional autonomy she needed, and was encouraged to, by him. Such self-emptying is always the condition for transcendence to a deeper level of spiritual awareness. The master's final farewell blessing to his most devoted disciple summed up his relationship to her: 'If I made you, be destroyed, If Mother made you, live!' (Nivedita: 1910, 278).

Ultimately, really Kali-worship helped her to redirect the intensity of her devotion to her charismatic and charming guru into a commitment to the struggle of India's people for their freedom. It was through Kali-worship that Nivedita was able to transcend her devotion for a person into a dedication to a cause. All her letters between 1900 and 1902, the year of Vivekananda's death, indicate her resolve to serve India. As she wrote on 19 July 1901 to her confidante, Josephine Macleod, her religious pilgrimage was now politically complete: 'I have identified myself with the Idea of Mother India, I have become the idea itself' (cited Reymond 1953: 262).

So within two weeks after her master's death on 4th July 1902, she was ready to withdraw from the Ramakrishna Mission. Since the Mission had deliberately chosen not to engage the government politically, so she did not want to compromise it. As she dedicated herself to a new cause beyond her school: 'Is it not by taking the national consciousness of the women, like that of the men, and setting it toward greater problems and responsibilities [than those of her school], that one can help? ... I think my task is to awake a nation, not to influence a few women. (Quoted Reymond 1953: 264).

Kali became the door though which she entered Bengali religious and political consciousness. Kali was both her nationalist symbol and personal myth. With her fierce rhetoric, it is little wonder that Vivekananda called her 'a real lioness', and her nationalist avatar was to confirm this. Nivedita's affinity to radical politics was already indicated by the friends she had in London and her contact with the Irish nationalists in the Home Rule movement then. She had begun with education believing that the school would be the agent of change but she had gradually come to conclude that insurrection was the only effective way to further the national cause.

Bengal was electric with nationalism and Nivedita was moving back to her radical London days, from neo-Vedantism to insurrection, from Kali to Kropotkin. Her nationalist involvement in Calcutta in the early 1900s did bring her into contact with moderates like Gopal Krishna Gokhale (1866-1915), R.C. Dutt (1848-1909) Jagdish Chandra Bose (1858-1937). However, she identified more with the radical extremists in the movement like Aurobindo Bose (1867-1950) with whom she had a natural affinity, but it was a more equal partnership than the guru-shishya, teacher-student, one she had with Vivekananda.

Her silence about her association with the extremists leaves some ambiguities. Already in 1902, she was under suspicion and definitely under police surveillance from 1906. There is no evidence that she was involved in direct violence, like planting bombs, though she seems to have had a supportive role 'behind the curtain'. She stood bail for Vivekanada's brother, Bhupendra Nath Dutt, who was charged with sedition in 1907, and she helped Aurobindo to get away in time to Pondicherry in 1910, then under the French.

In 1902 Aurobindo read *Kali, the Mother*, Nivedita's first book (1900) and admired it. She had heard of him as a revolutionary and offered herself to the cause: 'Count on me. I am your ally.' (cited Mazumdar, ed. 1968: 220) A friendship developed and Aurobindo invited her to be one of the five members of his short-lived Revolutionary Council of Bengal, which was to co-ordinate the various national societies with Aurobindo as its undercover leader and Nivedita as the exponent of anarchist and insurrectionist theory. She was even called the Mother and Joan of Arc of the Bengal Resistance by Barinda Bose, Aurobindo's younger brother.

At the Indian National Congress meeting in Calcutta in 1906 Aurobindo had emerged a spokesperson for the extremists and had succeeded with Tilak and others to force through a resolution supporting *swaraj*, self-rule. He had hoped to tilt the Congress into a more militant and confrontational mould but after the Surat Congress in 1907 he broke away. In 1906, Nivedita prompted Aurobindo to move to Calcutta on a permanent basis He was arrested on 5 May 1908 and tried for conspiracy but acquitted after a year's imprisonment. By April 1910, Aurobindo left for Pondicherry and was urging his political associates to give up all terrorist activity and negotiate their political space on the right side of the law.

When Nivedita retreated from the political stage it was ostensibly on grounds of health, but it could have been at the request of the leaders in the movement for their mutual safety. On her return to Calcutta in mid 1909, she got involved with the nationalist art movement centred there and devoted herself to what Aurobindo called the 'revival of the aesthetic mind of India.' She was now less directly involved politically but hoped that the art, which grew out of the nationalist struggle, would give wing to the 'free spirit' of the nation. In a keynote essay written in 1907 she proclaimed that *The Function of Art in Shaping Nationality* was to bind the nation into 'a firm and coherent whole, self-conscious, self-directed, self-controlled'. (Atmaprana, ed., 1982: 380)

Aurobindo always referred to his relationship with Nivedita as more political than spiritual. They were like-mined nationalist colleagues, who worked together for an independent India. Yet both shared an integral spiritual nationalism, grounded in their understanding of the *sanatan dharma*, which for Aurobindo embodied the soul of India. As he wrote in May 1909 in *Karmayogin*, the journal he edited: 'Nationalism is not politics but a religion, a creed, a faith. I say it again today, but I put it in another way. I say that it is the Sanatan Dharma which for us is nationalism. This Hindu nation was born with the Sanatan Dharma, and with it it grows... The Sanatan Dharma, that is nationalism.' (Aurobindo, 1972: 10)

For both of them nationalism was considered a religion come from God! The dedicated disciple and the fiery nationalist are two distinct but related aspects of the conversion Margaret Noble, the London radical, undergoes to become Sister Nivedita, the 'aggressive Hindu' and 'revolutionary nationalist'.

The world religion of the relativity of all truths that Vivekanada preached in the West was propagated at home in a more concrete form in Kali-worship. For him the Mother was the focus for the regeneration of India. In his preoccupation with the revival of his country, he felt the need for particularism before universalism, localisation before globalisation. Both were founded in the oneness of the Spirit. Nivedita understood the Swami's vision: 'Not in the Good alone but also in Evil, in Death as well as Life, in the West and in the East, in fact in diversity of all kinds, is to be read the revelation of Unity. From all points do the paths converge by which the One comes to the vision of man' (Atmaprana, ed. 1982: 380).

Thus, national unity as an organic whole of diverse parts was itself a part of a larger more universal human unity, the 'cosmo-national' in Nivedita's phrase. However, as concretised in Kali it becomes a more particularised mobiliser for national extremists as well. Kali becomes the inspiration for both Aurobindo and Nivedita to fire India into action and keep the flame of Vivekananda alive. A new Hinduism was needed to convert others to a synthesis of religion and politics on a worldwide scale. Vivekananda's preoccupation with 'manliness' and an assertive reading of the Gita is surely reflected here:

> We have wept long enough; no more weeping, but stand on your feet and be men. It is a man-making religion that we want. It is man-making theories that we want. It is man-making education all round that we want. And here is the test of truth – anything that makes you weak physically,

> intellectually and spiritually, reject as poison; there is no life in it, it cannot be true ... You will be nearer to Heaven through football than through a study of the Gita. You will understand Gita better with your biceps, your muscles, a little stronger. (Vivekananda 1951: III, 242)

In a 1905 pamphlet, Nivedita attempted to synthesise Vivekananda's message into the one ideal she termed *Aggressive Hinduism* (Atmaprana, ed., 1982: 489-511). She recalled her master's words to her in Kashmir: 'The aim of his whole life was, as he had said to me, "to make Hinduism aggressive, like Christianity and Islam"' (Nivedita 1910: 202). *Aggressive Hinduism* was also the summation of Nivedita's own hopes for India. She described it thus: 'Aggression is to be the dominant characteristic of the India that is today... aggression and the thoughts and ideals of aggression. Instead of passivity, activity; for the standard of weakness, the standard of strength; in place of the steadily yielding defence, the ringing cheers of the invading host.' (Atmaprana, ed. 1982: 492-3)

This was an impassioned cry not just to preserve custom, but also to create character, not merely to protect oneself but also to convert others. Following her master's injunction not to criticise an oppressed culture publicly, she seems to go to the other extreme of idealising all things Indian and Hindu: 'That which is Indian for India, I touch the feet of' (Atmaprana, ed. 1982: 145).

In *The Web of Indian Life* in the chapter 'A Study of Indian Caste', she argued that 'caste ought to be translated as honour' (Grover & Arora, ed. 1993: 85). For her it was a matter of 'noblesse oblige'. She did concede a downside: 'to be absolutely just, however, we must admit that the observance of caste law has entailed many foolish and irritating losses to society during the last fifty years' (Grover & Arora, ed. 1993: 95). Yet she insists that 'it cannot be denied that great benefits as well as great evils have accrued from caste' (ibid).

She did finally want change: 'If India is to regain national efficiency, this old device of the forefathers must be modified in the process – exactly how, the Indian people themselves can alone determine' (Grover and Arora, ed., 1993: 97). This is very much a top-down *savarna*, upper caste understanding, an idealised view of caste as varna that was held by many others at the time. However, it is hardly accepted any longer and would outrage the avarna, the outcaste generation today.

After her Swami's death, Nivedita underwent a further conversion. Her emphasis now turned from the mystic inspiration of

Vivekananda's neo-Vedanta to the Kshatriya warrior ethic she found in the *Bhagvad Gita*, which she called the 'gospel of Indian Revival' (Nivedita 1904: 234). In the early 1900s, the *Gita* was popularised and politicised by political radicals and religious revivalists as a call to arms. However, this was quite a different interpretation from the one Gandhi was to give it.

In this new dedication, there were strong religious overtones in her political agenda. For *Kali* and the *Gita* were her inspiration and motivation, her personal 'myth' and 'gospel', even as Kropotkin and Giuseppe Mazzini (1805-1872) became reference points for her understanding of anarchism and insurrection, of national liberation and unity. The nationalism she propagated was not necessarily exclusive or chauvinistic, but being religiously inspired it had an inevitable potential for morphing into a religious nationalism, as has happened today. Surely, this was something Vivekananda never intended, but it was something Nivedita never unequivocally condemned.

She wanted India to become obsessed with national consciousness. This was disconcerting to the colonial government in Calcutta and her proximity to the extremists only exacerbated their worst apprehensions. However, her understanding of nationalism was neither chauvinistic nor ethnocentric. In her understanding, all would contribute to the re-making of the Motherland. In the final analysis, her main concern was less with political ideologies and strategies of resistance than with the spiritual and religious side of nationalism. For her, behind all the concerns 'the social reform, the political agitation, religious movements, and economic grievances — there stands a greater reality, dominating and co-ordinating the whole, the Indian national idea, of which each is a part' (Grover & Arora ed. 1993: 190-1).

In one of the last issues of *Karmayogin*, the journal she edited for a brief while she wrote her valediction to active politics and her rededication to nationality as well. On 12 March 1910, as the conclusion to Aurobindo's series of essays on '*The Ideal of the Karmayogin*', she wrote: "O Nationality, come thou to me as joy or sorrow, as honour or as shame! Make me thine own!" (cited Grover and Arora 1993: 453)

At the personal level, her conversion that began with a charismatic guru, opened to the Impersonal Absolute. However, her guru always remained a reference point, and fidelity to him was always uncompromised, though once he was gone, she was on her own to interpret and carry forward his missions and ideals.

In some ways, the very otherness of the exotic colonies represented an attractive freedom to explore alternatives not available to women in the home country. This was often experienced as empowering and liberating by the privileged few, who dared to develop a certain empathy for indigenous causes and concerns. Missionary women could well be one such example; female converts to Hinduism were the other side of this. However, there was always a certain implicit imperial protection for white women in the patriarchal colonial context, even when they did cross over the colonial divide between ruler and ruled.

In such circumstances, the intensity of involvement between western women and eastern gurus is not unusual. We find it also with Gandhiji and with Madeleine Slade, whom he called Miraben. Surely, the emotional relationship of disciple with guru facilitates the communication of religious ideas and faith commitments. For the disciple, the guru stands in the place of divinity, but the true guru will wean the disciple away from such dependence, and never exploit it.

Vivekananda masterfully accompanied the conversion of Margaret Noble, as she left behind her feminine British self and converted into an aggressive Hindu nun, and grew into a new spirituality and mission as Sister Nivedita. As his disciple, she never lost her agency, and when her beloved master was no longer there, she was quite able to function on her own, even as her understanding evolved and new colleagues and new commitments engaged her dedication.

At the socio-cultural level, Nivedita's conversion was a part of the revival Vivekananda had initiated. Her resurgent Hinduism set limits to the critique she was willing to make of traditional Hinduism. Rather than reform she urged: 'We have to recreate the Dharma. We have to build again the 'Mahabharata' (Nivedita 1975: 85). She supported Ram Mohan Roy's campaign against sati, but she exalted the satis of the past: 'the entire world must prostrate itself in admiration before women who were capable of performing sati' (Nivedita 1975: 83). This did raise criticism in England and America, especially with mission societies concerned with child marriage and the status of women in India.

Here Nivedita was subordinating gender to nationalism. Was she coping with her own doubts as she propagated her faith to others? However, the critical question remains: was her 'aggressive Hinduism' the heart of her nationalist project or its outer limits? Such ambiguities do lend themselves to extremist interpretations. She saw nationality as a form of spirituality, the 'highest possible expression, for the time, of the spiritual life' (Atmaprana, ed., 1982: 134). The 're-establishment of Dharma' she sought was meant to bring 'a great, overflowing, complex, actual, ever-strong, ever-living consciousness of the common nationality' (ibid. 153). Her concern was the fulfilment of dharma, which was for her the national truth. This was the dharma of revival, rather than that of reform, of bringing the past into the present as valid for the future, rather than reinterpreting the past so, as to change the present to be relevant to the future.

Though in theory her politics was highly spiritual and extremist, in practice it was situated and cautious. There was a certain non-sectarian openness in her neo-Vedantic Hinduism when she said that just as 'a man may well claim to be a good Christian without being a Catholic...a man may well and rightly be servant of dharma, without calling himself a Hindu' (Grover and Arora, ed. 1993: 186). She urged us to see people as 'clothed with universal humanity' (ibid. 1993: 341-59).

As Vivekananda's dedicated disciple, her conversion was to his 'practical Vedanta', but later she extended this to the national cause, to a more active and direct political involvement than her guru's Ramakrishna Mission afforded. The transition was not without its ambiguities and contradictions.

The connection between neo-Hinduism and religious nationalism is apparent in both Nivedita and Aurobindo, both of whom drew their inspiration from Vivekananda. Yet, for the Ramakrishna Mission and his followers, Vivekananda had ruled out any direct engagement in politics. He wanted India to conquer the world with its spirituality. Aurobindo abandoned the political agenda in Pondicherry, Nivedita retreated into the Himalayas before her death. Others take up religious nationalism and make a selective interpretation of Vivekananda to claim legitimacy. Yet, once religious identity becomes the mobiliser for nationalism, there is the inevitable consequence of the nation-state being perceived as sacred rather than secular, the great danger of sacrificing religious pluralism to cultural nationalism.

These ambiguities and contradictions are inherent in the Hindu revival, for the spiritual ambitions of neo-Hinduism were ambiguous enough to nurture a nationalist chauvinism, and the deep-rooted tensions in the Hindu revival were contradictory enough to precipitate an extremist reaction. Vivekanada himself was not a political chauvinist or a religious communalist. His project to Hinduise India and universalise Hinduism was very much a spiritual endeavour, not a political programme. Even if what he propagated might seem to be a Hinduised internationalism, it has little in common with Savarkar's narrow parochial slogan to 'Hinduise all politics and militarise all Hindudom.' (cited Mckean 1996: 71)

Savarkar did make an exception to his own ideology and acknowledge Nivedita as a Hindu, even though her *janma bhoomi*, land of her birth, was not India, she made it her *punya bhoomi*, her holy land, because she adopted its culture and religion as her own. However, Nivedita's conversion was to the neo-Vedantism of Vivekananda, not the Hindutva of Savarkar. Even her understanding of nationality was closer to Vivekananda's universalism than to Savarkar's ethnocentricism. Anticipating the global-local dilemma she insisted: 'Only the tree that is firm in its own soil can offer us a perfect crown of leaf and blossom...cosmo-nationality consists in *holding the local idea in the world idea*' (Atmaprana, ed., 1982: 495 emphasis in text).

However, there are still ambiguities that have allowed a selective interpretation and a cooption by religious nationalists and fundamentalists, who claim Vivekanada's heritage. Nivedita facilitated rather than minimised this. Tagore and Gandhi were sensitively aware of the not-so-subtle political contradictions in the Hindu revival that became apparent only later. For Tagore, it was the contradiction between nationalism and internationalism, for Gandhi, it was between communal exclusiveness and religious universality. Nivedita experienced no separation between her Vedantic religion and her political nationalism.

Margaret Noble's quest begins in London with her political involvement and unfulfilled spiritual longings. It comes to India with Sister Nivedita embracing a neo-Vedantic spirituality of her guru, Swami Vivekananda. It moves into the nationalist movement with a kindred soul, Aurobindo, and finally disengages and reaches out to revive the nation though its own art. Yet all through, it is essentially a spiritual and religious quest, even though the concrete forms, in which her conversion expresses itself, are political. It was as much a dedication to the religion she converted to, as to the people she identified with. She asked rhetorically, 'For what is the real stuff of human tragedy, the hunger for bread or the longing for salvation?' (Grover and Arora, ed., 1993: 118) She has no doubt that a temporal hunger can never be more important than an eternal longing, for 'man does not live by bread alone.' Her life's quest is testimony to this deep-seated religious longing.

Nivedita is easily misunderstood for her militant nationalism, aggressive Hinduism, fiery politics and fierce rhetoric, but she also stood for a nobler, purer life, a freer, more divine world. There is a complex paradox involved in the quest of Sister Nivedita, the dedicated disciple and fiery nationalist. It is in her devotion to Kali, herself a paradoxical figure, through whom she lives out this paradox to personalise her quest and to syncretise her beliefs. It was for her a new beginning, a new birth: 'I set myself therefore to enter into Kali worship, as one would set oneself to learn a new language, or take birth deliberately, perhaps, in a new race.' (Nivedita, 1904: 395).

The trajectory of Sister Nivedita's conversion would seem to be the opposite of Pandita Ramabais. Though they were contemporaries, their paths were quite different. Yet, her conversion involved her in a movement, in which she could not escape the ambiguities and tensions of revivalist Hinduism and militant politics. If anything these are magnified in her peculiar situation of an outsider on the inside. She is a Hinduised Englishwoman, urging Hindu men to self-assertion and aggressive manliness, as she at the same time preaches to Hindu-women self-denial and feminine devotion.

Yet, her racial identity as a white woman under the British Raj makes her position uniquely different from that of the women, to whom she preached feminine submissiveness, and the men, whom she encouraged to manly vigour. Even when she was on the other side, her privileged connections were never completely severed, for the paternalist colonial Raj remained protective of its women even when they opposed it and was always ready to welcome them back into the fold. How many nationalist native women would have been visited socially by the vicereine, Lady Minto, as Nivedita was in 1910, once she was perceived as less of a threat by the government? (Boehmer, 2002: 104)

Rabindranath Tagore, who had met her in Calcutta in 1904, recalls how he was struck by this 'great-hearted Western woman', how 'she had won her access to the inmost hearts of our society by her supreme gift of empathy.' (Grover and Arora, ed. 1993: 443) She came not 'with the impertinent curiosity of a visitor ... She lived our life and came to know us by becoming one of ourselves.' (ibid.) Her life is a dramatic makeover of her Englishness in the process of her Hinduisation.

After her death in the Himalayas where she had retreated, Aurobindo recognised, that she was 'practically Indian in belief, culture and aspirations'. The yearnings of Margaret Noble, the English radical, were at last fulfilled in Sister Nivedita, the Vedantic sanyasin, no longer a visitor from the outside, but an insider who truly belonged. Surely, her own description of Aurobindo would best suit her too: 'a new seed grown on the ancient soil of India.' (Quoted Reymond 1953: 348)

Commonalities and Differences

These four case studies are paradigmatic in different ways. Ambedkar's quest for equality and justice leads him outside the Hindu fold to a Navayana Buddhism designed as a new vehicle for his people. Gandhi's experiments with truth and his reinterpretation of Hinduism create a new synthesis in an innovative version of the *sanatan dharma* that addresses and transcends many of the earlier critiques. Pandita Ramabai longs for an emancipation and salvation and her critique of patriarchy in traditional Hinduism is carried over to the Christian Church, where she feels constrained by its institutional and belief structures and eventually finds her salvation in a non-sectarian Christianity. Sister Nivedita journeys from an intensely personal relationship to her guru to a spiritual vision of reality in the neo-Vedantin Impersonal Absolute, and expresses this in a deep devotion to the national cause.

For Ambedkar, coming as he does from a situation of injustice and oppression, changing one's religious allegiance from a tradition that oppresses, to one in which he hopes to find liberation for himself and his people, is both legitimate and ethical. This applies not just to converting oneself but also to converting others. Both these are necessarily inherent in the right to freedom of conscience on which the right to religious freedom is based. Obviously, fraud, force or any other unfair means cannot be countenanced in any human interaction, and religious conversion is a sensitive area where such boundaries are unfortunately crossed.

For Gandhi, a religious tradition that oppresses must be reformed, not abandoned. He does not want to deny the legal right to convert oneself or to convert others, but he sees all religions as essentially equal and reformable. He does not object to someone changing their allegiance by converting to another religious tradition in some circumstances, but he cannot accept anyone converting others to their own tradition. He never encouraged this himself. He regards this as a negation in practice of the mutual respect religious tradition must have for each other. Even if propagation and conversion is mandated by a religion, there would still be a moral duty to follow its own conscience and offer her faith as a gift, leaving others the freedom to decline. This cannot amount to an ethical right to convert others to one's own faith, certainly never by taking advantage of their vulnerability.

There are instructive commonalities and differences here. Thus for Ambedkar, the essential issue is one of religious freedom and free choice; for Gandhi it is one of religious tolerance and mutual respect. Both are deeply committed secular persons and firmly convinced religious personalities. Both function within a perspective of fundamental rights and basic duties, though from their different vantage points, one stresses rights and the other duties. Each is coming from his or her own existential experience: Gandhi from that of a Vaishnava sanatani, Ambedkar from that of a Hindu outcaste. Their search is similar: for *dharma* and *moksha*, for *dhamma* and *nirvana*, respectively; but their paths are different as they cross and separate along the way.

In her pursuit of emancipation, Ramabai directs her critique against unacceptable social and institutional constraints. She seeks a religious salvation beyond these for herself and others. Nivedita's quest is for a dedication that will bring fulfilment, which she finds in practical Vedanta, consecrating herself to the service of India. Both are intensely committed, persevering pilgrims, willing to persuade others to join them in their pilgrimage, though they set off in very different directions. Ramabai begins as an insider, willing to be constructively critical, and ends her journey rather on the margins of the patriarchal society and institutional religion she opposed, claimed by neither. Nivedita's begins as an outsider, unwilling to publicly criticise and determined to belong to the religion and country of her adoption, and when she eventually does, she is immersed in the ambiguities and contradictions she had accepted.

Ambedkar and Gandhi were sensitive to issues of gender justice and equality, but both were father figures to their followers. The kind of incisive feminist critique that Ramabai offers could come only from a woman. However, the 'aggressive Hinduism' of Nivedita represents another kind of assertion by women, of a revivalism that serves the religious fundamentalists and extremists, who have used it to their own purposes. Today, we can look back and appreciate Ramabai's critique of patriarchy, even as we have come to recognise the paradox of Nivedita's dedication. Both were strong women, who have left their mark, and even when we may disagree with them, they command our respect. We may be cautious in our acceptance of their ideas, we cannot but be generous in our admiration of the lives.

6

Connecting Contested Issues

Dalit frustration – No Entry, No Exit – The Resilience of Caste – Meenakshipuram – Longing for Self-respect – The Wider Significance – Conversion as Protest and Quest – ***Tribal aspiration*** – The Staines Murders – The Politics of Hate – the Larger Context – The Devi Cult – Conflict in the Dangs – A Complex Heritage – Assimilation – Resistance – Response – Identity Construction – Significance of Religion – Conversion as Future Aspiration – ***Christian ambiguity*** – The Bishops' Dilemma – Openness of Truth – The Imperative of Equality – The Relativity of Culture – The Protestant Spectrum – The Catholic Transition – Creative Fidelity – ***Hindu tolerance*** – The Irrepressible Question – The Hindu Paradox – Recovering Tolerance – Gandhian Relevance – Nehruvian Rationalism – Neutrality or Respect – Conversion to Tolerance – ***Muslim diversity*** – Homogeneity and Demonisation – Unity not Uniformity – Indian Islam – Multiple Diversities – Modern Challenges – Subaltern Responses – ***Comparisons and contrasts*** – Dalits and Tribals – Christians, Hindus, Muslims

The diverse case studies in the earlier chapter address some contested issues in our contemporary situation. Thus, conversion movements among dalits and tribals to Christianity, led by the missionaries, have fallen short of the converts' expectations. It brought some improvement to their circumstances but not the breakthrough to the liberation they had initially hoped. Christian dalits and tribals are still marginalised in our society, even within the Christian community. The same can be said of the neo-Buddhist movement inspired by Ambedkar. He has become an icon, co-opted by dalit leaders more concerned with their own upward social mobility than with the uplift of the dalit masses.

Gandhi's views has been used to legitimise opposition to religious conversions, but the social and religious reforms that Gandhi had advocated have not kept pace with promises made or with dalit and tribal aspirations for change. Rather these are 'frozen into a social status quo that perpetuates 'old privileges and precipitates new prejudices'. Tribal religious traditions are deliberately Hinduised and tribal converts are reconverted in an organised manner, leaving the tribals confused, but not better off.

Christian communities today, especially Protestant ones, have reclaimed Ramabai, but her interrogation of Christian patriarchy and institutional exclusivism still underscores the ambiguity of Christians with regard to the dichotomy between theory and practice, as also dilemmas within each of these. This is not peculiar to the Christian tradition. Religious practice does tend to fall short of religious ideals. As in any human enterprise, preaching does not always faithfully mirror performance, nor is observance always consistent with belief. However, in striving to bridge this gap, new ambiguities must be faced and old certainties relativised.

Nivedita represents a whole tradition of Hindu assertiveness that now spills over into real aggression with the fundamentalists and extremists. These needs to be set in counterpoint to Hindu tolerance, that has all too easily and uncritically been proclaimed as characteristic of this tradition, while others are demonised as violent and intolerant. This is not an issue just for Hindus alone, but for extremists of all persuasions. Though all intolerance must be condemned, the tolerance of a majority community is more crucial than that of a minority one, because of the greater implications for society at large.

Today, Muslims projected as a pan-Islamic community, a uniform and integrated international *ummah*. Unfortunately, the richness and diversity of the Islamic world is discounted and dismissed. If the acceptance of diversity is the basis of tolerance, then negating or neglecting diversity cannot but have perverse consequences for tolerance and certainly for the sensitive issue of religious tolerance. It is in this context that appreciating the multiple facets of Indian Islam helps not only to exorcise the religious intolerance prevailing within that community, but also the intolerance it experiences from without.

Dalit frustration

The frustrating cruelty of caste oppression in the context of religious conversion brutally brought home to me in an encounter with a local activist, Avinash Gaikwad from the denotified tribes in Baramati on 17 August 2002.

In colonial times, the government had notified numerous nomadic communities as hereditary criminals with the Criminal Tribes Act in 1871. This was extended to the whole country by 1911. After Independence, these communities were 'denotified', the notification against them was withdrawn, and in 1950, the Act itself was abolished. These denotified communities are not scheduled and so are much worse off than the Scheduled Castes and Tribes, because they have no reservation quotas or any statutory affirmative action in their favour. Today, they are estimated to be some sixty million spread all through the country.

In a letter to the Prime Minister, dated 9 August 2002, Avinash had protested the terrible atrocities his people in the town suffered. They were routinely arrested, held without charge, and summarily found guilty in order to solve crimes, with which they could not have any possible connection. In a public announcement to the local newspapers, he had declared his people's intention to convert to Christianity en masse on the fifty-fifth anniversary of Independence.

The police then attempted to persuade him otherwise, promising help. His answer was to demand the release of all the denotified tribals held without charge in local lockups. But then, the police would not be able to explain their arrest in the first place and their convenient criminal investigation procedures would be compromised. Next, the RSS and their Sangh Parivar held a public meeting in the town and attempted to disuade them from the drastic step by once again, promising many benefits if they refrained. Their answer was that for fifty years, they had lived on promises, they wanted action now today and not tomorrow. The meeting ended in a confused postponement. Avinash then showed me an open letter from the local Church of Christ, Baramati, dated 9 August 2002. This was a public declaration distancing their Church from, and disowning, the proposed mass conversion.

Such instances need to be probe further and understood in their proper context, for they are not exceptional. I have had denotified tribals come to me and say, we are going to convert to Christianity. Moreover, I say, please do not, there will be a terrible backlash, this will complicate your life and may do you no good either. To my mind, these are certainly not strictly religious conversions but an anguished protest against, and a desperate attempt to escape, their tortured conditions. Can this be illegitimate social behaviour for citizens of our democratic secular state? Yet would any church be able to protect them from the vengeance that their conversion would bring upon them? So on being put on the spot, all I could say was that, like Ambedkar, they should study the matter long and hard, and then take a decision.

The dalit threat at Baramati is obviously an angry and despairing rejection of an imposed negative social identity and the economic injustice and political oppression of caste. At issue here is whether this is a truly religious conversion, an *atmaparivartan* preceding their *dharmantar*. It would take a generation or two to for such a group exodus to internalise their newly accepted faith. However, in terms of citizens' rights, can such a moving to stop by law or by self-proclaimed guardians of religion? There is civil legitimacy to such protest and rejection, uncomfortable and/or unacceptable as it may be to dominant castes and majoritarian religious communities. It must be addresses in terms of the real issues of oppression and marginalization that grind these people into the dust. No anti-conversion law can address this anguish.

At Barmati, the response to the would-be converts' frustration, by the police and the Sangh Parivar on one side, and the local church on the other, epitomises so acutely the 'no entry, no exit' dilemma that is forced on so many of the disempowered and voiceless in our land. Their own religious tradition pressurises them to stay in their oppressive circumstances. If they do try to break out of it, they are not accepted, certainly not as equals in the new community they convert to. This can only compound their frustration until it boils over and explodes in unanticipated ways.

Sometimes their threat has worked, at others they have carried it through and suffered drastic fallouts. Perhaps another Ambedkar might one day lead them out of their present fold to secure the identity and dignity that still eludes them. However, this time they may well be led in more than one direction to religious traditions that sharpen their protest against their oppressors. Indeed, some of their spokespersons, like V.T. Rajshekar, are already urging them to convert to Islam rather than Buddhism or Christianity, as this expresses a more telling protest today (Rajshekar 1983).

Dalit conversions include a quest for bettering themselves and more especially, a reaching out for greater equality and respect in society at large. Backward caste movements too have also been part of such a process, as conversions to Christianity in Andhra testify. These movements were more effective at registering a protest than in achieving the equality and respect that was sought.

Across all communities, religious and otherwise, caste in India has proved notoriously endemic. It defines Indian society even today. Earlier religious movements within Hindu society, particularly those among the *bhakti* cults, had opposed caste and sought greater equality. They were eventually encapsulated as religious sects and given their own niche in the caste hierarchy, becoming subcastes in the process. In choosing to convert to Buddhism, Ambedkar was looking for a 'new beginning'. However, his neo-Buddhist dalit converts are now facing the same plight that defined and contained earlier religious protest movements against caste hierarchy.

Indeed, whether dalit conversions were to Christianity or Islam, Sikhism or Buddhism, the egalitarian ethos of these traditions were not as resistant to caste hierarchies as their official teachings proclaimed. Often religious conversion met with less resistance when caste purity/pollution taboos were continued among the converts, indicating that in such cases caste was an even more defining marker of identity than religion. In these communities, caste hierarchies of their own prevailed and were perpetuated in practice by a rigorous endogamy. Inter-marriage was more likely across religious than caste boundaries. This is a carryover from the practice among indigenous religious traditions, as with Hindu and Sikh Jats, both agricultural castes, or Hindu and Jain Banias, both trading castes.

Among Christians, dalit entry into the ranks of the clergy was long resisted and contained within the lower echelons. Earlier this was even restricted by Papal decree, as in Kerala in 1832, which limited untouchable candidates to the priesthood to five a year. These were to be educated in faraway Bombay, not in Kerala, and they were to be assignment later to their own communities. Catholic dalits claim that though they are almost seventy per cent of Catholic Christians, the small percentage in their representation among the clergy bears no comparison to this and their presence in the upper hierarchy is just tokenism. The figures are difficult to compile but their sense of exclusion does have a credible and legitimate basis.

However, if religious conversion did not satisfactorily achieve the changed status converts had hoped for, this does not negate the real change it produced in their prospects for socio-economic advancement through improved heathcare and access to education, and most crucially in enhanced self-esteem. Indeed, conversion movements would not have been sustainable otherwise; frustration would have led to recidivism. To some extent, this has happened with neo-Buddhists, who lost their Scheduled Caste reservations and left to fend for themselves. To prevent this, Sikh dalits were put on the Schedule in 1950, and Buddhists in 1990. Christian dalits are now agitating for the same status. Oppressed as these outcastes already are, the additional burden of religious discrimination would be difficult to sustain without some support.

The Depressed Classes are always precariously placed in our society. At times, conversion to Christianity has meant a transference of dependence from the more exploitative patronage of the property owner to the more benevolent paternalism of the missionaries. Indeed, much of the resistance to their conversion was due to the loss it meant of bonded and cheap labour to the dominant castes. Often such change as conversion brought did not represent a complete liberation as might have been hope for, though it might have indicated some positive improvement in their life chances.

Today, liberation theology has proved to be an effective motivator and mobiliser for Christian involvement in social issues, and dalits have embraced it to project their demands nationally and even internationally, as they did at the United Nations World Conference Against Racism at Durban, South Africa, in August 2001. These dalits are now insisting not only on their separateness from caste Hindu traditions, but also on their distinctiveness within their respective religious traditions. Hence, their attempt to express their collective experience and to reconfigure their subaltern subjectivity as distinct from dominant caste groups with counter-cultural images, such as their drum, so evocative of a people who have no voice in their society, a symbol of divine power, rather than the sacred 'word', the mantra of priestly ritual.

The significance of caste as a factor that affects both converts and their opponents is dramatically illustrated by dalit conversions to Islam at Meenakshipuram in 1981, and its traumatic aftermath, is indicative of the typical response they have had to cope with. The Tamil Muslims have their early origins in trading communities with strong egalitarian traditions. In spite of the self-respect movement, caste feelings still run high in society globally and especially in southern Tamil Nadu, the site of many earlier mass conversion movements.

On 19 February 1981, two hundred dalit families of Meenakshipuram in Tirunelveli district in Tamil Nadu converted to Islam. On 23 May, twenty-seven more families followed suit. The movement spread to other villages in other districts. By 13 August, the Study Group of Parliamentary Affairs of the Tamil Nadu Government reported that the conversion wave had spread through the districts of Tirunelveli (numbering 1,000), Ramnathapuram (180), and Madurai (533), a total of 1713 conversions. There were threats by dalits to convert in Bangalore and Chennai, and even in Banaras. A major conversion movement to Islam seemed to be gaining momentum.

The initial reaction of other caste Hindus was empathetic as reported by *The Hindu*, a prestigious Chennai newspaper. They acknowledged the 'harassment, humiliation, and civil discrimination' (30 May), the 'social inequality and persecution' (27 June) that dalits suffered; they recognised the 'new awakening' (27 July), a 'new revolution' (15 July) among them.

But soon a reaction led by the VHP and other extremist Hindu organisations politicised the issue: now they saw a wider Islamic involvement naming specific organisations and targets (*The Hindu,* 3 October) and described this as an attack to ruin Hindu society (*Times of India,* 21 March). The Arya Samaj and other groups had earlier alleged the undue influence of foreign money and pan-Islamic interference (*The Hindu,* 30 May) and wanted to reconvert the dalits through a *shuddhi* (purification) ceremony (ibid. 25 July and 22 August). In later comments and publications, the dalits were accused of changing their dharma, religion, not for *dharmic*, religious/spiritual reasons, but for 'de-dharmic' (sic), secular ones (Dutt 1986: 44).

However, Mumtaz Ali Khan's *Sociological Inquiry* into the *Mass-Conversions of Meenakshipuram*, (1983) found little substance in such accusations. These dalits had made their decision after careful consideration without any wild expectations of immediate improvement in their lot. They had approached the South Indian Muslim Association in Tirunelveli, but were asked to wait. Only after repeated requests, which he felt in conscience he could not disregard, did Abdul Hasan Shathali Sahib, a local Muslim scholar, preside over their pledge of faith (Mathew 1982: 1031). There was some evidence of clothes and a borewell being gifted after the conversions, but the reconverts too were similarly benefited after their *shuddhi* (Khan 1983: 159). Claims that 20-30 per cent had reconverted were highly exaggerated, to say the least. Khan's *Inquiry* found only seven confirmed instances; most other claims were of families that had not converted in the first place, though they had expressed their intention to do so (ibid).

There was no evidence of foreign 'Gulf-money' being involved (ibid. 167). The Thevars, the regional dominant caste, and the local Brahmans (ibid. 1983: 158) supported this report. Caste discrimination against dalits had precipitated these events. The continuing practice of untouchability under various guises was the focus of the protest (ibid. 1983: 9). They were not unrealistic about discrimination against them ceasing altogether with conversion to Islam, but they wanted a 'minimum inequality' (ibid. 1983: 159). In a free democratic society this is hardly too much to aspire to after more than thirty years.

George Mathew's comprehensive analysis points to the 'feeling of brotherhood and sense of equality among Tamil Nadu Muslims' (Mathew 1982: 1033) as the reason for dalits preferring Islam to Christianity. Mathew sees these dalit conversions as 'functionally equivalent to village secession' (ibid: 1068). It 'questions the status quo' (ibid. 1071) and politicises religion in order to change the oppressive hierarchy.

Christian dalits too converted to Islam at Meenakshipuram to escape the caste oppression they experienced among their own Christians. 'For though Christianity, at the level of the charismatic founder was an egalitarian doctrine, at the level of sociological fact of the converted in Tamil Nadu it is highly hierarchical and caste ridden' (ibid.). Caste divisions extended even to the cemetery. As C. Krishna Murthy, a dalit leader in Thimmanaikem Palayam put it: 'By becoming Christians we cannot raise our social status by becoming Muslims we can' (*The Indian Express*, 3 July 1981). The story of Thankaraj at this time is significant. He was a dalit who eloped with a Thevar girl, converted to Islam and with the support of his Muslim friends was able to challenge the dominant caste and even resist police intervention on their behalf (*The Statesman*, 20 July 1981).

These were not the first 'mass' conversions in Tamil Nadu. From the 17th century, there were conversion movements to Christianity, especially in southern Tamil Nadu in the three districts of Madurai, Tirunelveli, and Ramanathapuram. Then as now, similar explanations of extrinsic interventions were made, rather than addressing the intrinsic conditions of the dalit communities converting. These districts still have a notorious reputation for dalit oppression. In Thanjavur, the green revolution rice bowl of the state, forty-two landless dalits were burned to death on 25 December 1968. Dalits are still subjected to harassment and humiliation: they are denied temple entry, discriminated against at work, their women are violated their children exploited. Their dependence on the dominant castes traps them in a hopeless situation, from which there is still little escape.

In Meenakshipuram, the Chakkiliyans, the poorest among the dalits there, did not convert, but the Pallars, the better off among them, who could challenge their subjugation by leaving the fold did so (Khan 1983: 158). Such conversions must be seen as part of the larger 'self-respect movement' that had launched a scathing critique and rejection of Brahmanism in South India. Not surprisingly, the main opposition to these conversions has come principally from the Hindu Munnani, a Brahman-dominated RSS organisation in Tamil Nadu. However, there is undoubtedly a social movement for change underway, and though it may not be revolutionary as yet, it is surely a demand for reform.

The conversion movement to Buddhism with Ambedkar had earlier presaged this longing for self-respect. Now at Meenakshipuram it was no longer Buddhism or even Christianity that seemed to be able to satisfy their longings. Conversion to Islam expressed dalit protest against caste more sharply and categorically in the context of the antagonisms and anxieties of Hindu nationalists and fundamentalists regarding Muslims.

Ambedkar's passionate rhetoric in a 1936 Marathi pamphlet *Mukti Kon Pathe.* (*What Path Freedom?*) captures in poetic form both this protest against caste oppression and this longing for human dignity:

> Religion is for man; man is not for religion.
> If you want to gain self-respect, change your religion.
> If you want to create a cooperating society, change your religion.
> If you want power, change your religion.
> If you want equality, change your religion.
> If you want independence, change your religion.
> If you want to make the world in which you live happy, change your religion.
> Why should you remain in a religion that does not value your manhood?

Why should you remain in a religion that does not let you enter its temples?
Why should you remain in a religion that does not give you water to drink?
Why should you remain in a religion that does not let you become educated?
Why should you remain in a religion that bars you from good jobs?
Why should you remain in a religion that dishonours you at every step?
That religion which forbids humanitarian behaviour between man and man is not a religion but a reckless penalty.
That religion which regards the recognition of man's self-respect as sin is not a religion but a sickness.
That religion which allows one to touch a foul animal but not a man is not a religion but a madness.
That religion which says that one class may not gain knowledge, may not acquire wealth, may not 'take up arms', is not a religion but a mockery of man's life.
That religion which teaches that the unlearned should remain unlearned, that the poor should remain poor, is not a religion but a punishment.
Do not say that men who treat animals with more respect than humans and who respect all Brahmans as Gods are religious.
Do not say that men who feed ants with sugar and let men go without water are religious.
Do not say that men who embrace another religion and push their own far from them hate society. (cited by Zelliot 1977: 121-123).

This impassioned plea from Ambedkar was in the context of the resolution for conversion passed by the All-Bombay District Mahar Conference in May 1936, but his trenchant cry has a wider relevance beyond Hinduism, as a critique of all religions that have sacrificed the poor and dispossessed them in this world with promises of the next.

The conversions at Meenakshipuram to Islam are not the only instance of mass conversions of dalits in contemporary India but it certainly is a poignant testimony to their plight. Indeed, the conversion movement among dalits is gaining momentum, rather than losing ground. An example among others is Udit Raj's movement. He was

Ram Raj before converting to Buddhism and founding the Lord Buddha Club in 1996, and the All India Confederation of SC/ST Organizations in 1997. A follower of Ambedkar, he now is leading a dalit movement to 'quit Hinduism' and join non-casteist religions. Hundreds of dalits in some places, thousands in others, have responded.

Dalits associations in Tamil Nadu have joined the movement. Some of their leaders like N. Natrajan and R. Tirumavalavan argue that dalits were never Hindus in the first place. Udit Raj too says he has not converted, just gone back to Buddhism, the original religion of the dalits, as Ambedkar had tried to establish. In Delhi on 4 November 2001, he planned a million-strong rally at which dalits would convert to Buddhism. However, the state government cancelled the rally three days before and barricaded the venue, preventing some 350,000 from attending. However, 50, 000 did manage to get through and convert publicly.

Surely, no preventive, much less repressive, measures will answer the issues these dalits are voicing, and neither the dalits nor their questions are likely to go away until both the opponents and proponents of conversion satisfactorily address them.

Dalits experience multiple and cumulative discriminations – psychological and social, economic and political, religious and cultural. These add up across many interrelated areas of their lives, each implicating the other in complex ways that leave such people trapped. A positive intervention in one area may be neutralised and reversed by the negative consequences this precipitates in another. Their life-situation denies them fair access to better their life-chances, and if they seek to escape the religious traditions that oppress them, those who oppose their seeking another future elsewhere resist them. These urge reform that dalits have waited for too long. There are others who take advantage of these dalits to coopt them to their own religious community, leaving them to same inequalities there. However, whose interests and concerns are at stake here? Who will speak for these dalits, voice their anguish, reflect their pain?

This is the cruel frustration of dalits. Religious conversion is a desperate protest against the stigma of caste. Yet this carries over into the new community, notwithstanding its religious teaching, and remains in society at large scale in spite of repeatedly proposed and well-intentioned religious reforms. Addressing the humiliation and oppression of caste will require more than a religious change, whether by conversion or reform. Religious revival, as nationalism or fundamentalism, has done little more than mere tokenism to improve their lot.

Only a deep and comprehensive social change can deal effectively with this. Those who oppose dalit conversion are often, though not always, the very ones who oppose secular reforms that would immensely benefit the dalits: such as affirmative action and an effective implementation of reservation quotas for them, land reforms and protective labour legislation, an employment guarantee scheme, or the many poverty alleviation programmes. These would benefit all those below the poverty line, where seventy per cent and more dalits are still trapped.

Atrocities against dalits are not just random violence against the weaker and more vulnerable in our society. There is a diabolic method in this unconscionable madness, even if it is not explicitly recognised. For this violence is used to reinforce caste barriers that seem threatened; and sometimes the greater the threat, the greater is the corresponding response. Atrocities on dalits are still endemic in our society and we seem unable and/or unwilling to exorcise them. Untouchability has been constitutional abolished, yet even today implicitly and explicitly its overt and covert practices are widely prevalent.

The lynching to death of five dalits as recently as 15 October 2002 in Haryana at Dulina, Jhajjar, outside the police post, poignantly underscores how little dalits are valued; in this instance, even less than cattle, as some prominent religious leaders among Hindu extremists indicated. The dalits were rumoured to have killed a cow in order to flay it. The government's response was to send the bovine carcass for a postmortem to ascertain the cause of death, while the 'mobsters' went free. After a public outcry, a case was registered and some persons were arrested, but they were release and are still out on bail.

The dalit conversions at Meenakshipuram dramatically and convincingly underline this: if conversion as protest is an essential part of dalit conversion movements, then conversion as a quest for self-respect is the necessary obverse of this. For in the final analysis religious conversion for dalits represents more than a protest against what they are subjected to. It is even more a quest for dignity and identity, for a chance for a better future, a hope in a more promising alternative. Emphatically, they have every right to this. Those who oppose their protest to save the status quo have no real understanding of their agonised quest. Those who take advantage of their anguish only to increase the numbers of their own communities, but negate or neglect their desperate human hopes and aspirations, do not respond to this deep quest either. Both are violators of dalit dignity and identity.

Tribal Aspiration

The burning to death in their jeep of Dr Graham Staines and his two young sons on the night of 22 January 1998 at Manoharpur in Orissa shocked the conscience of this nation. It focused attention on the issue of tribal conversions, but perhaps more on the proponents and the opponents, than on the plight of the tribals themselves.

Graham Staines, 58, was an Australian missionary doctor working among the leprosy-afflicted at a hospital in Baripada in Orissa. He had translated the Bible into the Ho language. He was involved in spreading the Gospel in the districts of Mayurbhanj and Keojhar, though he himself was not involved in any conversions. He had gone to Manoharpur to minister at a Christian camp that was held a few times in the year. It was about midnight that a mob of outsiders attacked the village shouting hostile slogans: 'Dara Singh zindabad, Bajrang Dal zindabad' ('long live Dara Singh, long live the Bajrang Dal', a militant Hindu organisation of the Sangh Parivar). They attacked people and set fire to the church house, and then to the jeep in which Graham and his two sons Philip, 10, and Timothy, 6, were sleeping. Their charred bodies were founding in the morning with Graham's arms around his sons. His wife Gladys, 49, and a daughter, Esther, 13, who had not come to the village that night, survived them.

A week after the murders, on 29 January, the government set up a commission of inquiry chaired by a judge of the Supreme Court, justice D. P. Wadhwa, whose report was submitted on 21 June 1999. In his concluding comments, he found the 'gruesome murder...a blot on the fair name of India known for its tolerance' (Raju ed. 1999: 269). He was emphatic that 'the murder of Graham Staines clearly has the effect of subverting the secular foundations of the India polity' (ibid, 270). However, the Report concluded: 'the act of murdering Staines and his two children was inspired by Dara Singh and his clout and no authority, organisation or any other person played any role in or in connection with the killings' (ibid. 280).

This shows the judge's preoccupation with the niceties of legal evidence. However, such legalities do not guarantee substantive justice.

It only makes the procedure consistent with the system. What the report did not probe, perhaps because it saw this as beyond its legal mandate, was the kind of poisonous climate of religious phobia that the hate-mongers had created, in Orissa and in the country, which could produce a murderer like Rabindra Pal, alias Dare Singh. His uncomprehending mother, Ramrati, 75, in Kajor Bujurag, a village in Auriya district of Uttar Pradesh, remembered him as someone who would not even hurt an insect intentionally. Surely, the hate-mongers that inspire these criminals must also bear responsibility for such murders. Hiding behind a smokescreen of legalities may stand up in a court of law, but it will not before a social conscience if, as the good judge wants, 'truth and reconciliation must prevail' (ibid. 269).

The report sees Dare Singh's resentment against the missionaries as the result of conversions in the area. There were some conversions and some tension between Christian and non-Christian tribal as converts withdrew from common village celebrations. The Commission did not go into the issue of how such feelings are transforms into a murderous rage. It does condemn religious fundamentalism and urges communal harmony, suggesting even that the National Foundation for Communal Harmony (NFCH) be urge to take this up.

The Commission's attention had been drawn to the Macpherson Report of 15 February 1999 (Raju ed., 1999: 263-) which had indicted the institutional racism of the British police force for the flawed investigation of the brutal murder of Stephen Lawrence, a black youth, by young white thugs on 22 April 1993 in south London. However, Justice Wadhwa did not see its relevance to the religious prejudice and hatred being institutionally promoted by fundamentalist and extremist organisations in this country.

The whole history of collective violence and its cynical political operation is ample testimony to our criminalised electorate politics. Dara Singh is symptomatic of this violence. Those who play the eerie music for this dance of death must bear as much, if not a greater burden of guilt, and must be named and tamed as well. The Sri Krishna Commission Report of 16 February 1998 that inquired into the Mumbai riots of December 1992 and January 1993 did indict such players — but even with the change of government had no action has been taken against them.

A Central Bureau of Investigation (CBI) court in Khurda finally convicted Dara Singh and twelve accomplices on 15 September 2003, and sentenced them on the 22 September — Dara Singh to death and the others to life imprisonment. Gladys Staines publicly pardoned the perpetrators and appealed for healing. John Staines, the brother, asked for mercy for all those convicted. On appeal, the Orissa High Court on 19 May 2005 commuted the death sentence to life imprisonment and acquitted eleven of the others convicted. However, the aftermath of tension and mistrust will linger in the area unless the root causes of such violence are addressed. There must be reconciliation and healing first, if there is now to be religious tolerance and communal harmony.

In an intense atmosphere of hate, a hopeless economic situation produces social failures and failed fortune-seekers, who readily displace their rage on easily identifiable victims. The frustrating poverty of people allows their discontent and vulnerability to exploited for such murderous purposes.

This politics of hate is certainly doing great harm to our social fabric, and tribal conversions are one more focal point in the violence done to tribal society. The converters too are implicated in this violence, if not actively as was once, then at least passively as happens even now. Evangelisers often seem all too innocent of the implications of winning tribal confidence with generous and genuine social interventions and then following this with persuasive and pervasive religious promotion. This may be an expression of religious freedom well within legal rights guaranteed by our Constitution, and may truly abide by ethical norms of social duties in a diverse society. However, there remains a further question of civic tolerance and political sensitivity.

In such situations of conflict and tension, the missionary may become a hero, and no one can take away from this, when the commitment is genuine and not fanatical, when it expresses selflessness and not ethnocentrism. However, at the end of day, the tribals are left in a strained and vitiated atmosphere. A divided community, in which their agency is not enhanced, whether it will be to accept or reject the new religion, or to stay with, or change from, the old. They become pawns in a larger political game in which rampaging elephants trample the grass.

Biswamoy Pati's *Identity, Hegemony, and Resistance: Towards a Social History of Conversions in Orissa, 1800-2000* (2003), is an incisive study of tribal conversions in one context, but it is not untypical of tribals elsewhere in this country. Already in precolonial times the Hinduisation process sought to bring tribals within the prevailing dominant hegemony. Tribal leaders claimed Kshatriya status, though their people were mostly assimilated as shudras in the *varna* system, while they kept their customs and traditions. Pati mentions "the Gonds of Sambalpur inventing new legends to re-locate themselves within the framework of Hinduism, and the Gond zamindar (property owner) wearing the 'sacred thread'' (Pati 2003: 9).

The British accelerated this process of integration with 'a set of terror campaigns of the coloniser and his privileged tenure holders.' (Pati 2003: 15). Thus, the colonial government and their feudal compradors progressively dispossessed and decimated the tribals, forcing them into survival strategies of various kinds of unpaid and bonded labour.

As happens in such circumstances a disaster finally precipitates a rebellion. Here it was the famine of 1866. The tribals revolted against the hated Paikas, the dominant caste in the region, with armed violence. A new plebian cult of the goddess Mahima Devi with its apocalyptic visions rapidly spread among these tribals, and 'not only resisted the varna order but posed a serious challenge to it' (Pati 2003: 18). The invention of the smallpox goddess, Dharma Pinnu, at this time is a similar instance of a people's cultural innovation under duress.

Christian missionaries came into the area with the reform movements of the late 19th century, marked with their own ambiguities to colonialism. As long as they were seen as identified with the colonial government, the tribals kept their distance. Where they were perceived as supporting their struggles, they flocked to them. The no-rent movement of 1939 led by the Lutheran Nathaniel Munda was one such example, though even here not all Christian's tribals joined in. Given the complexity of tribal aspirations and apprehensions in the prevailing situation, there were the inevitable differences among them.

There are parallels to this no-rent movement in Orissa in the earlier land rights movement of Jharkhand that was take-up by missionaries there. This had brought many tribals into the church. Here too the colonial government and the property owners opposed the missionaries. Again, the famine of 1895 precipitated a rebellion in 1897. The missionaries were far too cautious to join the revolt of Birsa Munda (1875-1900) against the non-tribal *dikkus*, the zamindars and their intermediaries, the *thikedars*. The rebellion was soon crushed and Birsa died in a Ranchi prison.

Against this background, Gandhi's reformism came to tribal regions with the nationalist movement and by incorporating them into the anti-colonial struggle, positively affirmed these people's dignity, but then further Hinduised their tribal identity. After Independence, the relationship of Christianity to the state necessarily changed. Churches could no longer be identifying with the government. The option for conversion acquired a new perspective: it now 'offered a defence against Hindu exploitation and the process of Hinduisation' (Pati 2003: 27). This is not very different to what happened in the northeast elsewhere.

David Hardiman's study of *The Coming of the Devi: Adivasi Assertion in Western India* (1987) reveals a parallel to the Mahima Devi cult in Orissa. In this instance, it was the Warli tribals in the Konkan coastal plain of the Bombay presidency in the 1920s. Like the Mahima cult, the movement originated as a smallpox propitiation ceremony to a mother goddess associated with soil fertility, Salabai. It began in Palghar taluka and moved north through Dahanu and Umbargaon into the Gujarat and the Dangs, where it was most intense, though it had little effect in Maharashtra.

The movement was an effort at self-assertion and self-protection against their most hated exploiters in the area, the Parsis. However, the movement was co-opted into Gandhi's nationalist movement that was sweeping through the area at the time. The British then suppressed it rather ruthlessly — for now, more than a law and order problem, it was pre-received to as a revolt against the colonial government. Today, few memories of this movement survive, even in Thane district, Maharashtra, where it began.

In his reconstruction, Hardiman establishes the religio-cultural inspiration for this revolt against economic exploitation. This was a religious movement concerned with the propitiation of a supernatural force. However, 'a large number took it to have a very different meaning, seeing it as a call for the adivasis to change their existing way of life and adopt a set of new social values. For them the Devi was the herald of a completely new way of life. Why did so many adivasis interpret the Devi in such a manner at this particular juncture?' (Hardiman, 1987: 67). It was surely, because it responded to more than their religious aspirations.

Indeed, as a religious movement, it experienced no opposition, but as soon as wage demands and social boycotts were added to the agenda it became a threat to the status quo and was vigorously opposed, especially by the Parsis against whom it was target. For the control of the Parsis over these tribals was most brutally exploitive. The movement's message was simple and direct: teetotalism, vegetarianism, non-violence, cleanliness, boycott of the Parsis (Hardiman 1987: 155).

There were Catholic missionaries working in this area, but at the time, they distanced themselves from such tribal movements, both religious and secular. They were supportive of the state and opposed to the Communists, whose agitation against the exploitation and suppression of tribals by the state and the property owners peaked between 1945— 1947 before it was suppressed by the state.

Interestingly, here Parsi Zoroastrian property owners and Muslim forest contractors opposed tribal conversions to Christianity. This could hardly be for reasons of religious concern. Rather, conversion was seen as giving the tribals access to mission schools and education, eventually affecting easily exploitable tribal labour on which the property owners grew rich. One Parsi property owner expressed their real concern at the time as recorded by a missionary: 'If you missionaries educate the tribals, who will then work for us?' This captures the resistance of such dominant groups here and elsewhere to any change in the status quo unfavourable to themselves.

The Dangs is a tribal district of southern Gujarat. Christian evangelical groups had been active in the area since the 19th century, but without much success. In 2001, the state population was 50.59 million, of which Christians were 0.6 per cent. In the Dangs out of 186, 712, Christians were 10 per cent or 18, 600.

In the mid-1980s, struggling for their very subsistence against the alienation of their traditional land rights by the state forest department, the tribals formed the Adivasi Bhumihin Kisan Hakka Sanrakshan Samiti (Committee for the Protection of the Rights of Landless Farmers). Neither the Gandhians in their ashrams nor the Christians in their missions supported the movement, while the state government considered this as a law and order problem.

Once in power, the BJP focussed on the issue of religious conversions to wrest control from the Congress in the Dangs. Spearheaded by militant organisations of the Sangh Parivar, attacks on Christians began in 1997, carried on though 1998, peaking in 1999. Charge and counter-charge were trade in this melee of conversion and reconversion.

Ghanshyam Shah, a well-respected Gujarati social scientist, reviewing the events in the Dangs, came to this damning conclusion: 'Instead of solving their basic issues of survival, the present agitation focusing on Christian missionaries has been fostered from the outside, diverting the prevailing tension and dividing the Dangis on religious lines which are a non-issue for the Dangis.' (Shah 1999: 118)

In the Indian context, 'tribal' or 'adivasi' still refers to a wide variety of communities, which before had remained relatively free from the control of outsiders. The colonial state subjugated and gradually brought them under its control. Some tribals had already made the transition from a social system based on segmented clan lineage to one based on hierarchical caste status.

As state formation spread, self-governing clans were integrated into the political system, often by coopting tribals leaders into a Kshatriya caste. Then, these people ceased to be tribal. This was not just a one-way abrupt process. D.D. Kosambi insists that 'THE ENTIRE COURSE OF INDIAN HISTORY SHOWS TRIBAL ELEMENTS BEING FUSED INTO A GENERAL SOCIETY', (Kosambi, 1975: 27 original all in capitals). Nevertheless, the trend was toward assimilation, not equal exchange. Yet, there remained non-hierarchical societies outside the *jati* system of sub-castes, though mostly isolated ones in more remote areas. Due to their geographic location, they served as 'bridge' or buffer communities between kingdoms, and so retained their autonomy as distinct communities, preserving their cultural identity.

The process of assimilation begins as tribal contacts with more dominant groups in the same social environment multiplied. These encounters with the non-tribals accelerated in the colonial period. Tribals were progressive integrated into a monetised political economy in ways that kept them at the bottom of the newly forming class stratification. We must be sensitive to inter-tribal diversity and recognise the complexity of tribal society in our country, for there are many tribal systems with their distinctive cultures and separate economies. We need to be aware of intra-tribal differentiation as well, since but for a few isolated and small communities, no tribe in India today subsists on a single mode of production.

The Scheduled Tribes are today an administrative category, constitutionally defined by presidential decree. As of 1976, there were 427 tribes in this schedule. However, it is not a completely arbitrary classification. These communities have common characteristics that justify this categorisation and legitimate constitutionally mandated affirmative action in their favour. Not all such groups have been included in the schedule. Many denotified and nomadic tribes are notable exceptions and an agitation is afoot to remedy this. In February 2006, the Government appointed a National Commission for Denotified, Nomadic and Semi-nomadic Tribes.

Since Independence, the Government of India's tribal policy was firstly articulate by the 'panchsheel' proposed by Nehru in 1959. This was to integrate the tribals into the national mainstream, keeping their distinctiveness; not to assimilate them into it, lest this be lost; nor to isolate them from it, leaving them behind. However, the development model imposed on them has been oppressively disruptive for tribal society. Those at the margins of a society are inevitably disadvantaged and exploited because of the unequal exchange between the centre and the periphery. With our tribals, this has meant both economic exploitation and cultural alienation, violating both their dignity and their identity. Assimilationists suggest overcoming the tribals' marginalised status by sacrificing their ethnic identity. The potential of a positive identity to mobilise the group is thus lost, leaving the tribals with a negative self-image and a deteriorating socio-economic status.

As we have seen in an earlier chapter, these tribals were classified by the Census as animists and later as Hindu. However, Hinduism itself is a constructed category from colonial times and refers to a wide spectrum of religious traditions. Tribal religious traditions do not fall into the mainstream sanatan dharma. They are organised into non-hierarchical clans, not hierarchical castes. This is enough to give them their own distinctive culture and identity. How 'Hindu' this is remains contested, and this contestation is especially acute where large numbers have converted to other religions, especially to various Christian denominations; or where tribal peoples have become the battleground for promoters of Hinduism and converters to Christianity.

Tribal resistance has recorded in numerous tribal revolts in colonial times and has continued with the many tribal movements against the government even today. The *Anthropological Survey of India* in 1976 identified as many as thirty-six on-going tribal movements. Still much more in continuity than discontinuity with the earlier colonial state, the post-colonial government all too often has treated tribal resistance as a law and order problem and suppressed it as ruthlessly as the colonialists before. However, as K.S. Singh, director general of the Anthropological Survey of India emphasizes; 'Behind all these movements lies the tribal's interminable search for identity and his urge to secure a better deal for himself' (Singh 1982: 1344).

The neglect of the cultural dimension, in particular in education, has further marginalised the tribals, leaving them still dependent on outsiders. Tribal self-reliance has been undermined not just by the expropriation and degradation of their material resources, but further by the negation and denigration of their cultural heritage. Various tribal movements have attempted to address these alienating processes by integrating cultural action into their struggle against social oppression and injustice. This will demand an appropriate collective pedagogy for a positive self-affirmation and an adaptive group identity. Religious conversion is very much a part of this search for such an identity, outside the earlier Hinduisation processes.

These resistance movements are a response to the ecological-cultural and economic-political marginalisation, to which our tribals have been increasing subjected. They reject assimilation as well as isolation. Overwhelmingly, their aspirations are for integration into our national society, but one that will respect their 'cultural autonomy', premised on an equal exchange. This is not an illegitimate or an unreasonable expectation in a diverse and democratic society. Because religion is so much a part of their culture, religious conversion is often an expression of their quest for autonomy.

In the rapid and radical changes sweeping through India, the tribals are clearly a vulnerable group. All too often, their identity as a tribal people is negated and their dignity as human persons violated. There is a connection between these two aspects of tribal life today: their marginalisation from the benefits of development and their relegation to the bottom of the social hierarchy. For it is the same process of change that first isolates tribals, negating their identity and denigrating their dignity, and then integrates and assimilates them with a 'forced division of labour' into a dysfunctional social system, to use this phrase in the sense Emile Durkheim did. Such coercive processes create dependencies and inequalities. After Independence, they have become more vigorous and cut deeper than ever before.

Cultural autonomy is legitimised by, and built around particular ethnic identities. Such social identities are constructed out of historical experiences and by human agencies. They are both imagined from within the community, and imputed from without. The more vulnerable a group is, the less agency it has, the greater is the imposition of an identity from without and its internalisation from within. We need to be sensitive to this social-cultural dimension involved in social interactions and not reduce them to an economic-political one.

Moreover, group identities are not static but in constant transition. Tribal communities are no exception.

Some have argued that tribal identity must inevitably be compromised, or even sacrificed for modern development. However, the loss of tribal identity will not be their loss alone; it would be a national impoverishment as well. Unfortunately, bureaucratic practice has not measured up to our high-minded national policies. To preserve the identity and dignity of these threatened people today, tribal ethnicity needs to be mobilised to overcome their minority status, so that in their integration into the national mainstream, their distinctive contribution will be appreciatively accepted, and the incisive challenge they pose honestly faced by this larger society.

However, a crucial difficulty of these people's movements, whether inspired by political ideology or cultural identity, by real interests or perceived concerns, has been to overcome group boundaries and extend them beyond caste and class, religion and community. The failure to broad-base their appeal has severely restricted their effectiveness. But then, the danger of being co-opted to another's cause is ever-present in a wider mobilisation. Religion has now become one more factor in this co-option, where the options for tribals are closing rather than opening.

The significance of religious cults, such as the ones described earlier, is critical though often missed. Usually, the tribals themselves, founded on a self-assertion that begins with a religious concern, lead such movements. They draw on their own religious tradition, and then go on to embrace a new secular political consciousness. To ignore such religiosity among our tribals, is to miss this hidden potential. However, the mass attraction of popular religion and its pertinacity among a folk people is always highly ambiguous; for it can be an effective motivator and mobiliser for real freedom and human fulfilment, as also horrible repression and dangerous superstition. Tribal brutalities against 'witches', usually helpless women, illustrates this.

However, outsiders, who may or may not have any genuine concern for tribal identity and culture, can also lead religious movements. Religious revivalists and fundamentalists have been quick to use religious-cultural appeals for their political agenda to co-opt people for their cause, even as the secular liberals and rationalists have ignored the potential for political liberation and economic justice embedded in such religious-cultural movements. Since the 1980s, the prominence of the Hindutva ideology, expressed as 'cultural nationalism', and its confrontation with evangelical churches in the country has strained the situation to the breaking-point, threatening innocent people in civil society. The Staines murders are a ghastly testimony to this politics of hate.

Whether it is assimilation, which tribals have resisted, or integration, which is not unproblematic, the reference point has been Hindu caste society. However, tribal anthropologists, such as Virginus Xaxa, discussing the *Transformation of Tribes in India* argue that tribes are 'communities' outside the caste system. Andre Beteille would place them more or less outside Hindu civilisation as well (Xaxa 1999: 1520). Caste hierarchy, so endemic to Hindu society, is not part of the internal social orgainisation of tribes. This puts a question mark over the real significance of the process of tribal Sanskritisaion and Hinduisation. Will this bring an alien hierarchy to the tribal clan structure?

The evolutionary change in tribal society is better understood in ecological terms as a transition from hunting-gathering, to shifting agriculture, to settled agriculture. This transformation of tribal to peasant leaves the question of tribal culture open to other points of reference, not merely how resilient it has remained and how Hinduised it has become. Once again, religion will play a key role in this changing tribal identity, and conversion to another religion, whether by social assimilation or decisive option, even if this is called re-conversion to their old one, becomes a sensitive and explosive issue. This is especially so when inter-religious relations are strained and intra-community tensions run high. Outsiders of whatever hue inevitably compound the situation further.

Tribal insurrection against exploitation and oppression is not a return to the past even when it is articulated in traditional terms. It is much more a demand for a reversal of unequal exchange relationships, for an equitable social inclusion and a respectful cultural autonomy. Tribal religious conversions must be placed in this context: their aspiration for change, for a future without an alienation from their past. This is something deeply human and characteristic of peoples in transition and under threat, as tribals in our country have long been and still are.

Christian Ambiguity

Rishikesh, which literally means the home of the seers, is a holy place of Hindu pilgrimage in the foothills of the Himalayas.

Sometime after Vatican II (1962-65), a number of Catholic bishops went for a retreat to the Divine Life Ashram, when Swami Chidananda was the Acharya. Inspired by the spirit of the Council, the bishops wanted an experience of inter-religious dialogue, and this was an early exposure. They asked Chidanandaji to speak to them and he said just this and left them: brothers, I have only one question to ask you. Are you as willing to be converts to us as you expect us to be willing to be converts to you? Whereupon there was a silence, and then confusion? What happened to the rest of the retreat is not our concern here, but clearly, the bishops were not quite ready for, and simply did not know how to face that question. It was one; they had not thought to ask themselves.

To answer positively would mean opening the possibility of conversion to another religion in good faith. This seems to imply conceding the incompleteness of one's own faith, and suggesting the superiority of the other's. Yet, to expect others to be open and to refuse to be open oneself negates the basis of an equal exchange. Conversion in this context would mean converters and proselytisers demanding of would-be converts and neophytes an openness they do not accept for themselves.

Respectful reciprocity is what the Swami was asking of the bishops. It was an awkward question, but a necessary one, not to be coveniently put away. His query touches delicate dilemmas especially, though not exclusively among Christians.

The three interrelated dilemmas elaborated here are pertinent to a religious pluralism and have a wider relevance beyond just the Christian tradition: religious truth as inclusive or exclusive in various religious traditions, religious believers as equal or unequal across and within their communities; a specific religious culture as relative or necessary to a particular religious tradition. The way one dilemma is resolved will affect the way the others are addressed. Thus inclusive religious truth, community equality and cultural relativity have an affinity that brings them together, just as exclusive religious truth, community inequality and cultural dominance do.

These dilemmas may well be rooted in the religious belief system itself but they inevitably precipitate ambiguities at the other levels of social interaction, especially with regard to conversion across religious communities and sects. Such ambiguities are inherent in any broad-based, multi-faceted religious tradition. The Christian response is a good illustration of this. The Orthodox Churches are far less affected by these dilemmas. They are mostly ethnic churches where a religion is identified with a community that makes little effort to extend this beyond itself. Here our focus is on the mainstream Protestant and Catholic responses to these dilemmas, not the fringe groups preaching 'hellfire and brimstone' to others. These have few ambiguities and fewer dilemmas.

Religions based on a creedal core of revelation, as contained in sacred texts, entrusted to a community and handed down over generations, claim privileged access to this truth. This sets them apart from the unbelievers. Depending on how exclusive the commitment to this truth is, the believers may consider openness to changing their faith to be a closed option, because of faith-commitments already made. Abandoning them for another religion is denigrated as 'apostasy'. It is not accepted as a genuine conversion.

Truth by its very nature must be inclusive of other truths. Only untruths must be excluded. However, openness to a new truth can be disturbing and threatening to older truth-commitments. Integrating both into a more inclusive faith-vision requires a far greater courage and a deeper commitment than staying with the old and familiar. Dismissing the new and unfamiliar as 'untruths' is far easier and simpler. Yet the human grasp of truth is always partial. Once this closes in on itself, it remains partial and impoverished, truncated and inadequate, a half-truth that is often worse than a lie. Opening it out to other truths, however partial, can only enhance and enrich it.

I am arguing against a religious dogmatism of 'no salvation outside my church'. This does not help openness to other communities. I am not urging an uncritical openness that amounts to an individualistic permissiveness of 'you have your truth and I have mine and never the twain shall meet'. This negates the basis of community. Nor am I suggesting a collective relativism of all truths being equal because all truths are partial. This undermines commitment to any truth. We need to search together for the point of convergence beyond our present horizon and to be enriched by each other on the pilgrimage there.

John Henry Newman is one such exemplary pilgrim. His seminal insight in his *Essay in Aid of a Grammar of Assent* explains how deep conviction can breed tolerance because it can afford to be accommodative to other views without the 'intellectual anxiety' of compromising its own core commitments. (Newman 1979: 167) Gandhi would agree: 'Intolerance betrays want of faith in one's own cause.' (*Young India* 2 Feb 1921)

When a religious tradition proclaims the essential equality of all humans before its deity, and then privileges an 'elected' few as 'a chosen race', 'a people set apart', a royal priesthood', it sets up a contradiction that poses the question of religious equality very starkly. Even to say that the privilege is to serve begs the question, for it, remains a privilege of the elite. Equality across this divide remains a dilemma for an egalitarian faith. Does this God love some more than others? If he does then he is partial, if he does not how he can privilege a few.

Such religious disparities in one area are likely to affect other non-religious areas of social interaction as well, often through prejudice and stereotyping: they have not been chosen like us. This happens even with neophytes, who are still culturally stereotyped, and in religious communities where caste and race prejudice still prevail. The aggression and intolerance of missionaries, proselytising non-believing 'savages' and 'pagans' and then treating the converts as lesser Christians, is evidence enough of religious beliefs bolstering social discrimination and cultural insensitivity.

These dilemmas of inequality are a challenge to any egalitarian faith tradition, and they are all the more prevalent, especially when a colonising power privileges its own religion over those of the colonised peoples. This was the social context of colonial Christianity where such anomalies were endemic. This burden of the past weighs heavily on Christians today. Religious equality, tolerance, and equal respect for religions, in our present situation of religious pluralism, acquire a new urgency. For this, the resources within these traditions must be mined even as religious harmony and social consensus must be facilitated from without.

The relationship between religion and culture is complex but easily misunderstood, often hijacked by conservatives, while discounted by progressives. Perhaps we can best illustrate this with language. Communicating in symbolic language defines us as humans. Language is essential even to communicate with oneself. We cannot be human without language, but no human being is predetermined to use any particular language. This may result from the accident of birth or deliberate choice. Yet, the syntax of the language must be observed, or communication will be stymied. Moreover, a literary tradition creates its own special heritage for a language that must be respected. This makes translation across languages difficult, but it does not make communication across them impossible. Translation can even bring out hidden nuances that might otherwise be lost.

So too, a religious tradition must be socially expressed in a culture. How this happens is often more a matter of historical accident rather than theological necessity. The first cultural expression of a religious faith may well be a privileged one, but it does not have to be the only one. It can, and needs to be further enriched by, other expressions in other cultures. As with language, a cultural tradition becomes the repository of a religious heritage, since the two are so closely related.

However, when this heritage makes the transition to another culture it will demand a credible and relevant translation into this new one, otherwise it will merely be ventriloquising the old. All universal religious traditions that travel across different cultures are thus challenged to contextualise themselves, in other words to inculturate, to reincarnate themselves in these new cultures. The dilemma is to express the old universal in a new specific.

In general, dominant groups in a society are not particularly sensitive or appreciative of subordinate cultures. They tend to treat them with patronising tokenism. Religious traditions of dominant groups are not notable exceptions to this, especially when 'lesser breeds without the Law', to use Rudyard Kipling has much quoted phrase, accept the religion of their masters, who still carry their 'white man's burden'. Colonial Christianity is a good illustration of this, but not the only one. Thus, pre-Islamic cultures tended to get 'Arabised' across the Muslim world, as indigenous ones in India get Brahminised, or Sanskritised.

There are always fringe groups in any large mainstream religious tradition that are not representative. Focusing on them would give a distorted overall picture. Being less centralised, Protestant sects cover a wide spectrum with some denominations outside the mainstream as represented by the World Council of Churches (WCC), either because they are too fundamentalist or too liberal. Yet within this mainstream, there are conservatives and progressives.

There are evangelical fundamentalists who use modern management techniques to estimate the cost-effectiveness of their strategies and make perspective plans estimating their budgets in terms of unit expenditure per baptism, dollars per soul. There are liberals too, for whom change of religious allegiance is not an issue because religious allegiance is itself a non-issue.

At the conference of Protestant missionaries in Tambaram, Tamil Nadu, in 1938, some Indian theologians broke ranks with the more traditional approaches, and formed the 'Rethinking Group'. They rejected the accepted standpoint of the discontinuity of Christianity with other religions. Pandipeddi Chenchiah regretted that the institutional Church has 'acquired as it were the same status as the original nucleuses' of the Gospel (Chenchiah 1939: 620). Conversion need not involve affiliation with any church, rather it would be a movement leading, not outside the Hindu fold but to an 'infusion of Hinduism by Christian ideals' (ibid. 50).

The debate on spiritualising conversion continuing through the 1940s and was taking up more in earnest after Independence. In 1966, Kaj Baago was a church historian in Bangalore. Questioned the legitimacy of conversions in post-colonial India, and called for abandoning them: 'The missionary task today cannot, therefore, be to draw men out of their religions into another religion, but rather to leave Christianity (the organised religion) and go inside Hinduism and Buddhism, accepting these religions as one's own, in so far as they do not conflict with Christ, and regarding them as the presupposition, the background and framework of the Christian gospel in Asia. Such a mission ... might lead to the creation of Hindu Christianity...' (Baago, 1966: 131-132).

There are others who, like Leslie Newbigin, bishop of the Church of South India in Chennai, contest this marginalising of the Church and insist on a visible community as a necessary expression of Christian commitment. For Newbigin conversion is a 'radical discontinuity' (Newbigin 1966: 312). It cannot be expressed in 'a purely mental relationship' that 'involves no visible solidarity with those who share that relationship' (ibid: 320).

However, M.M. Thomas, director of the Christian Institute for the Study of Religion and Society, Bangalore, who went on to become a leading figure at the WCC, rejects any separation of Christian salvation from secular humanisation. Instead, he proposes for Christians a 'Christ-centered secular fellowship of faith within the society, culture and religion in which they live, transforming their structures and values from within' (Thomas 1972: 73). Thomas thus rejects the idea of conversion and even the idea of a Hindu Christianity in favour of a secularisation of both.

In the context of conversions, this debate implies a distinction between accepting a personal fellowship with Christ and joining the collective membership of a Christian community. For some, such a personal commitment must be publicly confessed, and so this fellowship with Christ must be express in a community of faith, an assembly, which is actually what the word 'church', *ecclesia*, means. Others see no need for such an institutionalisation of commitment in a faith-community; the human community itself is enough to live this fellowship of faith and solidarity in the struggle for human liberation.

In a communitarian society like ours, constituted as it is of bounded communities rather than autonomous individuals, how relevant or viable such individualised faith-commitments in any religious tradition would be is still a moot point. The proliferation of religious movements and temple worship, of ashrams and gurus, even the explosion of popular religiosity in public life is an indicator of how powerful the social dimension of religious commitment is in our society. A privatised personal individualism, religious or otherwise, is not rooted in the consciousness of our people.

The spectrum we have sketched here stretches from a closed exclusive understanding of Christianity as discontinuous with other religious traditions to a more open, inclusive one, in harmony and solidarity with others. Inclusiveness, allows, for a greater willingness to contextualise the older tradition in a composite culture, say a Hindu-Christian one, and a greater readiness for secular fellowship in equality, like a civic association. Exclusiveness makes for resistance to both. The ambiguities in Protestant Christianity in confronting the dilemmas mentioned earlier, of truth, equality and culture, arise because both these tendencies are included within the same tradition.

The Catholic Church has a far more centralised tradition than the Protestant or the Orthodox ones, and though there is a plurality of perspectives, the range of differences is correspondingly smaller. Even its missionary ventures are more closely supervised, especially religious teaching and practice concerning neophytes. Sometimes, decisions from afar have had disastrous effects, as seen earlier with the suppression of the Malabar and Chinese rites in the early 18th century.

An extremely restricted understanding of 'no salvation outside the church' often motivated the colonial missionary effort. This did inspire many missionaries in good faith, both Catholic and Protestant, though the theological basis for such doctrine was always very dubious. To hold that people of goodwill through no fault of theirs would be condemned, if not baptised into the Church, is no longer tenable, if indeed, it ever was. Such an unqualified belief has now been condemned as heretical in the Catholic Church. At the time, however, such beliefs helped the colonial powers to mobilise missionary efforts, just as today it suits hostile adversaries to keep quoting it.

In the popular mind, there is still some ambiguity about the question of salvation outside the church. The early church had taught the 'baptism of desire', that extended the boundaries beyond the formal institutions to all persons of goodwill. With the expansion of the church over the Roman world, the question seemed to have lost its urgency. However, with the Muslim threat to medieval Europe, it became pertinent again, more so with the colonial expansion into new worlds, an aggressive and ethnocentric interpretation to the question gained prominence.

Such a narrowly exclusive understanding was hardly credible in the post-colonial world, and once again interpretations that are more inclusive were revived. Prominent among the more recent explanations was the one by Karl Rahner, a seminal theologian, who later greatly influenced the Second Vatican Council (1962-65). In 1961, Rahner lectured on Christianity and the non-Christian religions arguing that the universality of God's grace made salvation for all 'present as a hidden reality even outside the Church,' as a 'Christianity of an anonymous kind' (Rahner 1966: 133).

These 'anonymous Christians', were non-Christians, who were Christian without knowing it. However, others then too could speak of anonymous Buddhists as all those who seek enlightenment, and anonymous Muslims as all those who submit to God. This seemed an improved version of J.N. Farquhar's 'fulfilment theory' in 1913, where Christianity is *The Crown of Hinduism*, completing Hinduism without Hindus wanting it. In both these, salvation is still from Christianity.

Raymond Panikkar's '*Unknown Christ of Hinduism*', is a more positive affirmation of a non-Christian religion as a way of salvation. The Christian mission is to unveil this 'unknown Christ' hidden in Hinduism, who will then be the meeting point for the two. Here conversion: 'does not mean, speaking from a Christian point of view, a changing 'over' to another culture, another tradition or even 'another' religion, but a changing 'in', a changing into a new life, a new existence, a new creation, which is precisely the old one – and not another – but transformed, lifted up, risen again' (Panikkar 1964: 18).

However, the point of reference here again is still Christ. Mutuality would require that the 'unknown Hinduism of Christianity', or the hidden Vedanta of Christianity, as M.M. Thomas phrased it,

(Thomas 1976: 61) be accepted by Christians too, but this has not yet been seriously proposed, and to start with, there is surely an enormous ambiguity about it.

In the last century, there were some mystical approaches to religious conversion. This is exemplified by two Benedictine monks: Fr Jules Monchanin (1895-1957), later Swami Param Arubi Anandam, and Dom Henri Le Saux, later Swami Abhishiktananda (1910-1973), who found the experience of the Ultimate in both Hindu and Christian mystical traditions. Earlier Sufis and *bhaktas* did, and still do find such a mystical encounter in the Islamic and Hindu ones. For the truth of mysticism transcends allegiance to a local community or articulation in a specific culture.

The Second Vatican Council marks a watershed in the life of the Catholic Church. *Dignitatis Humanae*, its 'Declaration on Religious Freedom', affirms the right to religious freedom, founded on the dignity of the human person as rational and free. (No. 2) *Nostra Aetate*, its Declaration of the Relationship of the Church to Non-Christian Religions gives primary consideration 'to what human beings have in common and what promotes fellowship among them' (No. 1). Freedom of conscience is recognised as the cornerstone of human liberty and must be granted to all. Other religious traditions are recognised as salvific, but the parity of all religions is not addressed.

Inculturation is another area of ambiguity. The idea of 'incarnating' Christianity in a local culture goes back to Matteo Ricci and Robert de Nobili in the 17th century, but the Congregation for the Propagation of the Faith in Rome repressed it at the beginning of the 18th. Post-colonial Christianity has seen a strong revival of this, which has further strengthened and flowered after Vatican II encouraged inter-religious dialogue. However, as with the bishops at Rishikesh, Christians have still to come to terms with the challenge of an equal dialogue.

Criticism of Christian inculturation, or what Protestants call contextualisation has come from Hindu revivalists and nationalists on the political Right as well. They see this as a subversive attempt to convert Hindus by entering their citadel with the Trojan horse of inculturation and dialogue. The Marxist Left too has been suspicious of the church's option for the poor as a kind of religious subterfuge of 'false consciousnesses'. Christian ambiguity has not been very reassuring either.

However, inculturation has also been criticised within the church by liberation theology for its preoccupation with high culture and its neglect of issues regarding poverty and injustice. The argument here is that the inculturation of the faith must be into a 'culture of liberation', such as subordinate people aspire to, not into a 'culture of oppression' such as dominant groups are prone to. Liberation theology tends to see conversion too exclusively in economic-political terms and they have been criticised as being too secular and politicised, by those who do not want the religious and spiritual dimension of the church's mission compromised. These two dimensions, the religious and the secular, can indeed be integrated but they often remain distinct, and the resulting tensions are left unresolved.

The Catholic transition we have outlined above represents a movement from a rather defensive exclusiveness to a more welcoming inclusiveness in the Catholic understanding of religious truth and its bearing on salvation. This has once again reinforced the opening to other cultures, and reaffirmed the Church's commitment to social equality, especially with liberation theology and its preferential option for the poor. The institutional Church is not without its inherent ambiguities that remain unresolved and in tension, not just in popular Catholic religious understanding, but often even in the official stances taken.

Not all dilemmas must be conclusively or immediately resolved. Some must be lived in a creative tension, which may eventually lead to a deeper realisation and a more inclusive truth. Mystics have often indicated the 'coincidence of opposites' that cannot be comprehended rationally, much less articulated verbally, but only be experienced existentially. Nevertheless, dilemmas demand some response and this leaves scope for ambiguities.

I have attempted to outline the most pertinent dilemmas that impinge on the relationship of Christianity to other religions in a pluri-religious society, and on the implications this has for religious conversions. From Christian responses as indicated here, there is evidence of a certain pluralism within these traditions. Protestantism covers a broader spectrum as it is less centrally coordinated and controlled, but neither is Catholicism a monolithic belief system completely under a centralised Roman authority, as it is sometimes parodied.

Christianity is a creedal faith and to be faithful to its confession, some doctrines are defining as necessary to be held in order to belong.

However, these 'dogmas' are mostly articulated against heresies to be rejected. They are road signs along the way to the development of doctrine. There is stillroom for a creative fidelity that can interpret past tradition to be relevant to present realities, bringing newness to the old along the way. Indeed, Christians would be unfaithful to their founding inspiration if they did not read the 'signs of the times', as Jesus himself has urged his followers to do (Matthew 16: 3) and the Vatican Council recently reiterated.

Fundamentalists brook no change from what they define as authentic doctrine and practice. They forget that a tradition must change to stay alive. To remain static means inevitable death. Liberals seem to be too open to any change, with little regard to whether or not this new belief, or lack of it, puts them beyond the fold. Yet, even within the mainstream of a tradition, there are conservatives and progressives leaning to opposite, if not opposed sides. In discerning a path in-between, not necessarily the middle path but an authentic one, we can get overwhelmed and lost as ambiguities crowd in and dilemmas remain unresolved.

At Rishikesh, the bishops seem caught within the constraints of a dogmatic tradition as they are challenged to an equal dialogue. This raises critical questions. How inclusive is their religious truth? How egalitarian their commitment to others? How receptive their faith to another culture? Ambiguity rather than a 'creative fidelity' in response to such questions easily turns conversion, not into a respectful option, but into an aggressive encounter. This is what has been called 'proselytising' or conversion by unfair means, where the preoccupation is with winning numbers not with enhancing people's religious faith. Christians must find unambiguous ways of convincingly shunning this.

Coming as he does from a non-dogmatic tradition, Swami Chidanandaji's stance is distinct from that of the bishops as he poses his question. He seems to be inviting an equal exchange. Here the challenge moves to another level. Openness to the truth of the other demands an interrogation of one's own beliefs, not just tolerance of the other. Commitment to equality with others must be expressed not just in coexistence, but also in service to and struggle for the disadvantaged and the vulnerable. Cultural receptivity must make for diversity in unity, not an integration, where individualities are sub-summed and lost. If such challenges are not constructively met, encountering others can easily become appropriating and absorbing them into one's own community, where the old social inequalities and cultural dominance still prevail. This is another kind of conversion perhaps by less aggressive means.

In all religious traditions, their core beliefs will affect their openness in varying degrees, from a positive inclusive orientation to other faiths and different truths, to a negative exclusive emphasis on their own. Doctrinal faiths based on historical revelation may be more prone to exclusion; non-doctrinal traditions premised on a spiritual inspiration may be more inclined to inclusion. However, any religious tradition committed to its own beliefs and values, whether based on revelation or reason, must have some principle of internal critique. Otherwise, its beliefs and values will not be open to being interrogated from within. Moreover, in a pluralist religious society some principle of external critique, acceptable and applicable to other traditions and cultures, is as necessary, if the encounter between religions traditions is to be mutually enriching and not divisively acrimonious.

In exploring the relationship of *Christianity and World Religions*, the renowned theologian Hans Kung has 'sought to provide two things:

'1. Christian self-criticism in the light of other religions,
2. Christian criticism of the other religions in the light of the Gospel, (Kung, xvii; 1985)

Both these critiques are necessary to cope with ambiguities of the Christian response to the dilemmas they face. Too little attention has been given to a self-criticism, as the foundation for a critique of others, to bring out the ambiguities of one's own response. This is a first step and necessary for the second. Too much attention has been devoted to a critique of the others from various perspectives, bringing out the differences and focusing on the inherent dilemmas involved. This is a second step and must follow the first. For a critique of oneself must be a prior requirement for a criticism of the other.

The dilemmas of truth, equality and culture are not the only ones that confront Christians today. Neither are these peculiar to them alone. Ambiguity still characterises the Christian response. The Hindu answer to these is tolerance. However, this is something we can no longer take for granted as a reality on the ground. It must be critically examined, if only to save it from further erosion.

Hindu tolerance

On the morning of the 26 February 2002, coach S-6 of the Sabarmati Express was burning near Godhra station in Gujarat, following an altercation between local Muslims vendors and some Hindu *kar sevaks*, volunteer workers, returning from Ayodhya. What was first reports as an accident that evening on the national TV news, was later constructed by the Gujarat chief minister as a Pakistani conspiracy. The pogrom against Muslims that followed throughout the state is only the most recent in a continuing series of communal clashes in the sub-continent.

Why was there such unprecedented violence against the Muslims of Gujarat? Of all the Indian Muslim communities in the country, Gujarati Muslims are the most integrated into the mainstream. They are largely a business community there, not a once ruling or military elite, as the Muslims in north India. Gujarati Hindus too have often perceived as a non-militaristic business community, sometimes even denigrated as weak and effeminate. Their history has not produced a martial race, as classified by the colonial masters, or any great military rulers such as Rana Pratap (1540-1597) in Rajasthan to its north, or Chhatrapati Shivaji (1530-1580) in Maharashtra to the south.

Pogroms are generally against those, who are perceived to be different and resist any assimilation. There was hardly a strong case for this with Gujarati, as compared with other Muslims communities. Yet, after Independence, communal violence has become endemic in Gujarat. The socio-cultural differences between Hindus and Muslims there have been carefully reconstructed. The 'othering' of Muslims as 'Pakistani traitors' is now being counterpoised to a so-called Gujarati *asmita*, or identity, only to exaggerate and then take political advantage of the resulting divide. Now there seems to be an impenetrable barrier that helps only the fundamentalists on both sides.

Yet, even in the aftermath of the wave of such shocking violence in the state, the party which spearheaded the hate campaign and precipitated the slaughter was voted back to power, supposedly to protect long-suffering, tolerant Hindus from a conspiracy of aggressive, fanatic Muslims. However, the body count at the end of the carnage tells a completely different story. Invariably, more Muslims than Hindus are killed in such communal riots. Asghar Ali Engineer's *Comprehensive Account* of *Communal Riots After Independence* convincingly establishes this pattern (Engineer 2004).

This cultivated sense of collective hurt is nurtured on historical memories nursed from the raids of Mahmud of Ghaznavi (979-1030) and the many Muslims invasions thereafter. His sacking of the famous Somnath temple in 1024, on the coast of Kathiawar in Gujarat, is the centrepiece in this reading of history. Romila Thapar has demonstrated how complicated and controversial this actually was. (Thapar 2004) She uses Turko-Persian and Sanskrit sources on Somnath to establish through '*The Many Voices of a History*', how it was really the colonialist construction, which projects a Hindu versus Muslim divide in order to legitimise their rule by denigrating the Muslim rulers whom they replaced.

This 'divide and rule' policy was largely, but not solely responsible for the communal antagonisms that inflame the desire for redress, even vengeance, and which finally culminated in the collective frenzy of the Partition massacres in 1947. Communal carnage still shows little signs of abating. Gujarat suffered less than the Punjab or Bengal at the Partition. Yet, the first major communal riot in independent India was in 1969 in Ahmedabad, and now the state has become the vanguard of extremist Hindutva ideology.

It is not just against Muslims that such violence has erupted. After her Sikh bodyguards assassinated Indira Gandhi, the 1984 pogrom against the Sikhs in Delhi and other cities saw them mercilessly hunted down and massacred. Moreover, violence is certainly not the monopoly of any single community in South Asia. Whether, it is the ethnic cleansing in Assam. As the Nellie massacre in 1983, the insurgent tribals is in the northeast, separatists in Kashmir, Shia-Sunni violence in Uttar Pradesh and Pakistan, Bangladeshi suppression of the Chakma tribals in Chittagong, caste wars in Bihar, Shiv Sena machismo in Maharashtra, the Naxalite movement in Andhra and elsewhere, the Tamils and the Sinhala in Sri Lanka ... and the continuing atrocities against outcastes and women everywhere. The list is endless.

In such a sea of violence, what can Hindu tolerance mean? Hindu nationalists and fundamentalists perpetrate violence in the name of the majority community. Gujarat was considered a laboratory for this, after which the experiment was to extend to the rest of the country. Where does this leave mainstream Hinduism on the question of tolerance? Gujarat has become the most acutely defined contexts, in which this question is now raised in 2002, as perhaps it was with Delhi in 1984, or Nellie in 1983, or Punjab and Bengal in 1947, or... 1024 in Somnath. The question will not go away and we need to look beyond, or rather behind the events, to make some sense of them.

If intolerance and violence has not been an ethnic or religious monopoly in this South Asia, neither has tolerance and non-violence been the prerogative of any single tradition. We have the long-established traditions of Jain non-violence and Buddhist compassion.

Upanishadic's universalism, Sufi-*bhakti* mysticism and Christian charity ... These have been significant landmarks that can still inspire and challenge us today.

We have seen how, in the Mauryan period, the farsighted Buddhist Emperor Ashoka, his 12th major rock edict, issued the first recorded edict for tolerance. In medieval times, Emperor Akbar conceived of a state premised on religious tolerance. In the last century Gandhi's ahimsa, non-violence, was closest to the Jain inspiration, even though he himself claimed to belong to the *sanatan dharma*. Today, we seem to have abandoned Gandhi as our society is increasing mired in violence of all kinds and at all levels. We can hardly claim to be a non-violent society or even a tolerant one anymore.

Historically, in the Hindu tradition, the intellectual acceptance of pluralism and tolerance has been all too often in contradiction to the existential practice of exclusion and hierarchy. The suppression of Jainism in the south was perhaps more violent than the absorption of Buddhism elsewhere. The feudal battles between princes and the wars of Hindu and Muslim monarchs, colonial aggression, and the climax in the orgy of the Partition massacres are all evidence of a violent history in the sub-continent.

Sanjay Subrahmanyam, reflecting on the *Sectarian Violence and the State in Pre-colonial India*, soberly concludes: 'that medieval and late pre-colonial Indian society was violent, and the text and ideological statements produced in the epoch are often suffused with this violence. ... Nevertheless, there was relatively little harnessing of devices of collective memory or the recollection of 'historical grievances' to orchestrate mass violence.' (Subrahmanyam 1996: 58) This last is a more recent phenomenon. Fuelled by electoral politics, it threatens to spiral out of control. Nevertheless, it is not likely to be abandoned as long as it yields political returns.

Indeed, we seem to have reached a flashpoint in our continuing crisis, when even the acceptance of religious-cultural pluralism is contested by an aggressive 'cultural nationalism', which is really the intolerant imposition of the dominant castes, threatening the existence of other minorities. G. Balachandra concludes even more sombrely: 'Perhaps the most ominous social and political development in India in recent times is the rapid growth of aggressive Hindu chauvinism' (Balachandra 1996: 125).

Where can we situate Hindu tolerance in this trajectory of our history up to this point? As a non-creedal, non-dogmatic religious tradition, Hinduism has a remarkable basis for tolerance, but then orthodox social practice contradicts it. This is the central paradox of Hindu tolerance. It can be traced back into the four basic beliefs, identified by Bhikhu Parekh as grounding and overdetermining it: firstly, the primacy of conduct', of living rightly over believing correctly; secondlyl living according to dharma, as morally binding duties, some of which are common to all, *sadharan* dharma, and some specific to one's caste, *varnashrama* dharma; thirdly, uniquely individual karma, responsibility for one's action that carries over from past births to future ones; fourthly, religious pluralism, since 'different religions represent different and inherently partial visions of ultimate reality and contain both truth and error' (Parekh 2003: 48-49).

However, Parekh rightly shows how this theoretical grounding also 'overdetermines' Hindu tolerance. The importance given to ethical conduct and the moral duty of *sadharan* dharma, opens to a tolerance extended to all, but the same emphasis on *varnashrama* dharma leads to ostracising non-conformists. The only choice for individuals contesting their caste-imposed dharma is to move outside the system through *sanyas*, renunciation, and for groups the chance to better their castes status was through Sanskritisation. So we have the paradox of extensive freedom in religious beliefs and intensive conformity to social norms.

Moreover, once caste hierarchy excises the value of equality from the ideal of tolerance, religious pluralism itself becomes problematic. Not all dharmas are equal in the caste system. Lawmaker Manu is quite explicit and emphatic about this. *Adhikari-bheda*, (Ludden 1989: 277) hierarchically differential rights and duties, is patronising when perceived from the top and repressive when experienced from below.

Thus Sarvepalli Radhakrishnan, who so eloquently describes tolerance as 'the homage the finite mind pays to the inexhaustibility of the infinite' (Radhakrishnan 1939: 317) can also speak of caste as the democratic solution to group conflict: 'In dealing with the problem of the conflict of racial groups, Hinduism adopted the only safe course of democracy, viz, that each racial group should be allowed to develop the best in it without impeding the progress of others ...' (Radhakrishnan 1927: 97) Hence, 'Caste on its racial side becomes the affirmation of the infinite diversity of human groups.' On the individual side, it is 'a question of character' (ibid. 121).

Thus, the egalitarian possibilities in the Hindu theory of tolerance are overwritten by the hierarchical realities of caste. This affects not just religious plurality within the Hindu tradition, as we have just seen, but also the diversity of other traditions. For once differences are hierarchically systematised within, the temptation is to do the same without. Outsiders are 'encapsulated', contained within a social space, and given their niche in the system, the more empowered ones towards the top, the less Sanskritised ones towards the bottom. This has happened with most religious traditions and sects in their encounter with the bewildering complexity of Hindu traditions.

Yet, in its inclusivist theology, Hinduism has rich possibilities of reaching out to all, though once again such universalism can become 'overdetermined'. For when an overarching universalism integrates the specific diversities of other groups, it ends up absorbing unique identities as it assimilates distinctive differences. In this scenario, such inclusivism actually works against pluralism, though less aggressively, as may happen with exclusive religious traditions.

In either case, condescension is easily mistaken for tolerance, when it really means a patronising coexistence. If tolerance is not to be condescending, then it cannot be merely a matter of accepting diversities and integrating them, it must equally be one of allowing differences and respecting them. For it is not so much the similarities among people that makes them equal but mutual respect that enriches them, even when they hold different truths. Privileging one's own tradition and projecting it over others, even if this will be for its inclusive universalism, amounts to 'better salvation inside my church', which is a modified version of 'no salvation outside the church'.

Romanticising our own traditions and isolating ourselves in them is an inadequate and defensive response. Rather we need to creatively interrogate and constructively criticise them. There are positive possibilities in the paradoxes of our traditions that we must recover and draw on, for a more proactive understanding of tolerance, not just a passive coexistence of separate and bounded communities, if this were possible any more in our world today.

Certainly, there is a firm foundation for diversity and tolerance in Indian history and tradition that must be mined: the Jain concept of *anekantavada* (the many-sidedness of truth) and *syadvada* (the interrelatedness of all things); the Buddhist outreach in *sarvabhutadaya*, (universal compassion); the *atavistic* relativising of *mayavada* and *avidya*; the ancient ideal of *vasudhaiva kutumbakam*, (the universal family); the religious pluralism of Sufi-*bhakti* traditions, the heritage of our fakirs and *sant-kavis* (saints and poets) ... All this and more provides a basis for the legitimacy of religious diversity as a foundational truth. Once this is conceded, tolerance and non-violence become necessary consequences. This allows for more than just passive coexistence in mutual isolation; it can be reading as a call to dialogue and reciprocal enrichment, which can then become the point of departure for a committed response.

Nevertheless, much violence and intolerance is written into our wounded history and still survives in our collective memories, seeking redress and even revenge. In fact, tolerance as the distinctive feature of Hinduism is a 19th century reconstruction of the Hindu renaissance that began in Bengal, and had its own inherent ambiguities, towards the old and the new, the Indian and the western. Rather than resolving the paradoxes of Hinduism, it left them more sharply focused.

The most prominent architect of this renewal and reform, the most creative and innovative re-interpreter of Hinduism was Gandhi. His epic struggle for *purna swaraj* complete self-rule, was not just for political independence; it was a struggle for the very soul of India and not just Hinduism, a struggle that included the quest for *moksha*, liberation, not just for himself but for all.

Gandhi used the positive resources in the Hindu tradition to popularise his understanding of pluralism and tolerance that included more than just the religious. Moreover, he credited all religions with similar resources and the same fundamental values. Hence, Gandhi's relevance for any discourse on tolerance is seminal, whether in this country or abroad.

For Gandhi the unity of humankind was premises on the *advaitin* oneness of the cosmos. Unity in diversity was the integrating axis not just of Hindu, but of Indian culture. An enriched diversity would contribute to an invigorated pluralism and an enhanced unity. In Gandhi's understanding of Indian culture and civilisation, this was its strength and the reason for its survival.

Gandhi's understanding of the dharma he promoted was fundamentally grounded in his understanding of ahimsa and satya, and inseparable from either. Hence, rejecting the elite-mass dichotomy that privileged high culture and esoteric religion, he harnessed the old religious symbolism to electrifying effect, releasing people's energies and generating fearlessness among the masses. He realized that underpinning popular religiosity was an attachment to the moral order, to dharma over *adharma*, and that only the non-violent and fearless can be truly tolerant and compassionate, not the anxious and the insecure. For Gandhi, tolerance, like ahimsa, was a matter not of weakness, but of strength.

However, Gandhi's reformist Hinduism has its own inherent limitations, particularly on the issue of caste, as we have discussed earlier. Here his attempt to establish a basic social equality within the *varnashrama* dharma was doomed to be rejected by the more radical and militant movements on the right and on the left. More recently, the rediscovery of Gandhi by counter-cultural groups has called for a critical rethinking, not just an undiscerning repetition of his reformist programme (Hardiman 2003). I believe there is still is a radical relevance to his message today for our destructive and violent age.

To be sure, such a construction of tradition is already being contesting. The opposition to such pluralism is increasingly authoritarian and fascist, uninhibitedly ethnocentric and chauvinistic. This we must challenge not by denying our past, but by commenting on it; not by fleeing from the present crisis but by confronting it; not by escaping into utopia but providing for our future. Gandhi's *sarvadharma samabhava*, equal respect to all religions, is a good place to start as a contextual, relevant basis for such religious tolerance.

Nehru's understanding of tolerance, whether religious, social or political, was derived less from a reform or revival of Indian traditions, than inspired by the modernist Enlightenment. As a rationalist, Jawaharlal Nehru understood secularism in terms of the religious neutrality of the state, dharma *nirapekshata*, or indifference to religion. This 'indifference' could only mean equidistance from all religions. People's religiosity was to be respected by the secular state. However, the religious, tolerance premised on this remains somewhat alien to the masses even though it claimed constitutional legitimacy for itself.

Such statutory secular tolerance based on the European Enlightenment does not inspire mass support in this country. If it is to be liberating for the masses, it cannot be imposed as part of a dominant hegemony, as middle class rationalists are wont to urge. Grounding tolerance in middle-class sensibilities truncates it by excluding the mass of our people. This was the decisive difference between the Gandhian and the Nehruvian approach.

Unfortunately, the Gandhian discourse, which had dominated our freedom struggle was decisively upstaged by the Nehruvian one in the post-independence period. In the Indian context, its intrinsic weakness gradually led to a collapse from within. A dichotomy between the 'secular-minded elite and religiously-oriented masses' cannot be the basis for a project for tolerance, religious or otherwise. It inevitably turns out to be alien and then becomes oppressive, as some anti-secularists have argued.

This rationalist secularism of Nehru is particularly vulnerable to a religious backlash. The *Hindutvawadis* (followers of Hindutva) dismiss it as 'pseudo-secularism'. Their own 'positive-secularism' in a Hindu *rashtra* leaves little scope for religious tolerance, But then, Hinduism is a broad civilisational concept, whereas Hindutva is a narrow communal ideology.

Ashis Nandy, discussing *The Politics of Secularism and the Recovery of Religious Tolerance* argues that an aggressive secularism is not a viable facilitator for religious tolerance (Nandy 1992: 69-93). By putting religious traditions on the defensive, it makes them the more vulnerable to fundamentalism and extremism from within. For him cultural nationalism and nationalist secularism are both pathologies of civil society. He distinguishes between 'religion as ideology' and 'religion as faith'. From the second, he urges the recovery of traditional 'religious tolerance from everyday Hinduism, Islam, Buddhism, and/or Sikhism, rather than wish that ordinary Hindus, Muslims, Buddhists and Sikhs will learn tolerance from the various fashionable secular theories of statecraft (Nandy 1992: 86).

Nandy surely makes a point with his mistrust of secularism as the basis for popular religious tolerance, but neither is popular religiosity always benign nor tolerant. It has pathologies of its own. It needs to be exorcised of its demons and superstitions, freed from its prejudices and exclusions. A secularism premised on reason has the potential for such an exorcism; a secularism, which is democratic, can affirm religious freedom and tolerance against religious oppression and chauvinism. Nehru's dharma *nirapekshata* did have this potential but it was more for the westernised elite. Gandhi's *sarvadharma samabhava* has a wider, more inclusive appeal to all our peoples.

Nehru's religious neutrality is a secular tolerance that leaves religion to the private domain. At such, it intends a practical compromise: private religion, and public secularism. The aggressive secularism that often goes with a rationalist modernity progressively confines religion to more diminished spaces, expecting thereby to restrain its role in the public domain. However, religion is not so easily restricted, and the backlash can be equally aggressive, especially in a society like ours, where popular religiosity is so ingrained. Hostile religious feelings displaced from elsewhere are easily exploited as they simmer and finally burst into the public domain with destructive force. Such aggressions become pathological as religion mutates into an ideology and is no longer a matter of faith.

Gandhi's respect for all religions requires an engagement with religion that de-legitimises and defuses such hostile feelings and aggressive stances. He is realistically aware that there is always a proportion of tolerance and intolerance in all religious traditions. His approach is to face this contradiction and resolve it by tilting the balance in favour of tolerance and demanding mutual respect from all. This requires the state to be politically impartial and society to be religiously tolerant.

Hindu religious traditions have shown an amazing resilience. With no centralised organisation or authority and no continuous political patronage or power, they have survived over the centuries. The paradox of tolerance has been more accentuated when Hindus have been on the defensive. Yet, even in such circumstances, mutual respect and understanding is more reassuring and constructive than mutual recrimination and hostility. Gandhian tolerance is again crucially significant here because it reaches out in confidence and trust, not fear and insecurity. This is the challenge to Hindu tolerance today and to other religious traditions no less. Gandhi is our best guide in the struggle that may have only just begun.

In the secular modern world today, religions face the same critical threat. This puts all of them more or less on the defensive. For modernity with its rationality and instrumentality, its materialism and consumerism, represents a counter-point to traditional religion, to its spiritual values and theological beliefs. If people are unable or unwilling to cope with this threat, if they are isolated and left to their own resources, the 'discontents of modernity' are displaced onto others, and religious differences provide readily available scapegoats, though these may well be similarly placed in the same struggle. Gandhi would have us reach out to the others in mutual respect and solidarity to face the threat together, and not fight each other to fratricidal extinction.

A defensive internalising of an external threat often turns religious traditions in on themselves and makes them vulnerable to extremists and fundamentalists reinterpretations, even as they draw on its traditional resources in a desperate effort to cope with an imploding, globalising world. The Ramjanmabhoomi movement is a revealing example. The *maryada purush*, the dutiful, gentle Ram, respectful of his parents and concerned for his people, is reincarnated as Ram Raudra, the angry, avenging warrior, restoring the honour of his followers as they overwhelm their opponents. Such Ram sevaks, servants of Ram, seem to find a sense of efficacy in violence against accessible scapegoats.

This is regrettably regressive, and not to be confused with a people's movement struggling for justice and liberation from their oppressors. It is the very antithesis of Gandhi's inclusivist, universalising interpretation in the devotional song he popularised as almost the anthem of religious tolerance in his ashrams, and the *Ramrajaya* (the rule of Ram) he envisioned: *Ishwar, Allah tero nam, sab ko sanmati de Bhagwan*, which loosely translates thus: whether we call you God or Allah,... pray give us all true wisdom.

Traditional Hindu tolerance was premising on a gradation of dharmas systematised in caste. There can be harmony here only when the value premises and creedal assumptions are widely accepted, imposed from the top, and internalised at the bottom of the hierarchy. No other society has produced such an elaborate and rationalised stratification. In varying degrees, it has permeated all communities and religious traditions in this sub-continent.

However, when the basic values and assumed beliefs underpinning the system are challenged and rejected, the harmony cannot hold any longer. This is what our democratic churning, *manthan*, is doing to our society, and there is no indication either that it will find another balance of harmony and a basis for tolerance. The old hierarchy is being replaced with a new stratification, which cunningly legitimates itself in a hybrid of the old religion and the new politics. It is not officially premised on the dharma of caste, but it uses the power an electorate invests in numbers.

These are reconstructed into majorities and minorities, of dominant and subservient communities. When this is done in terms of the old religious differences, it results in religious nationalisms, which are easily mobilised by fundamentalists and extremists in the game of competitive politics.

Tolerance implies that the collective rights of groups are respected, and within groups individual rights are guarantee. It is a significant indicator of permeable inter-group boundaries and intra-group divisions, of a society's openness to share and exchange, its willingness to change social structures and revise religious traditions. Intolerance is often, used to seal group borders within and without, projecting hostility and demonising the other, to shore up the established structures of the status quo, regardless of their relevance or fairness.

In so far as religious conversions imply crossing group boundaries, they serve as sensitive indicators of tolerance. Too often, those who promote conversions have been guilty of a crude offensive intolerance in the name of religion, denigrating and antagonising the other. Those who resist conversions have then reacted defensively, sometimes with an equal measure of intolerance. The convert is caught between in a no man's land: induced to leave, pressured to stay.

What both sides need is a conversion to a tolerance that demands an equality, which in turn commands respect and a tolerance that respects the differences of others and supports the freedom to choose to be different. In religious matters, this goes beyond Gandhi, but it is very much in line with Ambedkar. Yet, as we have seen, Gandhi was too tolerant a man to forbid what he would not himself approve, and Ambedkar too much a liberal to compromise the legitimate freedoms of others.

In our imploding world, we realise that tolerance must be at the centre of our religious belief and practice to avoid an eventual religious meltdown as the warring faithful fight each other into exhaustion or irrelevance. Hinduism has rich resources for tolerance in its traditions, on which we can draw. What we need beyond Gandhi's *sarvadharma samabhava*, which can remain a somewhat abstract respect, is a more concrete equality in a *sarvadharmi samabhava* (equal respect for all believers). What we are experiencing now might just be the storm before the calm, and there still seems to be a long dark night ahead for South Asia.

Muslim diversity

The multiplicity of group variations in ethnicity and language, culture and religion, across and within groups, distinguishes a plural society. Further, overlapping and cross-cutting characteristics give rise to fuzzy boundaries between groups, and multiple identities within them. This makes polarisation across groups and homogenisation within them that more difficult.

My concern here is with the diversity of Muslim communities within the Islamic tradition. Given the obvious diversity of international Islam across countries and of Muslims within them, it is hard to justify the construction of a homogenous religious community of Muslims across these multiple dimensions. It would mean privileging religion as a constituent of identity, overriding and levelling all others. Why is this done for some religious traditions and not others? Are there underlying and unacknowledged reasons for this?

Part of the answer must be in the extent of secularisation in a society and its religious traditions therein. The attribution of homogeneity to a group can sharpen definitions of collective identities and polarise groups. Those who want to intensify an-versus-them divide can do this from the outside; those who want to mobilise an in-group feeling can do it from within. Either of these can be done for defensive or aggressive purposes.

Thus, pan-Islamism is constructed from without just as much as it is facilitated from within. People are often co-opted into this process because their leaders and elites give them no other option. They are panicked into supporting an alien agenda, thus compromising their real interests and concerns.

At the international level, the war against terror is doing this against Muslims across the globe. Why is Timothy McVeigh, who was executed on 11 June 2001 for bombing a federal government building at Oklahoma on 19 April 1995, killing hundreds of his fellow Americans, never called a Christian terrorist, while Osama bin Laden is identified as a Muslim one? Once a community is homogenised, a few terrorists are used to characterise a whole people. Such treacherous constructions need to be deconstructed and exposed for what they really are, the most unfortunate and opportunistic kind of prejudice.

In India too, the distinctive diversities of our numerous religious traditions are being erode from within and without, for political and chauvinist reasons that have no basis in our authentic religious traditions or our constitutionally defined citizenship.

Muslims from the north of the sub-continent, e.g., the plains of the Punjab, have more in common linguistically and culturally with their neighbours of other faiths, than with Muslims from the south, say the state of Tamil Nadu. In addition, vice versa for the Muslims in the south. The same holds for an east-west comparison, say between Bengal and Gujarat. Tamil Muslims have not been as Islamised as Muslims elsewhere in the north (Bayley 1989). Gujarati Muslims are so eclectic and indigenised in their region, especially Shia sects like the Bohras and the Khojas, that some conservative Sunnis even regard them as heretical.

Demonising a community is greatly facilitated by homogenising it first. Diversity is a bulwark against this. However, at both the international and national levels, Muslims are being aggressively homogenised from outside the community and then demonised as the hostile 'other'. This traps them into mobilising their communities in a defensive solidarity from within, and homogenises them further in a spiralling hostility. Both sides then become locked into a 'self-fulfilling prophecy', a 'they are all like that', and 'I-told-you-so' syndrome, from which neither party can easily escape. Such reciprocal hostility is simplified and self-justified. Acknowledging diversity allows for the complexity wherein to interrogate and comment on this constructed homogeneity and challenge the ground for such antagonisms.

Often this hostile other is constructed out of the need for an 'enemy' to consolidate group identity. At the international level, lost cold war warriors have found in the *Clash of Civilisations* their agenda for *Remaking the World Order* (Huntington 1996). However, the search for external enemies leads on to the quest for the internal 'other'. After 'othering' Islam, now the anxious question is '*Who are we?*' (Huntington 2004). In naming *The Challenges to America's National Identity*, Huntington now seeks to affirm its White Anglo-Saxon Protestant (WASP) identity by limiting non-white, non-English speaking immigration, especially Latinos, who are more resistant to absorption in the WASP culture. What Huntington is doing more sophisticatedly has happened more crudely in this sub-continent. The enmity between India and Pakistan has become internalised as communal hostilities against minorities in both countries.

The transcendent unity of God, *taw hid*, has been an uncompromising principle in Islam and its distinguishing characteristics among world religions. The unity of the Islamic community, the *ummah*, is founding on this religious principle. This unity in turn demands a radical equality in the community of believers, but this has not always obtained in Muslim society. However, neither the unity nor the equality require a cultural homogeneity across Muslim communities.

Nor are the religious principles of Islam completely exclusive. The Quran acknowledges the prophets of other religions, more positively than the Judaeo-Christian traditions sometimes do. Muslims are ones required to protect people of the book, and respect other religious traditions as willed by God, even though the same equality could not be extended to them. There are trends in Islam that consider all those who submit to God as Muslims already, others would require honouring the Prophet of Islam as well. For Islam was originally far more open theologically than its later institutional constructions.

From its earliest beginnings, there is a plurality of religious belief and practice within the *ummah*. The Shias and the Sunnis are one of the earliest and most enduring divisions in Islam, but there have been numerous other sects and denominations, interpretations and traditions, which have been accepted in mainstream Islam.

Culturally too, the process of Islamisation has allowed for distinct diversities, even in the Middle East, the cradle of Islam. In other places, the process of Islamisation has never been quite complete. Muslims in India and Indonesia are remarkably distinct from each other and even more so from Arab Muslims in the Middle East. Yet, they are extremely diverse within their own countries as well. The Arabisation of Islam is more closely associated with the Wahabism of the 18th century, now promoted and subsidised by the oil rich states, like Saudi Arabia. It has little to do with the Quranic origins of the *ummah* itself.

Pan-Islamic fundamentalism as an international phenomenon is very much a political reaction to the aggression of the modern western world. A triumphant, confident Islam was far more open to other and newer influences. The great Islamic empires in Spain, India and elsewhere exemplified this. Uniformity was not the inevitable end product of the Islamic principle of unity.

Historically, other heterodox religious traditions had been absorbed into its cultural environment and lost the dominance and distinctiveness they once might have had. Indian Islam's abiding concern with orthodoxy can only be read as a reaction to the perceived threat of an encompassing Hindu environment, though political dominance certainly helped the kind of ethnic self-confidence and openness needed to engage imaginatively with other local cultures and create a new composite one.

This certainly happened at the zenith of Mughal rule with Akbar and was carry even further with Dara Shukoh (1615-1659) the eldest and favourite son of Shahjahan (1628-1658). However, expediency at times dictated less enlightened and more chauvinistic policies that were disastrous in the long-term. The accession of Auranzeb to the Mughal throne and the execution of Dara Shukoh for heresy marked a turning point, precipitating subsequent divisions and antagonism that eventually came home to roost. If Akbar's is a positive, even a secular response of a Muslim ruler in a Hindu society, Aurangzeb's epitomises one of short-term opportunism.

T.N. Madan locates the roots of Islamic fundamentalism in India in the twin predicament of the threat of the Hindu cultural environment and the temptation of political expediency (Madan 1997: 13). The loss of Muslim power on the sub-continent with the expansion of colonial rule, particularly the backlash after 1857, rendered the crisis all the more acute.

With the Indian nationalist movement led by the Congress, dominated by Hindus and promising secularism, the sense of being engulfed in a Hindu sea and isolated in a secular world brought the crisis to a head. Jinnah's response with his Muslim League was political, protecting the interests of Muslims by mobilising Muslim nationalism. The more fundamentally religious response of Maulana Syed Abul A'la Maududi (1903-1979) and his Jama'at-i Ismaili founded in 1941, was not just a response to the seemingly threatening Hindu environment that might dominate post-colonial India. It was as much, if not more so, responding to the challenges of modernisation and the West.

However, neither of these religious or political responses went uncontested among the Muslims of India. Sayyid Ahmad Khan (1817-1898), the Indian modernist, saw the future in educating Muslims. In 1875, he established the Muslim Anglo-Oriental College at Aligarh, which later became Aligarh Muslim University in 1920. The *ulema* may have been religiously conservative, but very many did support a united India against Jinnah. Maulana Husain Ahmad Madni (1879-1957), who for decades served as the rector of the Deoband madrasa in Uttar Pradesh, and head of the Deobandi-dominated Jami'at ul-'Ulama-i Hind ('Union of the 'Ulama of India'), opposed the 'two-nation theory'. Basing himself on the Quran, he argued from for a 'united nationalism' in his book *Muttahida Qaumiyat Aur Islam* ('United Nationalism and Islam').

Even after the founding of Pakistan, Jinnah was committed to a secular ideology, not a sectarian one. According to Hamsa Alavi, Islamic fundamentalism was a late arrival among *Social Forces and Ideology in the Making of Pakistan*. (Alavi 2002). The Islamisation of Pakistan has used first to contain Bengali nationalism in what was then East Pakistan. This failed and the country was divided. Later, more cynically, it served General Zia ul Haq, who controlled the country from 1977 until his assassination in 1988, to shore up the feudal class and the military establishment.

However, this has not meant any greater cohesion for that society, only an endless proliferation of various extremist groups. The ethnic diversity among Muslims there and the religious differences within Islam itself have not been homogenised. With increasing frequency, it explodes in collective violence, threatening the continuing stability of that country.

The original composition of the *ummah* did not pretend to uniformity. Ethnic diversity of the Arabian tribal clans prevailed even within the Islamic religious unity represented by the *ummah*. Muslims came to the Indian sub-continent first as traders, then as conquerors, but the mass of local converts were from the intermediate and lower castes, hardly from the upper caste elites.

The controversy over the racial origins of Bengali Muslims is an instance of how Muslim elites, affirming their ethnic distinctiveness, distanced themselves from the Muslim masses. Thus, taking exception to the 1872 Census in Bengal, Khondkar Fazli Rabi, writing in 1895 on *The Origins of the Musalmans of Bengal*, claimed that the leading Muslim families were of foreign descent, 'the offspring of that dominant race who remained masters of the land for 562 years' (Rabi 1970: 43) as against the native converts who were mostly from the lower castes. Families such as the Saiads refrained from intermarrying with families of 'dubious' ancestry (Viswanathan 2001: 159).

Indeed, in the rest of the country no less, the distinction between foreign descendents and local converts coloured Muslim society. The blending of class and race here puts to question any monolithic understanding of Muslim identity. It reflects a feudal class structure that overlaid a regional caste hierarchy, of which was neither transcended, nor overridden by the unity demanded in the *ummah*.

The controversy over Urdu is a good example of how a language can be the meeting point of different religious communities or become the instrument of division and homogeneity among them. Urdu originated as the language in the camp of the Mongol armies and became the language of the people in the market by the time of the Mughal Empire in India. Persian was the court language and Arabic the religious one. As the Empire declined, Urdu replaced Persian as the language of administration only to be displaced again by English.

According to Imtiaz Ahmad, Urdu still represented the 'Ganga-Jamuni' culture, and was widely used by all communities in the north, and also by the ruling elite in the Nizam's domains in Hyderabad in the Deccan. The elites 'used Urdu for domestic and social communication and cultivated the culture that came to be associated with that language' (Ahmad 2002: 2285). The masses spoke a mixture of Urdu and local regional languages, which Gandhi referred to as Hindustani and had proposed as the national language in both the Urdu and Devnagri scripts. The *madrassas* taught Urdu so that the Quran could be read in Arabic, but for all practical purposes the language of instruction was the regional one in Assam, Bengal, Kerala, Tamil Nadu (ibid.).

After Independence, the aggressive promotion of Hindi, a language constructed out of the various north Indian dialects, put Urdu on the defensive, as it increasingly became identified with Muslims. Today many Muslims outside the Hindi heartland in the north report Urdu as their mother tongue, giving the illusion in the Census of Muslims as a homogenous linguistic group. This may suit the elites, but it only isolates the local Muslims from their regional language communities.

The proliferation of stratified groups in Muslim society forms their own peculiar hierarchy. Muslims in India often reflect the caste hierarchy of their regional social environment. Imtiaz Ahmad's extensive studies on Indian Muslims underscore the continuing existence of such hierarchies (Ahmad 1978). For instance, though caste is not acceptable as a religious principle in Islam, intermarriage between equals has some support in the Quranic tradition. This easily reproduced itself in the endogamy of caste (ibid. 14). Again, though caste purity and pollution has no theological basis among Muslims, the idea of social distance was elaborated by Islamic jurists into a system of grading birth and descent in terms of proximity to the Prophet.

Occupational specialisation too was ranked and differentially honoured. The worth of an occupation is easily associated and transferred onto its practitioners and with endogamy, this readily adds up to a hierarchy of closed occupational groups differentially valued. With economic and political disparities, it gets worked into the local *jajmani* system of patronage between unequal castes (ibid. 6). Certainly some such practices and characteristics of caste hierarchy were carried over and integrated into the local Islamic traditions from the caste communities that converted.

Hierarchies, unacceptable in principle, were eventually rationalised in practice. In varying degrees of rigidity, this has happened with other egalitarian religious traditions too, such as the feudal estates in Christian Europe. This is not to pretend that stratification in the Muslim communities reproduces caste hierarchies, but that these do have a significant function in differentiating and diversifying their communities.

With anxieties very similar to other religious traditions, Islam too faces religious and political challenges from the modern world (Goddard 1995: 151-154). The religious challenge is one of renewal and reform. Renewal, *tajdid*, is to make the old new again, to the reverse the present decline in belief and practice. There have been *mujadid*, 'renewers' before, like Abu Hamid al'Ghazali (1058-1111) who had an immense impact on the Islam of that time. Later, Jamal al-din al-Afghani (1839-1897) had urged a fresh use of *jihad*, independent reasoning in jurisprudence based on the Quran, and the *Hadith*, tradition. Closely related is reform, *islah*, which goes beyond renewal of the old traditions to relevancy in the contemporary situation. Sayyid Ahmad Khan distinguished between the eternally binding Quranic principles and the contextual details relevant to that time. Others have urged a return to the earliest sources of the Quran and the *Haddith* as the basis for reform, discarding later accretions.

The political challenge is seeing in the problematic relationship of Islam to the west, which once again presents a serious threat of the balance of power reversed in today's imploding world. However, even more pertinent is the relationship of religion to the state. The Egyptian Abd al-Raziq (1882-1947) has urged a separation between the two based on the Meccan period of the life of the Prophet, not the Medina one. Turkey is an aggressive example of such a separation but it is not the norm in Islamic countries.

In India, the complex history of the Partition in 1947 and its tragic aftermath is simplistically blamed on Muslims, at least in the popular Hindu understanding even today. This puts Indian Muslims on the defensive, and makes them vulnerable to Hindu nationalist jingoism. Nevertheless, there are numerous other bases for mutual antipathy. As a result, communal riots are still endemic in our society today, visiting a terrible vengeance on Muslims, who are held collectively responsible, supposedly for painful historical memories, carefully nurtured and kept alive for this very purpose rather than excised and healed.

Moreover, neither Pakistan nor Bangladesh has provided alternatives that are more attractive for Muslims in this sub-continent. Muslims thus understandably feel culturally and religiously threatened. An economic and political marginalisation readily follows, so that the cumulative consequence is that they are increasingly isolated in 'ghettos', which exploit their own as violently as the society around exploits the ghettos themselves. Every communal riot sees a further ghettoising of the Muslims in that area, further isolating them.

India has the largest Muslim population after Indonesia. Yet, in contrast to sub-Saharan Africa, where Islam is the fastest growing religion in the world, there is no significant recent Islamic conversion movement in India in any organised way. Conversions are mostly though inter-marriage, or at the initiative of the would-be converts themselves, such as the ones at Meenakshipuram. Today, Hindu hostility about conversions is more directed towards than Christians and Muslims.

However, there are a host of other underlying challenges and issues, and the responses have been complex and multi-dimensional. They vary from fundamentalist to liberal extremes. There has been diversity and dissent, debate and dialogue acknowledged within the tradition itself, though some would still want to push the limits even further to create more space for innovation and creativity. However, denigrating and pillorying a group, putting it on the defensive is not an effective way to encourage a relevant response.

More recently, Irfan Ahmad has credibly argued that the old upper class leadership has focused on the politics of identity that has served its own purposes, to the neglect of the backward classes and dalits among the Muslims. He now calls for a 'Different Jihad: Dalit Muslims' Challenge to Ashraf Hegemony' (Ahmad 2003: 4886-4891). The old leadership proved quite inadequate in the trauma of the Babri Masjid demolition in 1992 and the communal violence that followed in its wake, or in the horrendous genocide of Muslims in Gujarat in 2002.

Now a new leadership is emerging that does not take its cues from the older *ashraf* (noble) elites. Rather it proposes to make common cause with other oppressed peoples in a pluralist and liberating vision. Activist scholars, like Asghar Ali Engineer, have proposed a liberation theology derived from the Quran that inspires this movement. It is no longer satisfied with *taqlid*, blind imitation, but insists on opening again the gates of *jihad*, which were closed for the Sunnis in the 14th century.

These new leaders do not claim *ashraf* ancestry but identify themselves as the voice of lay Muslims from the backward and lower classes. They are still a small minority, but a growing and influential one. However, the dominant political mainstream in the country is still too engaged with the old leaders, who claim to represent the community, though actually they resist the 'Democratisation of Indian Muslims', as Anwar Alam convincingly argues (Alam 2003: 4881-4885), and perpetuate the authoritarian and conservative structures they thrive on themselves.

Officially called 'Other Backward Classes' (OBC), the backward caste movements among Muslims have begun more recently to gain momentum. In 1981, the Muslim Marathi Sahitya Parishad, a literary association, was formed that borrowed heavily from the Bahujan Samaj, the backward caste movement in Maharashtra. In the 1990s, a similar movement became active in Bengal, the Uttar Bango Anagrasar Muslim Samity, and by 1996, the All India Muslim OBC Orgnisation was holding its convention in New Delhi, much to the discomfiture of the older leadership who accused them of further dividing the Muslim community on caste lines. In 1994, the All India Backward Muslim Morch (AIBMM) was set- up by Dr M. Ejaz Ali in Patna to mobilise dalit Mulsims (Sikand 2001)

The reality of Muslim diversity makes any facile assumption of Muslim homogeneity untenable. Yet, this has often been the implicit ground for generalising Muslim intolerance from some instances to the community as a whole, while Hindu diversity has been assumed to be the basis for predicating tolerance as characteristic of that community. Both need to be critically reviewed.

Comparisons and contrasts

The contested issues elaborated in this chapter provide some comparisons and contrasts that may suggest some further reflections, though not all can be discussed here. Thus both dalits and tribals represent the 'other', who is different and interrogates our society. The dalit is the counter-point to caste hierarchy. From the bottom of the caste system, the dalit exposes its incompatibility with a free and egalitarian democratic ideal that our society proclaims. The tribal is the counter-point to cultural hegemony. From outside the dominant culture the tribal is a question mark on sustainability and fairness of the progress and development that our society has espoused. The controversies over conversion must be seen against this background.

For dalits, conversion as *dharmantar* represents, principally though not exclusively, their protest against caste oppression and their quest for liberation. For tribals likewise, it indicates their desire for change and their aspiration for progress. Neither wants to be trapped in their plight, is altered both would certainly want to influence how their situation.

With tribals, there is a temptation to idealise their past with a kind of 'back to nature' romanticism of Rousseau. With dalits the tendency is less, though Phule and Ambedkar have attempted to reconstruct a historical past, wherein dalits were the original inhabitants and masters of the land, until unscrupulous latecomers displaced them. However, that past is now too distant and too lost in mythic mists to be called back, though it does serve as a myth of origin for dalits in positively affirming ways. This tendency to idealise their past is more in evidence with tribals, but it is not by the tribals alone. At times outsiders too recall and romanticise the tribal past, though they have never been, nor are likely to be, a living part of it.

Contemporary dalits have been more Hinduised than tribals, and more assimilated into the caste system, albeit at the bottom. They even have their own caste hierarchy among the numerous dalit sub-castes. Tribals are still outside the caste system, but as they are increasingly Hinduised, they get more integrated into, and more conscious of, its hierarchy.

For dalits and tribals, religious conversion touches a sensitive nerve for all involved: converts, proponents and opponents. If caste hierarchy is the crucial issue for the dalits, cultural change is the critical one for our tribals. For dalits, conversion protests the oppression of caste hierarchy and is a quest for dignity. For tribals, conversion expresses a resistance to cultural hegemony and an affirmation of cultural identity. These are not two exclusive understandings of conversion in two dissimilar contexts, for there is obvious similarity between, and an overlapping across them, as in both instances, conversion is an assertion that rejects social dominance: for dalits, this is caste hierarchy, for tribals, it is cultural assimilation. Dalits too are in search of a positive identity, and tribals demand self-respect. However, their social situations have their own distinctiveness and their experience of religious conversion accordingly nuanced.

Dalits marginalised within the society, at the 'centre' as it were; tribals are isolated more outside it, at the 'periphery', it would seem. The quest for identity and the resistance to assimilation is the tribal response to the loss of their culture that they experience in their problematic integration into mainstream society. Dalits too are contesting their status in the social hierarchy, seeking a new identity and redefining their place in society.

Ambiguity is not the prerogative of Christians. Other religious traditions, even non-creedal ones, experience similar tensions and contradictions. With Christians shaking off an imperial past and seeking greater openness and a level playing field in a post-colonial, globalising world, ambiguity is of special pertinence to them. Openness, equality, relativity are themes that will have relevance for Muslims and Hindus. However, the pertinence of these to the issue of conversion is most apparent in Christianity, because the traditional answers to these issues are being discussed and debated. More than many other religious tradition, Christians have traditionally been preoccupied with orthodox doctrine rather than with orthodox practice, with doctrinal and moral theology, than with religious law and ritual. All this emphasises the ambiguities and dilemmas they must now confront.

Obviously, the paradox of tolerance affects Christians and Muslims as well as Hindus. The balance between acceptable tolerance and unacceptable intolerance remains fluid depending on how the relevant scriptures are read and interpreted. In the religious conflicts in the sub-continent, Hindu tolerance has been projected as a popular perception and thus, highlights the paradox there. With Gandhi, it even became an international cliché. Yet, no one can doubt Gandhi's tolerance or his Hinduism, and so both need to be historical contextual.

The challenge to Hindu tolerance by religious nationalists and extremists from within is what brings the paradox into sharper contemporary focus. Their selective co-option of a rich tradition is not always effective contested and challenged, let alone rescued and renewed, by moderates. However, after the general elections were in May 2004, some lost ground was regained.

Muslim diversity is historical well founded, but has become been more problematic today. They have put on the defensive against a neo-colonial west and from Hindu nationalism in this country. Their own fundamentalists from within the tradition aggressively promote pan-Islamism, even as extremists of other traditions from without project a homogenised Islam onto them. Other religions too have their share of extremists and fundamentalists who redefine and project their own interests into their religious community. Christian fundamentalists define a uniformity in faith, and Hindu extremists demand a cultural nationalism.

However, the concern here has been with the threat to the rich diversity of Indian Islam, particularly in the context of the communal constructions in the aftermath of the global war on terror, which has put Muslims on the defensive everywhere. Negating the diversity of Muslims only helps to deepen the religious divide — especially in South Asia, but elsewhere as well.

Taken together, the contemporary concerns, case studies, and contested issues presented so far question tired stereotypes and stale prejudice, and dare us to rethink our understanding of, and our stance on, conversion. To duck the challenge, to see it as a threat to the status quo, rather than an opportunity to break through to a new future, is to get stuck in a 'no win' stalemate.

7

Rethinking Conversion

Conversion as Process, not Event - Many Pilgrimages - Conversion to Each Other - *Conversion as Change and Affirmation* - Religious Identities - Social Space - Civil Society - Faith and Ideology - Affirming Dignity - *Conversion as Tolerance* - Mixed Motivations - Religious Options - Legal Repression - Limits and Levels – Dimensions of Understanding - Levels of understanding*Conversion as Dialogue* - Dialectics to Dialogue - Culture of Dialogue - Inter-religious Dialogue - Domains in Dialogue - Intra-Religious Dialogue - An Equal Dialogue – Inside/Outside - Pluralism and Relativism - *Conversion as Multiple Belongings* - Singular and Multiple Identities - Beyond Dialogue - *The Journey Ahead*

Conversion can bring new understanding to both traditions involved in the convert's journey. As persons on the margins, converts can make group boundaries more porous and groups themselves more tolerant, ir two-way critique of both traditions. However, this can be stymied by defensive or aggressive antagonisms, or even reversed.

When someone converts out of one group or community to another, perceived as rivals or adversaries, this cannot but cause hurt and resentment in the group which the convert leaves. When these feelings are self-centred, especially when supported by the collective egoism of a group, they easily mutate into narcissistic rage, manic or depressive. Whether of individuals or more so of groups, conversions enrage religious fundamentalists and extremists.

So too with converters, there often is a narcissistic grandiosity, paternalist and patriarchal. They feel convinced they have something to offer that cannot but be welcomed by the less fortunate outside their fold. Fanaticism and fundamentalism fuel such rage. Conquerors and colonialists have often been sponsors of such proselytising, and the backlash to this from defensive local hierarchies has been an understandable — if not always proportionate — reaction.

A critical introspection on both sides is needed to break through hackneyed discourses and invent almost a new language to talk about the real issues. Gauri Vishwanathan insightfully insists: 'Rethinking conversion in a modern, pluralistic world requires one to reclaim the language in which one can speak about conversion, not as violence but rather as movement and fluidity' (Viswanathan 2001: xv).

For a serious 'rethink' we need to engage with new perspectives to further an in-depth discussion. Conversion affects different people differently. We need more inclusive and comprehensive perspectives to understand our differences, even if we cannot reconcile them, to question ourselves less defensively and accept each other as different. There is still such a long journey ahead on this pilgrimage, but we can try to begin here.

Conversion as Process, not Event

Conversion by definition must involve change, more problematically so with a *dharmantar* and not just an *atmaparivartan*. However, it is simplistic to perceive conversion as a single, critical once-and-for-all event, an irreversible, point-of-no-return decision. Some conversions may be marked by such eventful decisiveness in the life of an individual or group. Yet, even in such cases, internalising the decisions, and realising the consequences of the subsequent events for oneself, and more so the impact of all this on others, will necessarily span a period of time.

An event may precipitate a decision; in turn, a decision can initiate a sequence of events. This is but the beginning of a process and other events and decisions will punctuate it as it develops. At some point in time along the way, this may add up to a real change of heart or a change of allegiance. When this happens, different spectators will perceive it differently, depending on where they situate themselves.

Such conversions by active assimilation or passive absorption are far more common in South Asia, both for individuals and groups, than the radical born-again experience that demands a renunciation of the old and a commitment to the new. The experience of a radical renunciation is not alien to Indic religious traditions, as when someone withdraws from the everyday *samsara* and retreats into *sanyas*.

This may well be a change of heart, an *atmaparivartan* and not yet an initiation into a new religious tradition, a *dharmantar*. More often, the new is added on to the old, not negated, as symbolised in some rites of initiation. Eventually but not necessarily, this adds up to a change of religious allegiance that is perhaps imperceptible at first and only recognisable after a lapse of time. This is what Sanskritisation has done to our tribals and Islamisation to some syncretic communities – for instance the Meos of Rajasthan, Khojas in Gujarat.

This will happen more easily with inclusive religious traditions than with more exclusive ones, but there is evidence of such eclecticism across most religious traditions. We have seen this in the context of traditions indigenous to South Asia, but other traditions have had equivalents too. Thus the Jews had 'friends of the synagogue', who attended the services, but were not formally initiated with circumcision. They were a bridge between the synagogue and the world outside. There were many such 'friends' among the Hellenistic Jews, who had spread through the Roman Empire, especially in the Eastern Mediterranean.

Kabir in the 15th, and Guru Nanak in the 16th century, tried explicitly to bring both Hindu and Islamic traditions together in a critique and interrogation of both. Nevertheless, eventually, new religious *panths* (sects) evolved, like the Kabir *panthis*, or even distinct religious denominations, as with the Sikhs distinguishing themselves from both Hindus and Muslims. Even today, there are vibrant syncretic religious traditions among various Hindu sub-castes, like the Meos in Rajasthan, and Muslim sects like the Khojas and the Dawoodi Bohras in western India. Such composite traditions are increasingly Hinduised and Islamised, as the case may be. Intense religious competition is alienating religious traditions from their spiritual resources and politicising them into jingoistic ideologies.

The early Christian churches had an adult catechumenate, an instruction programme for would-be converts and well-wishers, which did not always end with baptismal initiation. Most recently in India the Krista-bhakta movement initiated by some Catholic priests in 1992 from Matridham Ashram in Varanasi is gaining momentum and has spread to six districts in the region. This is basically an inculturated movement of *satsangs*, or prayer meetings, and *bhajans*, or devotional singing, centred on the ashram community, where all are welcome and the *Istadevtva*, the personal deity, is Jesus Christ, though the devotees are not converted to Christianity, and there is no formal *dharmantar* initiated with sacramental baptism.

Even when conversion is defined as a watershed event at a specific point in the life of an individual or group, the circumstances leading up to this are an implicit or explicit preparation for that event. There will be consequences thereafter to be dealt with too, more so with group than with individual conversions. Thus, conversion is better understood as a whole continuum of events that make up the process.

The events do follow a general pattern, yet each conversion unfolds in a unique sequence of personal and group decisions that will vary across different individuals and diverse groups. Moving the focus from a single conversion-event or even a disjointed sequence of them, to a more connected conversion process that is fluid and precarious, yet with some continuity and direction, opens up new perspectives and more space for dialogue.

In this perspective, conversion is not a decisive affirmation of one tradition and a derisive negation of the other. This does violence to the complexities of the conversion process itself. For as a process across constructed borders, conversion can question both sides. It has the capacity for commitment and interrogation in a more nuanced manner, to affirm and deny in complex and selective ways. As Gauri Viswanathan incisively affirms: 'to see conversion less as an endpoint than a starting point, a method of knowledge and communication, is the challenge of the moment' (Viswanathan 2001: xix). Conversion as process connects the beginnings to the end and tries not to get lost in the events in between.

The life journey in the case studies presented earlier illustrate this: Ambedkar, Ramabai and Nivedita all do this in their respective *dharmantars*, and Gandhi too, somewhat differently in his *atmaparivartan*.

Ambedkar's emphatic rejection of Brahmanic Hinduism unfortunately leads to an equally emphatic defensiveness on the part of most traditional Hindus, who then miss the challenge he poses to reform. Rather they react to bolster the status quo. This is what opponents of conversion often do with aggressive denunciation, and converters as readily provoke such negative reactions with belligerent recriminations of their own. Yet Ambedkar also interrogates Buddhism and reinterprets it so that his *Navayana* is more relevant to neo-Buddhist converts. As a spirituality for action in their quest for justice. This in turn challenges traditional Buddhism to engage in such issues as well.

Moderate reformers at first support Ramabai's rejection of Hindu patriarchy. However, once she leaves the fold she is out on her own. After her conversion, she continues to question Christian institutional patriarchy, much to the consternation of her Christian supporters. They cannot quite come to terms with this woman convert, now trying to convert their patriarchy to gender equality and justice, premised on the principles she has learnt from their Christian tradition itself. Her feminism remains a thorn in the side of patriarchy on both sides.

Nivedita is alienated from much of her Christian tradition in England, and she finds her deepest desires fulfilled in her guru Swami Vivekananda and his vision of the Vedanta as the universal religion. As she once reached beyond her Christian roots, she now travels beyond her Guru's vision. Her 'aggressive Hinduism' particularises her dedication to the Hindu nationalism of that time and inspires Hindu revolutionaries. In the end she is perhaps closer to her anarchist friends in London than to the Ram Krishna Mission she served after her initiation by her guru.

Gandhi's pursuit of truth leads him to a new synthesis of Hinduism that may not be a new religion but is as distant from traditional Brahmanism as from aggressive Hinduism today. For though Gandhi always claimed to belong to the *sanatan dharma*, he radically reinterprets Hinduism to spiritualise it. In the process, he marginalises far more from the tradition than he actually carries forward. He draws his inspiration from many religious streams, and eventually his piigrimage takes him beyond all of them, in his quest for a spirituality beyond any particular religion, one that is truly inter-religious, one might almost suspect trans-religious.

As with individuals, so too with groups. Conversion as a sequence of events is a fluid process that is more complex as it moves from the individual to the social, from the psychological to the socio-cultural.

Dalit conversions may begin in a sense of injustice that leads to protest, but then they must go on to affirm their newly realised dignity and define their new-found identity. If their conversion remains a negative protest event, without realising a re-affirmation and a redefinition of themselves in the process, they are likely to find themselves subordinated and paternalised in the new situation, where aspects of the old status quo are reconstructed to their continuing disadvantage.

We have seen how this happens with caste structures, when dalits convert to neo-Buddhism and Christianity. Conversion will be able to fulfil its liberating promise meaningfully only when it becomes a continuing process against such structural injustices. Left to chance or social drift, this is unlikely to happen, and the event of conversion becomes less relevant and even marginalised. At times, the conversion itself may be reversed, as has happened with some neo-Buddhists returning to their earlier religious tradition.

So too with tribals. If conversion is meant to assert their cultural autonomy against Hinduism and all the resentment that goes with this, the change may not help to maintain and enhance their autonomy in the new cultural domain of the community to which they give their allegiance. They may just as easily get assimilated and absorbed here as well, Christianised or Islamised. Once again, a process of cultural reconstruction that is positive and dynamic, not negative and static, is very necessary.

Conquest and trade once brought the major religious traditions into contact with each other. Often these encounters have been rife with anomalies and strife. Eventually in many instances, a peaceful coexistence evolved that at times was even mutually enriching. But there has also been much unresolved resentment and many bitter memories left behind in the wake of wars and conflicts. Conversions continue to bring these religious communities into existential and controversial contact and they easily become flashpoints in the ensuing exchange. These can be defensive and aggressive engagements, as often happens; or initiate a process of critique and meaningful dialogue, as they sometimes do.

Thus, much of the ambiguity, paradox and the diversity that we identified in these traditions can be rescued from being exploited from within by its own fundamentalists, and from without by other extremists. Constructive clarifications and imaginative reinterpretations can result in a positive process of exchange and dialogue. Yet only when the exchange itself is not defensive or aggressive can this happen. There must be tolerance before there can be dialogue. These are two perspectives on conversion, which we will pursue further.

Once conversion is seen as a process, not as an event, it is easier to perceive how it is not something confined to the so-called proselytising or missionary faiths. The difference between the endpoint and the starting point better defines conversion, rather than some event of initiation, however deliberate or arbitrary. At most it can symbolise this change, by itself it does not realise the transition on the ground. If the conversion process is understood as ongoing and multi-dimensional, then there is space for broader interpretations and genuine dialogue.

The dynamics of conversion processes are too complex for any simplistic one-dimensional understanding. There is the real danger of forcing a selected sequence of events into preconceived patterns that will reinforce old prejudices and fears. An open-ended interpretation must resist this temptation and question such presumptions and preconceptions.

If conversion, perceived as process rather than event, is to make space for tolerance and dialogue, it must be conceived as open-ended and not closed. For, a process closed to change, as sometimes opponents seem to want, or one preordained to a given outcome, as many proponents of conversion often desire, negates this space. Rather, the process of conversion must become a pilgrimage to a horizon that beckons all who dare to set out on this journey together, and invites them to be open to a conversion to each other.

Swami Chidananda's question to the bishops at his ashram in Rishikesh, discussed earlier, is really an invitation to set out on this pilgrimage. The bishops' apprehension is an indication of how faith-commitments once made constrain future options. Some faith-commitments are less constraining than others, but all such commitments are within a horizon of understanding and our journey together must not be one that negates an authentic experience on this side of that horizon, but rather one that reaches out to experiences beyond it as well. Perceived as a process, religious conversion is reaching out beyond one's horizons, and finally to the Ultimate.

Conversion as affirmation and change

Conversion as process necessarily implies change. Positively perceived change would mean personal betterment, or group/community progress. Conversion also involves changes in identity and allegiance and different players perceive and experience such changes differently. Religious conversion is problematic precisely because of this differential impact.

The changes in the old status quo precipitate challenges and threats on many fronts. Thus, improvement and progress for some may be loss and threat for others. Conversion for some is betrayal, for others liberation. With group or mass conversions, such changes are further complicated. Many of these tensions and confrontations are eventually expressed in an identity politics, as affected groups and communities mobilise themselves around collective identities to seek redress. Some of these are constructed as 'primordial', ascribed, indelible identities — and among these, religion is one of the most emotive ones.

Focusing on the conversion process, in which the converts' religious identities are deconstructed and reconstructed, helps to perceive religious identity itself as negotiated and flexible, not bound and sealed. Opponents of conversion are often opposed to this possibility and so prefer to close the door on it. Proponents want a one-sided change, as is obvious when they are so discomfited when their own faithful convert outside their fold.

Social identities are essentially constructed in reference to a group or community, and identity change in significant individuals or large groups will inevitably affect these groups and communities. In a plural and diverse society, such identity changes can easily upset a delicately balanced status quo. Imposing a rationalist secularism on a religious society is neither feasible nor acceptable to many religious communities, especially when these traditions run deep and social expression is a necessary dimension to this. Such attempts have only played into the hands of extremists and fundamentalists, for it allows them to panic the community and consolidate their position in it.

Identity change must be negotiated at the cultural and civic level before it is confused and manipulated at the political one. This can help contain and defuse identity politics, so that a more rational 'politics of interest' can preside. Indeed, religious traditions find their best and most creative expressions not in politics but in cultural and civic life.

Yet today, a clash of civilisations is premised on religious identities projected into transnational expressions that are inevitably political. Such political projections are hardly a requirement of religious identities in most traditional, and even in today's non-secular societies. All the world's major religious traditions have been able to find a place in Indic civilisation. This religious diversity was integral to Gandhi's 'India of My Dreams'. However, the 'discontents of modernity' have allowed religion to be co-opted to political purposes that are not religious but disguise themselves as such.

When they are constructed as inclusive and compatible, not as exclusive and antagonistic, social identities, especially religious ones, can find their expression in fidelity to their tradition and in harmony with others in society. For this, we need a less constrained and more open perspective on religious identity, one that acknowledges its necessary place in a society, without defining individuals and groups exclusively in terms of the religious communities to which they belong.

We have seen how religious fundamentalists and extremists emphasise a religious identity to subsume and consolidate other identities around a religious allegiance. Once such totalised identities are perceived as permanent and solidified, they cannot respond to change with any flexibility, and so become defensive and even aggressive. Yet under the present pressure of social change, collective identities cannot but be in flux, and ways of coping with the consequent anxiety become imperative. Conversion outside the fold is often among the most threatening of such identity changes.

A stable core identity can be layered and contextualised. This allows for inclusive and overlapping group and community boundaries. Since identities are both defined from within the group and imposed from without, intra- and inter-groups relationships will play a critical role in such identity construction. Threatening intra-group interactions between dominant and subordinate members will make for defensive insecure identities. Antagonistic inter-group encounters will promote exclusive and closed identities. Thus dysfunctional families induce negative and insecure personal identities in their individual members, while castes and racist groups project hostile and exclusive group identities for themselves and others in their societies.

We need to ground social identities in a viable social space where the positive and the secure, the generous and the inclusive are internalised and integrated in individuals and groups, lest they are transmuted by other less amenable group and social pressures. Such a space is found not with isolated individuals or in state politics, but in the intermediate social structures of civil society, the social space, where citizens live out their lives outside their families and the formal institutions of the state.

This would be a positive step in depolarising religious identities. If religion is located in such intermediate structures, it can find its social expression in the family and the community without being prejudiced by state politics, unless such politics itself is communalised and projects its interests and concerns into the civic community.

Politicians find it difficult to resist this temptation, but once indulged, it is even more difficult to reverse. For when religion explodes into electoral politics, there is no telling where it will lead or if the violence will be contained. Once one gets on this tiger, it is difficult to get off!

The recent history of the sub-continent is a telling indictment of such shortsighted politics. The change of social identity that religious conversions imply is one of the most provocative issues enmeshed in this. For insofar as conversions do impact other areas of social life, they become real concerns. We must deal with these within the appropriate social space, and not just in terms of electoral politics and its payoff.

If, following sociologist Ferdinand Tonnies, we consider 'community' as *Gemeinschaft*, i.e., based on more direct 'face-to-face relationships', and consequently the area of 'private space', then 'society' as *Geselleschaft* will be in the 'public space' of 'indirect relationships'. The first is more the sphere of family and religion, of particularised and personal interactions, the second more that of the economy and the polity, of more generalised and formal relationships. The state must be the guarantor of the personal and collective rights of citizens' at both levels: for instance, at the first, protecting gender rights from patriarchal domination and community rights against outside interference and manipulation; at the second, promoting economic justice and political freedom.

At both these levels, but especially at the second, the state must create a neutral space and a larger social unity wherein civil society can effectively function — not as a uniformity, where differences are suppressed — but with all the rich diversity that 'community' (*Gemeinschaft*), brings to 'society' (*Geselleschaft*). Society will then be a community of communities, just as at a more disaggregated level, the community will be a group of groups, and a neighborhood a family of families.

Some aggressive secularists have attempted to banish all religion from the public to the private sphere, with disastrously contrary effects. Situating religion in the domain of 'community' rather than 'society', as we have described these terms, allows for a religious expression in the family, the community and civil society. The state can then be neutral to religion and focus on the economic and political realities, which fall more properly within its secular domain.

When there are failures here, these are reflected in and projected into the religious sphere. Religion is thus drawn into the identity politics of the state and inevitably, conversion as a change in identity becomes extremely problematic to all concerned. Restraining religious identities to the family and the community in civil society provides a buffer against their co-option into state politics.

If community identities were inclusive enough to accommodate the new ones in some acceptable way, conversion as identity change would not mean a change of community, just as it does not necessarily demand a change of family, if the neophytes are accepted in the old one. Further, a change of one's family, as happen with marriage, does not always amount to a change of one's community. So too a change in community, as with religious conversion, need not necessarily mean a change in one's socio-cultural tradition, if this change is contained in a larger civilisational unity; for instance, Indic civilisation as embracing all religious communities under its cultural umbrella. I can still be a member of my family, my community, my society, after I convert to another religious tradition.

Thus a change in religious identity need not mean a change in cultural or political allegiance. This tends to be the case when conversion is historically associated with conquest and the imposition of an alien culture. It is only after the violence and oppression ceases that an authentic integration can bring about a civilisational unity, though this may at times take centuries to evolve.

An overarching civilisation is by itself no guarantee of inter-religious harmony. Blood-feuds within the clans, and even within families, are at times bloodier than those with distant outsiders are. The religious wars in Europe, especially between Christian denominations after the Protestant Reformation in the 16th century, have left wounded memories that are still to heal, as we see in Northern Ireland. For civil society to function effectively and harmoniously, even within a civilisational unity, there must be a corresponding politics operative at the level of the state.

For, if civic society simply reflects political parties and their divisions, then it is already a divided and contentious social space. Yet, if religious identities are not to be politically co-opted, politics must not be driven by religious vote banks, but restrained by more rational interests, focusing on real economic and political concerns.

Banning religion entirely from the public domain to the private space of individual behaviour is not a realistic option in a society as religious as ours. It violates people's deepest sensibilities and precipitates strong reactions. At times, this may be expressed in withdrawal from the larger society, or, as happens increasingly today, in hostility and even violent engagement against those perceived as a threat. In the first instant, whatever positive religious resources there might be are lost to society. In the second, the conflict easily spirals out of control.

Moreover, once religion is politicised in the public sphere, it betrays its own best inspiration, and becomes a political ideology, compromising its character as a religious faith. Religious leaders are no exception to the corruptions of power, and are all the more vulnerable to this once they are enmeshed in competitive politics. The pursuit of power, even when this is for the service of others, as politicians generally pretend, cannot but marginalise and alienate the religious experience itself, which is premised on faith and trust, not shrewd calculation. Inevitably, the arrogance of power hollows out faith, and ideology fills the vacuum.

If religion is to influence politics ethically and to spiritualise it, as Gandhi wanted, then this is best done through civil society, not party politics. For it is the values and commitments of civil society, and the structures and institutions based on these, that are best able to bring an ethical and human dimension to state politics, rather than the hurly-burly of competition for political power in the promotion of collective interests.

However, restricting religion to community and civil society, difficult as this is to achieve, is still only the first step. For civil society and state politics are necessarily related. They cannot be completely compartmentalised, for the interacting subjects are the same persons on either side of the divide. Most politicians are eager to extend their power by co-opting religious interests and institutions, just as many religious leaders are not averse to extending their influence by projecting their religious concerns into state politics. Both blatantly exploit the religious commitments and beliefs of their people.

Once religious group allegiance is projected into the state, any change in allegiance, such as the change religious conversion brings, will have political implications, which often have little to do with the religion itself. Moreover, religious allegiance can be a matter of intense and even exclusive commitment. This has proved effective in mobilising groups in competition and hostility to each other.

There is need for a compact between leaders and among peoples to give religion its appropriate space in community and civil society, and not to politicise it. A religious tradition, which relates persons in a faith-community, demands a social expression. However, there is no requirement that this be projected to the rest of society, or into the politics of the state. Citizens of a state need a political ideology, but this need not be extended into politicising community or family relations. Containing identity politics with such a compact can only be by consensus, not compulsion.

This requires a delicate balance of interests and power. Changes in identity, even at the level of community and civil society, can upset this balance and affect public order, especially where this amounts to a change in group allegiance. In so far as it implies an identity change, religious conversion will inevitably be a destabilising factor, when it cannot be accommodated within the status quo. But then again, precisely in critiquing and challenging the establishment, it makes its contribution to religious communities and secular societies.

Most religious traditions have an enormous potential for social liberation. In setting off a process of interrogation, conversion can — but does not always — bring this into the open. The resistance to liberation theology and the kind of spirituality and social interventions it inspires, in conservative religious traditions and in secular establishments, is testimony to this potential.

For the quest for identity that conversion implies is not distinct or separate from the pursuit of dignity that often motivates this quest. This demand for social respect by the oppressed is bound to upset the status quo of old hierarchies and prevailing privileges. Yet even if the motivation for such conversions is not entirely religious but inevitably mixed and complex, it can still be a legitimate desire for change that must not be denied. Unfortunately, such aspirations have not always been fulfilled and converts are often left with an understandable sense of betrayal.

For dalits and tribals and other subordinated groups in society, religious conversion has meant and been pursued, both as a change of identity and an affirmation of dignity. If this upsets the status quo, then the disturbance to public order must be judged not in terms of the old order that denied these people a positive identity and a human dignity, but by how they are affirmed in the new one. As we have seen, religious change by itself does not address the entire issue, and a new religious identity by itself can leave many unfulfilled and broken promises unless confirmed and consolidated with real social dignity.

Conversion as tolerance

As a process that brings identity change, conversion can be experienced as problematic and provocative. It implies changes that cannot be wished away. Yet, if the changes are not too sudden or drastic, and the identities involved are open and inclusive, if there is a climate of tolerance, then such conversions are less likely to be fraught with tensions and confrontations.

Conversion out of personal conviction is easier to justify in terms of religious freedom, though there are some groups and communities that are intolerant even of this. The individual encapsulated in the collective is not allowed to break free. Conversion of a part is often perceived as a threat to the unity and identity of the whole. Even where religious freedom is acknowledged as a value, religious conversion, especially of significant or crucially placed persons, such as community or opinion leaders, may well evoke a sense of betrayal and provoke a resentful and hostile reaction.

When the conversions are accelerated and the numbers large, the effects can be far more precipitous and often violent, as at Meenakshipuram. Proponents and opponents get locked into irreconcilable differences, in which might becomes right, and the converts themselves reduced to pawns in a larger battle, in which the first casualty is religious tolerance. The atrocities against the tribals in Orissa and elsewhere, the aggressive proselytising, the vicious attacks, the intimidating re-conversions, are all testimonies to this.

If we accept that most human motivation, consciously or unconsciously, is invariably mixed, then religious conversion involves complex dynamics that affect other human and social dimensions, in which religion itself is necessarily implicated. When political leaders of a dominant community convert with their people, this is less contested by those not converting; but not so when subordinate groups disaffiliate themselves from the dominant social group's religious tradition and convert to another.

In earlier times, a conquered or colonised people often did follow their leaders into the religion of their conquerors. More recently, groups of people have left their traditional religious fold in protest against the dominant groups there. There is more than a religious motivation involved here and we find ourselves wondering how far such conversions are to be accepted or opposed.

Mass conversions do have a corresponding impact on the social order. They provide a good indicator of religious tolerance and of the respect for human freedom this implies: for proponents, when their proselytising exploits the vulnerability of their converts; and for opponents, when their intimidation thwarts the would-be converts from exercising their choice. Dalit and tribal conversions, whether to Buddhism led by Ambedkar, or to Christianity following the missionaries, or more recently to Islam, need to be seen in this perspective, and the motivations of the proponents and opponents are as much to be scrutinised as those of the converts are.

A truly religious conversion requires the exercise of free choice made on religious grounds. Oftentimes with mass conversions, the choice may well be freely made, perhaps not with the most enlightened considerations. Yet it can be an act of trust in a leader that does not take away from their freedom. It may not be a truly religious option, but a matter of political protest, social mobility or economic advantage. Yet none of this necessarily adds up to compulsion, religious or otherwise.

At other times, it could well be vice versa: a choice regarding religion but not so freely made, because of other intervening circumstances. Choosing to convert out of compulsive fear, psychological or physical, undermines freedom, just as the threat of force, or the imposition of unjust alternatives - conversion or exile - negates it. Fraud or unfair inducement takes advantage of vulnerable people. It implies a false choice because of deceit, or improper incentive, not an informed decision.

Yet to jump to conclusions of unfair force or deliberate fraud in every conversion is precipitously obfuscating, or at best benignly patronising. It is difficult to claim that large-scale conversions are entirely motivated religiously. Pretending to deal with them within an exclusively religious discourse only confuses issues further. Banning conversions or containing them through legislation may restrict people's religious options. Neither confronts the real issues for all those involved: proponents, opponents and especially the converts themselves, which, as we have discussed, are multi-dimensional and complex.

Certainly, it would be an unfair curtailment of legitimate civil liberties and democratic rights to ban even an organised attempt to propagate and persuade others of one's own views and beliefs, whether religious, political, cultural or otherwise, provided this did not violate the freedom of others. However, religious conversion has become an extremely sensitive issue, especially when it gets caught up and distorted in electoral politics. Where this involves an organised attempt at mass conversions backed by financial, political, and institutional power, the backlash can be explosive to the point of undermining public order.

The massive force and fraud in our electoral politics is not a reason to ban elections, but an imperative to reform them. Yet in spite of the Supreme Court urging this, our legislators are still unwilling to impose effective legal restraints on their corrupt electoral practices. How is it that the political exploitation of these vulnerable voters does not evoke the same outrage as religious conversions? Is political suffrage less important than religious affiliation? Is our tolerance for fraud, force and unfair inducement less in religious matters than in electoral politics? Which does the greater damage to our polity and people, the corruption of our electoral system or the conversion of some people to another religious tradition?

The Representation of Peoples' Act, Article 123 (2), includes as corrupt practice any appeal to vote based on a candidate's religion, race, caste or language. As Bhanu Pratap Mehta perceives it, this is premised on 'the idea that "religious speech" appeals to the emotions, unleashes uncontrollable passions, and impairs reason' (Mehta 2003: 56). Clearly, the intention of the Act is to rule out appeals based on any invidious identity of the voters, from which the law intends to distance the electoral process. Especially with regard to religion in this country, such identity politics has too often degenerated into the politics of hate with its corrosive religious communalism eroding the legitimacy of a secular state, and favouring various kinds of theocracies.

This implicates the courts in distinguishing between the religious and the non-religious. Since religion overlaps with the other areas of social life, appeals to religion are often disguised as appeals to culture or even history. Hindutva can then be presented as a cultural nationalism to the electorate, in spite of the implications of its religious exclusiveness and its hostile construction of religious majorities and minorities. The Ram janmabhoomi controversy is projected as a matter of history, while the mass appeal made to the electorate is premised on the basis of their faith! The courts then are left to decide where the religious issue ends and the cultural or historical one begins. The point at issue is not the legitimacy of hate politics, but whether this is best dealt with through legislation and in the courts, or whether it must be countered in the larger arena of civil society, and how.

Historically, confrontation and controversy have been accepted ways of settling such differences. History witnesses to numerous such instances, and even today genocide as the 'final solution' and ethnic cleansing as ways of getting there, are still promoted and practiced by some zealots, who have used religious violence as a strategy to mobilise support and redraw the political map in blood, regardless of the human cost involved.

Yet repression by force only makes for unstable and dangerous situations. It sows the seeds of disaffection that will eventually explode into violence in some not-too-distant future. We have still to learn that — particularly in matters of conscience — human beings cannot be forced, or imposed upon for an indefinite length of time.

The antagonistic interactions between religious communities may be to an extent contained by legislation restraining it in view of public order. Yet, in spite of good intentions, the legislation itself cannot be a substitute for the tolerance within and between these religious communities. Conversions put this to the test, particularly mass conversions. Moreover, it is not just the tolerance of the opponents that is questioned, but equally, if not more, that of the proponents. Whether or not these show respect for the vulnerability of the groups they seek to convert, is as much a question of tolerance, as it is for the opponents, who may or may not show respect for the wishes of the would-be converts they seek to protect.

The limits of tolerance must be set up within a regime of human rights. The United Nations does this at an international level, the Indian Constitution for our citizens. They provide a reference point and context, normatively binding on both the state and civil society.

However, to be sustainable in strained circumstances, our tolerance must go beyond these norms. It must be founded on positive values that are sensitive to the other, and expressed in multiple ways in diverse arenas of inter-personal and social encounter. To mention but a few: being non-authoritarian and non-judgmental in personal relations, a non-dogmatic religious openness, a positive appreciation of cultures and languages other than one's own, a commitment to equitable gender relations, a respect for egalitarian group rights and fundamental individual rights, an ecological awareness and aesthetic sensitivity ...

Now if tolerance is to be an active and positive response to coping with our differences, it must be more than a passive acceptance of these norms and values. Indeed, we can distinguish levels of tolerance from reluctant forbearance to joyful acceptance. What are the limits to which tolerance can be constructively extended?

Lest our understanding of tolerance be impractical and naive, we distinguish four levels of tolerance following Raimundo Panikkar (Panikkar 1983: 20-36). The first is tolerance as a practical necessity, i.e., bearing with a lesser evil for the sake of a greater good. This amounts to a political and pragmatic acceptance of necessary or inevitable evils.

The second level is based on the realisation that the human grasp of any truth is always partial. Certainly, this is true of religious or even revealed truth, because the human recipient is limited. Such an intellectual or philosophic realisation makes us cautious in absolutising our own 'truths', and even more so in rejecting those of others we disagree with. From such philosophically founded tolerance comes respect.

At the third level, ethical or religious tolerance derives from the moral imperative to love and care for others, especially those different from us, even our enemies. This tolerance is far more demanding than the acceptance and respect at the earlier levels of tolerance. Yet the different 'other' here is still the 'object' of one's love. Such love can even make us celebrate our differences, but it cannot overcome or transcend them completely in a higher unity.

Overcoming this objectification of the other is 'a mystical experience of tolerance'. Panikkar explains this tolerance as 'the way one being exists in another and expresses the radical interdependence of all that exists' (ibid.23). In the final analysis, only this kind of mystical or spiritual tolerance can overcome and transcend the contradictions and conflicts between religious traditions, bringing them into a higher communion.

These levels of tolerance can best be clarified by situating Gandhi's ahimsa along the continuum. Gandhi's tolerance is never just political pragmatism. He realizes that the truths we grasp are necessarily partial. They need to be complemented by the partial truths of others. Beyond intellectual realisation, he is sensitive to the moral responsibility for others we must own, and he reaches out to all in non-violence, which he describes more positively as love. In the final analysis, Gandhi's ahimsa is intelligible only as a mystical-spiritual union, a condition and presage of moksha.

Further, the level of tolerance we live by is not something arbitrarily chosen. It is set by the way the 'other' is perceived by the 'self'. From perceiving the other as practical obstacle, to positive complement, to moral obligation, to mystical-spiritual fulfilment, our perception of the other is always complex. Yet in a given context, one or the other perception will be the more operative, and so limit the level of tolerance correspondingly.

Thus, if the other is pragmatically perceived as a limitation on — or an instrument for —oneself, at worst an obstacle or at best a means for my own fulfillment, then only a pragmatic level of tolerance as a practical necessity is possible. If the other is realistically perceived as complementary to oneself in overcoming one's own limitations, then a more positive level of tolerance is possible in my relationship to the other, at least intellectually. Where the other is perceived as someone the self has a moral responsibility for, this brings tolerance to the level of ethics, religious or secular. Finally, at the mystical-spiritual level of tolerance the other is perceived as the necessary fulfilment of oneself. This demands a tolerance beyond politics and philosophy, even beyond religion and ethics.

With Panikkar again, we can distinguish two dimensions of understanding, reaching across these levels of tolerance: myth and ideology. 'Myth' here is not understood in the pejorative sense as opposed to fact, but rather as the 'horizon of intelligibility' (Panikkar 1983: 101) and hence a form of consciousness. It is the taken-for-granted, unquestioned, pre-understanding, something that is accepted in 'faith'; not an irrational, blind faith, but a non-rational, pre-articulate understanding. Joseph Campbell describes *The Power of Myth* (1991) as a collective dream that expresses the unarticulated depths of a people's unconscious, their deepest longings that they themselves may not be consciously aware of. More than ever, we need such collective dreams for our societies today". For 'myth' is a story, a narrative that poetically, not conceptually, points to an eternal truth. An imaginative, not merely rational grasp can be only expressed in symbol and metaphor.

Once it is rationally articulated, myth is demythicised and so is our faith, in a 'passage from *mythos* to *logos*', (Panikkar 1983: 21) from myth to reason as the articulated conscious word. This then develops into an 'ideology': 'the more or less coherent ensemble of ideas that make up critical awareness, i.e., the doctrinal system that enables you to locate yourself rationally...a spacio-temporal system constructed by the logos as a function of its concrete historical moment' (ibid.). We need ideologies as well to locate ourselves in social space and interpret our role therein at a given moment of our history. However, 'ideology' has a greater affinity for the political and intellectual level of tolerance, as 'myth' has for the religious and mystical one.

The more articulate and coherent, comprehensive and compelling an ideology is, the more likely it is to reduce other ways of understanding to its own terms, or reject them, if they cannot be fitted into its own presumptions. Consequently, there is less space for tolerance in the area it marks out for its truth. To be open to alternative insights, to broader and deeper perspectives, the ideologies we use must be open and non-dogmatic, critical and non-authoritarian. This will depend on the myth, the pre-understanding, from which it derives. For the more extensive and intense a myth's meaningfulness is, the richer and denser its symbolism, the more open and accommodating the ideology built on it.

Whether or not an ideology develops into an open or closed system of understanding finally depends on the myth from which it derives. The farther the myth's horizons stretch and the more openness and space it allows, the richer will be the texture of its themes and the greater the intensity and density of meaningfulness it will evoke. Hence, we can conclude with Panikkar: '*the tolerance you have is directly proportional to the myth you live and inversely proportional to the ideology you follow*' (ibid. 20 emphasis in original).

All this may seem somewhat laboured and abstract but it has a crucial relevance for our understanding and practice of tolerance, especially religious tolerance. For in our religious understanding, faith is the realm of 'myth', as an imaginative, intuitive, non-rational comprehension that makes our worldview meaningful, and theology is the realm of ideology as the rational articulation that attempts to spell out its meaning. The deepest roots of religious tolerance lie in our religious 'myths', the collective dreams we live by, while theology, the rational doctrine we follow, is the 'ideology' that explains religious intolerance. For faith is a matter of the heart, theology of the head; if the two are not intimately connected, our collective personalities would be schizophrenic.

At times of rapid change and consequent tensions, such collective pathologies are not uncommon. To break through to a sane and healthy tolerance, we need a *metanoia*, a radical change of our myths to escape the *paranoia*, the delusions, of our ideologies, whether religious, political or otherwise. This is a utopian ideal for any society, but it is still an ideal we can reach out to even if it remains beyond our grasp. This is the conversion we all most need, conversion to tolerance, one that will both interrogate and analyze all those involved. What kind of *atmaparivartan* and/or *dharmantar* would this imply?

Conversion as dialogue

Any dialogue inevitably becomes problematic and unstable if tolerance is pursued by just one party, without some reciprocity by the other. Especially in strained circumstances, tolerance needs dialogue to be sustainable. But tolerance itself is the necessary condition of dialogue, which is essentially at least a two-sided engagement. Hence, just as conversion as process involves change, so too does conversion as tolerance implies dialogue.

The level of tolerance we accept sets the context for the degree of dialogue we are able to pursue. As with tolerance, dialogue can be pragmatic and political, and restrict itself to adjusting and coping with differences, or it can be intellectual and philosophical and seek to complement the truth of each partner. Further, dialogue may be ethically and religiously motivated to grow in the love and concern of each partner, or mystically inspired to culminate in a higher union of both, in a deeper comprehension of truth and love.

Conversion as a process of critique and interrogation can be pursued in a context of conflict or cooperation. Tolerance is the critical divide between the two. The first approach we call 'dialectic', to 'read against', to position one stance against another so that something new emerges in and through the conflict. The second is a 'dialogic' approach, to 'speak towards', to reach out from one's own understanding and try to understand the other. Just as what begins in conflict is most constructive when it ends in cooperation, so too conversation communicates more productively than contestation, and dialogue opens venues beyond dialectics.

Dialectics is based on a difference of opposites, on thesis and anti-thesis, from which the synthesis emerges. Dialogue is premised on differences as complementary, brought together in a conversation, awaiting the moment of coherence, of fulfilment, of a 'fusion' of different horizons that will bring a new and more enriching perspective to each others' truths, harmonising and enhancing, relativising and contextualising them.

In this 'difference' we must find the basis of dialogue, in which 'myself' and the 'other' are both discovered and enriched. As we unveil our 'self' in the 'other' and the 'other' in our 'self', we find that our deepest identity and bonding transcends all differences in an immanent I-thou communion. Indeed, dialogue is the most constructive and creative practice of tolerance, the only effective way to really cope with the bewildering diversity that challenges and confounds us, as a precarious legacy and a precious treasure.

Fundamentally, dialogue is opening myself to another so that the truth of the other spoken to me can question and so reveal my truth, that is often hidden from me. Thus, 'dialogue is a way of knowing myself and of disentangling my own point of view from other viewpoints and from me.' (Panikkar, 1983: 242). For Panikkar 'dialogue' is a most fundamental condition of human existence. It is our way of being, for to be human is to be in dialogue with others, in communication, in contact with them. That is why solitary confinement is such a terrifying and dehumanising punishment.

Dialogue and conversation, then, are intrinsic to the human condition, the very language of our existence, the necessary site for interpreting all our experience. For we are constructed and deconstructed in dialogue with ourselves and others, as the German philosopher, Hans Georg Gadamer (1900-2002), insists, 'the conversation that we are is one that never ends' (Gadamer 1989: 95).

A conversation necessarily involves another and so reaches beyond oneself, or else it might well become a monologue, or worse, a dialogue of the deaf, where everyone talks and no one listens. Self-talk is not dialogue. All genuine dialogue must be 'to recognise oneself (or one's own) in the other and find a home abroad – this is the basic movement of spirit whose being consists in this return to itself from otherness.' (Gadamer 1975: 15) A further challenge is to recognise the alien other in oneself and realise the basic human commonalities that bind us all together, reaching beyond our differences.

Dialogue, then, goes beyond dialectics for 'dialectics' is the optimism of reason. Dialogue 'is the optimism of the heart' (Panikkar 1983: 243). With Gramsci the 'pessimism of the intelligence' must yield to 'the optimism of the will' (Gramsci 1996: 175). For as Blaise Pascal has wisely counselled: 'the heart has its reasons that reason, knows not of' (Pascal 1958: 222). Indeed, a genuine dialogue pertains less to the dialectical mind than to the compassionate heart. For this, we must dare beyond the constraints of dialectical reason, which no doubt has its uses, as also its limitations.

Hegemony cannot but result in the culture of silence, leaving people voiceless while their leaders speak for them. Silence and suspicion are good neighbours. Each encourages the other in a reciprocal manipulation, feeding stereotypes, encouraging falsehocds, spawning rumours, spreading disinformation, fuelling odium and mistrust. Such a 'culture of suspicion' is the very contradiction of a 'culture of dialogue'. If we grant that dialogue is essential to the human condition, then it must be a dialogue that breaks the silence and opens communication, discredits suspicion and creates trust.

There is always the danger of celebrating our own 'difference' in isolation and seclusion from others, and not in dialogue with them. Such an inwardly turned dialogue eventually becomes a monologue, whether of individuals or of groups. This inbreeding can only lead to a genetic decline of the group's cultural and intellectual DNA. About others, the outsiders, it 'shades over into the celebration of indifference, non-engagement and indecision' (Gadamer 1989: 90). This further negates creative pluralism, undermines respectful tolerance and destroys any real possibility of a culture of dialogue.

Most often, these prejudices and negative sentiments are embedded in the myths and ideologies we live by and act from. To be a constructive engagement at the four levels of tolerance identified earlier, a culture of dialogue must include both myth and ideology. For in their mutual encounter, myths are deepened and enriched, and in their reciprocal exchange ideologies become more open and refined. Such a culture of dialogue will demand a radical change, a metanoia of our hearts, to free us from the paranoia of each other.

Human beings are meant to be interrelated and interactive, not isolated and alone. In all the four dimensions discussed in chapter four — the psycho-social, the socio-cultural, the eco-political, the socio-religious — human development and growth, both personal and social, can only be through interaction and interrelationship. Thus at the psycho-socio level, to be an authentic human person one must be inter-personal or risk a dangerous neurosis or even a psychosis. At the socio-cultural one, to truly assimilate one's own culture one must be inter-cultural, and a really cultured society would have to be inter-cultural as well. At the eco-political level, it is only through egalitarian participation and equitable exchange that a progressive economic and political development is possible for individuals and communities, for nations and societies. Finally, at the socio-religious level, to be authentically religious in one's own tradition one must be inter-religiously involved in others, for to be to be true to itself and discover its own religious depths, a religious tradition needs to reach out to other religious traditions in concord, not confrontation.

The imperative for dialogue can now be summed up in a few pertinent sutras:

to be a person is to be inter-personal;
to be cultured is to be inter-cultural;
to develop is to participate and exchange;
to be religious is to be inter-religious;

Psychologists have convinced us of the first; sociologists are trying to teach us the second; political economists are promoting the third; theologians are coming to realize the fourth.

In 1995, the 34th General Congregation of the Society of Jesus in Decree 5 gave a particularly relevant mandate for dialogue to the Jesuits: 'to be religious today is to be inter-religious in the sense that a positive relationship with believers of other faiths is a requirement in a world of religious pluralism.' (Dec. 5, No.130), Raimundo Panikkar rightly insists that 'dialogue is not a bare methodology but an essential part of the religious act par excellence' (Panikkar 1978: 10). Conversion is at the crossroads of such inter-religious dialogue, and ought to be an opportunity to reach out to, not a threat to retreat from. Swami Chidanandaji's incisive question to the bishops at Rishikesh dramatically illustrates just this.

As with tolerance, so too with dialogue, we must distinguish various levels and dimensions of this involvement with one another, for dialogue is surely more than a verbal exchange. Recently, Catholics have been urged by their Church to engage in a four-fold dialogue (Pontifical Council for Inter-Religious Dialogue 1991: no. 42):

1. '*The dialogue of life*, where people strive to live in an open and neighbourly spirit...'
2. '*The dialogue of action*', in which we 'collaborate for the integral development and liberation of people'.
3. '*The dialogue of religious experience*, where persons, rooted in their own religious traditions, share their spiritual riches...'
4. '*The dialogue of theological exchange*, where specialists seek to deepen their understanding of their respective religious heritages...'

Such a distinction of domains, of life, action, experience, articulation, not a separation between them, allows for a multiplicity of diverse dialogues with a variety of different partners, even with non-believers outside any religious tradition. Indeed, such transparency among believers and non-believers would make even an 'extra-religious' dialogue challenging and fruitful for both sides.

Moreover, dialogue implies a reciprocity between the 'self' and the 'other' that can take place in various types of encounter and exchange between persons and groups. A more nuanced understanding of dialogue requires a specification of various kinds of involvement of the 'self' with the 'other'. For in each of these areas of exchange we distinguish degrees of dialogue corresponding to the levels of tolerance, premised on differing understandings of the self and the other, and the encounter between the two as delineated above.

At the pragmatic level of tolerance, where the other is perceived as the limitation of the self, dialogue becomes a practical way of overcoming differences, rather than by confrontation that could result either in the assimilation or in elimination of the other. At the intellectual level, where the other is seen as complementary to the self, dialogue seeks to overcome the limitations of the self with help of the other, rather than instrumentalist the other in the pursuit of self-interest. At the ethical level, the self accepts moral responsibility for the other and reaches out to the other to establish relationships of equity and equality. Here dialogue becomes a sharing of mutual responsibilities. At the mystical level, the other is perceived beyond a limitation, a complement, or an obligation, as the fulfilment of the self. Here dialogue calls for a celebration of one another.

In this perspective, the dialogue of life is at the level of sharing and encounter of our myths, which is then deepened in the dialogue of religious experiences. This can be an even deeper level of not just mythic communication but of mystical experience as well. Collaborative action requires some level of ideological and political consensus, which can then be intensified and sharpened in a theological exchange. Thus, life and experience are at the level of 'myth' and mysticism; action and theology at that of 'ideology' and politics.

All this will demand a more liberal and humanist approach within each tradition. Hence, an intra-religious dialogue is a necessary condition for an inter-religious one, otherwise we will have a debate not a dialogue, controversy not complementarity. Panikkar has described the intra-religious dialogue at the personal level thus: 'an inner dialogue within myself, an encounter in depth of my personal religiousness, having met another religious experience on that very intimate level. In other words, if *interreligious* dialogue is to be real dialogue, an *intrareligious* dialogue must accompany it, i.e., in must begin with my questioning myself and the relativity of my beliefs (which does not mean *relativism*), accepting the challenge of a change, a conversation and the risk of upsetting my traditional patterns' (Panikkar 1978: 40).

Intra-religious dialogue will at times involve the pain of re-education. As St. Augustine of Hippo confessed: *Question mihi factus sum* (I am become a question to myself!). I must face the question I am if I am to face the question that the other is to me. Facing such questioning is surely even more problematic when it comes to groups and communities.

For unless the plurality within a religious tradition is encouraged, differences celebrated, tolerance sensitised, it is unlikely that any of these can be carried over to an inter-religious dialogue. For a religious tradition that is homogenising, insensitive and intolerant to its own diversity from within cannot be open to being enriched by the diversity and difference of others from without.

What we need then is an intra-religious dialogue so that we can see, each in their own tradition, what we can do for ourselves as a preparation for a dialogue, where we can do something for each other. If we can be non-defensive, then we will be able to initiate a non-violent and open dialogue with other religious traditions, and perhaps even with the fundamentalists within them. Moreover, what holds for individuals holds equally for groups and communities. Hence, beyond a personal understanding of intra-religious dialogue, there is need for a community or collective one, a dialogue within a religious tradition between various groups across different perspectives.

Ninian Smart, the Ideologist, somewhat provocatively suggests, 'God has created many religions so that they may keep each other honest. By mutual criticism and hopefully friendly rivalry they can help to prevent the myopias and corruptions which seem everywhere the concomitants of human worldviews and in particular religious ones' (Smart 1993: 64).

We all need this collective metanoia, an *atmaparivartan*, and in our engagement with each other, we may well find we ourselves have undergone a religious change, a *dharmantar*, in our life and our world. Swami Chidanandaji was asking for such openness from the bishops.

An engagement in dialogue can be inspired by an obedience and fidelity to one's own religious tradition, which may well indicate or even mandate this. This is but a first step. A further and more challenging one must then be taken: to rediscover at a greater depth what this obedience and fidelity must mean through the encounter with other religious traditions, in the questions and responses arising therein. This can only be done honestly in a dialogue of equal partners. Such an *equal* dialogue is of the utmost importance to tap the resources of our rich heritage.

For any dialogue that starts with the assumptions of superiority on one side, or has a hidden agenda intending assimilation or absorption, propaganda or conversion of the other can never be an equal exchange. In the end all unequal exchange, whether between classes, castes, genders or even between communities, regions, etc., eventually becomes exploitative and oppressive. To be truly creative, dialogue must be open and free, beginning with mutual respect and continuing in reciprocal enrichment.

Dogmatic religious traditions find it problematic to concede that those outside their revelation and beliefs have an equal access to the truth. They feel themselves privileged in this regard, and compromise in this matter is tantamount to being disloyal to their faith. In such a perspective, a clash of religious traditions becomes unavoidable and peace and harmony is only possible in a secular space. This is precisely the argument of the rationalist, and history would seem to justify their stance. In Europe, the religious wars ended with the secularisation of societies and the marginalisation of religious traditions themselves.

Nevertheless, if inter-religious dialogue between such exclusive religious traditions is more difficult, it is also more necessary. The challenge is to move religious traditions from being exclusive to being inclusive, or at least to find some common ground for a dialogue. This demands a distinction between the perspectives of the insider and the outsider. The challenge is for the partners in the dialogue to give up their insider perspective and take an outsider one by positioning themselves on common, perhaps higher ground. Here all the partners to the dialogue can be equal.

This requires that we bracket away our own convictions and commitments not to abandon or betray them, but to hold them in abeyance as we reach out to each other, as in any attempt at resolving differences. This makes eminent sense in a pragmatic approach to conflict resolution. It would surely not take a great leap of faith to do the same for an inter-religious dialogue of equal partners. In a family quarrel, the common good of the family grounds the appeal for harmony; in gender debates, our common humanity must be the accepted point of reference; in inter-religious dialogue, the joint purpose is to explore, rather than resolve differences.

From an insider's perspective, differing truths cannot lay claim to equal validity, unless they are relativised, or brought into harmony at a higher level of unity. This harmony may require an outsider's perspective if the insider's one is not inclusive enough. Without compromising itself, an insider perspective must grant the right to hold, and the duty to respect different opinions, even those incompatible with one's own. For in civil society the other's legitimate right to freedom and claim to respect must not be compromised by imposing one's own dogmatic beliefs or prevailing practice. This makes dialogue possible even between believers and atheists – an extra-religious dialogue.

For the believers of the creedal religions, claiming privilege for their truth, an equal dialogue may not be a matter of 'equal truth', yet it must always be one of 'equal freedom'. No one standpoint must be privileged, but all critiqued and challenged. Given the diversity of our plural-religious traditions today, the only common currency viable is our common humanity and a basic humanism derived from this. Any apparent controversy between truth and right, between tolerance and justice must be resolved at this level.

For given the multiple polarities delineated across sharp divides on the contentious issue of conversion, any attempt to clear a common ground for an equal dialogue must begin with a reciprocity of perspectives, i.e., seeing ourselves as others see us, a necessary exercise for individuals and groups, for communities and other agents as well. This means positioning oneself beyond one's own perspective and situating oneself within reach of the other's. This will in turn have its own problems, but only on such a common ground, can all engage as equal partners and set the conditions for a deeper inter-religious dialogue.

To those outside the faith community, these creedal religions may well be perceived as unwilling or unable to face the challenge of an equal dialogue: 'My truth is truer than yours'. Such religious traditions need a relevant intra-religious dialogue to be more open and inclusive. We are all conscience-bound to follow the truth wherever it leads. From an insider perspective, when a creedal religion holds its truth to be revealed, the objective possibility of one's conscience leading one outside the fold, as it were, is extremely problematic. Is this always 'apostasy'? At least the insider must grant the subjective possibility of this happening in good faith. Nevertheless, crucial questions remain. How inclusive is one's perspective? How informed is one's conscience?

The non-creedal religions are generally not constrained by exclusive beliefs. However, inclusiveness too must go with its own cautions. It must not fall into relativism or degenerate into permissiveness; neither must it become a process of appropriation and absorption into a higher unity, wherein the distinctiveness of each tradition is conflated, not just subsumed. The all-inclusiveness of some universalists at times seems to imply just this. 'My truth includes yours, but not vice versa'. A valid inclusiveness would demand the integration of diversities into an enriching and higher unity so that we have'diversity-in-unity' rather than a 'unity-in-diversity'.

White light includes the wavelengths of all the seven colours, yet the rainbow has its own especial beauty. So too, the polyphonic voices in dialogue make the symphony.

At Rishikesh, the bishops seem caught within the constraints of a dogmatic tradition and are unwilling or unable to face the challenge of an equal dialogue. An open and inclusive intra-religious dialogue as urged by the Second Vatican Council would be a necessary and enabling preparation for this. In contrast to the bishops is the openness and inclusiveness of Swami Chidananda who, from his insider perspective is not constrained by exclusive beliefs, nor is his purpose to absorb or assimilate the other.

The implications of God's redeeming feature and truth as active outside one's own religious tradition is something that exclusivist, dogmatic religious traditions cannot readily come to terms with. Many of the faithful in the creedal religions, especially those claiming to be divinely revealed, still struggle with this. Many more have not quite thought through the implications of religious pluralism and too easily confuse it with religious relativism.

However, we must be emphatic about the difference. Relativism, whether religious, ethical or political, when this is associated with non-commitment, ends up reinforcing the status quo, where all are equal but some more so than others. This is hardly compatible with an authentic humanism, whether religious, ethical or political.

Pluralism, as Raimon Panikkar explains, is the necessary consequence of 'recognising the contingency of everything that is human' (Panikkar 1998: 120). The human is never the ultimate absolute but always in relationship to it. This does not amount to relativism.

For pluralism is not about the equality of differing and contradictory of truth, but about equal respect for others, who hold different truths. We owe this respect to others, even as we expect the same for ourselves.

For all humans are finite and can only hold a part of the infinite truth. Indeed, we are capable of grasping truth, but there is always more beyond our reach. Even among those we do comprehend, there is a hierarchy of truths: some are more fundamental and must be held more dearly than others, some more partial than others and more easily relativised. Equating all truths is to devalue them all. Mahatma Gandhi's truth cannot possibly be equated with Nathuram Godse's convictions, though even he must respectfully be given a fair trial.

In our multi-cultural and pluri-religious society, pluralism is a psychological challenge, a cultural imperative, an economic political necessity, a theological given. We need a pluralism inspired by a humanist, liberating, this-worldly ethic, premised on tolerance and sustained by dialogue. For a genuine pluralism is possible only within such a context. Tolerance and dialogue are defining ways of being human in our pluralist world. This demands an *atmaparivartan* that is open to a *dharmantar*.

Conversion as multiple belongings

In a diverse and complex pluralist society, where there are fuzzy boundaries between, and common characteristics across groups, there will inevitably be multiple identities. How these are contextualised and prioritised, and played out for both individuals and groups, is necessarily a function of the situation. A father of a family would not play the same role to his younger boss in his office; a Brahmin may be particular about his ritual taboos in his home, yet dispense with them without difficulty outside it.

The complications and contradictions arise when all other identities are collapsed into single, solitary, totalising, exclusive one. This becomes the key identity dictating one dominant role in any situation. Once a boss always a boss; if a Brahmin, everywhere a Brahmin. This can lead to some unfortunate exaggerations, though in fact most practical persons find ways of pragmatic adjustment. With groups, such identities may be more complex and more easily exploited, politically and otherwise.

When such totalising happens with religious identities, serious clashes and conflicts can be precipitated. Not surprisingly, conversion in such circumstances is unacceptable and opposed. For such totalising identities, inevitably tend to be singular, not plural, and consequently claim a comprehensive allegiance, a total belonging. For example with regard to one's caste identity, one can belong only to one caste. To try — or claim — to belong to two makes one an outcaste in the hierarchy.

Inclusive, flexible identities allow for multiple belongings. When group boundaries overlap, one can belong to more than one, without compromising oneself and find room enough to adjust to their various claims, e.g., of one's family by birth, by marriage, by adoption... If conversion in understood as process and change, as tolerance and dialogue, if exclusive and rigid religious identities of individuals and communities yield to more inclusive and flexible ones, then multiple belongings are possible, and indeed necessary.

Religious traditions do not exist in isolation. They necessarily overlap and relate to other areas of society and culture. Religious identities are as complex and multiple as the religious traditions from which they derive. Inevitably, these will be embedded in other areas of society and if they are exclusive and inflexible, then there will be cause for serious strains and tensions in a plural society. These can be resolved and overt conflict avoided either by dominance or by withdrawal, both of which undermine pluralism, one by hegemony the other by exclusion.

Private — as distinct from public — space as the arena for religious expression has been the approach of the secular rationalist. We have argued for a broader perspective of distinguishing community and society to restrain the political expression of religion in the polity, while allowing for its social expression in the community. Dialogue can open social and community space for multiple belongings. However, if the religious identity of community is exclusive and totalising, its interaction in society becomes problematic, and conversion as a change of identity and allegiance will be a threat to this community, and disruptive in that society.

Examples from medicine and linguistics can be enlightening. Beyond a superficial eclecticism, the different schools of medicine are derived from different cultures and they do not always agree in many aspects. Yet they can be complementary to each other in a more comprehensive approach to sickness, and together can contribute towards a more holistic understanding of health and healing. We can then belong to more than one school of medicine, and even practice them wherever these are not incompatible. This is good example for inter-religious practice.

Multi-lingualism can provide a deeper insight into multiple belongings. We speak different languages in different contexts. Learning a new language does not demand that we abandon the old one, rather it enriches our understanding and facility in both. Each new language represents a whole other universe, a worldview of its own. We must enter into this to really absorb the deep structures of its syntax and access the hidden treasures of its symbolic universe and worldview. This is an apt metaphor for inter-religious endeavour.

To pursue the metaphor further in the context of religious conversion, it would mean 'learning a second first language – learning a new way of seeing and being in the world - in the same manner as that in which we learned our first language' (Schreiter 1994: 45). Raimundo Panikkar's description of his own journey captures most evocatively this sense of multiple belonging: 'I "left" as a Christian, "found myself" a Hindu, and I "return" as a Buddhist, without having ceased to be a Christian' (Panikkar 1978: 2).

The journey ahead

By those opposing it, conversion has been perceived as subversion, as atrocity, as *adharma*. Those promoting conversion consider it a protest against oppression, religious and secular, as an aspiration for betterment, spiritual and otherwise. The converts themselves, experience it as a revolt and a quest, a liberation and an affirmation, a complex process of changing social identities and affirming human dignity.

The more intransigent and hostile opponents are often on the defensive, though what exactly they are defending is not very clear since their opposition is often enough expressed less in support for the would-be converts than in anger towards the so-called converters. Easily provoked, their defensiveness often turns into rage and aggression, as with religious fundamentalists and nationalists, who become self-legitimating extremists rejecting any *dharmantar* and even an *atmaparivartan* within their tradition that challenges or disagrees with their stance.

There are equally aggressive promoters of conversion who have done little to remedy or discourage this negative perception of the hostile opponent. Denigrating and rubbishing other religious traditions, they betray an inability to dialogue, not just with others outside their religious tradition, but also even with dissenters within their own fold. For such proselytisers, conversion becomes a game of numbers and religion an ideology that serves other than religious purposes. For these, even a *dharmantar* into their fold, if it questions their stance and challenges their religious institutions, is unacceptable.

There are also the more moderate and reasonable among the opponents, whose objections and goodwill cannot be dismissed in good faith. These are outraged by the arrogance of propagandising proselytisers. There are those who genuinely want to share the truth that has enlightened them, and changed their lives, to reach out with the compassion they themselves have experienced. Many missionaries and monks, Buddhists and rishis, Sufis and fakirs have been exemplary in this. For such missionaries, conversion is promoted as fulfilment and freedom, as liberation and moksha, as enlightenment and nirvana, a breakthrough to a new understanding and commitment that brings a change of heart and may eventually bring even a new religious allegiance.

For the converts, conversion is often more complex and mixed than they themselves are aware. It can be a protest against oppression, a quest for liberation, an aspiration for betterment, a search for a new identity, an affirmation of human dignity. For the more critical seekers, conversion becomes a two-way interrogation of both traditions, the old and new. For some it becomes a personal discovery of solidarity with, and dedication to, a brave new world.

We cannot pretend to wish away intractable religious differences. With many of these, we have still not come to terms. We cannot any more settle religious differences within, much less between, religious traditions through controversy and violence. No truly religious person can disagree with this, or the crying need for peace and harmony in our world. Only a few fundamentalists and extremists would, whose religious worldview is closed and exclusive? Yet even with such as these we must still exercise tolerance and attempt dialogue. Already, too much blood and tears have been shed on this 'clash of civilisations'. Globalized terrorism is only the end of this road, on which we are now skidding along to a 'clash of barbarisms'.

Religious conversion remains a sensitive flashpoint that brings these differences to surface and compels us to confront them. I have tried to map the history and geography of this bitterly contested and violent terrain. In rethinking conversion, I am attempting to open a way forward through this dangerously mined territory. The journey ahead will surely demand an enlightened agenda of its own.

8

Religious Disarmament

Models of and Models for - *Faith and Reason* - New Sutras for Old Dichotomies - Right Belief, Right Practice - *Towards a Global/Universal Ethic* - the Paradox - The Ethical Imperative - A Global Ethic - A Compelling Search - Mapping a New Landscape - *Freeing the Imagination* - Mismatches and Misunderstandings - Human Rights and Religious Liberty - Person and Community - *Many Dharmas* – Introspection and Interrogation - Beyond Introspection

Any vision of utopia is necessarily beyond our present horizon, but it can still serve as a critique of our present reality, a reference point for our goals and endeavours. In *The Interpretation of Cultures,* Clifford Geertz makes a pertinent distinction between two models with regard to culture as a symbol system (Geertz 1973: 93). A model *of* social reality helps to understand and interpret it, while a model *for* reality serves to respond to and change it. We must of course begin with understanding in order to change. The challenge is not only to interpret the world as the philosophers have done, but to change it, as Karl Marx famously proclaimed in the eleventh of *The Theses on Feuerbach*.

We can only do this from a common ground on which we can begin to build a consensus for such models. A first step will attempt to clear some open space on the controversial theme of faith and reason. Without some common understanding on the relationship and function of faith and reason, any discussion on religion is already condemned to misunderstanding, or worse.

As a committed Christian believer and a professional social scientist, this will also indicate how I position myself in this discussion. Any viable agenda for the future must be premised on a constructive comprehension of the relationship between the two. Both will require a critique to find this common ground that will include believers within and across religious traditions, and to reach out to secular rationalists outside these. This ought to enable us to map or at least have some idea of where there is agreement, where disagreement, and what still remains contested.

Based on such a critical understanding, we can then attempt to sketch an ethical approach acceptable to our different religious traditions to enable us to engage in a fourfold dialogue, premised on multiple levels of tolerance. The contemporary attempts to articulate a global ethic can well serve as our guide in this quest, and be the basis for an agenda that is grounded in the past, built in the present, embraces the future.

Faith and Reason

Too easily, a dichotomy posited between faith and reason is perceived as two alternate ways in our quest for truth. Such binary opposites are typical of western thought. Our contention here, as with eastern thought more generally, is that faith and reason are complementary, not contradictory ways of seeking truth. After all, more than just truth as knowledge, it is truth as reality, satya, that cannot be contradictory. Otherwise reality itself would be absurd. Faith and reason must both be included in a more comprehensive understanding, which would thereby be the more human for being the more inclusive and holistic. However, we must first refine our understanding of what we mean by 'faith' and 'reason' to explore more incisively the dialectic between the two.

An increasing religious revivalism and fundamentalism seems to be spreading like inkblots on the global map across countries and even continents. The 'Age of Reason' once seemed to have 'freed' us from our faith. However, with the end of the Enlightenment, critical reason has turned on itself and now undermines our confidence in the older rationalist optimism. This has not helped to re-find our faith, while a post-modern age is putting to question all the grand narratives that once seemed to epitomise the cutting edge of our evolving rationality. For lack of more feasible faith-perspectives and more viable scientific worldviews, we seem to be careering into a corrosive relativism.

'Faith' in this context is not exclusively religious faith, but rather faith in all its dimensions: personal and inter-personal, in community and society. 'Reason' here refers to the modernist Enlightenment and more particularly to the inspiration drawn from it: from the privileging of the experimental science to the abstract logic of philosophers, like Emanuel Kant (1724-1804). In such a perspective, it is 'faith' that makes the basic pre-judgements, which are then interrogated by 'reason'. This new understanding is further subsumed into a more refined pre-judgement based on a more meaningful faith, proceeding progressively in a question-answer dialogue, wherein each interrogates the other, bringing both together in a more inclusive approach.

Between global secularism and religious revivalism, the dichotomy between faith and reason is sharpened. We need a more insightful understanding of 'reason' than the 'Age of Reason' gave us, a more incisive comprehension of 'faith' than the new religious movements, proffer, especially the fundamentalist and revivalist ones today. Our query: *what does being 'reasonable' mean to faith, and again what does being 'faithful' to reason require?*

A binary opposition between faith and reason eventually leads to an unbridgeable divide between them. This all too easily deteriorates into a schizophrenia between religious intolerance and rationalist dogmatism. More generally, within the horizon of eastern thought, there is a more inclusive understanding as expressed in our first sutra: *faith and reason are complementary, not contradictory, ways of seeking the truth*.

More conventionally, faith is understood as giving one's assent to a truth on the testimony of another. Its credibility rests on the trustworthiness of the testifier, and not on the content of the belief itself. Hence our second sutra: *what we believe depends on whom we trust*.

Now a reasoned assent to truth is not dependent on extrinsic testimony, but on a rational methodology that leads not to 'belief' but to 'knowledge'. This very method rests on basic premises like the reality and intelligibility of the world we live in, which cannot be logically proven, but must be existentially experienced. The collapse of old certainties with the critique of the old rationalist methodologies has today demonstrated the limits of the old Enlightenment rationalism and has led to alternative investigative approaches. Hence, in accepting the validity of a positivist methodology, we must also acknowledge its limitations. And so our third sutra: *a rational methodology transgressing its inherent limitations can never yield 'rightly reasoned' knowledge.*

Further, the sociology of knowledge has convincingly demonstrated how our underlying presumptions and pre-judgements are not subject to reason so much as socially derived from the 'unconscious ideologies' of the status quo, and fundamental options of vested interests. Consequently our fourth sutra: *where we position ourselves influences how we reason.*

Moreover, in 'faith' we must distinguish the 'content of belief', which is contingent, and the 'act of faith', which is necessary to live our interdependent lives and demand some measure of trust beyond oneself. If we grant that we are not the ground of our own being, then this 'faith' must transcend and reach beyond the horizon of the human. In an empirical-rationalist framé of reference, there is no room for such faith, that is, for 'what ultimately concerns man', as Paul Tillich described religion (Tillich 1958: 2). Hence our fifth sutra: *whether or not we believe depends on our self-understanding.*

In this sense Panikkar rightly insists on 'Faith as a Constitutive Human Dimension' (Panikkar 1983: 187-229) and the content of faith must fulfil, not negate this, i.e., belief must humanise the believers, not dehumanise them or demonise others. Tolerance then becomes the sign of 'good faith'. Therefore, our sixth sutra: *if to believe is human, then what we believe must make us more human, not less.*

Being more human is precisely the test of 'good faith', whereas with 'blind faith', the act of faith becomes compulsive rather than free, and fixated on promises of certainty and security and perhaps even grandiosity and ecstasy, rather than expressing trust and dependency. Hence sutra seven: *faith that is 'blind' is never truly humanising; faith that is not humanising is to that extent 'bad faith'.*

Now the language of faith communicates at the various levels of meaning, from the literal and the direct, to the symbolic and the metaphoric. Rather than an experimental methodology with the objective emphasis it demands, this needs a more self-reflexive and experiential methodology, which while being subjective is neither arbitrary nor irrational, but focuses on 'meaning' and 'meaningfulness', rather than merely measuring quantities and determining cause and effect. Thus our eighth sutra: *a self-reflexive and experiential methodology is meaningful to the discourse of faith; a rationalist-empirical one is alien to it.*

The basis for an enriching religious dialogue cannot be so much the *content of faith*, which may vary across different cultural and religious traditions. Rather because the *act of faith is constitutively human, it necessarily has a common religious basis across varying cultures and traditions*. This is our ninth sutra.

Today religious revivalism justifies the unreasonable and even the irrational in the name of faith, while a rationalist secularism dismisses all religious beliefs as irrational and unscientific. This merely turns the dilemma between faith and reason into an irresolvable dichotomy, not a constructive dialectic nor a creative dialogue. Therefore, our tenth sutra: *an inclusive humanism must embrace both 'meaningful faith', as well as 'sensitised reason'*. For it is only thus that we will be able to bring a healing wholeness to our bruised, broken world.

People confused and angered by the convulsive changes around them often seek security in the dogmatic affirmation of absolutes and uncritical submission to an authority, whether this 'faith' be religious or ideological, or even rationalist under the pretence of 'science'. There are fundamentalists in regard to reason, just as there are others on matters of faith. The temptation to fall into one or the other affects us all in varying degrees, though it is easy to point out the speck of compromise in the eyes of those struggling in their search for relevance, and to miss the beam of self-righteous complacency in one's own. And so to conclude with our last sutra: *the dialectic between faith and reason must be pursued in the context of tolerance and dialogue or it will degenerate into a hostile debate across an unbridgeable divide*. The worse danger, of course, is to fall into the 'fundamentalist trap' on one or the other side of the divide.

The content of faith refers to doctrine, both theological and moral, and defines orthodox and heterodox belief. This remains an intellectual abstraction. The concrete act of faith, as an act of trust in, and of surrender to, an ultimate beyond oneself, is an existential engagement to be lived in practice. Right belief implies conviction that has meaning, right practice demands commitment that affirms value. If belief and practice are to be humanising and open, not dogmatic and closed, they must be tested by reason. For this, reason itself must be sensitive to the relevant convictions and value commitments of faith. This is the dialectic between faith and reason. That can help steer us between fideism (the doctrine that knowledge depends on faith or revelation) and rationalism.

Gandhi sets up such a dialectic between faith and reason, in the context of a religious tradition, to make a genuinely new and creative synthesis of his religious belief and practice, even as he develops a powerful critique of rationalism. He is indeed the epitome of a person who requires his faith to be reasonable in terms of making his humanity authentic, just as he would demand that his reason be truly faithful to this humanity as well. For Gandhi, truth was the reality that possessed him and to which he surrendered in faith, more than the knowledge and understanding he grasped with his reason.

Much has been made of Gandhi's religious sense and sensitivity, but not enough has been said by way of examining the rational basis for this. We can see that Gandhi's 'inner voice', to which he gave such great importance in discerning and authenticating his life, was very much an experiential, intuitive self-reflective reasoning. But then again he refuses to be overwhelmed by reason. He is only one aware of its limitations.

Perhaps what rationalists have never examined is their own faith in 'rationality', and how easily this becomes another politically and/or socially committed ideology. Gandhi explicitly challenges modern rationalists to do this, even as he interrogates the traditional and popular faith of his people. For him human authenticity will be the measure for this critique for both faith and reason. The human is measured by God, not just the God who is Truth, but rather the Truth that is God, grasped with faith, yielded to as reasonable.

Gandhi can serve as our model for the dialectic process between faith and reason we must all engage in: firstly, each with our inner voice in conscience, then with each other in dialogue within and across religious traditions and cultural commitments, political ideologies and religious discourses. In a tension-fraught and conflict-ridden situation that religious conversion has precipitated in many societies, this dialect of faith and reason is the only way for us to begin to clear some common ground in tolerance for dialogue.

Most religious traditions go through a pendulum swing between the relative emphasis they place at different times on faith or reason. Usually, in their early beginnings, they tend to be more critical and open, later they get encrusted in ritual and embedded in institutions. The process of renewal must be a continuing call and the faith-reason dialectic response is the most rewarding and effective. Religious conversion, both as *atmaparivartan* within a tradition and as a *dharmantar* across them, focuses attention on this tension, which too often is met with fideistic suppression or rationalist dismissal, rather than a humanist and ethical critique.

Towards a global/universal Ethic

The atrocities of the last century have shocked us into the compelling need for some minimal standards of conduct between nations and among peoples. After two world wars and still continuing genocides of innocent and defenceless peoples, not to mention gross violation of fundamental human rights and basic freedoms in the name of 'political ideals' or ideological utopias, the urgency of a global ethic presses upon us with ever greater desperation. Violence as the 'argument of last resort' has become common currency. However, the violent resolution of conflict has only resulted in increasing violence and decreasing reconciliation, so that unresolved issues leave a trail of terror. The only answer to violence in our world seems to be more violence.

Given the inherent plurality of our world today, differences are bound to arise. We cannot escape the consequent ambiguities, no matter how much we may hanker after the old 'moral monism' and its secure certainties. While the dynamics of our present crisis forces on us the necessity of overarching universal standards, the same process makes this so much the more difficult with the pluralities it breeds. Without a commitment to a global ethic, we cannot effectively address this moral paradox.

A passive acceptance of this endemic and intransigent pluralism often leads to an uncritical relativism that does not allow for any mediating norms of justice and fair play. If everything is equally good or bad, right or wrong, then such value-neutral pluralism undermines the social solidarity and consensus on which society is premised. Without commonly accepted values, there can be no generally legitimated norms, since norms are derived from values and hence without either, there can be no viable critique for change. At best the status quo prevails, the relative status of groups remains unchanged and structural injustices unaddressed; at worst, the powerful impose a hegemony, against which there is no effective appeal but only symbolic, ritual protest. This does not make for an equal dialogue between partners.

Yet rejecting such relativism too hastily will lead to the opposite extreme that is unable to understand — let alone appreciate — differences, especially moral ones. For 'moral monism also runs the constant danger of grossly misunderstanding other ways of life and spells a hermeneutic disaster' (Parekh 2000: 49) i.e., misinterpretation confounding misunderstanding. How then do we cope with the collective threats we have created for ourselves in a pluralist universe of religious cultures and political ideologies? How can we come to an effective common agenda?

Anthony Giddens indicates four possible ways of dealing with a 'clash of values': through geographic segregation, active exit, positive dialogue and finally force or violence (Giddens 1994: 19). The first two are not viable in a globalizing world today. There is no safe haven now, no exit from the global cauldron, in which we are all being churned. Force and violence even as options of last resort are hardly viable any more, as the means of such violence have escalated to impossible levels of horror.

This leaves us with dialogue as a means to both resolve and celebrate 'difference' as a way of being more richly human.

The Parliament of World Religions in 1993 passed the 'Declaration Towards a Global Ethic'. Hans Kung, one of the key drafters of the Declaration, has elaborated this in three contemporary global challenges to which he proposes three corresponding responses (Kung 1998)

The first is the dangerous polarisation between believers and non-believers, the religious and the secular, the clerical and the non-clerical ... This can be readily illustrated with numerous examples from the West and the East, the North and the South. Hence the corresponding realisation: there is no survival of democracy without a coalition of believers and non-believers in mutual respect. This will demand some overarching commonality, in other words, a consensus for the foundation of our solidarity.

Secondly, the 'clash of civilisations' emphasised by Samuel Huntington (Huntington: 1996) threatens violence and has precipitated conflict, not just between nations, but inside them, not just among communities, but within them. At the state and community levels, group and individual ones, violent conflict has resulted in a massive loss of life and livelihood, in immense human suffering and wounded, unhealed memories. Now as Huntington rightly insists, religion is still at the core of culture and civilisation. This is so even in the fairly secularised, post-Christian west. Hence the logical conclusion: there will be no peace between civilisations without peace between religions; and there will be no peace between religion without dialogue between them. In other words, inter-religious dialogue becomes an ethical imperative.

Finally, religious revival and the fundamentalism that goes with it, leads to irreconcilable dogmatic differences. As we have seen, globalisation sharpens such differences in a diverse but imploding world. We need a new world order to contain such differences and resolve them, but there will be no new world order without a new global ethic. Hence, the ethical imperative must be at the heart of this quest for a new global order.

Kung (1998) makes an earnest attempt to found a global ethic on two basic principles: "'Every human being must be treated humanely', and 'what you wish done to yourself, do to others'". These principles would apply to all spheres of life: political, economic, religious; and at all levels: individual, group, community, nation, state.

These principles must be given some substantive content in terms of moral values: justice, truth, humanity, compassion, love...Further, these values must be spelt out in behavioural norms: non-violence and respect for life, social solidarity and a just economic order, tolerance and truthfulness, gender relations in terms of equality, partnership and respect.

Finally, these norms need to be worked out into concrete rights and duties, spelt out in an internationally recognised charter, like the UN declaration, but more importantly made effective at various levels by suitable structures and sanctions, legitimated and empowered to protect these values and implement the respective norms, to hold agencies to account and remedy violations. In other words, an ethic that is founded on values, which are grounded in cultures, made operational in norms, which are effectively enforced. All this would seem to add up to a utopia. However, considering the alternatives, it may well be a journey of a thousand miles that we must begin now with a few faltering steps. Alternatively, we may tumble ever further into ethical relativity and moral chaos.

However, the real problem with any proposed universal global ethic is that it stays at rather general levels of articulation in order to get a wider range of acceptance. To get a broad general assent, such lists of universal rights become so vague as to be virtually vacuous, but if they are made more specific, cultural differences could easily lead to a breakdown in the universal consensus. Gender relations and individual versus community claims are only the more obvious cross-cultural differences on which such a consensus is still quite elusive. Religious rights and values, norms and practices are another even more contentious arena.

Kung (1993: 86) has urged that what is truly human, the '*humanum*' (Kung 1993: 86) as the ideal of a fully developed human existence, must be the ground on which a universal ethic is premised and ethical differences, from varying cultural and religious traditions, resolved. These traditions have different understandings of what constitutes the 'truly human'. In the 'The Search for a Global Ethic', Jean Potter argues rightly that though we may concede 'a universal human nature that has moral implications', even so 'the commonalities of human nature are consistent with substantively different moral codes' (Porter, Jean, 2001: 119). Commonalities by themselves are not sufficient to generate a universally binding ethical code but they are a practical starting point for a viable working consensus.

However, there are countervailing 'little traditions' within every 'great tradition' that can become the critical points of departure to expand this common ground in an on-going process in search of this elusive universal ethic. We must grant that a universally accepted understanding of the 'truly human' is beyond our horizons at present. Yet, we can at least begin to discern the direction in which we must move to expand those horizons, and approach more closely to an ideal beyond our grasp but not quite outside our vision!

For while human moral codes are social constructs, in practice, specific norms draw on more universal values. Among these is an acknowledgement of a growing common ground that is more than trite generalities and empty platitudes. There are at least some species specific needs and inclinations that ground such universal values: 'values of the sanctity of human life, universal human rights, the preservation of species and care for future as well as present generations of children may perhaps be arrived at defensively, but they are certainly not negative values. They imply ethics of individual and collective responsibility, which (as value claims) are able to override divisions of interest' (Giddens 1994: 20).

This must be the starting point of a global ethic, which is yet an incomplete but not a directionless search, an ongoing, perhaps even a never-ending process, but one whose evolution leaves open the possibilities for progress as well as regress. A globalising world defines our moral responsibility even more acutely and compels this search for an authentic global ethic. This it is evidence of an ethical universal, pointing us to a truly humane 'humanism' we are still trying to uncover.

Mapping a new landscape

Today we need a global pluralism that will allow space not just for diversity, but also beyond it for a postcolonial sensitivity that will decolonise our mind and free our imagination. We need to be able to cope with multiple identities and to accept a radically new hybridisation. For this, we must first map the new social landscape today. It is becoming apparent even in the west that modernity is not singular or uniform, but decidedly multiple and diverse.

Simple binary choices are no longer viable now, for binary models substitute one kind of homogeneity for another (Sarkar 2002: 186). We need multiple frames of references, multiple selves, multiple identities to function in our world today (Goonatilake 1997: 232).

For a discourse that remains within the framework of binary opposition lacks the resources for creatively imagining how, as the World Social Forum insists, 'Another World Is Possible', where complex multiple identities reflect a new creativity in imaging possible lives. The task in this context of rethinking religious conversion is to map a brave new world into the global and the local, to locate it within the multi-dimensional processes at work in an ever-changing complex, to measure this against our tolerance, and to risk ourselves in dialogue.

In a constructive agenda for the future, conversion as process must be oriented more in terms of continuity and harmony, than in discontinuity and contention. As change, it must be more an affirmation than a negation. As tolerance, it must be more ethical and religious, mystical and spiritual, than just pragmatic and political, or intellectual and philosophic. As dialogue, it must be engaged in at all four levels of life, action, experience and articulation, in free and equal, not coercive and alienating, partnership.

The faith-reason dialectic can serve to make faith critical and reason faithful, and forge a consensus for a universal global ethic. Once some common ground has been cleared, on which diverse understandings meet, we can situate ourselves more adequately to address the many different perspectives and polarities that agitate the various players on the numerous issues that divide them on religious conversion.

Whether explicitly the category is used or, not all religious traditions convert, both in terms of an *atmaparivartan* as well as a *dharmantar*, some by way of absorption and integration, others by spreading the message they feel commissioned to. Some traditions do this more explicitly, others more implicitly. Too often mismatches and misunderstandings stifle any constructive agenda. Clearing this minefield has left many retreating, defeated and maimed in the encounter. Yet there is no other viable way around.

In August 1948, the World Council of Churches (WCC) in its 'Declaration on Religious Liberty' (WCC 1948: 229-32) affirmed that 'freedom of religion is an essential and integral aspect of human freedom', and defined it to include the 'freedom to choose ... religious beliefs' and to 'propagate and persuade' others. Under Christian influence the UN's 'Universal Declaration on Human Rights' in December 1948, proclaimed in Article 18 the universal right to 'change' and to 'manifest', one's religion or belief in 'teaching, practice and observance.'

These are clearly individual rights and liberties. By the 1960s, the understanding of human rights broadened to include a second order of rights, i.e., economic, social and cultural ones. This marked a shift from a civil-libertarian understanding of rights to a more collective communitarian one. Community and group rights were now recognised with individual ones.

In 1966, the UN 'International Covenant on Civil and Political Rights' declared in Article 18 (2): 'No one shall be subject to coercion which would impair his freedom to have or to adopt a religion or belief of his choice.' This was considered necessary to allow for freedom of choice and at the same time to protect individuals from over-zealous proselytisers. Religious freedom now emphasised the right to change or maintain one's faith, not the right to convert or proselytise others. In 1977, our own Supreme Court in its judgement on the Freedom of Religion Acts of Madhya Pradesh and Orissa reflected this view.

Protection against proselytisation is now seen as the right of a community to its own religious tradition, much in the same way as the right to its own language and culture. Without this no group or community can feel any real acceptance in society. This is why they are contested with such political passion. Religion is an intrinsic part of these cultural rights. What this actually means in the concrete context of religious freedom and rights needs to be creatively and imaginatively worked through.

Individual rights are founded on the human person's inviolable dignity, whereas cultural and religious rights are grounded in the ethnic community's distinctive identity. What is experienced as a person-community tension in a society is carried over into the area of individual and community rights. A resolution of such tensions must be premised on an understanding of person and community as complementary, not contrary, of the human individual as necessarily person-in-community, in inter-dependent relationship, not in self-sufficient isolation; of human groups as a community of inter-related persons, not an aggregate of individuals.

There is a delicate balance between person and community, and religious freedom must be sensitive to both. Cultural collective rights cannot override fundamental individual ones, nor vice versa. For instance, a right to culture cannot mean that a patriarchal tradition is exempted from gender justice, or that a community can forbid the right of an individual to learn or speak another language: so too, individual liberty must respect public order, and freedom of speech must be sensitive to community and public sentiment.

There are differences not only between the individual and the group, but also between groups and peoples. At the level of the group, differences can be even more intractable and uncompromising than at the individual level. There is a dilemma here, but if we concede a priority to the universally human (a global ethic), over the culturally specific (cultural customs or religious rituals), then a constructive reconciliation is possible. A homogenising universalism must not override and negate cultural and religious diversities. These must be respected and even celebrated. However, neither the right to culture and religion are unconditional. For cultural and religious rights cannot contradict more fundamental human rights, rather they can only be legitimate in the context of a culture of rights and in a religious tradition of tolerance.

With religious conversion, it is of crucial importance that when group identities are reconstructed, the human dignity of sub-groups and persons is not violated. For only when cultural and religious rights are an extension, not a curtailment, of fundamental and human rights can they claim legitimacy in the larger civil and political society. Only a sustained commitment to tolerance guarantees equal treatment and dignity for groups, much as it does for individual persons. This is Gandhi's insight of equal respect and he so effectively based his practice of ahimsa and satyagraha on such an ethic.

Many dharmas

The Hindu concept of dharma is not the best equivalent of 'religion'. Although religion can be translated as one kind of dharma, in general dharma is not adequately translated as 'religion'. The concept is richer and needs to be refined further. Thus, *sadhana* dharma would mean religious spirituality, while *samaj* dharma refers to the binding obligations of one's place in society. Further *svadharma* is the obligation of personal conscience we all experience, and may not always be the same as that internalised in one's *samaj* dharma.

An *atmaparivartan* pertains to one's *sadhana* dharma and *svadharma*. It may often be more in continuity than in disjunction with one's past, but is still within the same religious tradition. A *dharmantar* inevitably means a change in *samaj* dharma and so impacts the inter-group and community relationships in a society. Understandably, religious traditions are far more challenged and threatened by a *dharmantar* than an *atmaparivartan*.

Religious conversion pertains to religious belief and practice, but to perceive it only at this level is to leave out more than is comprehended. The change in religious identity and the allegiance it implies has an inevitable social impact on the religious traditions to which these changing identities and allegiance are bound. It is here that differences must be faced and reconciled where possible, rather than just those in doctrinal conflicts or ritual disputes.

Hence, the closer a society is tied in with the prevailing status quo, in terms of binding relationships between religious and ethnic groups, among members within and across these, the more affected it will be when there is a change of identity or allegiance that upsets the prevailing structures of the social system. Consequently, religious conversion is more opposed in hierarchical and closed societies than in more egalitarian and open ones. Thus caste society opposes conversion whether of dalits or of Brahmins, while tribal societies find the conversion of members of their clans less objectionable.

Societies that favour freedom, personal and social, can be expected to be more open to individuals and groups exercising their freedom of choice even with regard to religious conversion. All religious traditions in principle, if not in practice, claim to privilege such freedom. Yet, when this choice goes against these same communities, there is ambiguity and equivocation, mostly justified in terms of community and tradition at the cost of persons or groups converting.

The more a society emphasises *samaj* dharma over *svadharma* the more a *dharmantar* will affect and threaten it, especially if this happens with significant individuals or sizeable groups. Vice versa, the more a society privileges *svadharma* and *sadhana* dharma the more freedom of choice it will be able to accommodate. Authoritarian religious fundamentalists stress *samaj dharma* and collective conformity in their endeavour at revival, while democratic religious reformists will emphasise *svadharma* and personal commitment in the efforts at renewal. An *atmaparivartan* in the *sadhana* dharma on both sides could begin the search for a meeting point, beginning with the intra-religious, to reach out to the inter-religious.

Yet, necessary as it certainly is, it would be naïve to pretend that a theoretical discussion about intellectual perspectives would be adequate to address the issues and concerns on the ground without a committed and enlightened practical agenda. The first step proposed here has been to clear some common ground using the faith-reason dialectic from which to reach across differences with tolerance in dialogue. Unfortunately, it is not usual for the extremists on either side of this divide, whether proponents or opponents of conversion, to be open to such an introspection. However, an interrogation from without only leads to a defensiveness within, and further confirms their extremism and deepens their divisions. Caught in between are the would-be converts who sometimes feel too pressured and helpless to make such a critical introspection for themselves, though they too, like the others, do need such an examination of conscience.

However, there are moderates and seekers on both sides, and critical and courageous converts to whom such an appeal can be made. I believe there are many more of these than we imagine. Unfortunately, it is the implicit support of the more mainstream moderates, which fundamentalists claim and use to justify their extremism. When this aggressive extremism is allowed to hide behind the silence of their communities, then such silence can be bloody, even for those in the community itself. When moderate voices deny legitimacy to suicidal jihadis, trishul-wielding *swayamsevaks* and rampaging crusaders, they undermine the community support base, moral and otherwise, of such extremists. Deprived of legitimacy and support, new recruitment to such fanaticism will eventually dwindle.

There is much need for a serious and honest introspection by all involved: what are our religious concerns affirming? What are they negating? Where and how do our other non-religious interests intervene? Perhaps a large part of our real issues may be less religious than psychological and social, political and economic. These must be addressed as such, and not obfuscated with religion out of pragmatic expediency and political short-sightedness. Hopefully, such soul-searching questions on religious conversion will be honestly faced by both the converter and converted, opponents and proponents, the unconverted and the would-be converts too. This will help initiate a practical agenda to address our real preoccupations more adequately.

In our tense and polarised situation, to avoid such an introspection is to expose ourselves and society to great risk. It is urgent and imperative that the powerful and dominant be more sensitive and introspective on these issues, than the subordinate and oppressed. For the protection of the rights of the weaker must be the greater responsibility of the stronger, just as the more powerful ought to be more tolerant than the more helpless.

Freeing the imagination

Coping in our complex world of fuzzy community boundaries, of historical discontinuities and disintegrating structures, demands multiple identities for the varying, diverse situations that engulf us. We need to free our imagination and project a new creativity beyond a narcissism of victimhood and submissiveness, or of grandiosity and arrogance. We need to imagine other worlds and other lives in the interstices beyond the binary oppositions in which we entrap ourselves.

It is also possible that for the sake of public order and communal harmony religious leaders come to an agreement to tread lightly in this arena of religious conversions. Such agreements have been worked out before in some sensitive situations, as between the Roman and the Orthodox Churches with 'Practical Rules' in the joint declaration at Balamand, Lebanon. (*Information Service* 1993: 98, No. 22). In view of larger ecumenical concerns, the agreement between these churches was not to encourage individual conversions. Likewise in 1995, the World Council of Churches' joint working group announced a similar agreement between Catholics and Protestants (*ibid.* 1996: 82, No. s 34-37). The committee on inter-religious affairs of the Catholic Bishops

Conference of the US in its 'Reflection on Covenant and Mission' on 12 August 2002 declared it unacceptable to target Jews in their evangelisation.

As recently as 12 – 16 May 2006 at Lariano in Italy, an inter-religious meeting of representatives from Buddhism, Christianity, Hinduism, Islam, Judaism and Yoruba religion, was hosted by the Pontifical Council for Inter-Religious Dialogue, Vatican City, and the Office on Interreligious Relations and Dialogue of the World Council of Churches, Geneva, on "Conversion: Assessing the Reality". Their concluding reflections and recommendations are an apt example of the kind of religious disarmament urged in our discourse here and are important enough to be quoted at length: (*Vidyajyoti*, Vol. 70, No. 8 Aug. 2006: pp. 625- 628)

1. All of us believe that religions should be a source of uniting and ennobling of humans. Religion, understood and practiced in the light of the core principles and ideals of each of our faiths, can be a reliable guide to meeting the many challenges before humankind.
2. Freedom of religion is a fundamental, inviolable and non-negotiable right of every human being in every country in the world. Freedom of religion connotes the freedom, without any obstruction, to practice one's own faith, freedom to propagate the teachings of one's faith to people of one's own and other faiths, and also the freedom to embrace another faith out of one's own free choice.
3. We affirm that while everyone has a right to invite others to an understanding of their faith, it should not be exercised by violating other's rights and religious sensibilities. At the same time, all should heal themselves from the obsession of converting others.
4. Freedom of religion enjoins upon all of us the equally non-negotiable responsibility to respect faiths other than our own, and never to denigrate, vilify or misrepresent them for affirming superiority of our faith.
5. We acknowledge that errors have been perpetrated and injustice committed by the adherents of every faith. Therefore, it is incumbent on every community to conduct honest self-critical examination of its historical conduct as well as its doctrinal/ theological precepts. Such self-criticism and repentance should lead to necessary reforms *inter alia* on the issue of conversion.

6. A particular reform, we would commend to practitioners and establishments of all faiths is to ensure that conversion by "unethical" means are discouraged and rejected by all. There should be transparency in the practice of inviting others to one's faith.
7. While deeply appreciating humanitarian work by faith communities, we feel that it should be conducted without any ulterior motives. In the area of humanitarian service in times of need, what we can do together, we should not do separately.
8. No faith organization should take advantage of vulnerable sections of society, such as children and the disabled.
9. During our dialogue, we recognized the need to be sensitive to the religious language and theological concepts in different faiths. Members of each faith should listen to how people of other faiths perceive them. This is necessary to remove and avoid misunderstandings, and to promote better appreciation of each other's faiths.
10. We see the need of usefulness of a continuing exercisely to collectively evolve a "code of conduct" on conversion, which all faiths should follow. We therefore feel that inter-religious dialogues on the issue of conversion should continue at various levels.

(Vidyajyoti, 2007 : 625-678)

Nothing prevents an extension of similar agreements in South Asia and elsewhere, but this can only be by mutual acceptance between the partners in the dialogue and not by an imposition of the powerful or an enforced abridgement of weaker citizens' rights. A more effective and sensible approach to defuse such tensions is to find ways of transforming and liberalising religio-cultural traditions from within, rather than subjecting them to the threat of destruction or humiliation by denigration from without. This only provokes defensiveness and resistance, sometimes even escalating violence.

However, to try to freeze the status quo is to trap people in the very situations from which they seek to escape in order to affirm the identity and dignity that have too long been denied them. Whether this be motivated by religious conviction and spiritual enlightenment, or by social equality and political freedom, or whatever else, their choice to convert is still well within their rights. It must not be negated by those who might be offended by this nor manipulated by those who would take advantage of them.

We need to heed Jesus' own harsh and uncompromising condemnation of the kind of proselytisation he encountered among the scribes and Pharisees of his time, for it surely applies to many religious fundamentalists today (Matthew 23: 13). We would do well to hear him urging his disciples to preach in poverty and powerlessness: 'Take no gold, nor silver, nor copper in your belts, no bag for your journey, nor two tunics, nor scandals, nor a staff ...' (Matthew 10: 9 - 10).

We need to rediscover the *nishkamakarma* (disinterested action) of the Bhagvadgita and the compassion of the *bodhisattvas*. We must turn the Islamic jihad to the internal struggle for reform that it was originally intended to be, and not let it get lost in the external one of revivalism and violence. We need to urge Christian crusaders to address the ethical crises in their own societies and not seek to impose a Christian salvation on unsuspecting others. We need a Gandhi to guide us once again into the powerful, peaceful depths of ahimsa and satyagraha.

In this context, Gandhi's favourite talisman of the last Indian can help us free ourselves from excessive introversion and reach out imaginatively to engage our world:

> 'Whenever in doubt recall the face of the poorest and the weakest man whom you may have seen, and ask yourself if the step you contemplate is going to be of any use to him.' (CW 89: 125).

I would be like to turn around to this talisman. For we need not just to interrogate ourselves on how our decisions will affect the last and least, but rather to allow the poorest and weakest to affect, or rather 'infect' our decisions and our worldview. What place do the poorest and the weakest have on my decisions and worldview? In the discernments for my decisions, how central are they to my deliberations? Beyond any introspection, this is the interrogation to which any stance on conversion must be subjected, and to which we must respond from where we stand and who we are, whether as proponents or opponents, converts or would-be ones ourselves.

Religion is not just a large and critical part of our culture; it is at the core of culture, especially in a society where popular religiosity is predominant and religious traditions central. Religious beliefs and institutional interests also dig themselves into self-defensive bunkers, and trench warfare becomes a battle of attrition in the attempt to overrun and dislodge each other. Religious conversion can bring about an intensification of religious differences and antagonisms or it can be the occasion to review and resolve them.

When a culture entrenches its values and vested interests as non-negotiable, a *Cultural Disarmament* is the only *Way to Peace* (Panikkar 1995). Today we need similar commitment to a 'religious disarmament' to open a way to intra-/inter-religious harmony and intra-/inter-communal peace.

In the final analysis, a 'rethink' on religious conversion in this country must lead us to this: a struggle, a jihad, for the 'Soul of India', not just for 'souls in India'; an endeavour to sow the good seed of a meaningful, relevant faith for a hundredfold harvest of peace, premised on tolerance and justice, forgiveness and reconciliation. The father of our nation would surely bless such a venture for the *India of My Dreams*.

Bibliography

Adhav, S.M., ed., 1979, *Pandita Ramabai*, Christian Literature Society, Chennai.

Adhav, S.M. ed. 1958, *Pandita Ramabai Centenary Souvenir*, Bombay.

Ahmad, Imtiaz, 2002, "Urdu and Madrasa Education", *Economic and Political Weekly*, 37, No. 24, 15 Jun., pp. 2285-2287.

Ahmad, Imtiaz, ed. 1978, *Caste and Social Stratification among Muslims in India*, Manohar, N. Delhi.

Ahmad, Irfan, 2003, "Á Different Jihad: Dalit Muslim' Challenge to Asraf Hegemony", *Economic and Political Weekly*, Vol. 38, No. 46, 15 Nov., pp. 4886-4891.

Ahmed, Akbar, 1999, *Islam Today: A Short Introduction to the Muslim World*, I. B. Tauris, London.

All India Reporter, (AIR) Madhya Pradesh, 1975.

AIR, Orissa, 1973:120 See Ch. 2.5 p. 4.

AIR, Supreme Court, 1977.

Alam, Anwar, 2003, "Democratisation of Indian Muslims: Some Reflections", *Economic and Political Weekly*, Vol. 38, No. 46, 15 Nov., pp. 4881-4885.

Alavi, Hamsa, 2002, "Social Forces and Ideology in the Making of Pakistan", *Economic and Political Weekly*, Vol. 37, No. 51, 21 Dec., pp. 5119-5124.

Aloysius, G. 1997, *Nationalism without a Nation in India*, Oxford Univ. Press, Delhi.

Ambedkar, 1945, *What Congress and Gandhi have Done to the Untouchables* Thacker and Company, Mumbai.

Anderson, Benediet 1983, *Imagined Communities: Reflections on the Origin and Spread of Nationalism*, Verso, London.

Armstrong, Karen, 2000, *The Battle for God*, Alfred, A. Knopf, New York.

Armstrong, Karen, 1994, *a History of God: The 4000-Year Quest of Judaism, Christianity and Islam*, Alfred A. Knopf, New York.

Atmaprana, Pravrajika, 1961, *Sister Nivedita of Ramakrisha-Vivekananda*, Sister Nivedita Girls' School, Calcutta.

Atmaprana, Pravrajika, ed., 1982, *Studies from an Eastern Home, Complete Works of Sister Nivedita*, 2nd ed., Vol. 2, Advaita Ashrama, Calcutta.

Augustine, John S., ed., 1993, *Religious Fundamentalism: An Asian Perspective*, Asian Theological Research Institute, Bangalore.

Aurobindo, 1972, *Karmayogin, Early Political Writings*, Vol. 2, Sri Aurobindo Birth Centenury Library, Pondicherry.

Aurobindo, 1918, *'The Ideal of Karmayogin'*, Sri Aurobindo Ashram, Pondicherry.

Balachandra, G., 1996, "Religion and Nationalism in Modern India", in Basu and Subrahmanyam eds., op. cit., pp. 81-128.

Bapat, Ram, 1995, *Pandita Ramabai: Faith and Reason in the Shadow of the East and West*, Dalmia and Stietencron, op. cit., pp. 224-252.

Bayley, Susan, 1989, *Saints, Goddesses and Kings: Muslims and Christians in South Indian Society, 1700 - 1900,* Cambridge Univ. Press, Cambridge, UK.

Basham A. L., 1975, *A Cultural History of India*, Clarendon Press, Oxford.

Basham A. L., 1989, *The Origins and Development of Classical Hinduism*, ed. and annotated by Kenneth G. Zysk, Oxford Univ. Press, New Delhi.

Basu, Kaushik and Sanjay Subrahmanyam, 1996, *'Unravelling the Nation: Sectarian Violence and India's Secular Identity'*, Penguin, New Delhi.

Boehmer, Elleke, 2002, *Empire, the National, and the Postcolonial, 1890 - 1920: Resistance and Interaction*, Oxford Univ. Press. Delhi.

Bose, Nirmal Kumar, 1994, *The Structure of Hindu Society*, rev. ed., earlier ed. 1975, Orient Longman, New Delhi.

Buhlmann, Walbert, 1977, *The Coming of the Third Church*, Orbis Books, New York.

Bultmann, Rudolf, 1961, *Kerygma and Myth*, Harper and Row, New York.

Campell, Joseph, 1991, *The Power of Myth*, Anchor Books, New York.

Carr, E. H., 1990, *What Is History*, Penguin, England.

Catholic Bishops Conference of the United States of America, 2002, "Reflection on Covenant and Mission", Committee on Inter-religious Affairs, Washington D.C.

Chakravarti, Uma, 1998, *Rewriting History: The Life and Theme of Pandita Ramabai*, Kali for Women, N. Delhi.

Chambers, Robert, 1983. *Rural Development: Putting the Last First*, Longman, London.

Chenchiah, Pandipeddi, 1939, "Jesus and Non-Christian Faiths", in Devasahayam and A. N. Sundarisanam (eds.), *Rethinking Christianity in India*, Christian Literary Society, Madras, pp. 47-62.

Census 1911, Volume-II (India Report). Government of India, N. Delhi.

Conn, Walter E, ed., *Conversion: Perspectives on Personal and Social Transformation*, Alba House, New York.

Constitutional Assembly Debates: Official Report, (CAD) 1948, 7 Vols., Government of India Manager of Publications, Delhi.

Cort, John E., ed., 1998, *Open Boundaries: Jain Communities and Cultures in Indian History*, New York Press, New York.

Baago, Kaj, 1966, "The Post Colonial Crisis of Missions", *International Review of Missions*, Vol. 60, No. 221, Jan., pp. 322-32.

Dallmayr, Fred R., 1989, "Hermeneutics and Deconstruction: Gadamer and Derrida in Dialogue", in eds., Michelfelder and Palmer, op. cit., pp.75-92.

Dalmia, Vasudha and Heinrich Von Stietencron ed., 1995, *Representing Hinduism:'The Construction of Religious Traditions and National Identity'*, Sage Publication, N. Delhi.

Das, Bhagwan, ed., 1963, *'Thus Spake Ambedkar'*, Vol. 1- 4, Bheem Patrika, Publications, Jullander.

Das, Veena, ed. 1992, *Mirrors of Violence: Communities, Riots and Survivors in South Asia*, Oxford University Press: Delhi.

D'Costa Anthony, 1965, Heras Institute, Mumbai.

Devadason, E. D, 1977, 'Supreme Court Judgement on the Orissa Freedom of Religion Act, 1967, National Historian Council Review, Vol. 97, No. 9, Sept., pp. 433 – 437.

Devasahayam and A. N. Sundarisanam (eds.) 1939, *Rethinking Christianity in India*, Christian Literary Society, Madras.

"Dialogue and Proclamation", 1991, Pontifical Council for Inter-Religious Dialogue, Vatican City, cited Vidyajyoti, 2007, op. cit.

Dutt, Dev, 1986, "Conversions: A Viewpoint", in Swarup, ed. op.cit, pp. 35-46.

Dutta, R. C., 1906, *History of India*, Vol. 1, Croloier Society, London, Baroda edition.

Dwyer, Rachael, 2006, *Filiming the Gods: Religion and Indian Cinema*, Routledge, Taylor, Francis Group, London, New York.

Eaton, Richard , 2004, "Approaches to the Study of Conversion to Islam in India" in ed. David N. Lorenzen, *Religious Movements in South Asia 600 - 1800*, Oxford Univ. Press, Delhi, pp. 106 - 127.

Eaton, Richard, 1984, "Conversion to Christianity among the Nagas: 1876 - 1871", *'The Indian Economic and Social History Review'*, Vol. 212, No. 1, Sage, Delhi, pp. 1 - 44.

Eaton, Richard, 1994, *The Rise of Islam and the Bengal Frontier, 1204 - 1760*, Oxford Univ. Press, Delhi.

Engineer, Asghar Ali, 2004, *Communal Riots After Independence: A Comprehensive Account*, Shipra Pub., Delhi.

Fernando, Leonard & G. Gispert-Sauch, 2004, *Christianity in India*, Penguin, N. Delhi.

Frykenberg, Robert Eric 2003, *Christian Missionaries in India: 'Cross-Cultural Communication since 1500 with Special reference to Caste', Conversion and Colonialism*, William B. Eerdmans Publ., Grand Rapids, Michigan & Cambridge, UK.

Fuchs, Stephen, 1992, "The Religion of Indian Tribals", in Buddhadeb Chaudhuri, ed., *Tribal Transformation*, Inter-India Publication, N. Delhi, Vol. V, pp. 23-51.

Fukuyama, Francis, *'The End of History and the Last Man'*, Avon Books, New York, 1992.

Gadamer, Hans-Georg, 1975, *Truth and Method*, Seabury Press, New York.

Gadamer, Hans-Georg, 1989, "Destruktion and Deconstruction.", in ed.s, Michelfelder and Palmer, op. cit., pp. 102, 113.

Ganaveer, Ratnakar, ed.1981, *Mahad Samatá Sangar* (Marathi), Jalgaon: Ratnamitra Prakashan, Bhusaval.

Gandhi, M. K., 1941, *Christian Missions: 'Their Place in India'*, ed., Bharatan Kumarappa, Ahmedabad, Navajivan Publishing House.

Gandhi, M. K., 1950, *'Hindu Dharma'*, ed., Bharatan Kumarappa, Ahmedabad Navajivan Publishing House.

Gandhi, Mohandas K., *Collected Works*, 1958 - 89, 100 vols, Government of India, N. Delhi. Referred to in text as CW.

Geertz, Clifford, 1973, '*The Interpretation of Cultures*', Fontana Press, New York.

Ghurye, G. S. 1963, '*The Scheduled Tribes*', Popular Prakashan, Mumbai, 3rd ed.

Ghruye, G. S. 1969, '*Caste and Race in India*', Popular Prakashan, Mumbai.

Giddens, Anthony, 1994, *Beyond Left and Right: 'The Future Radical Politics'*, Polity Press, Cambridge, UK.

A Global Ethic: 'The Declaration of the Parliament of the World's Religion', 1998: 11- 40, Continuum, New York.

Goddard, Hugh, 1995, *Christians and Muslims: From Double Standards to Mutual Understanding,* Curzon Press, Surrey, England.

Goel, Sita Ram, 1998, *Vindicated by Time: The Niyogi Committee Report on Christian Missionary Activity*, Voice of India, N. Delhi.

Golwalkar, M.S., 1939, *We, or our Nationhood Defined*, Bharat Publications, Nagpur.

Golwalkar, M.S, 1980, *Bunch of Thoughts*, Jagarana Prakashana, Bangalore.

Goonatilake, Susantha. 1997, "The self wondering between cultural localisation and globalization", in eds, Nederveen and Parekh, op.cit., pp. 225 - 239.

Gore, M.S. 1993, *The Social Context of an Ideology: Ambedkar's Political and Social Thought, Sage. N. Delhi.*

Graham, Carol, 1946, *Azariah of Dornakal*, SCM Press, London.

Gramsci, Antonio, 1996, *Selections from the Prison Notebooks*, ed., trans., Quintin Hoare and Geoffrey Nowell Smith, Orient Longman, Madras.

Grover, Verinder & Ranjana Arora, ed., 1993, *Sister Nivedita: 'Her Contribution to Political Economic and Social Developmen't*, Deep and Deep, N. Delhi.

Gupta, Dipankar, 1999, "Secularization and Minoritisation", in ed. Kumar Anand, *Nation-Building in India: Culture, Power and Society*, Radiant Publishers, N. Delhi. pp.75-84.

Hardiman, David, 1987, *The Coming of the Devi: Adivasi Assertion in Western India*, Oxford University Press, Bombay.

Hardiman, David, 2003, *Gandhi in His Times and Ours: The global legacy of his ideas*, Hurst, London.

Hardy, Friedheim, 1995, "A Radical Reassesment of the Vedic Heritage -The *Acaryahrdayam* and it Wider Implications" ed. Dalmia and Stietencron, op. cit. pp. 35-50.

Heras, Henry, 1933, *The Conversion Policy of the Jesuits in India*, Indian Historical Research Institute, Mumbai, pp. 39-44.

Hodge, J. Z., 1946, *Bishop Azariah of Dronakal*, Christian Literature Society for India, Madras.

Horne, Francis, 1967, *The Illusion of Permanence: British Imperialism in India*, Princeton Univ. Press, Princeton.

Horton, Robin, 1975, "On the Rationality of Conversion," Part I, *Africa,* Vol. 45, no. 3, 1975, pp. 219 - 235, and 1975, Part II, *Africa*, Vol. 45, no. 4, pp. 373 - 399. Also 1971, "African Conversion," *Africa*, 41, 2, Apr. pp. 85-108.

Huntington, Samuel P. 1996, *The Clash of Civilizations and the Remaking of World Order*, Simon and Schuster, New York.

Huntington, Samuel P., 2004, *Who Are We? The Challenges to America's National Identity*, Simon and Schuster.

Information Service, 1993, No. 83, (II), pp. 95 - 99, Vatican City.

Information Service, 1996, No. 91, (I-II), pp. 77 - 83, Vatican City.

Iyer, Raghavan, 1973. *The Moral and Political Thought of Mahatma Gandhi*, Oxford Univ. Press, Oxford.

Jaffrelot, Christophe, 2005, *Dr. Ambedkar and Untouchability*, Hurst, London.

Jinnah, Mohamed Ali, 1948, *Speeches of the Quaid-i-Azam Mohammad Ali Jinnah as Governor General of Pakistan*, Sind Observer Press, Karachi.

Jordens, J.T.F. 1998, *Gandhi's Religion: A Homespun Shawl*, MacMillan Press, London,

Joshi, Barbara, 1984, *Untouchable! Voices of Dalit Liberation*, 2nd ed. Books, London.

Kabir, Humayun, 1955, *The Indian Heritage*, Asia Pub. House, Mumbai.

Kakar, Sudhir, 1992, "Some Unconscious Aspects of Ethinic Violence", in ed. Veena Das, op. cit., pp. 135 - 145.

Kakar, Sudhir. 1993. "Reflections on Religious Group Identity," *Seminar*, No. 402, pp. 50 - 55.

Kaviraj, Sudipto, 1992, "The Imaginary Institution of India", in Parthna Chatterjee and Gyanendra Pandey, eds., *Subaltern Studies VII*, Oxford Univ. Press, Delhi.

Kim, Sebastian, 2003, *In Search of Identity: Debates on Religious Conversions in India*, Oxford Univ. Press, Delhi.

Keer, Dhananjay, 1962, *Dr. Ambedkar: Life and Mission*, 2nd ed., Popular Prakashan, Mumbai.

Kellenberger, ed. 1993, *Inter-Religious Models and Criteria*, MacMillan, London.

Khan, Mumtaz Ali, 1983, *Mass-Conversions of Meenakshipuram: 'A Sociological Enquiry'*, The Chirstian Literature Society, Chennai.

Kosmbi, D. D., 1962, *Myth and Reality: Studies in the Formation of Indian Culture*, Popular Prakashan, Mumbai.

Kosambi, D. D., 1975, *An Introduction to the Study of Indian History*, 2nd revised ed. Popular Prakashan, Mumbai.

Kosambi, Meera, 2000, *Pandita Ramabai Through Her Own Words: Selected Works*, Oxford Uni. Press, N. Delhi.

Kumar Anand, 1999, *Nation-Building in India: Culture, Power and Society*, Radiant Publishers, N. Delhi.

Kumarappa, Bharatan, ed., 1941, *M. K., Gandhi: Christian Missions: Their Place in India*, Ahmedabad, Navajivan Publishing House.

Kumarappa, Bharatan, ed., 1950. *M. K. Gandhi: Hindu Dharma*, Ahmedabad, Navajivan Publishing House.

Kung, Hans, 1985, *Christianity and the World Relgions: Paths of Dialogue with Islam, Hinduism, and Buddhism*, Trans. Peter Heinegg, William, Collins and Sons, Glasgow.

Kung, Hans, 1998, *A Global Ethic for Global Politics and Economics*, Oxford Univ. Press, Oxford.

Kung, Hans, 1993, *Global Responsibility: In Search of a New World Ethic*, Continuum, New York.

Lele, Jayant, 1995, *Hindutva: The Emergence of the Right*, Earthworm Books, Madras.

Lonergan, Bernard, 1978, "The Dimensions of Conversion," in ed. Walter E. Conn, op. cit. *Conversion: Perspectives on Personal and Social Transformation*, pp. 15-21. Reprinted from *Method in Theology*, pp. 237-43.

Lorenzen, David N., ed, 2004, *Religious Movements in South Asia 600 - 1800*, Oxford Univ. Press, Delhi.

Ludden, David, 1989, *Peasant History of South India*, Oxford Univ. Press, Delhi.

MacNincol, Nicol and Vishal Mangalwadi, 1996, *Pandita Ramabai: A Builder of Modern India*, Nivedita Good Books, Mussoorie, India.

Majumdar, R.C., 1963, *Hindu Colonies in the Far East*, 2nd. Ed., K. L. Firma, Kolkata.

Madan, T. N., 1997, *Modern Myths, Locked Minds: Secularism and Fundamentalism in India*, Oxford Univ. Press, N. Delhi.

Malraux, Andre, 1970, *Antimemoirs*, Penguin, England.

Marak, Krickwin C., and Plamthodathil S, Jacob, 2000, *Conversion in a Pluralist Context: Perspectives and Perceptions*, Indian Society for the Promotion of Christian Knowledge, Delhi.

Mathew, George, 1982, "Politicisation of Religion: Conversions to Islam in Tamil Nadu", *Economic and Political Weekly*, Vol. 17, No. 25, 19 Jun., pp. 1027-34, and No. 26, 26 Jun., pp. 1063-72.

Mathew, P.D., 2002, *Freedom of Religion and a Debate on Religious Conversions*, Indian Social Institute, N. Delhi.

Mazumdar In A.K.,ed., 1968, *Nivedita commemoration Volume*, Vivekananda Janmotsava Samiti, Calcutta.

McKean, Lise, 1996, *Divine Enterprise: Gurus and the Hindu Nationalist Movement*, Univ. of Chicago, Chicago.

Mehta, Bhanu Pratap, 2003, "Passion and Constraint", *Seminar*, No. 521, Jan. pp. 54-57.

Menon, Nivedita, 2004, "Citizenship and the Passive Revolution: Interpreting the First Amendment", *Economic and Political Weekly*, Vol. 39, No. 18, 1 May, pp. 1802-1819.

Michelfelder. Diane P. and Richard E. Palmer, eds., 1989, *Dialogue and Deconstruction: 'The Gadamer-Derrida Encounter'*, State Univ. of New York.

Moon, Vasant, ed. 1979, *'Revolution and Counter-Revolution in Ancient India'*, in *Dr. Babasaheb Ambedkar: 'Writings and Speeches'*, 1987(a), Vol. 3, Dept. of Education, Govt. of Maharashtra, Mumbai.

Moon, Vasant, ed. 1979. *Dr. Babasaheb Ambedkar: Writings and Speeches*, Bombay: Dept. of Education, Got. of Maharashtra, Vol. 1

———, ed. 1982, Vol. 2.

———, ed. 1987(a), Vol. 3.

———, ed. 1987(b), Vol. 4.

———, ed. 1990(a), Vol. 7.

———, ed. 1990(b), Vol. 8.

———, ed. 1991, Vol. 9.

Muller, Max Friedrich, 1899, *Auld Lang Syne. Second Series: 'My Indian Friends'*, Longmans, Green, London.

Myrdal, Gunnar, 1968, *Asian Drama: An Inquiry into the Poverty of Nations*, Penguin, Britain.

Nanda, B. R., 1985. *Gandhi and His Critics*, Oxford Univ. Press, Delhi.

Nandy, Ashis, 1980. *At the Edge of Psychology: Essays in Politics and Culture*, Oxford University Press, Delhi.

Nandy, Ashis, 1995, *Creating a Nationality: The Ramjanmabhoomi Movement and the Fear of the Self*, Oxford Univ. Press, Delhi.

Nandy, Ashis, 1993, "Fundamentalism", in ed. John S. Augustine, *Religious Fundamentalism: An Asian Perspective*, Asian Theological Research Institute, Bangalore, pp. 1 – 10.

Nandy, Ashis, 1983, *The Intimate Enemy: The Loss and Recovery of Self under Colonialism*, Oxford Univ. Press. Delhi.

Nandy, Ashis, 1992, "The Politics of Secularism and the Recovery of Religious Tolerance", in Veena Das, ed. op. cit., pp. 69-93.

Nederveen Pieterse, Jan and Bhikhu Paarekh, eds., 1997, *The Decolonization of Immagination: 'Culture, Knowledge and Power'*, Oxfoprd Univ. Press, Delhi.

Nehru, Jawaharlal, 1947, *The Discovery of India*, Signet press, Calcutta.

Newbigin, Leslie, 1966, "Conversion", *National Christian Council* Review, Vol. 87, No. 8 Aug., pp. 309-23.

Newman, John Henry, 1956, *Apologia Pro Vita Sua*, Doubleday, New York.

Newman, John Henry, 1979, *An Essay in Aid of a Grammar of Ascent*, Notre Dame Univ. Press, South Bend, Illinois.

Nivedita, Sister, 1975, *'Sister Nivedita's' Lectures and Writings*, Sister Nivedita's Girls School, Calcutta.

Nivedita, Sister, 1910, *The Master as I Saw Him*, Longmans, Green, & Co., London.

Nivedita, 1904, *'The Web of Indian Life'*, William Heinemann, London.

Oddie, G. A., ed. 1977, *Religion in South Asia: Religious Conversion and Revivalist Movements in South Asia in Medieval and Modern Times*, Manohar, N. Delhi.

Oddie, G. A., ed., 1977a, *Religious Conversion Movements in South Asian: Continuities and Change, 1800-1900*, Curzon Press, Surrey, England.

Omvedt, Gail, 2003, *Buddhism in India: Challenging Brahmanism and Caste*, Sage, N. Delhi.

Omvedt, Gail, 1994, *Dalits and the Democratic Revolution: Dr. Ambedkar and the Dalit Movement in Colonial India*, Sage, New Delhi.

Omvedt, Gail, 1995, *Dalit Visions: The anti-caste movement and the construction of an Indian identity*, Orient Longman, New Delhi.

Omvedt, Gail, 2000, "Gandhi and Ambedkar: Why the Confronation?" in ed. M. L. Ranga, *B. R. Ambedkar: Life, Work and Relevance*, Manohar, N. Delhi.

Pal, Mahendra, 1990, "Ambedkar - Life and Conversion Movement", in ed. Sanghason Singh, ed., *Ambedkar on Buddhist Conversion and Its Impact*, op.cit., pp. 50-64.

Panikkar, Raimon, 1995, *Cultural Disarmament: The Way to Peace*, Westminister John Knox Press, Louisville, Kentuky.

Panikkar, Raim, 1978, *'The Interreligious Dialogue'*, Paulist Press, New York.

Panikkar, Raimundo, 1983, *Myth, Faith, and Hermeneutics*, Asian Trading, Bangalore.

Panikkar, Raimon, 1998, "Religion, Philosophy and Culture", *Inter Culture — Special Issue*, No 135, Oct, pp. 99 - 120.

Panikkar, Raimundo, 1987, "Towards a Dialogical Dialogue", *Inter Culture*, Vol. 20, No. 4, Oct., pp. 21 - 26.

Panikkar, Raymond, 1964, *'The Unknown Christ of Hinduism'*, Darton, Longman and Todd, London.

Parekh, Bhikhu, 1995, *Gandhi's Political Philosophy: 'A Critical Appreciation'*, Ajanta, Delhi.

Parekh, Bhikhu, 2000, *Rethinking Multiculturalism: Cultural Diversity and Political Theory*, Macmillan, London.

Parekh, Bhikhu, 2003, "Some Reflections on the Hindu Theory of Tolerance", *Seminar*, No. 521, Jan.

Pati, Biswamoy, 2003, *Identity, Hegemony, Resistance: Towards a Social History of Conversions in Orissa, 1800-2000*, Three Esasy Collective, New Delhi.

Peterson, Indira Viswanathan, 1998, "Sramanas Against the Tamil Way of Life: Jains as Others in Tamil Saiva Literature", in *Open Boundaries: Jain Communities and Cultures in Indian History*, ed. John E. Cort, New York Press, New York, 1998, pp. 163 - 185.

Phadke, Y.D., 1993, *Visavya Shatakatil Maharashtra* (Marathi) Shre Vidya Prakashan, Pune, Vol. 4

Porter, Jean., 2001, "The search for a Global Ethic", *Theological Studies*, Vol. 62, No. 1, pp. 105-121.

Prashad, Vijay, 1996, "The Untouchable Question", *Economic and Political Weekly*, Vol. 31, No. 9, 2nd. March., pp. 551-560.

Rabi, Khondkar Fazli, 1970, *The Origins of the Musalmans of Bengal*, Society for Pakistan Studies, Dacca.

Radhakrishnan. S., 1939, *Eastern Religions and Western Thought,* Oxford Univ. Press, Oxford.

Radhakrishnan, Sarvepalli, 1927, *The Hindu View of Life*, George Allen and Unwin, London.

Rahner, Karl., 1966, *Theological Investigations*, Vol. 5, Darton, Longman and Todd, London.

Rajshekar, V. T., 1983, *'Ambedkar and His Conversions'*, Dalit Sahitya Akademy, Bangalore.

Raju, M. C., ed., 1999, *Wadhwa Commission Report: A Critique*, Media House, Delhi.

Ramabai, Pandita Saraswati, *A Testimony of Our Inexhaustible Treasure*, Kedgaon (Poona), Ramabai Mukti Mission, 1907, (1992 reprint).

Ranga, M. L., 2000, ed., *B. R. Ambedkar: Life, Work and Relevance*, Manohar, New Delhi.

Rao, B. Shiva, 1967-1968, *The Framing of India's Constitution: Selected Documents*, Vol.s. Indian Institute of Public Administration, N. Delhi,

Ratnagar, Shereen. 2000, *'The End of the Great Harappan Tradition'*, Manohar. Delhi.

Reymond, Lizelle, 1953, *The Dedicated: 'A Biography of Nivedita'*, The John Day Company, New York.

Report of the Christian Missionary Activities, Enquiry Committee, Madhya Pradesh, 1956. Vols. 1 and 2. (Popularly called the Niyogi Report, after its chairman)

Robinson, Neal, 1999, *Islam: A Concise Introduction*, Curzon Press, Surrey, England.

Robinson, Rowena. 1998, *Conversion, Continuity and Change Lived Christianity in Southern Goa*, Sage, New Delhi.

Sarkar Sumit, 2002, *Beyond Nationalist Frames: 'Relocating Postmodernism, Hindutva, History'*, Permanent Black, Delhi.

Sangharakshata, 1986, *Ambedkar and Buddhism*, Windhorse Pub., Norwich, Norfolk,.

Savarkar, V. D., 1964, *Hindu Rastra Darshan*, in *Samagra Savarkar Wangmaya*, Vol. 6, Pune, Maharashtra Prantik Hindusabbha.

Savarkar, V. D., 1971, *'Hindu-Pad-Padshash'*, Bharati Sahitya Sadan, 4th ed., New Delhi, 1st ed. 1925.

Savarkar, V. D., 1989, *Hindutva: Who Is a Hindu?* Bharati Sahitya Sadan, 6th ed., New Delhi, 1st ed. 1923.

Schreiter 1994, *The New Catholicity: Theology between the Global and the Local*, Maryknoll, New York.

Sengupta, Padmini, 1970, *Pandita Rambai; Her Life And Work*, Asia Publ. House, Bombay.

Shah, A. B., ed., 1977, *The Letters and Correspondence of Pandita Ramabai* Maharashtra State Board for Literature and Culture, Mumbai.

Shah, Ghanshyam, 1999, "Conversion, Reconversion and the State: Recent Events in the Dangs", *Economic and Political Weekly*, Vol. 34, No. 6, 6 Feb., pp. 312-318.

Sharma Arvind, 1996, *Hinduism for Our Times*, Oxford Univ. Press, Delhi.

Sharma, Jyotirmaya, 2003, *Hindutva: Exploring the Idea of Hindu Nationalism*, Penguin, Viking, New Delhi.

Singh, K. S. 1982, "Transformation of Tribal Society", *Economic and Political Weekly*, Vol. 16, No. 33, 14 Aug., pp. 1376-1384.

Singh, Sanghason, ed., 1990, *Ambedkar on Buddhist Conversion and Its Impact*, Eastern Book Linkers, Delhi.

Shodhan, Amrita, *A Question of Community: Religious Groups and Colonial Law*, Samya, Calcutta, 2001,

Source Material on Dr. Babasaheb Ambedkar and the Movement of Untouchables, 1982, vol. I, Govt. of Maharashtra, Bombay.

Smart, Ninian, 1993, "Models for Understanding the Relations between Religions", in ed. J. Kellenberger, op. cit., pp. 57 - 68.

Smith, David, 2003, *Hinduism and Modernity*, Blackwell Oub., Oxford.

Subrahmanyam, Sanjay, 1996, "Before the Leviathan: Sectarian Violence and the State in Precolonial India", in Basu and Subrahmanyam eds., op.cit. pp. 44-80.

Swarup, Devendra, ed., *Politics of Conversion*, Deendayal Research Institute, Delhi, 1986.

Tambikuttu, E. R. ed., *History of the Tamils from Prehistoric Times to AD 1800*, General Publishers, Colombo.

Thapar, Romila, 1961, *Ashoka and the Decline of the Mauryas*, Oxford Univ. Press, London.

Thapar, Romila, 1966, *A History of India*, Penguin, England.

Thapar, Romila, 2004, *The Many Voices of History*, Penguin, N. Delhi.

Thapar, Romila, 1989, "Imagined Religious Communities? Ancient History and the Modern Search for a Hindu Indenity", in Lorenzen, ed., op. cit. pp. 333 - 359.

Thomas, M. M. 1976, *The Acknowledged Christ of the Indian Renaissance*, SCM, London.

Thomas, M. M. 1972, "Baptism, the Church and Koinonia", *Religion and Society*, Vol. 19, No. 1 Mar. pp. 69-90.

Tillich, Paul, 1958, *Dynamics of Faith*, Harper and Row, New York.

Vidyajyoti : Journal of Theological Reflection, Vol. 70, No. 8, Aug. 2007, pp. 625-678.

Viswanathan, Gauri, 2001, *Outside the Fold: Conversion Modernity and Belief*, Oxford Univ. Press, Delhi.

Vivekananda, Swami, 1951, *The Complete Works of Swami Vivekananda*, Kolkotta, Advaita Ashram, 1962.

Vivekananda, Swami, 1962, *Selections from the Works of Swami Vivekananda*, Kolkotta, Advaita Ashram.

Vidyajyoti: Journal of Theological Refection, Vol. 70, No. 8, Aug. 2007, pp 625-678.

World Council of Churches (WCC), 1948, *The Church and the International Order*, Student Christian Movement (SCM) Press, London.

Xaxa, Virginus, 1999, "Transformation of Tribes in India: Terms of Discourse", *Economic and Political Weekly*, Vol. 34, No. 24, 12 June, pp. 1519-1524.

Zelliot, Eleanor, 1996, *From Untouchable to Dalit: Essays on the Ambedkar Movement*, Manohar, New Delhi.

Zelliot, Eleanor, 1997, "The Psychological Dimension of the Buddhist Movement in India", in ed., Oddie, G. A., 1977, op. cit.

Index

A

Abbasids of Baghdad, 52
Abrahamic religions, 100
Acchutananda, 143
Acharyahridayam, 40
Ad-Dharm qaum, 143
Adi-Andhra, 143
Adi-Hindu identity, 143
Adi-Karnataka movement, 143
Adivasi Bhumihin Kisan Hakka Sanrakshan Samiti, 218
Adivasis, 31, 42, 83, 217
Advaita, 39
Advaita Vedanta, 39
Afghanistan, 46
Africa, 50
Age of Reason, 140
Agricultural Relief Act, 178
Ahimsa, 157
Ahmad, Imtiaz, 250
Ahmad, Irfan, 253
Ahmed, Akbar, 60
Akbar the Great, 57
Al Qaeda, 50
Alam, Anwar, 254
Alavi, Hamsa, 249
Aligarh Muslim University, 249
All India Backward Muslim Morcha, 254
All India Depressed Classes Political Conference , 149
All India Dravida Anna Munnetra Kazhagam, 84
All India Muslim OBC, 254
All India Suppressed Classes Conference at Lahore, 145
Allah, 24, 33, 54, 244
Allen, Isaac, 183
Aloysius, G., 146
Ambiguities, 74, 86, 115, 130, 141, 138, 184
Ambiguity, 201-02, 230-31, 223
American Baptists, 71
Anderson, Benedict, 113
Andhra Pradesh, 74, 75
Andrews, C.F, 75, 132, 165, 169

Anglican Church, 73, 121, 171, 181-83, 185
Anglicans, 74, 97, 121, 129, 175, 190
Animists, 42, 220
Annihilation, 100, 104, 107, 149
Anonymous, 230
Anthropological Survey of India, 220
Anti-conversion law, 14, 204
Antyodaya, 132,161
Arabisation, 62, 126, 248
Armstrong, Karen, 99, 138
Arunachal Pradesh Freedom of Indigenous Religions, 84
Arya Mahila Samaj, 174
Arya Samaj, 43, 102, 132, 207
Aryan' race, 38
Asceticism, 44-45, 160, 179
Ashoka, Emperor, 45
Ataturk, 54
Atharva-Veda, 39
Atmaparivartan, 19, 24-25, 141-42, 154, 156, 164, 169, 183, 204, 259, 260, 278, 283, 287, 289, 297, 302, 304, 305
Atrocities, 22, 123, 61, 79, 91, 96, 104, 132, 153, 212, 236, 271, 297
Auranzeb, 248
Axial Age, 89, 99, 100
Ayodhya, 235
Azad, Maulana, 169

B

Babri Masjid, 22, 253
Babur, 57
Backward castes, 72, 126
Baghdad, 52, 55
Bahiskrit Hitakari Sabha, 145
Bahujan Samaj, 254
Bajrang Dal, 213
Bakhtiyar, Mohammad, 58
Balachandra, 237
Bali, 31, 41
Bandung Conference in 1955, 19
Bangladesh, 60, 87, 257
Bania (merchant) community, 65
Bapat, Ram, 171
Baptist, 71, 72, 74, 121
Baramati, 203, 204
Basham, 36-39
Bayley, 59, 246
Belgian and German missionaries, 71
Bellah, Robert, 153
Belloc, Hillarie, 63
Bengal, 43, 57, 58, 59, 60, 69, 70, 71, 83, 92, 171, 189, 190, 236, 240, 246, 249, 250, 251, 254
Bengal Resistance, 190
Beteille, Andre, 223
Bhagat, Anandibai, 174
Bhagavad-Gita, 157
Bhakti, 39, 41, 44, 61, 62, 112, 131, 136, 143, 157, 177, 205, 237, 240
Bhandarkar, R.G., 174, 176
Bharatiya Janta Party (BJP), 79, 93
Bible, 68, 69, 92, 168, 176, 183, 213
Bihari, Bipin Medhavi, 173
Bijapur, 65
Bin, Osama Laden, 50
Bishops, 63, 67, 71, 201, 224, 231, 233, 264, 281, 283, 286, 306
Bohras, 247
Bombay presidency, 144, 217
Bonded and cheap labour, 206
Bonded labour, 216
Bose, Aurobindo, 189

Bose, Barinda, 190
Bose, N.K., 28
Brahmabandhab Upadhyay, 77
Brahmanism, 38, 40, 44, 46, 47
Brahmo religion, 174
Brahmo Samaj, 171
British colonial rule, 55
Buddha, 46-48
Buddhism, 40, 44, 45
Buddhist, 42, 46
Buhlmann, Walbert, 64
Byzantine, 50, 63

C

Caliphs, 51
Carey, William, 69
Carr, H. E., 35
Caste, 41, 42, 44
Catholic Union of India, 83
Catholicism, 97, 121, 129, 134, 232
Catholics, 20, 69, 70, 71, 97, 121, 182, 281, 306
Census, 220, 250-51
Central Asia, 38, 52, 63
Central Bureau of Investigation (CBI), 214
Chaitanya, 41
Chakma tribals, 236
Chakravarti, Uma, 172
Chandra, Jagdish Bose, 189
Chapman, Sara Bull, 187
Charity, 237
Charter of, 65, 137
Chenchiah, Pandipeddi, 228
Chennai, 22, 64, 207, 228
Chhattisgarh, 70, 83
Chicago, 179, 186
Chidananda, Swami, 224
Chinese rites, 67, 68, 229
Chinmayananda mission, 43
Chitpavan Brahman, 174
Chittagong, 236
Chola kings, 45
Chotanagpur, 70, 71
Christendom, 63
Christian Missionary Enquiry Committee, 82
Christianity, 34
Churches, 217, 223, 224, 225, 227
Citizenship, 21, 119, 123, 246
Civil liberties, 123, 132, 133, 138, 272
Civil rights, 98, 138
Colonialism, 76
Colonialism, 60, 68, 122, 147, 167
Columbia University, 143, 144
Common civil code, 90
Community, 91, 102, 103, 104, 106
Confucianism, 100
Congress socialists, 148
Constantine the Great, 63
Constantinople, 51, 52, 63
Constituent Assembly, 79, 82, 87, 89, 90
Coromandel, 59, 66
Criminal Tribes Act in 1871, 203
Crusades, 20, 27, 49, 50

D

D., justice P. Wadhwa, 213
Da, Vasco Gama, 64
Dalit, 201, 202, 203, 204
Dalit Panthers, 155
Damascus, 49, 135
Dangs, 201, 217, 218
Darwish, Mahmoud, 32

D'Costa, Anthony, 66
De, Afonso Albuquerque, 65
De, John Britton, 68
De, Robert Nobili, 231
Democracy, 36, 37, 55, 56, 82
Demography, 64
Deoband School, 54
Depressed Castes, 169
Depressed Classes, 72, 74, 75, 149, 154, 206
Devadason, 85
Dharma, 39, 44, 49
Dharma nirapekshata, 88, 112, 241, 242
Dharmantar, 127, 141, 142, 154, 156
Digambar Jainism, 45
Disarmament, 291, 307, 310
Divide-and-rule policy, 55, 87
Dom Henri Le Saux, 231
Draft Constitution, 80, 81
Dravidian culture, 38
D'Souza, Jerome, 80
Duff, Alexander, 69
Dumont, Louis, 147
Durkheim, Emile, 221
Dutta, R.C., 41

E

Eastern Orthodox Churches, 27
Eaton, Richard, 58
Ecumenical Councils, 63
Ejaz, M. Ali, 254
Electoral politics, 133, 148, 151, 237, 267
Elwin, Verrier, 132
Engineer, Ali, Asghar, 235
England, 97, 129, 174, 262
Enlightenment, 292, 293, 290, 294
Ethnic cleansing, 11, 20, 56, 236, 274
Ethnicity, 97, 119, 222, 245
Ethno-nationalism, 91
Europe, 91, 97, 108
European Union, 63, 108
Evangelicals, 25
Evangelisers, 33, 215
Extremists, 202, 212, 243, 244

F

Faguji, Kisan Bansode, 143
Falsafah, 62
Farquhar, J.N., 230
Fazli, Khondkar Rabi, 250
Fernando, 64
Ford, Henry, 34
Freedom of conscience, 81, 84, 88, 89, 113, 116
Freedom of Religion, 137, 302, 307
Freedom of Religion Acts, 302
Froebel, Freidrich, 186
Frykenberg, 63, 64, 73
Fukuyama, Francis, 55
Fundamental rights, 79, 106, 109, 113, 123, 133, 199, 123
Fundamentalism, 138, 151, 168, 212

G

Gaikwad, Avinash, 203
Gandhi, Mahatma, 287
Gavai, G.A., 143
Geertz, Clifford, 291
Gender, 148, 172
General Allenby, 49
Geneva, 307
Genocide, 11, 105, 253, 297
George Uglow Pope, 73
Geraldine, Sr, 182
German missionaries, 71

Gharvapasi, 25
Ghurye, G.S., 151
Giddens, Anthony, 298
Golwalkar, M.S., 95
Gonds of Sambalpur, 216
Gore, S. M., 142, 148, 150, 151, 156, 159
Goreh, Nehemiah, 171
Government of India's tribal policy, 220
Gramsci, Antonio, 33
Grant, Charles, 69
Great Revolt of 1857, 60
Griffiths, Bede, 77
Guardian, The, 162
Gujarat, 217, 218, 234
Gujarat Freedom of Religion Act, 2003, 84
Gupta, Dipankar, 114
Gupta period, 40, 46, 47
Guru Nanak, 41, 112, 124
Guru Nanak Panth, 124

H

Had, British annexed Assam, 71
Hadith, 252
Hamid, Abu al'Ghazali, 252
Harappa, 38
Hardiman, David, 217
Hare Krishna sect, 97
Harijan, 146, 159, 162, 163, 164, 167, 168
Harijans, 146, 164
Hasan, Abdul Shathali Sahib, 207
Hebrew, 26, 176
Henry, John Newman, 121
Heras, Henry, 66
Heterogeneity, 41, 43, 128
High Court, 43, 215
Hindu Code Bill, 42, 90
Hindu Mahasabha, 95, 143
Hindu Munnani, 209
Hindu nationalism, 256, 262
Hindu personal law, 42, 90
Hindu rashtra, 90, 93
Hindu renaissance, 60, 240
Hindu theory of, 239
Hindu tolerance, 201, 202
Hinduisation, 215, 217
Hindutva, 222, 236
Hindutvawadis, 33, 242
Home Rule movement, 189
Horton, Robin, 58
Human rights, 76, 81
Huns, 57
Huntington, Samuel, 55
Husain, Maulana Ahmad Madni, 249
Huxley, Thomas, 186

I

Ilyas, Muhammad, 54
Inculturation, 231, 232
Indian Converts (Regulation and Registration) Bill, 82
Indian National Congress, 86, 93, 148
Indic civilisation, 44, 46
Indigenous Religions Act, 84
Inquisition, 66
Iran, 54, 92
Irish Republican Army (IRA), 50
Ishtadevta, 181
Islam, 150
Islamic states, 62, 103
Islamic tradition, 245, 251, 260
Islamic world, 20, 55, 62

Islamisation, 53, 57, 59

J

Jaffrelot, 159
Jainism, 28, 30, 40
Jamaat-i-Ismaili, 54
Japan, 46
Jati, 29, 95, 219
Jesuits, 65, 66, 67, 70, 281
Jesus Christ, 182, 261
Jethmalani, Ram, 85
Jews, 51, 53
Jharkhand, 70, 82
Jihadis, 50, 305
Jinnah Mohammed, Ali, 86
Jnanadev, 177
Joshi, Jethalal, 82
Jotirao, Mahatma Phule, 93

K

Kabir, 41, 57
Kabir, Humayun, 57
Kabir Panth, 70
Kakar, Sudhir, 106
Kali worship, 197
Kant, Emanuel, 293
Kapilavastu, 48
Karma, 39, 44, 49
Karve, Maharshi, 171
Kashmir, 173, 192
Kaviraj, Sudipto, 42
Kenneth, John Galbraith, 151
Kerala, 57, 64
Kesari, 178
Keshab Chandra Sen, 173
Khan, Ali, Mumtaz, 207
Khilafat, 86
Khojas, 247, 260
Khomeini, Ayatollah, 54
Kipling, Rudyard, 227
Kohima, 71, 72
Kolkata, 69, 121, 173
Konkan, 142, 217
Koran, 168
Kosambi, D.D., 219
Kosambi, Meera, 172
Krishna, C. Murthy, 208
Krishna Consciousness movement, 43
Krishna, Gopal Gokhale, 189
Krishnamachari, 80, 81
Krista-bhakta movement, 260
Kropotkin, Peter, 186
Kshatriyas, 170
Kumarappa, 165
Kung, Hans, 234

L

Lady Ripon, 186
Lariano, 9, 10, 307
Latin America, 25, 127
Lebanon, 306
Lele, Jayant, 131
Liberalism, 92, 135
Liberals, 222, 227
Liberation theology, 127
Lingayats of Karnataka, 29, 41
Linguistic nationalism, 107
Literalism, 101, 103
Livens, Constance, 71
Lodi, Ibrahim, 57
London, 143, 186
Lonergan, Bernard, 134
Lord Buddha Club, 211
Ludden, David, 45

M

MacLeod, Josephine, 187
Macpherson Report, 214

Madan, T.N., 249
Madhya Pradesh, 70, 82, 83, 84, 302
Madhya Pradesh Dharma Swatantrya Adhiniyam, 83
Madhya Pradesh High Court, 84
Madras Presidency, 173
Madurai, 207, 208
Mahabharata, 39
Mahabodhi Society, 153
Mahadev, Justice Govind Ranade, 93
Mahanubhav Panth, 40
Mahar caste, 151
Maharaj, Shahu, 144
Maharashtra, 142, 143
Maharatta, 177
Mahima Devi, 216, 217
Majumdar, C.R., 41
Malabar rites, 68
Malayan archipelago, 41
Malraux, Andre, 19
Manusmruti, 152
Marak, 72
Marathas, 57, 177
Margs, 28
Marriages, inter-caste, 104
Marx, Karl, 151
Marxists, 148, 161
Mathew, George, 208
Matteo Ricci, 231
Maulvis, 62
Mauryan Empire, 45
Mauryan period, 47, 237
Mayavaram, 69
Mazhab, 25
Mazhabi Sikhs, 73, 150
Mazzini, Giuseppe, 193
McVeigh, Timothy, 246
Medina, 102, 252
Meenakshipuram, 96, 201
Meheru'llah, Munshi, 60
Mennonite Amish, 97
Meos of Rajasthan, 260
Metanoia, 277, 280
Methodist, 175
Middle East, 38, 51
Minorities, 36, 53
Minto, Lady, 197
Miraben (Madeleine Slade, 163
Missionaries, 156
Modernisation, 98, 249
Modernity, 160, 242
Mohen-jo-daro, 38
Moksha, 49, 131
Monchanin, Jules, 231
Mongols, 52, 55
Monks, 44, 45
Monotheism, 58
Moors, 50
Moral Majority, 92
Moral majority, 51
Moral policing, 22
Mosque, 49
Mosque, 57
Mughals, 52, 54
Mukkuvars, 67
Muller, Max, 93
Munda, Birsa, 216
Munis, 28
Munshi, M. K., 79, 80
Murdoch, Iris, 160
Muslim League, 82, 249
Muslim Marathi Sahitya Parishad, 254
Muslim nationalism, 87, 93, 249
Muslim personal law, 90
Myanmar, 88
Myrdal, Gunnar, 90

Mysticism, 231, 237, 282
Mythos, 134, 276

N

Nagaland, 72
Nagas, 71, 72
Nagpur, 70, 75, 95
Nalanda, 47
Nandy, Ashis, 102
Narayanan, R. K., 79
Nath, Bhupendra Dutt, 190
National Foundation for Communal Harmony (NFCH), 214
National freedom struggle, 86
Nationalism, 37, 40, 48, 54, 75
Navayana Buddhism, 153, 198
Naxalite movement, 236
Nehru, Jawaharlal, 241
Nellie, 15, 236
Neo-Hinduism and religious nationalism, 195
Nepal, 21, 48, 88
New Testament, 67, 70
Nirvana, 153, 199, 290
Niyogi Report, 82, 83
No-rent movement in Orissa, 216
Noble, Margaret, 186
Non-Brahmin movement, 144, 178
North Africa, 50, 53
Northern Ireland, 268

O

Of, conversion minors, 80
Oklahoma, 246
Old Testament, 131
Omvedt, Gail, 47
Opium Wars, 76
Orientalism, 41
Orientalist, 40, 60
Orissa Freedom of Religion Act, 83
Orissa High Court, 215
Orthodox, 12, 27, 43, 65, 101, 159, 174, 178, 224, 256, 295, 306
Other Backward Classes' (OBC), 254
Ottoman, 51, 52, 54
Oxford, 121, 175

P

Pakistan, 36, 56
Pakistan Constituent Assembly, 94
Pandarasamis, 68, 73
Pandharpur, 174
Panikkar, Raimundo, 281
Panipat, 57
Panth, 40, 61
'Parangis', caste, 68
Parayas, 74
Parekh, Bhikhu, 157
Parliament, 179, 186
Parliament of World Religions, 298
Pascal, Blaise, 279
Patel, Vallabhbhai, 80
Paternalism, 85, 133
Pati, Biswamoy, 215
Patna State Freedom of Religion Act, 1942, 79
Patriarchy, 125, 141
Persian empire, 50
Peshwas, 177
Pestalozzi, Johann, 186
Pharisees, 27, 309
Pluralism, 21, 62, 64, 89, 90, 92, 101, 103, 107, 108, 109, 110, 115, 116, 134, 135, 183, 195, 226, 237-258, 280-81, 286-88, 297, 301

Pogrom, 9, 11
Polytheism, 58
Pondicherry, 190
Poona Pact, 145
Porter, Jean, 300
Portuguese, 64-68, 130
Poverty alleviation programmes, 212
Prarthana Samaj, 171, 174
Prasad, Rajendra, 80
Pratap, Bhanu Mehta, 85
Pratap, Rana, 235
Prophet, 247, 248, 251
Proselytisation, 302, 309
Protestant Christianity, 229
Protestant Reformation, 63, 268
Protestants, 20, 68, 69, 70, 71, 73, 231, 306
Pune, 93, 172
Punjab, 59, 73, 143, 145, 236, 246
Punya, 43, 196
Puranas, 47, 173
Purity and pollution, 251
Purna swaraj, 90, 240

R

Radhakrishnan, Sarvepalli, 238
Rahner, Karl, 230
Raj, Udit, 210
Rajah, M.S., 143
Rajasthan, 235, 260
Rajshekar, V.T., 204
Ram, Mangoo, 143
Ram Rajya, 102
Ramabai Association, 175
Ramabai, Pandita, 134
Ramakrishna Mission, 187, 189
Ramakrishna Paramhansa, 184
Ramanathpuram, 69
Ramjanmabhoomi movement, 244
Rammohan, 83
Ramsey MacDonald Award, 145
Rashtriya Swayamsevak Sangh, 93
Rationalism, 111, 112
Reformation in medieval Europe, 20
Regulation Act II of 1827, 177
Religion, 150, 151
Renaissance, 60, 240
Representation of Peoples' Act, 273
Republican Party of India, 149
Revivalism, 200, 292, 293, 295, 309
Revolutionary Council of Bengal, 190
Right to freedom, 22, 285
Right to Religious Freedom, 79, 198, 231
Rights, 89, 98, 104, 106
Rights and duties, 86, 129
Rishikesh, 223, 231
Roman Empire, 63, 260
Rome, 31, 63, 65
Round Table Conference, 147, 149
Rousseau, 255
Rowena Robinson, 66
Rudolf Acquaviva, 67
Ruskin, 157, 186

S

Sadharan dharma, 238
Sadhus, 27
Safavid, 54
Sage Agastya, 41
Sahib, Pocker, 82
Saiva, 45
Salaudin, 49
Sampradayas, 28

Samuel, Vedanayagam Azariah, 74
Sanatan dharma, (eternal religion), 44
Sandhurst, Lord, 176
Sangh Parivar, 203, 204
Sangharakshata, 152, 153
Sankhya system, 39
Sanskritisation, 59, 126
Sant-kavis, 28, 41, 177, 240
Sant-kavis (saints and poets), 240
Santoshi Mata, 39
Saracens, 51, 55
Sarkar, Sumit, 61
Sarna religion, 42
Sartre, Jean-Paul, 100
Sarvadharma samabhav, 112
Sati, 178, 194
Satsangs, 261
Satya Shodhak, 144
Satyagraha, 145, 157
Saul of Tarsus, 26, 135
Savarkar, V. D., 43, 47, 86, 87, 94, 95, 156, 196
Savarna sanatanis, 142
Scheduled Castes, 151, 203
Scheduled Tribes, 42, 219
Schweitzer, Albert, 163
Secularising, 21
Secularism, 241, 242
Self-respect movement, 207, 209
Seljuks, 52
Sen, Amartya, 32
Shah, A.B., 171
Shah, Ghanshyam, 218
Shahjahan, 248
Shaivism, 40, 45
Shankar, Bhawani Niyogi, 82
Sharada Sadan, 175
Shariah, 62
Sharma, Arvind, 43
Sharma, Jyotirmaya, 43
Shastri, Anant Dongre, 172
Shaw, Bernard, 186
Shias, 52, 248
Shiv Sena, 236
Shivaji, Chhatrapati, 235
Shodhan, Amrita, 36
Shramana tradition, 28, 44
Shudras, 48, 149
Shukoh, Dara, 248
Sikhism, 205, 242
Simon Commission, 72, 147
Sindh, 38, 57
Singh, Dara, 213
Singh, K.S., 220
Smart, Ninian, 283
Soares-Prabhu, George, 112
Society of Jesus, 68, 281
Somnath, 235, 236
South Africa, 31, 206
South Asia, 20, 32
South Asian Association for Regional Cooperation, 87
South Indian Muslim Association, 207
Southern Baptists, 97
Spain, 91, 248
Staines, Graham, 213
Stanley, William Jones, 60
State, Raigarh Conversion Act, 79
Statesman, 208
Sub-Saharan Africa, 52, 253
Sufis, 231, 290
Suleiman, 51
Sunni schools of law, 102
Sunni Tablighi Jammat, 54

Sunnis, 247, 248
Supreme Court, 213, 273
Surguja State Apostasy Act, 80
Swami Abhishekananda, 77
Swaraj, purna, 90
Swatantrya Adhiniyam, 83
Sword of Islam, 47, 51
Syrian Christians, 64, 65

T

Tagore, Rabindranath, 197
Taj Mahal, 61
Tambikuttu, E. R., 41
Tamil literature, 45
Tamil Nadu, 84, 96
Tamil Nadu Prohibition of Forcible Conversion of R, 84
Tantra, 44, 148
Taranath, 47
Terrorism, 50, 94
Testament, 131, 143
Thanjavur, 69, 209
Thapar, Romila, 38
Theology, 52, 57
Thomas, 64
Thomas, M.M., 228
Thomas, St., 64
Timbuktu, 52
Times of India, 147, 152
Tirumavalavan, R., 211
Tirunelveli, 207, 208
Tolerance, 20, 23, 35, 45, 47, 53, 61, 66, 81, 82, 86, 87, 92, 106, , 201, 202, 213, 287, 288, 290, 292, 294, 295, 296, 299, 301, 303, 305, 310, 319, 320
Tonnies, Ferdinand, 267
Tukaram, 112, 177
Two-nation theory, 36, 249
Tyagi, O.P., 84

U

Udaipur State Anti-conversion Act, 1946, 80
Ulema, 62, 249
Umar-ibn-Khattab, 51
United Liberation Front of Assam (ULFA), 50
United Nations, 206, 274
United Nations World Conference Against Racism, 206
United Presbyterian Mission, 73
United Provinces, 73
Universalism, 106, 191
Untouchability, 146, 147, 158
Untouchability League, 146
Untouchables, 145, 146
Upanishad, Brihadraranyaka, 39
Upanishads, 39, 112
Uprising of the Pintos, 66
Urdu, 61, 250
Uttar Pradesh, 214, 236

V

Vaishnava sanatani, 199
Vaishnavism, 40, 84
Valmiki, 102
Vaman, Narayan Tilak, 77
Varanasi, 10, 260
Varkaris of Maharashtra, 30
Varna system, 158, 216
Varnashrama dharma, 238, 241
Vatican, 224, 230
Vatican Council, 77, 230
Vedanta, 39, 230, 262

Vedapramanya, 44
Vedas, 38, 40
Vedic age, 60
Vedic civilisation, 93
Vedic religion, 39, 112
Verma, Justice J. S., 95
Violence, 9, 11, 14, 15, 20, 21, 22, 26, 28, 33, 45, 56, 60, 61, 79, 80, 86, 87, 104, 108, 115, 120, 122, 123, 212, 214, 250, 261, 267, 268, 274, 312, 313, 316, 322
Violence in, 235, 236
Vishwa Hindu Parishad (VHP, 22
Viswanath, Indira Peterson, 45
Viswanathan, Gauri, 97

W

Wahabism, 248
Wantage, 174, 181, 183
West Bengal, 43, 70
Westphalia, 21
World Council of Churches, 77, 227
World Parliament of Religions, 179, 298
World Social Forum, 301

Y

Yeola, 142, 149
Young India, 157, 158

Z

Zelliot, 144, 149, 210
Zia-ul-Haq, President, 94
Zoroastrians, 29